DATE DUE

Victimology

The International Library of Criminology, Criminal Justice and Penology
Series Editors: Gerald Mars and David Nelken

Victimology

Edited by

Paul Rock

Professor of Sociology and Director of the Mannheim Centre for the Study of Criminology and Criminal Justice at the London School of Economics and Political Science

Dartmouth
Aldershot · Brookfield USA · Hong Kong · Singapore · Sydney

Published by
Dartmouth Publishing Company Limited
Gower House
Croft Road
Aldershot
Hants GU11 3HR
England

Dartmouth Publishing Company
Old Post Road
Brookfield
Vermont 05036
USA

British Library Cataloguing in Publication Data
Victimology. – (International Library of
Criminology & Criminal Justice)
  I. Rock, Paul II. Series
  362.88

Library of Congress Cataloging-in-Publication Data
Victimology / edited by Paul Rock and the London School of Economics
  and Political Science.
      p. cm. — (The International library of criminology and
criminal justice)
  Includes bibliographical references and index.
  ISBN 1-85521-405-9 : $129.95 (est.)
  1. Victims of crimes. I. Rock, Paul Elliott. II. London School
of Economics and Political Science. III. Series.
HV6250.25.V56 1993
362.88—dc20

93-36618
CIP

ISBN 1 85521 405 9

Printed in Great Britain by Galliard (Printers) Ltd, Great Yarmouth

Contents

PART IV   REMEDIES AND CONCLUSIONS

Acknowledgements

The editor and publishers wish to thank the following for permission to use copyright material.

American Medical Association for the essay: C. Henry Kempe, Frederic N. Silverman, Brandt F. Steele, William Droegemueller and Henry K. Silver (1962), 'The Battered-Child Syndrome', *The Journal of the American Medical Association*, **181**, pp. 105–12. Copyright © 1962 American Medical Association.

American Sociological Association for the essay: Lawrence E. Cohen and Marcus Felson (1979), 'Social Change and Crime Rate Trends: A Routine Activity Approach', *American Sociological Review*, **44**, pp. 588–608.

Blackwell Publishers for the essays: Ronald Clarke, Paul Ekblom, Mike Hough and Pat Mayhew (1985), 'Elderly Victims of Crime and Exposure to Risk', *The Howard Journal*, **24**, pp. 1–9 and with the permission of the Controller of Her Majesty's Stationery Office. Jane Morgan and Lucia Zedner (1992), 'The Victim's Charter: A New Deal for Child Victims?', *The Howard Journal*, **31**, pp. 294–307.

Ronald Clarke, Paul Ekblom, Mike Hough and Pat Mayhew (1985), 'Elderly Victims of Crime and Exposure to Risk', *The Howard Journal*, **24**, pp. 1–9. Crown Copyright. Reproduced with the permission of The Controller of HMSO.

The Notre Dame Law Review for the essay: Michael Ash (1972), 'On Witnesses: A Radical Critique of Criminal Court Procedures', *Notre Dame Lawyer*, **48**, pp. 386–425. Reprinted with permission. Copyright © by *Notre Dame Law Review*, University of Notre Dame.

The Observer for the essay: M. Fry (1957), 'Justice for Victims'. Reproduced in the *Journal of Public Law*, **8**, 1959. First published in *The Observer*, 10 November 1957. Copyright © The Observer.

Oxford University Press for the essays: Nils Christie (1977), 'Conflicts as Property', *The British Journal of Criminology*, **17**, pp. 1–15; Pat Mayhew and Lorna J.F. Smith (1985), 'Crime in England and Wales and Scotland: A British Crime Survey Comparison', *The British Journal of Criminology*, **25**, pp. 148–59. Crown Copyright. Reproduced with the permission of The Controller of HMSO; A.E. Bottoms, R.I. Mayby and Monica A. Walker (1987), 'A Localised Crime Survey in Contrasting Areas of a City', *The British Journal of Criminology*, **27**, pp. 125–54; Susan J. Smith (1982), 'Victimisation in the Inner City: A British Case Study', *The British Journal of Criminology*, **22**, pp. 386–402; Natalie Polvi, Terah Looman, Charlie Humphries and Ken Pease (1991), 'The Time Course of

Repeat Burglary Victimization', *The British Journal of Criminology*, **31**, pp. 411–4; Mike Maguire (1980), 'The Impact of Burglary upon Victims', *The British Journal of Criminology*, **20**, pp. 261–75; Joanna Shapland (1984), 'Victims, the Criminal Justice System and Compensation', *The British Journal of Criminology*, **24**, pp. 131–49.

The Progressive for the essay: Michelle Wasserman (1973), 'Rape: Breaking the Silence', *The Progressive*, pp. 19–23.

Sage Publications Inc. for the essay: J. Garofalo (1979), 'Victimization and Fear of Crime', *Journal of Research in Crime and Delinquency*, **16**, pp. 80–97. Reprinted with permission of Sage Publications Inc.

Victimology Inc. for the essays: Mike Maguire (1985), 'Victims' Needs and Victim Services', *Victimology*, **10**, pp. 539–59. Copyright © 1985 Victimology Inc. All rights reserved; E. Fattah (1979), 'Some Recent Theoretical Trends in Victimology', *Victimology*, **4**, pp. 198–213. Copyright © 1979 Victimology Inc. All rights reserved.

Every effort has been made to trace all the copyright holders, but if any have been inadvertently overlooked the publishers will be pleased to make the necessary arrangements at the first opportunity.

Series Preface

The International Library of Criminology, Criminal Justice and Penology, represents an important publishing initiative designed to bring together the most significant journal essays in contemporary criminology, criminal justice and penology. The series makes available to researchers, teachers and students an extensive range of essays which are indispensable for obtaining an overview of the latest theories and findings in this fast changing subject.

This series consists of volumes dealing with criminological schools and theories as well as with approaches to particular areas of crime, criminal justice and penology. Each volume is edited by a recognised authority who has selected twenty or so of the best journal articles in the field of their special competence and provided an informative introduction giving a summary of the field and the relevance of the articles chosen. The original pagination is retained for ease of reference.

The difficulties of keeping on top of the steadily growing literature in criminology are complicated by the many disciplines from which its theories and findings are drawn (sociology, law, sociology of law, psychology, psychiatry, philosophy and economics are the most obvious). The development of new specialisms with their own journals (policing, victimology, mediation) as well as the debates between rival schools of thought (feminist criminology, left realism, critical criminology, abolitionism etc.) that contribute overviews offering syntheses of the state of the art. These problems are addressed by the INTERNATIONAL LIBRARY in making available for research and teaching the key essays from specialist journals.

GERALD MARS
Visiting Professor of Risk Management, Cranfield University

DAVID NELKEN
Visiting Professor of Law (Criminology), University College London

Introduction

Victims attract a level of interest, both as a subject of criminological enquiry and as a focus of criminal justice policy, unimaginable a decade ago. Far from being a compartmentalised topic for research, the recognition of victims has resulted in a major reorientation of criminological thinking.[1]

Victimology is a relatively amorphous discipline that was conceived in the late 1940s[2] to study the victims of crime; it attained maturity perhaps in the 1980s[3] and came, in time, to produce a set of arguments that obliged criminologists to think hard about their own discipline and the questions that it should ask. It can probably best be appreciated by a wide and general introduction that explains how it attained its special character.

The Neglect of the Victim

If victims have been established as objects of intellectual enquiry, it has been only recently and within a restricted sphere of activity and interest. Not much notice is taken of them outside criminology and the politics of criminal justice. They are quite invisible to sociology and the other social sciences[4] (and there is no reason to imagine why the situation should ever have been otherwise). They are effectively invisible in legal circles, being what Joanna Shapland once called 'non-person[s] in the eyes of the professional participants'.[5] They certainly do not figure large in the formal study and practice of criminal law in Britain or North America.[6] Legal statutes, texts and dictionaries do not refer expressly to them.[7] They have no legal standing at all unless it is as members of a larger population of witnesses who claim to have direct knowledge of some crime. For the most part, they are taken to be no more than *alleged* victims, creatures of uncertain status, until their assertions have been put to the test in trials.[8] Indeed, it is the victimologist's claim that victims lost control over 'their' crimes, problems and conflicts long ago, with the rise of the centralized State. Their role as the injured party has since been usurped by the State.[9] It is against the State that criminals are deemed in law to have offended and it is in the State's name that prosecutions are brought.

Even criminology and the sociology of deviance – disciplines concentrated most squarely on the analysis of crime, criminals and criminal justice – tended somehow to obliterate the victim for a very long while, failing to see what, in retrospect, should probably have been evident all along. Such omissions occur continually. They are an ineluctable part of any discipline, a consequence of the truth marked by Burke when he said that 'a way of seeing is always a way of not seeing'.[10] The price of organizing, specializing and accumulating knowledge about any area is a systematic neglect of the other matters thrown out of focus and beyond the margins. Precisely because criminology is an empirically-driven discipline, it has tended to ignore those things that do not bear the name of crime, criminals and criminal justice.

Consider the works of succeeding waves of criminological theorists. The more positivist criminologists of the 1940s and 1950s, the criminologists with roots in statistics, medicine, psychiatry and psychology, certainly approached criminality as if it were a thing-like entity residing in persons or structures, bounded and entire in itself, somehow analytically isolated from the phenomena and processes around it. For practical scientific purposes, the causes of crime have been thought to lie in criminals, and it is crimes and criminals that criminologists have examined.[11] At best, victims became shadowy, background figures who played no recognized part in causal explanation.[12] (It is interesting that, when positivist criminologists did eventually take to studying victims, they did so as if they were mirror-criminals, and proceeded to look for a thing called 'victimicity' that could serve as an analogue to the criminality of the criminal.)

The structural-functionalist criminologists of the 1950s and 1960s wished principally to show how crime and deviance buoyed up social systems. Crime was functional. If it *did* indeed inflict distress, they argued, it was as an epiphenomenal matter that should be disregarded.[13] What really signified were the effects wrought at a deeper level. Epiphenomenal too were the minute, embedded details and circumstances of crime. What criminals and those about them might actually have to say about crime was of little worth: the ideas of lay people on the social scene were, after all, no more than the unscientific thoughts of minds blind to the hidden structures of society. Structural-functionalists did not rely on interviewing or ethnography (what could such methods have told them?), and they could not have noticed what many of the participants in criminal events would have seen and heard all the time.

The more radical criminologists of the 1960s and 1970s regarded crime variously as a spirited or half-spirited gesture against capitalism,[14] a predictable result of capitalism's possessive individualism[15] or as an ideological distraction from the real besetting ills of capitalism.[16] They did not talk about the pain and suffering that crime inflicted. Such talk, they might have maintained, would have taken the afflictions of the bourgeoisie more seriously than they deserved, belittled the political import of the deviant act, attended too much to things of the surface or constituted a form of collusion with the hegemonic project of an oppressive politics. It was mere mystification, a kind of false consciousness to be dispelled by the application of scientific socialism.[17] Talk about victims would have been reactionary indeed.

Interactionists, phenomenologists and other phenomenalists of the 1960s and 1970s were perhaps the most intellectually culpable of all because *they* had worked with a body of ideas that had pointed insistently at the need to understand the social and symbolic interdependencies of deviance. *They* should have seen the victim (and, indeed, a very few, such as Lonnie Athens,[18] had done so). Yet theirs was a predominantly *appreciative* stance[19] that encouraged the study of the more sympathetic and harmless deviants who fringed the sociologist's own world. (One eminent interactionist was heard to mutter *sotto voce* at a conference, 'after all, we were only writing about ourselves'.) And some seemed to have been persuaded by Schur and others at an early stage to concentrate on crimes *without* victims,[20] the expressive forms of deviation that seemed to hurt no one, that were amenable to ethnographic research and did little more than illustrate the capriciousness of rule-making[21] and rule-enforcement.[22] Such deviants did not create an abundance of visible victims worthy of study.

Perhaps, then, it is not very remarkable that victims were not seen clearly, that they were not thought interesting enough to prompt consideration. And many victims are inconspicuous enough anyway unless the scholar deliberately goes to seek them out: they are often immobilized and withdrawn in the immediate aftermath of crime; do not regard themselves as members of a distinct group and may, indeed, believe themselves to be uniquely afflicted; do not usually linger long in the role of victim; may not refer to themselves as *victims* but use some other, more familiar, title to explain their condition; and may actually resent the very word *victim* but prefer instead to talk about themselves as survivors. Only when the experience of crime has been particularly shocking and traumatic are victims likely to take on a lasting public identity, the most poignant examples being the immediate victims of rape, sexual abuse, incest and violence and, at a remove, the families and friends who form the secondary victims of homicide, arson and drunken driving. Representatives of those victims *have* banded together, but they are quite evidently not the victims of commonplace crime (victims from whom they are inclined to distance themselves), and their organizations are few and new, almost all having been created since the 1970s. They are sometimes angry and frustrated; indeed, one group, Mothers Against Drunken Driving, has adopted the acronym of MADD. They succeeded in reviving the spectre of the victim-vigilante so feared by the policy-makers and criminologists of Britain and North America. They were probably best left alone.

The Rediscovery of the Victim

In short, criminologists, lawyers and criminal justice policy-makers have been relatively incurious about victims, have not regarded victims and victimization as particularly problematic, and have actually been a little alarmed about the prospect of stirring victims up politically. They were likely to busy themselves with the victim only in very special circumstances, when questions about criminological or political issues inadvertently illuminated victims and, in so doing, gave them an odd, almost accidental, appearance. But victims having been thus illuminated, a few people began to be intrigued by what could be seen, made them a more deliberate object of study, shifted intellectual focus to become as much 'victimologist' as criminologist, and moved on to build an organization to husband their infant ideas.

Let me illustrate. One early and important problem was the measurement of crime. There was an interest, as the criminologists were wont to say, in 'improving the criminal justice data base'. Criminology and criminal justice policy-makers wished to learn more about what they conceived to be the 'real' rates and movements of crime, aware that official rates reflected the vagaries of public reporting and bureaucratic recording practices;[23] they wished to reach down, as Sellin[24] and others conceived it, to the very sites of crime where most could be learned. Household surveys might more effectively disclose the *true* volume of crime in its guise as victimization.[25] The introduction to the first British Crime Survey reflected that:

> The discovery over the last decades of some of the shortcomings of statistics of recorded offences as a measure of the volume of crime is more properly seen as a rediscovery of what generations of statisticians and criminologists have pointed out: variations over time or place in recorded crime rates can reflect the processes by which the statistics are compiled as much as the conditions they are intended to depict. ... It is one thing to identify the shortcomings of statistics or recorded offences as a measure of crime, quite another to provide an alternative. Only recently has a research technique been developed with this aim in mind – the sample survey of victimisation, or 'crime survey'.[26]

Experimentally in the 1960s at first, and then recurrently, there were the massive US National

Crime Surveys. They were followed by surveys in Canada, Australia, Ireland, Finland and Scotland, England and Wales and elsewhere in the 1980s. Many were repeated at intervals to generate what were called 'trend data'.

One of the first roles in which victims came to view, then, was as indices or numbers in improved measures to count crime. However, it was not to be very long before they began to achieve some independence of character, becoming seen as analytically distinct from the crimes and criminals they were helping to enumerate.[27] It was not to be long, too, before statisticians and criminologists turned to crime surveys to explore phenomena other than crime rates: the fear of crime,[28] the geography of crime,[29] the links between 'routine activities' and crime,[30] attitudes towards the police,[31] and the particular victimization of women,[32] the young and the elderly. There were local surveys to look more closely at the relations between gender, class, race and victimization in small areas.[33] Surveys were to become part of the furniture of any modern criminal justice system and were to release a great explosion of new information and ideas that transformed criminology.

Crime was revealed as more prevalent and more distressing than many criminologists had formerly supposed; it was shown to be particularly distressing for the very groups that radical and other criminologists had adopted as their own: the poor, women and members of ethnic minorities. It could not be dismissed merely as political protest, class justice, false consciousness, an artifact of bureaucratic procedures or the creation of 'moral panics'. In a grand gesture of recantation, two radical criminologists said that they had believed 'that property offences are directed solely against the bourgeoisie and that violence against the person is carried out by amateur Robin Hoods in the course of their righteous attempts to redistribute wealth. All of this is, alas, untrue'.[34] Tracts of radical criminology were reformed and renamed to become 'left realism', the word 'realism' denoting the radicals' responsiveness to the new facts disclosed by crime surveys. Left realism began to address issues once wholly taboo: the control of crime, the improvement of policing practices, and the links between race and deviance.[35] It cooperated with the central and local state when such a practice would formerly have been denounced as cooptation, correctionalism and reformism. Its methods were transformed: what had once been disparaged as positivistic, piecemeal and empiricist was now embraced, as realists conducted surveys and mounted experimental crime prevention projects.

A second role was that of helpmeet in the reform of criminal justice and the penal system. The angry, vindictive, obstructive victim was imagined to be an impediment to change that could be removed only by appeasement.[36] Thus criminal injuries compensation was instituted in New Zealand and the United Kingdom in the early 1960s to defuse the wrath of victims of violence and so ease the abolition of corporal and capital punishment. Victim-offender reconciliation projects were instituted during the 'fiscal crisis' of the 1970s to allow the diversion of offenders from custody, the closure of prisons and a reduction in the rate of prison expansion. It was reasoned that an unforgiving and frightened community had to be mollified and pacified before prisons were reformed.[37]

It was only when victims were actually confronted, when they met their offenders and the reformers who organized their meetings, that their suffering, neglect, isolation and frustration began to become apparent. Only then did reformers and criminologists think beyond a domineering penology and a preoccupation with the offender's lot. They began to investigate the social psychology of victimization, seeing its effects as more long-lasting, more complex and with more ramifications than had hitherto been supposed. The impact of crime was undoubtedly more complicated than the description thrown up by the simplifying and impersonal questions of a crime survey that may have been conducted some time after the event.[38] Impact certainly could not be predicted neatly. One surprise was that the social and psychological consequences of property crime were not dissimilar to those of crimes against the person.[39] Both forms of crime could be experienced as invasive, contaminating, alienating and debasing. Property crime was more than a problem that could be put right merely by hardening targets, reducing opportunity, monetary compensation or more extensive insurance. Another surprise was that many victims and offenders are not unlike: there seems to be a pool of people who frequent crime-ridden areas and prey on one another. Indeed, one study in London reported that 'to a considerable extent the police deal with a limited clientele of people who tend to be in trouble both as victims and as offenders ... people who tend to be repeatedly victims also have a much higher average chance of being arrested'.[40] The result, said Antilla, was that the earlier criminological stereotypes of black and white, of discrete offenders and discrete victims, had to be replaced by 'grey versus grey'.[41] Crime, it appears, is committed most frequently by the poor against the poor, against the least adequately protected and insured residents of the inner city areas of Western countries. Those with the least suffer the most, and they do so in part because they live so near the offender.

A third role emerged out of the dialectic between a feminist politics and practical services for abused, battered and assaulted women. Rape crisis centres[42] and refuges for battered women were established or re-established in the early 1970s in North America and elsewhere.[43] They arose out of, and illustrated, arguments about the lot of women under patriarchy.[44] Women were victimized frequently, painfully and sometimes invisibly. Theirs was a private 'domestic' suffering that had come to public view only after concerted campaigns.[45] The assaulted woman, it was claimed with justifiable vehemence, was not a mere subject of false consciousness or moral panics. She needed a champion. Her victimization needed to be noticed.[46]

Criminologists, in particular the radical criminologists criticized by radical women, gave ground. They trimmed. For a while, they acknowledged the woman victim as a solitary exception to their larger arguments. Then they capitulated altogether: they conceded that much crime was brutal, disorganizing and disagreeable, a source of very real problems in everyday life. There was much less talk about deep structures, ideological distortions and mystification. Jones and his colleagues were constrained to write about 'a general tendency in radical thought to idealize [its] historical subject (in this case the working class) and to play down intra-group conflict, blemishes and social disorganization. But the power of the feminist case resulted in a sort of cognitive schizophrenia amongst radicals. ...'[47] Revelations about crimes against women prompted criminologists to think anew about the relations between violence, power and gender, as well as about the uses of formal and informal control in private and public space.

The list could be extended. New political and criminological practices have given victims numerous, proliferating forms. Consider the work done in the 1970s to win back victims in their guise as witnesses estranged from the criminal justice system by the indifference and cruelty of the trial system (work done in the service of more efficient prosecutions[48]); the rediscovery of children abused, battered and victimized directly or indirectly,[49] and the consequences of a decline of faith in the effectiveness of formal agencies of criminal justice, a decline that prompted politicians, policy-makers and criminologists to turn away from the established repertoire of detection, adjudication and punishment to a new cooperation with the 'community'. The community was deemed to include victims, bystanders and their representatives; they too were wooed assiduously in the 1980s,[50] coming to the fore as important sources of knowledge and control.[51] 'Community policing' and 'multi-agency work' gave the victim a new visibility.

It was not easy to accommodate all these new actors and discoveries and to map out a field for them: the very word 'victimology' was an ungainly neologism. Victimologists themselves made some inflated claims and said some idiosyncratic things, particularly at the very beginning, opening themselves to the charge of eccentricity (Calvin Becker said in 1981 that 'it is difficult to restrain the urge to dismiss victimology as the lunatic fringe of criminology'[52]). The new discipline occasionally met with opposition, obstacles and incredulity: Viano remarked that 'any new field ... initially struggles to develop its terminology, define its boundaries, justify its existence, gain respectability and eventually claim its place among the already established disciplines. ... Victimology is no exception'.[53]

So it was that victimology began to be established in the 1970s[54] as a result of victims entering criminology unbidden. They entered awkwardly, obliquely and in disguise, taking their places without coordination, having no planned or clear relation to one another, jumbled together solely because they shared a common name.

It was inevitable that what was thus formed bore the mark of its origins. Victimology is, in effect, a sub-discipline of criminology, the only discipline even remotely attentive to victims, the discipline that sired victimology despite itself. Like criminology, it is an empirically-driven science, a *rendez-vous* science defined by its attention to all things associated with victims,[55] rather than a science unified by a common theory, practice, profession or institution. Like criminology, it may be described as diffuse, synthetic and loosely-integrated. Such a dispersed set of ideas lacks shape, and there has been a persistent fear that victimology lacks definition, a centre and a body of unifying argument.[56] It was also inevitable that some of the terminology, methods and concepts of criminology were simply transposed to victimology: they were the intellectual materials most readily to hand. Thus the prospectus for the World Society of Victimology is at once a criminological programme in all but name and a compendium of almost everything ever linked with victims:

> From its beginning, victimology has been an international and an interdisciplinary subject. The need for information about the victim's contribution to the commission of crime, the offender-victim relationship, the victim's vulnerability and recidivism, the victim's role in the criminal justice system, the potential victim's fear of crime and attitudes towards legislation and law enforcement stimulated victimological research throughout the world. Victim service centers, victim-witness assistance programs, rape crisis centers, victim advocates offering comprehensive integrated responses to the legal, financial, social and emotional needs of the innocent crime victim and his family have been established in many countries.

This book reflects the emerging structure of that discipline by marshalling some of the very different manifestations and arguments that brought victims back into scholarly research. What now remains is to build victims more securely into research and analysis. Criminal encounters should be treated as the centre of evolving webs of actors and audiences, actions and reactions, relations and meanings, that can fan out to affect the worlds and lives of people about them. Only then would it be possible to begin charting the larger social and psychological significance of crime.

Notes

1. L. Zedner, 'Victims' in M. Maguire *et al.* (eds), *The Oxford Handbook of Criminology*, forthcoming.
2. *The Oxford English Dictionary* gives the earliest usage of the word as 1956 in an article by B. Mendelsohn ('Une nouvelle branche de la science bio-psycho-sociale: Victimologie', *Revue internationale de criminologie et de police technique*, 1956, **10**). Victimology actually seems to have been a creature of the decade before, the 1940s, Mendelsohn's article itself having first appeared in *The American Law Review*, **13** (4) in 1947. Other instances were in the work of H. Ellenberger (1954), 'Relation psychologique entre le criminel et sa victime', *Revue internationale de criminologie et de police technique*, **8**, and H. von Hentig (1948), *The Criminal and His Victim: Studies in the Sociology of Crime*, New York: Yale University Press. Another contender, cited by Zedner, was Frederick Wertham who proposed a 'science of victimology' in *The Show of Violence*, London: Victor Gollancz, 1949. More generally, see B. Mendelsohn, 'The Origins of the Doctrine of Victimology' in I. Drapkin and E. Viano (eds) (1974), *Victimology*, Lexington, MA: D.C. Heath.
3. It was during the 1980s that a great spate of important books and articles marked the coming of age of victimology. See, for example, G. Chambers and A. Millar (1983), *Investigating Sexual Assault*, Edinburgh: HMSO; E. Fattah (ed.) (1986), *From Crime Policy to Victim Policy*, London: Macmillan; M. Maguire (1982), *Burglary in a Dwelling*, London: Heinemann; and J. Shapland *et al.* (1985), *Victims and the Criminal Justice System*, Aldershot: Gower.
4. Thus there is no listing for 'victim' and its linked words in the *Penguin Dictionary of Sociology*, London: Penguin, 1988; the *Encyclopedia of Sociology*, Guilford, Conn: Dushkin, 1974; *A Blackwell Dictionary of Twentieth-Century Social Thought*, Oxford: Blackwell, 1993; *The Social Science Encyclopedia*, London: Routledge, 1989; and all similar works of reference which include terms taken to be of interest to the sociologist and the social scientist. The lone exception is *The Macmillan Student Encyclopedia of Sociology*, London: Macmillan, 1983, which includes a rather tetchy entry on victimology that I prepared as one of the subject editors.
5. J. Shapland (1983), 'Victim Assistance and the Criminal Justice System', paper delivered to the 33rd International Course in Criminology, Vancouver, March, p. 8.
6. Thus the US Department of Justice declared that 'traditionally, both public attention and the criminal justice system have focused on criminal offenders. Criminal justice resources have been used to pursue, judge, and imprison offenders and have paid little attention to their victims'. *Victims of Crime*, Washington DC: Bureau of Justice Statistics, US Department of Justice, 1981, p. 1.
7. For instance 'victim' and words stemming from it are not to be found in *Harrap's Dictionary of Law and Society*, Bromley: Harrap, 1979 or in *A Concise Dictionary of Law*, Oxford: Oxford University Press, 1990.
8. See M. Mears (1990), 'Rape and the Radical Lawyer', *The Law Society's Gazette*, 28 March, Number 12.
9. See S. Schafer (1968), *The Victim and his Criminal*, New York: Random House and N. Christie (1977), 'Conflicts as Property', *British Journal of Criminology*, **17** (Chapter 2 in this volume).
10. K. Burke (1935), *Permanence and Change*, New York: New Republic Inc., p. 70.
11. And that examination would take place in prisons, hospitals and psychiatrists' consulting rooms where no victims could be seen. Criminals themselves, it should be noted, are not often anxious to consider their victims when they talk about crime. See M. Wright (1977), *Making Amends: Criminals, Victims and Society*, Chichester: Barry Rose.
12. It is no surprise that the edited volume that celebrated the birth and development of a more positivist version of criminology should make no mention of victims. H. Mannheim (ed.) (1960), *Pioneers in Criminology*, London: Stevens.

13. It was David Matza's contention that they failed utterly to note the pathos of crime. See D. Matza (1969), *Becoming Deviant*, Englewood Cliffs, New Jersey: Prentice-Hall.

14. See S. Hall *et al.* (1976), *Resistance through Ritual*, London: Hutchinson.

15. See I. Taylor *et al.* (1973), *The New Criminology*, London: Routledge and Kegan Paul.

16. See S. Hall *et al.* (1978), *Policing the Crisis*, London: Macmillan.

17. See S. Box (1971), *Deviance, Reality and Society*, London: Holt, Rinehart and Winston; S. Box (1983), *Power, Crime and Mystification*, London: Tavistock; and F. Pearce (1976), *Crimes of the Powerful*, London: Pluto Press.

18. See L. Athens (1980), *Violent Criminal Acts and Actors: A Symbolic Interactionist Study*, London: Routledge and Kegan Paul, and L. Athens (1988), *The Creation of Dangerous Violent Criminals*, London: Routledge.

19. See D. Matza, *Becoming Deviant, op. cit.*

20. See E. Schur (1965), *Crimes Without Victims*, Englewood Cliffs, New Jersey: Prentice-Hall.

21. See E. Sutherland and D. Cressey (1960), *Principles of Criminology*, Chicago: Lippincott.

22. See S. Cohen (1972), *Folk Devils and Moral Panics*, London: MacGibbon and Kee; J. Young (1971), *The Drugtakers*, London: MacGibbon and Kee.

23. See, for instance, J. Kitsuse and A. Cicourel (1963), 'A Note on the Use of Official Statistics', *Social Problems*, **11**.

24. See T. Sellin, 'The Significance of Records of Crime' in M. Wolfgang *et al.* (eds) (1962), *The Sociology of Crime and Delinquency*, New York: John Wiley.

25. See P. Ennis (1967), *Criminal Victimization in the United States: A Report of a National Survey*, Washington DC: Department of Justice.

26. M. Hough and P. Mayhew (1983), *The British Crime Survey: First Report*, London: HMSO, p. 1.

27. I have discussed the evolving significance of victims in the Canadian Urban Victimization Surveys in my *A View from the Shadows, op. cit.*, Chapter 5, and in the British Crime Surveys in my *Helping Victims of Crime: The Home Office and the Rise of Victim Support*, Oxford: Oxford University Press, 1990, Chapter 7.

28. See M. Maxfield (1984), *The Fear of Crime in England and Wales*, London: HMSO.

29. See S. Smith (1987), *Crime, Space and Society*, London: Cambridge University Press.

30. See L. Cohen and M. Felson (1979), 'Social Change and Crime Rate Trends: A Routine Activity Approach', *American Sociological Review*, **44** (Chapter 8 in this volume).

31. See W. Skogan (1990), *The Police and Public in England and Wales: A British Crime Survey Report*, London: HMSO.

32. See L. Smith (1989), *Concerns about Rape*, London: HMSO, and L. Smith (1989), *Domestic Violence*, London: HMSO.

33. See T. Jones *et al.* (1986), *The Islington Crime Survey*, Aldershot: Gower; R. Kinsey (unpublished); and *Merseyside Crime Survey*, Liverpool, 1984.

34. J. Lea and J. Young (1984), *What is to be Done about Law and Order?*, London: Penguin, p. 262.

35. See, for example, J. Lowman and B. MacLean (1993), *Realist Criminology in the 1990s*, Toronto: University of Toronto Press.

36. See, for instance, Justice (1962), *Compensation for Victims of Crimes of Violence*, London: Stevens. C.H. Rolph, a campaigner for criminal injuries compensation in England and Wales, wrote 'the law for centuries has required the citizen to smother his natural desire for revenge and leave it to the police and the courts to deal with the offender. The disabled man's injury is the State's injury. When he was coshed, the community was coshed. Vengeance is mine, saith the State; but it does not repay. ... Last November the Home Secretary was presented with a petition ... signed by 87,000 people asking for heavier sentences on violent criminals, the revival of flogging, and "adequate compensation for victims – as far as possible at the expense of their attackers"' (C.H. Rolph, 'Wild Justice', *New Statesman*, 18 January 1958).

37. See M. Wright (1982), *Making Good: Prisons, Punishment and Beyond*, London: Burnett Books; J. Hudson and B. Galaway (eds) (1977), *Restitution in Criminal Justice*, Lexington, MA: Lexington Books, and J. Hudson and B. Galaway (eds) (1980), *Victims, Offenders and Alternative Sanctions*, Lexington, MA: Lexington Books.

38. See E. Fattah (1979), 'Some Recent Theoretical Trends in Victimology', *Victimology*, **4** (2),

(Chapter 19 in this volume).

39. See M. Maguire (1980), 'The Impact of Burglary Upon Victims', *British Journal of Criminology*, **20** (3), July (Chapter 10 in this volume).
40. D. Smith (1983), *Police and People in London*, London: Policy Studies Institute, Volume 1, p. 124.
41. I. Antilla (1964), 'Victimology – A New Territory in Criminology', *Scandinavian Studies in Criminology*, **5**, p. 8.
42. See M. Wasserman (1973), 'Rape: Breaking the Silence', *The Progressive*, November (Chapter 15 in this volume).
43. See E. Pizzey (1974), *Scream Quietly or the Neighbours Will Hear*, Harmondsworth: Penguin.
44. Center for Women Policy Studies (1981), *Programs Providing Services to Battered Women*, Washington D.C.: Z. Adler (1987), *Rape on Trial*, London: Routledge and Kegan Paul; and R. Hall (1985), *Ask Any Woman: A London Inquiry into Rape and Sexual Assault*, London: Falling Wall Press.
45. See J. Hanmer, 'Violence to Women: From Private Sorrow to Public Issue' in G. Ashworth and L. Bonnerjea (eds) (1985), *The Invisible Decade: UK Women and the UN Decade 1976–1985*, Aldershot: Gower.
46. See, for example, C. Smart (1977), *Women, Crime and Criminology*, London: Routledge and Kegan Paul.
47. T. Jones *et al.*, *The Islington Crime Survey*, *op. cit.*, pp. 2–3.
48. See, for example, *Remembering Forgotten Victims*, Sacramento, California: Office of the Attorney General, 1980; and M. Knudten *et al.*, 'Will Anyone be Left to Testify?' in E. Flynn and J. Conrad (eds) (1978), *New and Old Criminology*, Washington D.C.: LEAA.
49. See J. Morgan and L. Zedner (1992), *Child Victims*, Oxford: Clarendon Press.
50. See the essays in T. Hope and M. Shaw (eds) (1988), *Communities and Crime Reduction*, London: HMSO.
51. See J. Shapland and J. Vagg (1988), *Policing by the Public*, London: Routledge.
52. C. Becker (1981), *Criminal Theories of Causation and Victims' Contributions to the Etiology of Crime*, Ph.D. dissertation, University of Cambridge, p. 4.
53. E. Viano (1976), Introduction to *Victims and Society*, Washington: Visage Press, p. 3.
54. There were to be a number of volumes championing victimology published during that decade: the journal *Victimology* and the International Symposium on Victimology were both founded in 1976.
55. See K. Levine (1978), 'Empiricism in Victimological Research', *Victimology*, **3** (1-2).
56. There has been rather persistent anxiety that victimology does not possess a distinct theory. For example, it was reported at the Second International Symposium on Victimology that 'there were more data offered ... than [there] were theories and hypotheses. There are few victimological theories available to scholars'. E. Flynn (1977), 'Report on the Discussion Sections of the Second International Symposium on Victimology', *Victimology*, **2** (1), Spring, p. 34.

Part I
The Birth of Victimology

[1]

THE ORIGIN OF THE DOCTRINE OF VICTIMOLOGY

by

B. MENDELSOHN, Lawyer

Jerusalem – Israel

The idea of Victimology occurred to my mind in the following manner:

A) As the natural corollary of the conception set forth in my first study *Method to be used by counsel for the defence in the researches made into the personality of the criminal* (Revue de Droit Pénal et de Criminologie, Bruxelles, août–sept.–oct. 1937, page 877). Convinced that a 'well conducted defence cannot be based on untruth' (page 883), I once more took the trouble that I had previously taken at the outset of my profession as a barrister, of drawing up for my own use, a scientific method of study of a criminal case. In general this method consists of the following measures (which explains my gradual evolution towards the conception of Victimology). a) A questionnaire containing more than 300 questions, concerning the branches of criminology and associated sciences (pages 882-883) couched, as far as possible, in simple language. b) The same questionnaire is given to the accused and to some of those around him, with the object of being able to complete and compare the material collected and to go through the proofs. c) To the sources of information indicated above is added, of course, the report of the trial in the lower court, and what the accused testifies (independently of the replies given in the questionnaire), the opinion of the expert witnesses, and the results of a social enquiry — when such is necessary and is possible in practice. (I have presented this method here only in rough outline for the purposes of demonstration.) Thus the defence comes to be the result of the best documented facts and the application of well established law. By this method I have in detail gone into: 'The personality of the accused from the bio-psycho-social point of view and, parallelly, into the 'data concerning the personality of the victims' and even of their social relations (page 883). This method has been applied by me throughout my practice of the profession of a barrister specializing in criminology.

B) As one of the results of the application of the method indicated above (A), I have published my study on *Rape in criminology* (Giustizia Penale, Roma, 1940, Parte I-a — I presupposti del diritto penale, VI della 5-a serie, Fasc. I-II-III-IV), which appeared after the outbreak of the second world war. This time I have concentrated my researches *on the victim* from the bio-psycho-social point of view, and his relationships with the delinquent, within the framework of rape and — to some degree — of other crimes against morality. Chapter II treats the subject of: 'The phases of the struggle for possession between the aggressor and the victim. The extent to which the woman is able to resist rape'. I pointed out the possibility of resistance on the part of the woman by the almost inexpugnable position she occupies on account of the topography of the sexual organs in the female body ... They have the following features: a) 'They are not situated at the extremities of the body, exposed to attack; b) they are sheltered in the most hidden place of the external portion of the human body; c) They do not constitute a prominence but a cavity — that is to say, they are sheltered within the body; d) 'They are protected by two lower limbs that

240

possess a great mobility, a great radius of action of defensive and offensive nature and a great power of resistance and are served by the most powerful muscles in the human system, sustaining and transporting all the weight of the body. I would add: the various muscles have well deserved the title of: Castitatis custodese! The following exceptions are mentioned: (I) A very great disproportion between the physical strength of the aggressor (or aggressors) and that of the victim. (II) The state of unconsciousness of the victim (early age, anaesthesia, fainting, drunkenness, hypnotism, alterations of the mental state, stupefiants, etc.). (III) The element of surprise in an abnormal position favourable to the neutralization of the resistance of the victim and to the perpetration of sexual intercourse. (IV) Threats strong enough to break down the will to resist. Finally, I remarked that, from the psychological point of view, the resistance of the victim may be lessened also by the circumstances listed here: (1) The familial, authoritative or hierarchical relations existing between the accused and the victim. (2) The volcanic temperament of the victim, which may obscure the reasoning faculty. (3) The libertine social surroundings of the victim . . . (4) The superiority of the social milieu of the accused in relation to that of the victim.

Chapter II — at the end — points out that it is absolutely necessary to take into consideration the degree of exhaustion of the victim, and also that the power of the aggressor should not be appraised by that of the individual in his normal condition but according to what it is when under the influence of his unleashed primitive instincts; that his physical strength is the resultant of the combination of two primitive instincts: the sexual and the aggressive; and that his strength may be exaggerated by the morbid sexuality of the delinquent, or by alcohol, etc.; or it may be diminished by a violent blow. To avoid a mistaken interpretation the following remark was added: 'we are far from admitting that a woman must either fight for the defence of her virginity like an athlete in an arena or else be considered to be at fault — such is not the theme of our study. Moreover, no juridical law can demand that anyone should be a hero! The point that we wish to make is simply that the court — whose appreciation of the facts is of sovereign quality — should be careful to take account of all the real possibilities of the woman's defence, every time that it is not a question of rape but of a consented act or a simulated resistance. In every case it must weigh up all the circumstances which may throw light on the happenings.'

Attention is also drawn to threats that may really intimidate the victim, taking into consideration her personality, that may force her to yield from fear, and that may be directed against some other member of the family (Garraud, Garçon, etc.). Chapter IV treats the problem of 'the degree of specific credibility of the woman with regard to her complaints about offences against her modesty'. The victims are divided from the psychological and juridical point of view into the following categories and the subject is developed in detail (here I only indicate the title of each category). I) Adult witnesses. II) Minor boys between the ages of 16 and majority (article 79 of the French code of criminal procedure and article 161 of the Roumanian code. Charles II) have the right to give evidence under oath in the same way as other witnesses. III) Minors below 15 years of age do not take the oath and are heard only as informers. IV) The statements of young girls under the age of 15 when giving evidence should be received with greater caution than those of minor boys of the same age. V) The depositions of girls under 16 years should be taken with still more reserve in questions of assaults against decency. VI) Depositions of the group of minor girls. VII) Minors with pathological constitutions. Chapter II ends with the conclusion — from the juridical point of view — that the sexual act is possible only under the following circumstances: 1) With the consent of the woman, or in cases of simulated resistance — which does not constitute a crime; 2) without the consent of the victim, and in spite of the latter's resistance – which is a crime; 3) with the consent of the victim but with resistance reduced in proportion to the intimidation, the intellectual and social level, the physical disproportion, the degree of consciousness and the position in which the victim has been surprised. In these conditions the sexual act is a crime.

I think that there is a way of treating this subject which fits perfectly into a treatise on victimology. The title *Rape in victimology* would harmonize better with the contents of my article.

C) As a result of the same manner of thinking and as a consequence of the method set forth above (A), it is applied to several cases of 'crimes passionnels' in which I have pleaded before the Court of Criminal Justice in Bucharest between 1934 and 1951. It was while preparing for the trial of Stephan Codreanu arraigned in 1945 for a crime passionnel that I began to elaborate the doctrine of Victimology. It was a case of double murder: The accused had with premeditation killed his wife and her lover. He had for several years continued to live with his wife after the divorce. He was always invited by her to stay on the first and the fifteenth of the month, under the pretext of preparing the lessons with their little daughter, whom he adored. He would eat with the family and she poured out all her sweetness to keep him for the night, but the next day she would turn him out of the house, having first of all taken all his money. The lover — a young soldier — would ridicule him. He was sentenced to 12 years, but the sentence was mitigated and he was released after 5 or 6 years. There can be no doubt that, had it had not been for the perversity of his former wife, he would never have been guilty of two crimes.

D) In 1946 the manuscript *New bio-psycho-social horizons: victimology* was circulated among the specialists of Bucharest (medico-legal experts, psychiatrists, psychoanalysts, barristers). This manuscript was intended for a work of considerable size, but I have only published the summaries of a few chapters in specialist reviews.

E) In March 1947, at the invitation of the Roumanian Society of Psychiatry, I made a communication on Victimology in the amphitheatre of the State Hospital 'Coltzea' in Bucharest.

F) In 1948, Prof. Dr. Hans van Hentig published in Yale a very interesting study entitled *The criminal and his victim,* and in 1954 Prof. Dr. Henry Ellenberger (Topeka, Kansas) made an important contribution to this subject in his study *Relations psychologiques entre le criminel et sa victime* (Revue internationale de criminologie et de police technique, No. 2/1954, Genève). I have quoted these two studies because — in contrast to various other works that only skim over the question — these attack the very essence of these problems. Between the studies of Prof. van Hentig and Prof. Ellenberger on the one hand, and ours on the other hand, there are statements and viewpoints that are identical, even though the terms employed are different. Thus, what we designate as the 'penal couple' — that is to say, the victim-criminal — appears in Prof. van Hentig's work under the name of 'doer-sufferer'; and what we have named 'Victimology' is called 'Victimogenesis' by Prof. Ellenberger. It is also interesting to note that the training of the two authors is completely different, one being a psychiatrist and the other a barrister specializing in criminology. What is especially noteworthy is that this new scientific conception took concrete form after the second world war, almost simultaneously at the two different sides of the globe, in two worlds completely separated from one another and without any intellectual contact between them, Roumania being at that time completely shut off behind the Iron Curtain. These facts confirm our opinion that Victimology is a scientific reality which impresses itself on the human consciousness by its scientific quality. Nevertheless, we must point out a fundamental difference between the points of view of Prof. van Hentig and Prof. Ellenberger on the one hand and of ourselves on the other hand. The former consider the study of the victim as a chapter of criminology, whereas we consider it as a separate science, which, because of its structure and its aim should be independent. The reasons which have led us to this conclusion can be found in my study *Victimology, present day science — La victimologie, science actuelle* (Revue de Droit Pénal et de Criminologie, Bruxelles, avril 1957, page 519).

242

G) The same text appeared under the title of *A new branch of bio-psychosocial science: Victimology* (Revue Internationale de Criminologie et de Police Technique, Genève No. 2/ 1956). *Victimologie* (Etudes Internationales de Psycho-sociologie Criminelle, Paris No. 1/ 1956) was a summary of a part of our incomplete and unpublished study: *Horizons nouveaux bio-psycho-sociaux: la victimologie.*
H) In 1954 at the International Congress on Social Defence at Antwerp, my work was mentioned for the first time in the general report by Judge Versele (Brussels).

The spread of the idea of victimology in various countries
My *Victimology* appeared in English and French in several papers. In Japanese in the Japanese Journal of Legal Medicine and Criminology, Vol. 24, No. 6/1958, published in continuation of the report of Prof. Dr. Shufu Yoshimasu, professor of the Section of Psychological Medicine, and in the translation of Dr. Osamu Nakata, assistant professor in the Medical University of Tokyo.

In Paris the daily newspaper *Combat* in its issues of 6.6.1958, 27.8.1958, and 21.8.1958 published articles under the signature of Alexandre Wexliard (Paris, at the present time professor at the University of Ankara) and M. Mellot, the former adopting the idea of Victimology in its entirety — with powerful supporting arguments — and the latter only admitting it within the scope of criminology.

Geneva: On several occasions during the debates at the meeting of the European consultative group on the prevention of crime and the treatment of offenders (1958) the problems of Victimology were mentioned.

Belgium: At the suggestion of Prof. Paul Cornil, the Dutch–Belgian conferences dedicated their meetings of December 19 and 21, 1958, to the problem of Victimology. Four papers were read respectively by the professors: Paul Cornil (Brussels), Nagel (Leiden), Callewaert (Ghent), and Noach (Utrecht). Several meetings were held in 1958 on Victimology during the University Seminar on Criminology and the programme contained a study of Victimology on its agenda.

Prof. Paul Cornil opened the new academic year of the University seminar on criminology with a lecture on Victimology. A certain number of sessions were reserved for a study of this doctrine. A victimological *movement* began to take shape in Belgium and developed in the following years. The April number 1959 of Revue de Droit Pénal et de Criminologie was dedicated to Victimology (120 pages). This number contained the following articles: Prof. Paul Cornil, *The contribution of Victimology to criminological science.* Prof. Willy Callewaert, barrister (Ghent), *Victimology and fraud.* B. Mendelsohn (Jerusalem), *Victimology — a present day science.* Prof. Dr. Dellaert (Louvain), *First comparison of criminal psychology and Victimology.* Aimé Racine, barrister (Brussels), *The child as the victim of immoral acts committed on its person by an ascendant.* L. de Bray (Brussels), *Some observations on the victims of crimes.* This number also published some detailed accounts of the discussions, suggestions and resolutions adopted by the Dutch–Belgian conferences.

Gerda de Bock, director of the course of studies at the University of Ghent, presented a report *Justice et publicité* to the Belgian and Luxemburg Assembly on Penal Law. Published in the Rev. de Droit Pénal et de Criminologie (Brussels), No. 1/1960, p. 35-65. Beginning with page 57 the subject is treated from the point of view of Victimology. The results are related to a careful social enquiry in Ghent. Though no victimological question was introduced into the questionnaire, the subjects of the enquiry, of their own account, supplied data concerning problems of Victimology. They were of sufficient value to be recorded and shown in the results of the work.

Italy: (1958) Professor Dr. Domenico Macaggi of the Faculty of Law and director of the Medico-Legal Institute has included Victimology in the list of subjects for theses for the Doctorate. A thesis on Victimology has been prepared by Miss Maria Grazia Anduini-Plaisant.

243

The Netherlands: Prof. Dr. W. H. Nagel, V*ictimologie,* Tijdschrift voor Strafrecht LXVIII (1959). Prof. Dr. W. M. E. Noach, *Het Slachtoffer en de rechtspraak,* Strafrechtspraak. (An anthology.) 1959). p. 29–43.

France: Etudes internationales de psycho-sociologie criminelle No. 4/1959 includes an article critically analysing the matter under the title *La Victimologie* and bearing the signature of Me. Claude-Roland Souchet, barrister of the Paris courts. The same appeared in La Vie Judiciaire in its number of December 1959. I was invited to take part in the International Congress of social prophylaxis (Paris, September 26, 1959) under the presidence of Mr. M. Patin, president of the Supreme Court, Criminal Section, and to present a report from the victimological point of view on a selected subject, but was unable to participate.

Dr. N. Duc, *Considérations sur la criminologie et la victimologie des attentats aux moeurs à propos de 35 cas personnels* (Annales de Médecine Légale, Paris, Année XLI, No. 1/ 1961, pages 55-58). Abstracted in English in Excerpta Criminologica, No. 5/1961, page 455.

Dr. Louis Gayral, director of studies in the Faculty of Medicine of Toulouse. In his work on general psychiatry, in the chapter on forensic medicine, he introduces some considerations on Victimology.

Jean Geraud, Professor in the Faculty of Medicine of Toulouse, established Victimology as a subject for the degree of doctor.

Dr. R. Lafon, *Quelques propos sur la Victimologie* (Annales de Médecine Légale, Paris, Année XLI, No. 1/1961, page 24) (Excerpta Criminologica No. 4/1961, page 349).

Dr. R. Lafon, Dr. J. Trivas, Dr. J.-L. Faure and Dr. R. Pouget, *Victimologie et criminologie des attentats sexuels sur les enfants et les adolescents* (Annales de Médecine Légale, Paris, Année XLI, 1961, p. 97-106) (Excerpta Criminologica No. 5, 1961, p. 454) Cl. R. Souchet, barrister-at-law, Paris: *La Victimologie,* in Etudes Internationales de Psycho-sociologie Criminelle, Paris, No. 4/1958, pages 13-14). Idem reprinted in La Vie Judiciaire, Paris, December 1958. Idem summary published in Excerpta Criminologica, No. 1/1960, page 24.

Argentina: Prof. Luis Jemenes de Assua gave in 1958 a series of lectures on Victimology at the institute of penal law and criminology of the University of Buenos Aires, for candidates for the degree of doctor. Prof. L. H. de Assua, together with Dr. Eduardo Aguira Abarrio, Dr. Maria H. Pen, Dr. Octavio Iturbe of the Board of Governors of the Institute and the students who had taken the course, collect these studies together in a book on Victimology.

Dr. O. Iturbe gave a lecture on Victimology at the Criminological Society. He also published a study on the same subject called *Victimologia, nuevo enfoque criminologica de la victima del delito,* in 'La Revista Penal y Penitenciaria' No. 87-90, Enero-Diciembre 1958. Tome XXI, pages 199-223. (Excerpta Criminologica, No. 1/1960, 23).

Japan: Dr. Shûfu Yoshimasu, professor of Medical Psychology of the Faculty of Medicine, and Prof. Dr. Tanemotu Furuhata, president of the Japanese Academy of Criminology decided to organize a symposium on the problems of Victimology. It took place at the Tokyo Medical and Dental University on 14th November 1959. The programme was as follows: (1) Introduction — Prof. Dr. T. Furuhata, president of the Japanese Association of Criminology. (2) Prospect of Victimology — Dr. O. Nakata, Associate Professor of Tokyo Medical and Dental University. (3) On the Victim of Female Homicide — Dr. K. Hirose. (4) Victimology from the viewpoint of Crime Prevention — T. Onojima, Chief of the Section of Crime Prevention, Tokyo Metropolitan Police. (5) On the Concept of Victimology — Prof. Dr. S. Yoshimasu, University of Tokyo. These studies were published in the Japanese Journal of Legal Medicine and Criminology, Tokyo, Vol. 25, No. 6/1959. Prof. Dr. Shûfu Yoshimasu published a study called *Studien über 200 Mörder von ihren kriminellen Lebenskurven aus gesehen,* in the review Folia Psychiatria et Neurologica Japonica (1958) Tokyo, in which Victimology is taken into consideration.

Dr. Tetsuya Hirose, collaborator of Professor Dr. Yoshimasu in the Institute of Mental Research of the University of Tokyo, *Psychiatrische Untersuchungen an den Mörderinnen.*

244

Beobachtungen an den 50 strafgefangenen Mörderinnen und Totschlägerinnen und ihre kriminelle Katamnese. The doctrine of Victimology is taken into consideration.

Dr. Yoshiske Ikeda of the Institute of Mental Research of the University of Tokyo (Prof. Dr. Shufu Yoshimasu), *Industrial psychiatric study on the human factors in the causation of accidents.* The doctrine of Victimology is considered.

Federal Republic of Germany: Klaus Bermann (University of Heidelberg) is preparing his doctoral thesis on Victimology in the Law Faculty of Mainz. Edgar Lenz, Assessor Frankfurt/Main, *Der Betrogene,* thesis for the degree of doctor in the Law Faculty of Mainz (Referent: Prof. Dr Mergen, Co-referent: Prof. Dr. Klug, lithographed work, 192 pages).

Israel: The delinquent and his victim (Haavarian Vekorbano) appeared in the daily paper 'Haaretz' on May 28th, 1962. It was from the pen of Mr. Menahem Horovitz (Jerusalem), member of the committee of the Israelian Society of Criminology, who completely accepts the doctrine.

In regard to research in this field we have been greatly impressed by the promising studies by Dr. Reuben Rothenberg of Tel Aviv, psychiatrist. He deals with especially the psychiatric and psycho-analytical aspects of the problems of Victimology. He intends shortly to give a lecture on the subject with a presentation of cases before the Neurological Society under the title of *The relations between victimology and psychiatry.* The following are the main points he will take up:

1. Victimology as a social doctrine: a. Its history. b. The founder, his experience, his researches. The researches of psychiatrists, psychologists and jurists. c. The importance of the epoch of social cataclysm provoked by Hitlerism; the Eichmann trial.

2. Two mutually opposed positions — positive and negative — concerning the victim: a. In crimes against life: Murders — examples. b. In crimes of financial character: fraud. c. Treatment: hypnosis or suggestion.

3. The problem of the persecuted-persecutor in Freudian cases. The author of the crime becomes the victim and vice versa.

4. Rape in victimology; the problem of the Oedipus complex.

5. The relations to other doctrines.

Conclusions: A separate science or only a section of a science? An important contribution to Victimology has been made by Professor Baruk, who, with his characteristic foresight, has written articles and given lectures in national and international conferences on this conception and its perspectives. He says: (letter of 1.7.1957.) '... Victimology in the end will win general assent'.

In summary, the following aspects of the opinions expressed about the conception of Victimology are emphasized:

a) The specialists who expressed their points of view on Victimology, whether in articles in the scientific or the daily press, or in correspondence with me, were unanimous in recognizing the fact that the bio-psycho-social and legal aspects of the victim have been neglected and that a fundamental change of opinion is taking place.

b) The majority — almost the unanimous opinion — is in favour of Victimology, but solely within the bounds of Criminology.

c) The minority — which is becoming less of a minority — supports my view that Victimology should be a separate and autonomous science, should have its own institutions and should be allowed to develop for the well-being and progress of humanity.

[2]

THE BRITISH JOURNAL
OF
CRIMINOLOGY

Vol. 17   January 1977   No. 1

CONFLICTS AS PROPERTY*

NILS CHRISTIE (Oslo) †

Abstract

CONFLICTS are seen as important elements in society. Highly industrialised societies do not have too much internal conflict, they have too little. We have to organise social systems so that conflicts are both nurtured and made visible and also see to it that professionals do not monopolise the handling of them. Victims of crime have in particular lost their rights to participate. A court procedure that restores the participants' rights to their own conflicts is outlined.

Introduction

Maybe we should not have any criminology. Maybe we should rather abolish institutes, not open them. Maybe the social consequences of criminology are more dubious than we like to think.

I think they are. And I think this relates to my topic—conflicts as property. My suspicion is that criminology to some extent has amplified a process where conflicts have been taken away from the parties directly involved and thereby have either disappeared or become other people's property. In both cases a deplorable outcome. Conflicts ought to be used, not only left in erosion. And they ought to be used, and become useful, for those originally involved in the conflict. Conflicts *might* hurt individuals as well as social systems. That is what we learn in school. That is why we have officials. Without them, private vengeance and vendettas will blossom. We have learned this so solidly that we have lost track of the other side of the coin: our industrialised large-scale society is not one with too many internal conflicts. It is one with too little. Conflicts might kill, but too little of them might paralyse. I will

* Foundation Lecture of the Centre for Criminological Studies, University of Sheffield, delivered March 31, 1976. Valuable comments on preliminary drafts of the manuscript were received from Vigdis Christie, Tove Stang Dahl and Annika Snare.
† Professor of Criminology, University of Oslo.

NILS CHRISTIE

use this occasion to give a sketch of this situation. It cannot be more than a sketch. This paper represents the beginning of the development of some ideas, not the polished end-product.

On Happenings and Non-Happenings

Let us take our point of departure far away. Let us move to Tanzania. Let us approach our problem from the sunny hillside of the Arusha province. Here, inside a relatively large house in a very small village, a sort of happening took place. The house was overcrowded. Most grown-ups from the village and several from adjoining ones were there. It was a happy happening, fast talking, jokes, smiles, eager attention, not a sentence was to be lost. It was circus, it was drama. It was a court case.

The conflict this time was between a man and a woman. They had been engaged. He had invested a lot in the relationship through a long period, until she broke it off. Now he wanted it back. Gold and silver and money were easily decided on, but what about utilities already worn, and what about general expenses?

The outcome is of no interest in our context. But the framework for conflict solution is. Five elements ought to be particularly mentioned:

1. The parties, the former lovers, were in *the centre* of the room and in the centre of everyone's attention. They talked often and were eagerly listened to.

2. Close to them were relatives and friends who also took part. But they did not *take over*.

3. There was also participation from the general audience with short questions, information, or jokes.

4. The judges, three local party secretaries, were extremely inactive. They were obviously ignorant with regard to village matters. All the other people in the room were experts. They were experts on norms as well as actions. And they crystallised norms and clarified what had happened through participation in the procedure.

5. No reporters attended. They were all there.

My personal knowledge when it comes to British courts is limited indeed. I have some vague memories of juvenile courts where I counted some 15 or 20 persons present, mostly social workers using the room for preparatory work or small conferences A child or a young person must have attended, but except for the judge, or maybe it was the clerk, nobody seemed to pay any particular attention. The child or young person was most probably utterly confused as to who was who and for what, a fact confirmed in a small study by Peter Scott (1959). In the United States of America, Martha Baum (1968) has made similar observations. Recently, Bottoms and McClean (1976) have added another important observation: "There is one truth which is seldom revealed in the literature of the law or in studies of the administration of criminal justice. It is a truth which was made evident to all those involved in this research project as they sat through the cases which made up our sample. The truth is that, for the most part, the business of the criminal courts is dull, commonplace, ordinary and after a while downright tedious".

But let me keep quiet about your system, and instead concentrate on my

CONFLICTS AS PROPERTY

own. And let me assure you: what goes on is no happening. It is all a nega-
tion of the Tanzanian case. What is striking in nearly all the Scandinavian
cases is the greyness, the dullness, and the lack of any important audience.
Courts are not central elements in the daily life of our citizens, but peripheral
in four major ways:—

1. They are situated in the administrative centres of the towns, outside the
territories of ordinary people.

2. Within these centres they are often centralised within one or two large
buildings of considerable complexity. Lawyers often complain that they need
months to find their way within these buildings It does not demand much
fantasy to imagine the situation of parties or public when they are trapped
within these structures. A comparative study of court architecture might
become equally relevant for the sociology of law as Oscar Newman's (1972)
study of defensible space is for criminology. But even without any study, I
feel it safe to say that both physical situation and architectural design are
strong indicators that courts in Scandinavia belong to the administrators of
law.

3. This impression is strengthened when you enter the courtroom itself—
if you are lucky enough to find your way to it. Here again, the periphery of
the parties is the striking observation. The parties are represented, and it is
these representatives and the judge or judges who express the little activity
that is activated within these rooms. Honoré Daumier's famous drawings
from the courts are as representative for Scandinavia as they are for France.

There are variations. In the small cities, or in the countryside, the courts
are more easily reached than in the larger towns. And at the very lowest end
of the court system—the so-called arbitration boards—the parties are sometimes less heavily represented through experts in law. But the symbol of the
whole system is the Supreme Court where the directly involved parties do not
even attend their own court cases.

4. I have not yet made any distinction between civil and criminal conflicts. But it was not by chance that the Tanzania case was a civil one. Full
participation in your own conflict presupposes elements of civil law. The key
element in a criminal proceeding is that the proceeding is converted from
something between the concrete parties into a conflict between one of the
parties and the state. So, in a modern criminal trial, two important things
have happened. First, the parties are being *represented*. Secondly, the one
party that is represented by the state, namely the victim, is so thoroughly
represented that she or he for most of the proceedings is pushed completely
out of the arena, reduced to the triggerer-off of the whole thing. She or he is
a sort of double loser; first, *vis-à-vis* the offender, but secondly and often in a
more crippling manner by being denied rights to full participation in what
might have been one of the more important ritual encounters in life. The
victim has lost the case to the state.

Professional Thieves

As we all know, there are many honourable as well as dishonourable reasons
behind this development. The honourable ones have to do with the state's

NILS CHRISTIE

need for conflict reduction and certainly also its wishes for the protection of
the victim. It is rather obvious. So is also the less honourable temptation for
the state, or Emperor, or whoever is in power, to use the criminal case for
personal gain. Offenders might pay for their sins. Authorities have in time
past shown considerable willingness, in representing the victim, to act as
receivers of the money or other property from the offender. Those days are
gone; the crime control system is not run for profit. And yet they are not
gone. There are, in all banality, many interests at stake here, most of them
related to professionalisation.

Lawyers are particularly good at stealing conflicts. They are trained for
it. They are trained to prevent and solve conflicts. They are socialised into a
sub-culture with a surprisingly high agreement concerning interpretation of
norms, and regarding what sort of information can be accepted as relevant
in each case. Many among us have, as laymen, experienced the sad moments
of truth when our lawyers tell us that our best arguments in our fight against
our neighbour are without any legal relevance whatsoever and that we for
God's sake ought to keep quiet about them in court. Instead they pick out
arguments we might find irrelevant or even wrong to use. My favourite
example took place just after the war. One of my country's absolutely top
defenders told with pride how he had just rescued a poor client. The client had
collaborated with the Germans. The prosecutor claimed that the client
had been one of the key people in the organisation of the Nazi movement. He
had been one of the master-minds behind it all. The defender, however, saved
his client. He saved him by pointing out to the jury how weak, how lacking
in ability, how obviously deficient his client was, socially as well as organisa-
tionally. His client could simply not have been one of the organisers among
the collaborators; he was without talents. And he won his case. His client
got a very minor sentence as a very minor figure. The defender ended his
story by telling me—with some indignation—that neither the accused, nor
his wife, had ever thanked him, they had not even talked to him afterwards.

Conflicts become the property of lawyers. But lawyers don't hide that it is
conflicts they handle. And the organisational framework of the courts underlines this point. The opposing parties, the judge, the ban against privileged
communication within the court system, the lack of encouragement for
specialisation—specialists cannot be internally controlled—it all underlines
that this is an organisation for the handling of conflicts. *Treatment personnel*
are in another position. They are more interested in *converting the image of the
case from one of conflict into one of non-conflict.* The basic model of healers is not
one of opposing parties, but one where one party has to be helped in the
direction of one generally accepted goal—the preservation or restoration of
health. They are not trained into a system where it is important that parties
can control each other. There is, in the ideal case, nothing to control, because
there is only one goal. Specialisation is encouraged. It increases the amount
of available knowledge, and the loss of internal control is of no relevance. A
conflict perspective creates unpleasant doubts with regard to the healer's
suitability for the job. A non-conflict perspective is a precondition for defining crime as a legitimate target for treatment.

4

CONFLICTS AS PROPERTY

One way of reducing attention to the conflict is reduced attention given to the victim. Another is concentrated attention given to those attributes in the criminal's background which the healer is particularly trained to handle. Biological defects are perfect. So also are personality defects when they are established far back in time—far away from the recent conflict. And so are also the whole row of explanatory variables that criminology might offer. We have, in criminology, to a large extent functioned as an auxiliary science for the professionals within the crime control system. We have focused on the offender, made her or him into an object for study, manipulation and control. We have added to all those forces that have reduced the victim to a nonentity and the offender to a thing. And this critique is perhaps not only relevant for the old criminology, but also for the new criminology. While the old one explained crime from personal defects or social handicaps, the new criminology explains crime as the result of broad economic conflicts. The old criminology loses the conflicts, the new one converts them from inter-personal conflicts to class conflicts. And they are. They are class conflicts—also. But, by stressing this, the conflicts are again taken away from the directly involved parties. So, as a preliminary statement: Criminal conflicts have either become *other people's property*—primarily the property of lawyers—or it has been in other people's interests to *define conflicts away*.

Structural Thieves

But there is more to it than professional manipulation of conflicts. Changes in the basic social structure have worked in the same way.

What I particularly have in mind are *two types of segmentation* easily observed in highly industrialised societies. First, there is the question of segmentation *in space*. We function each day, as migrants moving between sets of people which do not need to have any link—except through the mover. Often, there-fore, we know our work-mates only as work-mates, neighbours only as neigh-bours, fellow cross-country skiers only as fellow cross-country skiers. We get to know them as *roles*, not as total persons. This situation is accentuated by the extreme degree of division of labour we accept to live with. Only experts can evaluate each other according to individual—personal—competence. Out-side the speciality we have to fall back on a general evaluation of the supposed importance of the work. Except between specialists, we cannot evaluate how good anybody is in his work, only how good, in the sense of important, the role is. Through all this, we get limited possibilities for understanding other people's behaviour. Their behaviour will also get limited relevance for us. Role-players are more easily exchanged than persons.

The second type of segmentation has to do with what I would like to call our re-establishment of caste-society. I am not saying class-society, even though there are obvious tendencies also in that direction. In my framework, however, I find the elements of caste even more important. What I have in mind is the segregation based on biological attributes such as sex, colour, physical handicaps or the number of winters that have passed since birth. Age is particularly important. It is an attribute nearly perfectly synchronised to a modern complex industrialised society. It is a continuous variable where

5

NILS CHRISTIE

we can introduce as many intervals as we might need. We can split the population in two: children and adults. But we also can split it in ten: babies, pre-school children, school-children, teenagers, older youth, adults, pre-pensioned, pensioned, old people, the senile. And most important: the cutting points can be moved up and down according to social needs. The concept " teenager " was particularly suitable 10 years ago. It would not have caught on if social realities had not been in accordance with the word. Today the concept is not often used in my country. The condition of youth is not over at 19. Young people have to wait even longer before they are allowed to enter the work force. The caste of those outside the work force has been extended far into the twenties. At the same time departure from the work force—if you ever were admitted, if you were not kept completely out because of race or sex-attributes—is brought forward into the early sixties in a person's life. In my tiny country of four million inhabitants, we have 800,000 persons segregated within the educational system. Increased scarcity of work has immediately led authorities to increase the capacity of educational incarceration. Another 600,000 are pensioners.

Segmentation according to space and according to caste attributes has several consequences. First and foremost it leads into a *depersonalisation* of social life. Individuals are to a smaller extent linked to each other in close social networks where they are confronted with *all* the significant roles of the significant others. This creates a situation with limited amounts of information with regard to each other. We do know less about other people, and get limited possibilities both for understanding and for prediction of their behaviour. If a conflict is created, we are less able to cope with this situation. Not only are professionals there, able and willing to take the conflict away, but we are also more willing to give it away.

Secondly, segmentation leads to destruction of certain conflicts even before they get going. The depersonalisation and mobility within industrial society melt away some essential conditions for living conflicts; those between parties that mean a lot to each other. What I have particularly in mind is crime against other people's honour, libel or defamation of character. All the Scandinavian countries have had a dramatic decrease in this form of crime. In my interpretation, this is not because honour has become more respected, but because there is less honour to respect. The various forms of segmentation mean that human beings are inter-related in ways where they simply mean less to each other. When they are hurt, they are only hurt partially. And if they are troubled, they can easily move away. And after all, who cares? Nobody knows me. In my evaluation, the decrease in the crimes of infamy and libel is one of the most interesting and sad symptoms of dangerous developments within modern industrialised societies. The decrease here is clearly related to social conditions that lead to increase in other forms of crime brought to the attention of the authorities. It is an important goal for crime prevention to re-create social conditions which lead to an increase in the number of crimes against other people's honour.

A third consequence of segmentation according to space and age is that certain conflicts are made completely invisible, and thereby don't get any

6

decent solution whatsoever. I have here in mind conflicts at the two extremes of a continuum. On the one extreme we have the over-privatised ones, those taking place against individuals captured within one of the segments. Wife beating or child battering represent examples. The more isolated a segment is, the more the weakest among parties is alone, open for abuse. Inghe and Riemer (1943) made the classical study many years ago of a related phenomenon in their book on incest. Their major point was that the social isolation of certain categories of proletarised Swedish farm-workers was the necessary condition for this type of crime. Poverty meant that the parties within the nuclear family became completely dependent on each other. Isolation meant that the weakest parties within the family had no external network where they could appeal for help. The physical strength of the husband got an undue importance. At the other extreme we have crimes done by large economic organisations against individuals too weak and ignorant to be able even to realise they have been victimised. In both cases the goal for crime prevention might be to re-create social conditions which make the conflicts visible and thereafter manageable.

Conflicts as Property

Conflicts are taken away, given away, melt away, or are made invisible. Does it matter, does it really matter?

Most of us would probably agree that we ought to protect the invisible victims just mentioned. Many would also nod approvingly to ideas saying that states, or Governments, or other authorities ought to stop stealing fines, and instead let the poor victim receive this money. I at least would approve such an arragement. But I will not go into that problem area here and now. Material compensation is not what I have in mind with the formulation " conflicts as property ". It is the *conflict itself* that represents the most interesting property taken away, not the goods originally taken away from the victim, or given back to him. In our types of society, conflicts are more scarce than property. And they are immensely more valuable.

They are valuable in several ways. Let me start at the societal level, since here I have already presented the necessary fragments of analysis that might allow us to see what the problem is. Highly industrialised societies face major problems in organising their members in ways such that a decent quota take part in any activity at all. Segmentation according to age and sex can be seen as shrewd methods for segregation. Participation is such a scarcity that insiders create monopolies against outsiders, particularly with regard to work. In this perspective, it will easily be seen that conflicts represent a *potential for activity, for participation*. Modern criminal control systems represent one of the many cases of lost opportunities for involving citizens in tasks that are of immediate importance to them. Ours is a society of task-monopolists.

The victim is a particularly heavy loser in this situation. Not only has he suffered, lost materially or become hurt, physically or otherwise. And not only does the state take the compensation. But above all he has lost participation in his own case. It is the Crown that comes into the spotlight, not the victim. It is the Crown that describes the losses, not the victim. It is the Crown

NILS CHRISTIE

that appears in the newspaper, very seldom the victim. It is the Crown that gets a chance to talk to the offender, and neither the Crown nor the offender are particularly interested in carrying on that conversation. The prosecutor is fed-up long since. The victim would not have been. He might have been scared to death, panic-stricken, or furious. But he would not have been un-involved. It would have been one of the important days in his life. Something that belonged to him has been taken away from that victim.[1]

But the big loser is us—to the extent that society is us. This loss is first and foremost a loss in *opportunities for norm-clarification*. It is a loss of pedagogical possibilities. It is a loss of opportunities for a continuous discussion of what represents the law of the land. How wrong was the thief, how right was the victim? Lawyers are, as we saw, trained into agreement on what is relevant in a case. But that means a trained incapacity in letting the parties decide what *they* think is relevant. It means that it is difficult to stage what we might call a political debate in the court. When the victim is small and the offender big—in size or power—how blameworthy then is the crime? And what about the opposite case, the small thief and the big house-owner? If the offender is well educated, ought he then to suffer more. or maybe less, for his sins? Or if he is black, or if he is young, or if the other party is an insurance company, or if his wife has just left him, or if his factory will break down if he has to go to jail, or if his daughter will lose her fiancé, or if he was drunk, or if he was sad, or if he was mad? There is no end to it. And maybe there ought to be none. Maybe Barotse law as described by Max Gluckman (1967) is a better instrument for norm-clarification, allowing the conflicting parties to bring in the whole chain of old complaints and arguments each time. Maybe decisions on relevance and on the weight of what is found relevant ought to be taken away from legal scholars, the chief ideologists of crime control systems, and brought back for free decisions in the court-rooms.

A further general loss—both for the victim and for society in general—has to do with anxiety-level and misconceptions. It is again the possibilities for personalised encounters I have in mind. The victim is so totally out of the case that he has no chance, ever, to come to know the offender. We leave him outside, angry, maybe humiliated through a cross-examination in court, without any human contact with the offender. He has no alternative. He will need all the classical stereotypes around " the criminal " to get a grasp on the whole thing. He has a need for understanding, but is instead a non-person in a Kafka play. Of course, he will go away more frightened than ever, more in need than ever of an explanation of criminals as non-human.

The offender represents a more complicated case. Not much introspection is needed to see that direct victim-participation might be experienced as painful indeed. Most of us would shy away from a confrontation of this character. That is the first reaction. But the second one is slightly more posi-tive. Human beings have reasons for their actions. If the situation is staged so that reasons can be given (reasons as the parties see them, not only the selection lawyers have decided to classify as relevant), in such a case maybe the situation would not be all that humiliating. And, particularly, if the situa-

[1] For a preliminary report on victim dissatisfaction, see Vennard (1976).

CONFLICTS AS PROPERTY

tion was staged in such a manner that the central question was not meting out guilt, but a thorough discussion of what could be done to undo the deed, then the situation might change. And this is exactly what ought to happen when the victim is re-introduced in the case. Serious attention will centre on the victim's losses. That leads to a natural attention as to how they can be softened. It leads into a discussion of restitution. The offender gets a possibility to change his position from being a listener to a discussion—often a highly unintelligible one—of how much pain he ought to receive, into a participant in a discussion of how he could make it good again. The offender has lost the opportunity to explain himself to a person whose evaluation of him might have mattered. He has thereby also lost one of the most important possibilities for being forgiven. Compared to the humiliations in an ordinary court—vividly described by Pat Carlen (1976) in a recent issue of the *British Journal of Criminology*—this is not obviously any bad deal for the criminal.

But let me add that I think we should do it quite independently of his wishes. It is not health-control we are discussing. It is crime control. If criminals are shocked by the initial thought of close confrontation with the victim, preferably a confrontation in the very local neighbourhood of one of the parties, what then? I know from recent conversations on these matters that most people sentenced are shocked. After all, they prefer distance from the victim, from neighbours, from listeners and maybe also from their own court case through the vocabulary and the behavioural science experts who might happen to be present. They are perfectly willing to give away their property right to the conflict. So the question is more: are *we* willing to let them give it away? Are we willing to give them this easy way out? [2]

Let me be quite explicit on one point: I am not suggesting these ideas out of any particular interest in the treatment or improvement of criminals. I am not basing my reasoning on a belief that a more personalised meeting between offender and victim would lead to reduced recidivism. Maybe it would. I think it would. As it is now, the offender has lost the opportunity for participation in a personal confrontation of a very serious nature. He has lost the opportunity to receive a type of blame that it would be very difficult to neutralise. However, I would have suggested these arrangements even if it was absolutely certain they had no effects on recidivism, maybe even if they had a negative effect. I would have done that because of the other, more general gains. And let me also add—it is not much to lose. As we all know today, at least nearly all, we have not been able to invent any cure for crime. Except for execution, castration or incarceration for life, no measure has a proven minimum of efficiency compared to any other measure. We might as well react to crime according to what closely involved parties find is just and in accordance with general values in society.

With this last statement, as with most of the others I have made, I raise many more problems than I answer. Statements on criminal politics, particularly from those with the burden of responsibility, are usually filled with

---

[2] I tend to take the same position with regard to a criminal's property right to his own conflict as John Locke on property rights to one's own life—one has no right to give it away (*cf.* C. B. MacPherson (1962)).

NILS CHRISTIE

answers. It is questions we need. The gravity of our topic makes us much too pedantic and thereby useless as paradigm-changers.

A Victim-Oriented Court

There is clearly a model of neighbourhood courts behind my reasoning. But it is one with some peculiar features, and it is only these I will discuss in what follows.

First and foremost; it is a *victim-oriented* organisation. Not in its initial stage, though. The first stage will be a traditional one where it is established whether it is true that the law has been broken, and whether it was this particular person who broke it.

Then comes the second stage, which in these courts would be of the utmost importance. That would be the stage where the victim's situation was considered, where every detail regarding what had happened—legally relevant or not—was brought to the court's attention. Particularly important here would be detailed consideration regarding what could be done for him, first and foremost by the offender, secondly by the local neighbourhood, thirdly by the state. Could the harm be compensated, the window repaired, the lock replaced, the wall painted, the loss of time because the car was stolen given back through garden work or washing of the car ten Sundays in a row? Or maybe, when this discussion started, the damage was not so important as it looked in documents written to impress insurance companies? Could physical suffering become slightly less painful by any action from the offender, during days, months or years? But, in addition, had the community exhausted all resources that might have offered help? Was it absolutely certain that the local hospital could not do anything? What about a helping hand from the janitor twice a day if the offender took over the cleaning of the basement every Saturday? None of these ideas is unknown or untried, particularly not in England. But we need an organisation for the systematic application of them.

Only after this stage was passed, and it ought to take hours, maybe days, to pass it, only then would come the time for an eventual decision on punishment. Punishment, then, becomes that suffering which the judge found necessary to apply *in addition to* those unintended constructive sufferings the offender would go through in his restitutive actions *vis-à-vis* the victim. Maybe nothing could be done or nothing would be done. But neighbourhoods might find it intolerable that nothing happened. Local courts out of tune with local values are not local courts. That is just the trouble with them, seen from the liberal reformer's point of view.

A fourth stage has to be added. That is the stage for service to the offender. His general social and personal situation is by now well-known to the court. The discussion of his possibilities for restoring the victim's situation cannot be carried out without at the same time giving information about the offender's situation. This might have exposed needs for social, educational, medical or religious action—not to prevent further crime, but because needs ought to be met. Courts are public arenas, needs are made visible. But it is important that this stage comes *after* sentencing. Otherwise we get a re-emergence of the whole array of so-called "special measures"—compulsory treatments—very often only euphemisms for indeterminate imprisonment.

Through these four stages, these courts would represent a blend of elements from civil and criminal courts, but with a strong emphasis on the civil side.

A Lay-Oriented Court

The second major peculiarity with the court model I have in mind is that it will be one with an extreme degree of lay-orientation. This is essential when conflicts are seen as property that ought to be shared. It is with conflicts as with so many good things: they are in no unlimited supply. Conflicts can be cared for, protected, nurtured. But there are limits. If some are given more access in the disposal of conflicts, others are getting less. It is as simple as that.

Specialisation in conflict solution is the major enemy; specialisation that in due—or undue—time leads to professionalisation. That is when the specialists get sufficient power to claim that they have acquired special gifts, mostly through education, gifts so powerful that it is obvious that they can only be handled by the certified craftsman.

With a clarification of the enemy, we are also able to specify the goal; let us reduce specialisation and particularly our dependence on the professionals within the crime control system to the utmost.

The ideal is clear; it ought to be a court of equals representing themselves. When they are able to find a solution between themselves, no judges are needed. When they are not, the judges ought also to be their equals.

Maybe the judge would be the easiest to replace, if we made a serious attempt to bring our present courts nearer to this model of lay orientation. We have lay judges already, in principle. But that is a far cry from realities. What we have, both in England and in my own country, is a sort of specialised non-specialist. First, they are used *again and again*. Secondly, some are even *trained*, given special courses or sent on excursions to foreign countries to learn about how to behave as a lay judge. Thirdly, most of them do also represent an extremely *biased sample* of the population with regard to sex, age, education, income, class [3] and personal experience as criminals. With real lay judges, I conceive of a system where nobody was given the right to take part in conflict solution more than a few times, and then had to wait until all other community members had had the same experience.

Should lawyers be admitted to court? We had an old law in Norway that forbids them to enter the rural districts. Maybe they should be admitted in stage one where it is decided if the man is guilty. I am not sure. Experts are as cancer to any lay body. It is exactly as Ivan Illich describes for the educational system in general. Each time you increase the length of compulsory education in a society, each time you also decrease the same population's trust in what they have learned and understood quite by themselves.

Behaviour experts represent the same dilemma. Is there a place for them in this model? Ought there to be any place? In stage 1, decisions on facts, certainly not. In stage 3, decisions on eventual punishment, certainly not. It is too obvious to waste words on. We have the painful row of mistakes from

[3] For the most recent documentation, see Baldwin (1976).

NILS CHRISTIE

Lombroso, through the movement for social defence and up to recent
attempts to dispose of supposedly dangerous people through predictions of
who they are and when they are not dangerous any more. Let these ideas
die, without further comments.

The real problem has to do with the service function of behaviour experts.
Social scientists can be perceived as functional answers to a segmented society.
Most of us have lost the physical possibility to experience the totality, both
on the social system level and on the personality level. Psychologists can be
seen as historians for the individual; sociologists have much of the same function for the social system. Social workers are oil in the machinery, a sort of
security counsel. Can we function without them, would the victim and the
offender be worse off?

Maybe. But it would be immensely difficult to get such a court to function
if they were all there. Our theme is social conflict. Who is not at least made
slightly uneasy in the handling of her or his own social conflicts if we get to
know that there is an expert on this very matter at the same table? I have no
clear answer, only strong feelings behind a vague conclusion: let us have as
few behaviour experts as we dare to. And if we have any, let us for God's
sake not have any that specialise in crime and conflict resolution. Let us
have generalised experts with a solid base outside the crime control system.
And a last point with relevance for both behaviour experts and lawyers: if
we find them unavoidable in certain cases or at certain stages, let us try to
get across to them the problems they create for broad social participation. Let
us try to get them to perceive themselves as resource-persons, answering when
asked, but not domineering, not in the centre. They might help to stage
conflicts, not take them over.

Rolling Stones

There are hundreds of blocks against getting such a system to operate within
our western culture. Let me only mention three major ones. They are:
  1. There is a lack of neighbourhoods.
  2. There are too few victims.
  3. There are too many professionals around.

With lack of neighbourhoods I have in mind the very same phenomenon
I described as a consequence of industrialised living; segmentation according
to space and age. Much of our trouble stems from killed neighbourhoods or
killed local communities. How can we then thrust towards neighbourhoods a
task that presupposes they are highly alive? I have no really good arguments,
only two weak ones. First, it is not quite that bad. The death is not complete.
Secondly, one of the major ideas behind the formulation ' Conflicts as
Property ' is that it is neighbourhood-property. It is not private. It belongs
to the system. It is intended as a vitaliser for neighbourhoods. The more fainting the neighbourhood is, the more we need neighbourhood courts as one of
the many functions any social system needs for not dying through lack of
challenge.

Equally bad is the lack of victims. Here I have particularly in mind the
lack of personal victims. The problem behind this is again the large units in

CONFLICTS AS PROPERTY

industrialised society. Woolworth or British Rail are not good victims. But again I will say: there is not a complete lack of personal victims, and their needs ought to get priority. But we should not forget the large organisations. They, or their boards, would certainly prefer not to have to appear as victims in 5000 neighbourhood courts all over the country. But maybe they ought to be compelled to appear. If the complaint is serious enough to bring the offender into the ranks of the criminal, then the victim ought to appear. A related problem has to do with insurance companies—the industrialised alternative to friendship or kinship. Again we have a case where the crutches deteriorate the condition. Insurance takes the consequences of crime away. We will therefore have to take insurance away. Or rather: we will have to keep the possibilities for compensation through the insurance companies back until in the procedure I have described it has been proved behond all possible doubt that there are no other alternatives left—particularly that the offender has no possibilities whatsoever. Such a solution will create more paper-work, less predictability, more aggression from customers. And the solution will not necessarily be seen as good from the perspective of the policy-holder. But it will help to protect conflicts as social fuel.

None of these troubles can, however, compete with the third and last I will comment on: the abundance of professionals. We know it all from our own personal biographies or personal observations. And in addition we get it confirmed from all sorts of social science research: the educational system of any society is not necessarily synchronised with any needs for the product of this system. Once upon a time we thought there was a direct causal relation from the number of highly educated persons in a country to the Gross National Product. Today we suspect the relationship to go the other way, if we are at all willing to use GNP as a meaningful indicator. We also know that most educational systems are extremely class-biased. We know that most academic people have had profitable investments in our education, that we fight for the same for our children, and that we also often have vested interests in making our part of the educational system even bigger. More schools for more lawyers, social workers, sociologists, criminologists. While I am *talking* deprofessionalisation, we are increasing the capacity to be able to fill up the whole world with them.

There is no solid base for optimism. On the other hand insights about the situation, and goal formulation, is a pre-condition for action. Of course, the crime control system is not the domineering one in our type of society. But it has some importance. And occurrences here are unusually well suited as pedagogical illustrations of general trends in society. There is also some room for manoeuvre. And when we hit the limits, or are hit by them, this collision represents in itself a renewed argument for more broadly conceived changes.

Another source for hope: ideas formulated here are not quite so isolated or in dissonance with the mainstream of thinking when we leave our crime control area and enter other institutions. I have already mentioned Ivan Illich with his attempts to get learning away from the teachers and back to active human beings. Compulsory learning, compulsory medication and compulsory consummation of conflict solutions have interesting similarities.

NILS CHRISTIE

When Ivan Illich and Paulo Freire are listened to, and my impression is that they increasingly are, the crime control system will also become more easily influenced.

Another, but related, major shift in paradigm is about to happen within the whole field of technology. Partly, it is the lessons from the third world that now are more easily seen, partly it is the experience from the ecology debate. The globe is obviously suffering from what we, through our technique, are doing to her. Social systems in the third world are equally obviously suffering. So the suspicion starts. Maybe the first world can't take all this technology either. Maybe some of the old social thinkers were not so dumb after all. Maybe social systems can be perceived as biological ones. And maybe there are certain types of large-scale technology that kill social systems, as they kill globes. Schumacher (1973) with his book *Small is Beautiful* and the related Institute for Intermediate Technology come in here. So do also the numerous attempts, particularly by several outstanding Institutes for Peace Research, to show the dangers in the concept of Gross National Product, and replace it with indicators that take care of dignity, equity and justice. The perspective developed in Johan Galtung's research group on World Indicators might prove extremely useful also within our own field of crime control.

There is also a political phenomenon opening vistas. At least in Scandinavia social democrats and related groupings have considerable power, but are without an explicated ideology regarding the goals for a reconstructed society. This vacuum is being felt by many, and creates a willingness to accept and even expect considerable institutional experimentation.

Then to my very last point: what about the universities in this picture? What about the new Centre in Sheffield? The answer has probably to be the old one: universities have to re-emphasise the old tasks of understanding and of criticising. But the task of training professionals ought to be looked into with renewed scepticism. Let us re-establish the credibility of encounters between critical human beings: low-paid, highly regarded, but with no extra power—outside the weight of their good ideas. That is as it ought to be.

REFERENCES

BALDWIN, J (1976) "The Social Composition of the Magistracy" *Brit. J Criminol.*, **16**, 171–174.

BAUM, M. AND WHEELER, S. (1968). "Becoming an inmate," Ch. 7, pp. 153–187, in Wheeler, S. (ed.), *Controlling Delinquents*. New York: Wiley.

BOTTOMS, A. E. AND McCLEAN, J. D. (1976). *Defendants in the Criminal Process*. London: Routledge and Kegan Paul.

CARLEN, P. (1976). "The Staging of Magistrates' Justice." *Brit. J. Criminol.*, **16**, 48–55.

GLUCKMAN, M. (1967). *The Judicial Process among the Barotse of Northern Rhodesia* Manchester University Press.

KINBERG, O., INGHE, G., AND RIEMER, S. (1943). *Incest-Problemet i Sverige*. Sth.

CONFLICTS AS PROPERTY

MacPHERSON, C. B. (1962). *The Political Theory of Possessive Individualism: Hobbes to Locke.* London: Oxford University Press.

NEWMAN, O. (1972). *Defensible Space: People and Design in the Violent City.* London: Architectural Press.

SCHUMACHER, E. F. (1973). *Small is Beautiful: A Study of Economics as if People Mattered.* London: Blond and Briggs.

SCOTT, P. D. (1959). "Juvenile Courts: the Juvenile's Point of View." *Brit. J. Delinq.*, 9, 200–210.

VENNARD, J. (1976). "Justice and Recompense for Victims of Crime." *New Society*, 36, 378–380.

Part II
Crime Surveys

[3]

BRIT.J.CRIMINOL. Vol. 25 No. 6 APRIL 1985

CRIME IN ENGLAND AND WALES AND SCOTLAND: A BRITISH CRIME SURVEY COMPARISON

PAT MAYHEW and LORNA J F SMITH (London)*

OFFENCES recorded by the police have to date been the most accessible basis for comparing the level of crime in different countries, despite well-known problems of differences in the content of the criminal law, and in the classification, definition and counting of offences. Such figures have for some time served as the basis of Scotland's more criminal reputation as compared with England and Wales, though in fact they do not support the image of Scotland as particularly more violent. On the face of it, the relative positions of the two countries according to police figures has been confirmed by a recent reassessment (Smith, 1983) in which comparability was improved by reaggregating Scottish classifications of "crimes" to reflect more closely the categories of "notifiable offences" used in England and Wales. Smith's comparison found that, for all offence categories except one, Scotland in 1981 (and figures for previous years were similar) had a higher rate of recorded crime per capita than England and Wales (see Table 1). The exception was violence against the person.

TABLE 1

Rates per 10,000 population of recorded crimes in Scotland and notifiable offences in England and Wales, 1981

	England and Wales	Scotland
Violence against the person	20	15
Sexual offences	4	4
Burglary[1]	147	185
Robbery	4	8
Theft and handling stolen goods	325	389
Fraud and forgery	22	42
Criminal damage[2]	78	120

Notes:
[1] Residential and non-residential burglary.
[2] Including damage to the value of £20 or less.

Smith herself, however, was sceptical whether recorded offences accurately reflect the volume of crime committed in the two countries—for two main reasons. First, different proportions of offences may be reported to the

* Respectively, principal research officer and senior research officer, Home Office Research and Planning Unit.

CRIME IN ENGLAND AND WALES AND SCOTLAND: A B.C.S. COMPARISON

police by the public, and any dissimilarity here would have an obvious effect on the amount of crime available to the police to record. Secondly, she argues that the procedures for recording crime in Scotland differ from those in England and Wales in ways which would seem to promote higher levels of recorded offences in Scotland for the same amount of crime. One possible difference arises from the fact that there are more formal rules for counting offences in England and Wales than in Scotland. How important these are is unclear; notable variations between police forces south of the border suggest that what is chosen for recording is more important than how it is counted. For example, "no crime" practices can significantly affect recorded crime levels. So too can the treatment of TIC offences: Farrington and Dowds (1985) found that in three counties in England and Wales between four and 25 per cent. of offences came to police notice on admission by the offender. In Scotland, offences are not "taken into consideration" in sentencing and this may lead to smaller numbers of offences being revealed by police questioning.

Other differences in counting practices may also serve to keep the figures for England and Wales relatively lower than those for Scotland. In particular, for instance, some repetitive crimes committed over a period of time (*e.g.* some frauds) may be counted as a single "continuous" offence in England and Wales though in Scotland each instance is counted separately. A more important factor may be that in Scotland different infractions involved in a criminal incident are separately recorded, whereas in England and Wales lower counts are produced by the system of recording only the most serious element when more than one infraction of the law occurs. Sexual offences and offences of violence against the person are, nevertheless, treated as exceptions to the general England and Wales rule, so that where more than one victim is involved one offence is generally counted for each victim; in Scotland, multiple-victim incidents of violence may be counted as one rather than several crimes. This difference, together with the fact that some incidents of robbery and assaults with attempt to rob are treated dissimilarly in the two countries, may underlie the anomalous position of violent offences: the per capita rate of violence against the person was a third higher in England and Wales in 1981 than in Scotland, whereas robbery (the other category which by definition requires some degree of violence) was about half the Scottish rate.

"Crime" (or "victim") surveys (in which representative samples of the population are asked to recount offences of which they have been a victim over a given period) seem to offer new possibilities for comparing crime rates between different countries or geographical regions. On the face of it, such surveys can circumvent some major difficulties of comparison; they are not necessarily bound to the methods of classification and counting used by the police, and—more important—offences can be included whether or not they are reported to and recorded by the police. In practice, criminologists who have used crime surveys for comparative purposes have had to grapple with a host of problems relating to differences in survey methodology, a point taken up at the end of the paper.

PAT MAYHEW AND LORNA J. F. SMITH

The British Crime Survey as a Basis for Comparison

With regard to England and Wales and Scotland, however, the 1982 British Crime Survey (BCS) provides an unusually tight basis for a between-country comparison drawing on information given by 11,000 respondents in England and Wales and 5,000 in Scotland about their recent experience of crime and a number of other crime-related issues (for fuller details see Hough and Mayhew, 1983 and Chambers and Tombs, 1984). The BCS was designed to maximise comparability of results: notably, fieldwork was conducted at the same time by the same survey organisation (Social and Community Planning Research); all respondents were asked about the same offences in the same way; and reports of victimisation were coded by the same people using the same system of classification.[1]

This is not to say that the BCS information on crime levels is comprehensive or flawless. Not all offences are included (*e.g.* shoplifting or fraud) since the crime survey method uncovers only offences which have clearly identifiable individuals as victims. There will be deficiencies, too, in the measurement of those offences which are covered: people fail to report in interview all the relevant incidents they have experienced and, if asked about victimisation in a specific time period, they will report incidents which fall outside it. Also, crime survey estimates are based only on a sample of the population and error may arise on this account, all the more so for rarer crimes such as robbery and sexual assaults. These limitations need to be acknowledged in comparing BCS estimates of crime with the levels recorded in *Criminal Statistics*. Nonetheless, for the purposes of assessing *differences* in the levels of crime in England and Wales and Scotland, no systematic biases need be expected from the way the BCS was conducted.

The differences in crime

The BCS paints a rather different picture of crime in the two countries than do official statistics. Contrary to offences recorded by the police, there is little difference in the level of most offences. (For definitions of offence types, see Hough and Mayhew, 1983, pp. 52–55.) Table 2 shows BCS

---

[1] Interviewing for the BCS took place early in 1982. One person aged 16 or over was interviewed in each household. A response rate of 80 per cent. was achieved in England and Wales, giving an unweighted sample of 10,905; in Scotland the rate was 81 per cent., sample = 5,031. After appropriate weighting, the samples were meant to give a representative cross-section of those living in private households in England, Wales and Scotland whose addresses appear in the Electoral Register. "Screening" questions based on ordinary-language descriptions of legal definitions of offences were used to identify victims who then completed a "victim form" for each offence reported. These offences were divided into two types: "personal" offences (*e.g.* sexual offences, robberies etc.) where there was usually one victim per offence, and "household" offences (*e.g.* burglary and car theft) where more than one member of the household could regard themselves as victims. For the former, respondents were asked about their own experience; for the latter, about incidents affecting any household member. From the "victim form", incidents where it was clear that the law had been breached were classified under different offence headings at the coding stage. To facilitate comparison with offence classifications in *Criminal Statistics*, instructions for classification were drawn up in consultation with the statistical departments of the Home Office and the Scottish Home and Health Department, and with personnel in police forces (see also footnote 4).

CRIME IN ENGLAND AND WALES AND SCOTLAND: A B.C.S. COMPARISON

TABLE 2

Offences in England and Wales and Scotland: BCS estimates for 1981

	England and Wales	Scotland
Household offences	Rate per 10,000 households	
1. Criminal damage	1,494	1,435
2. Theft from motor vehicle (owners)	1,040	1,512*
3. Burglary	410	408
4 Theft of motor vehicle (owners)	232	280
5. Bicycle theft (owners)	287	278
6. Theft in a dwelling	78	31*
7. Other household theft	835	797
Personal offences	Rate per 10,000 people aged 16+	
8. Common assault	396	345
9. Thefts from the person	112	134
10. Wounding	98	44*
11. Robbery	42	38
12. Sexual offences[2]	16	34
13. Other personal theft	413	453

Notes:
[1] Categories 3, 7, 8, 9, 11, 12 and 13 include attempts.
[2] Only women were asked about sexual offences; rates are per 10,000 females.
* Differences in rates are not statistically significant except for those offence categories starred, where the probability of the differences being due to chance is less than 5 per cent. (difference between means, two-tailed test, using complex sampling errors).

estimates of crimes rates in 1981 expressed per 10,000 households for household offences, and per 10,000 adults for personal offences. Rates for thefts of and from motor vehicles (motor-cycles, mopeds, cars, vans, etc.) are expressed on the basis of those owning such vehicles; the rate for bicycle theft is also expressed on the basis of owners.

As the rates in Table 2 are derived from a sample they should not be considered precise. (For instance, with 95 per cent. certainty, the rate of criminal damage per 10,000 households in Scotland could have fallen beween 1,721 and 1,149; in England and Wales it could have been between 1,676 and 1,312.) Nevertheless, allowing for sampling error, the conclusion from Table 2 is that for 10 of the 13 offence categories the rate of crime in England and Wales and Scotland was not significantly different; observed differences in some of the 10 categories could have arisen simply as a result of sampling error.

There are three exceptions where rates significantly differ. In England and Wales, woundings and thefts in a dwelling were more prevalent, while for thefts from motor vehicles (though not thefts of them) Scotland took the lead. With regard to wounding, the higher rate in England and Wales may be somewhat suspect given that assaultive offences are considered to be the least validly measured by victim survey techniques (see, for example, Skogan, 1981). The higher rate bears out the picture from the much broader category of crimes of violence recorded by the police, though—as already indicated—this in itself may be particularly unreliable. As the term

PAT MAYHEW AND LORNA J. F. SMITH

implies, theft in a dwelling is committed *inside* a home by someone who is entitled to be there (*e.g.* a party guest, workman, etc.), and why these offences were lower in Scotland eludes easy explanation. It seems implausible, for instance, that the Scots would be less prepared to define such acts as criminal.

With regard to thefts from motor vehicles, the significantly higher rate in Scotland derives only from the figures shown in Table 2 calculated on the basis of *vehicle-owning households* (of which there are fewer in Scotland than in England and Wales). When the level of thefts from vehicles in the two countries is compared on the basis of *all* households, the difference disappears.[2] In other words, the rate of offending was the same, but in Scotland it was concentrated on a smaller number of possible targets. Those who did own vehicles in Scotland, then, faced higher risks of having property taken from their cars or vans than owners in the south, though thefts from vehicles posed an equivalent burden on the police in the two countries. It is likely that parking habits contribute to the higher risks faced by Scottish vehicle-owners. BCS findings show that those who normally have to park overnight on the streets face a higher risk of theft both of and from vehicles. And in Scotland, some 33 per cent. of vehicle owners said they usually parked overnight on the street compared to 24 per cent in England and Wales.

Reporting to the police

Given the similarity of most offence rates in Scotland and England and Wales as measured by the BCS, what can the survey offer in the way of an explanation for the fact that Scottish statistics of offences known to the police are higher? One reason could be that there are differences in reporting behaviour on the part of the public; more recorded crime in Scotland might result from Scots being more likely to tell the police after they had been victims of an offence. The BCS provides some support for this. Although in both countries the level at which different types of offence were reported varied markedly (with, for example, the police being informed of virtually all thefts of motor vehicles as against roughly a quarter of incidents of criminal damage) there was a general tendency for Scots to report more offences. Thus, taking all 13 offence categories together, some 37 per cent. of offences were reported to the police in Scotland compared to 31 per cent. in England and Wales (p<0.01; see Table 3). Nevertheless, higher reporting rates in Scotland are not consistent across individual offence categories, and most of the differences are not very statistically robust.

As far as the evidence does suggest higher reporting in Scotland, one reason for this may be the differences in the way in which the police are viewed in the two countries. It might be hypothesised that the Scots are more satisfied with their police force and have more faith in the police

---

[2] On the basis of all households, the rate per 10,000 households of theft from motor vehicles was 837 in Scotland and 700 England and Wales. The rate of theft of motor vehicles was 155 in Scotland and 156 in England and Wales. The rate of bicycle theft in Scotland was 96 and 118 in England and Wales.

CRIME IN ENGLAND AND WALES AND SCOTLAND: A B.C.S. COMPARISON

TABLE 3

Percentage of BCS offences reported to the police[1]

	England and Wales	Scotland
Household offences		
Criminal damage	22	29
Theft from motor vehicle	30	43*
Burglary	66	58
Theft of motor vehicle	95	94
Bicycle theft	64	66
Theft in a dwelling	18	33
Other household theft	25	21
Personal offences		
Common assault	26	35
Thefts from the person	31	41
Wounding[2]	39	66
Robbery	47	64
Sexual offences[2]	28	0
Other personal theft	24	35*
All offences	31	37*

Weighted data; unweighted n=4,595 (England and Wales), 2,111 (Scotland). Incidents which occurred in 1982 are included.
* Differences in reporting levels are not statistically significant except for those offence categories starred, where the probability of the differences being due to chance is less than 5 per cent. (difference between proportions, two-tailed test, allowing for complex sampling design).
Notes:
  [1] The information in this table derived from the BCS question: "Did the police come to know about the matter?"
  [2] The percentage of wounding and sexual offences given as reported to the police in Scotland differs slightly from figures given in Table 3 of Chambers and Tombs (1984) where a different definition of the offences is taken to aid comparability with *Criminal Statistics*.

dealing effectively with complaints of victimisation. On this score, BCS results do not provide much in the way of confirmation. Comparing the reasons given by respondents for *not* reporting to the police, more victims of household offences in England and Wales indicated that they thought the police would or could do nothing about the incident ($p < 0.01$). However, this did not apply for personal offences, and in no other way did the pattern of reasons for non-reporting indicate less faith in the police south of the border. Similarly, in response to questions about police performance at a local level, large and again strikingly similar proportions of respondents in both countries expressed favourable attitudes. And victims who had reported crimes to the police showed equal satisfaction with the way in which their cases were handled.

Given this lack of differences, the suggestion of rather higher levels of reporting in Scotland demands other explanations. One possible reason is that there are different policing levels in the two countries; Smith's (1983) paper shows some 242 police per 100,000 population in England and Wales in 1981 as against a higher (though not markedly higher) figure of 255 for Scotland (perhaps explained by the larger areas of low population). Another possibility is that more Scots notify the police because they intend to make insurance claims. Evidence from the 1980/81 Family Expenditure Survey showed that 82 per cent. of households in Scotland had household

PAT MAYHEW AND LORNA J. F. SMITH

insurance cover compared to 75 per cent. in England and Wales, while a BCS question to victims on whether they had received any recompense from an insurance company for stolen property also indicated a rather higher repayment rate for Scottish victims (p<0·05). This provides some support for the idea that higher reporting in Scotland is affected by insurance considerations, though the matter must be treated as far from settled. Reporting levels for burglary in Scotland, for instance, were actually lower (though not reliably so statistically) than in England and Wales.

Recording by the police

For whatever reason, then, more reporting by Scottish victims provides a partial explanation for the higher rates in crime in police figures, though it is unlikely to account for all the difference. In addition, the Scottish police may simply record more of the crimes they come to know about. The slightly higher levels of police personnel in Scotland may play a part here, though it is more likely that other differences are at work. As indicated above, there are various known procedural differences (*e.g.* the absence of systematic "counting rules" such as exist in England and Wales, and, more likely, the counting of each element in a criminal incident) which may inflate the level of recorded crime. Nor can other less obvious variations in police recording practice be ruled out (*cf.* Bottomley and Coleman, 1981; Farrington and Dowds, 1985).

In both the fuller reports of BCS results for England and Wales (Hough and Mayhew, 1983) and Scotland (Chambers and Tombs, 1984), comparisons are made between figures derived from respective *Criminal Statistics* and the level of certain types of offences in 1981 as estimated by the BCS. The main purpose of these comparisons was to expose the extent of the so-called "dark figure" of crime. But by comparing the numbers of offences *recorded* by the police with BCS estimates of the numbers of offences *reported* to them, some examination is also possible of whether the proportion of reported offences which are recorded by the police is higher in Scotland.

In both countries, "dark figure" comparisons were made only for those offence categories which could be reliably matched with *Criminal Statistics* categories.[3] The sub-sets of the 13 BCS offence categories compared with *Criminal Statistics* were not the same. (For instance, the Scottish comparison included common assault while that for England and Wales did not; theft from vehicles was included for England and Wales but not for Scotland; etc.) In all, seven offence types were common to both comparisons (criminal damage, burglary, theft of motor vehicles, bicycle theft,

---

[3] In England and Wales, three offence groups (common assault, other household theft and other personal theft) were omitted from the comparison with *Criminal Statistics* because they did not correspond with distinct categories of "notifiable offences" in *Criminal Statistics*. In Scotland, five offences groups were omitted: theft from a motor vehicle, theft in a dwelling, other household theft, theft from the person, and other personal theft. All of these involved particular types of thefts which are not differentiated in Scottish *Criminal Statistics*.

CRIME IN ENGLAND AND WALES AND SCOTLAND: A B.C.S. COMPARISON

wounding, sexual offences and robbery). Of these, three are especially problematic: sexual offences because of the very small numbers of victimisations and some differences in the way they are dealt with in the comparisons; criminal damage because of particular limitations in comparing BCS estimates with *Criminal Statistics* in Scotland[4]; and thefts of motor vehicles because in both England and Wales and Scotland the number of offences recorded by the police was in excess of the number estimated from the BCS.[5] The scope, therefore, for examining whether the BCS indicates that a higher proportion of reported offences are recorded in Scotland is limited. And the comparison is problematic for other reasons:[6] so much so indeed that the reports of BCS results for both England and Wales and Scotland made little mention of the shortfall between the recorded levels of offences and those estimated to have been reported. With all the problems acknowledged, nevertheless, some comparison is appropriate here. Of the four offence categories for which a comparison is reasonable, a greater proportion of the estimated number of reported woundings and bicycle thefts were recorded in *Criminal Statistics* in England and Wales than in Scotland. Conversely, more reported robberies and burglaries were recorded in Scotland. On the face of it, then, these results give little support to the idea that the higher level of offences recorded by the police in Scotland is associated with more reported offences finding their way into police records.

Summary

Designed as a survey of crime in both England and Wales and Scotland, the 1982 BCS was an unusually good vehicle for a comparative study. So far, too, it provides the only basis for comparison using victim survey figures. The survey was repeated in England and Wales early in 1984, but Scotland did not participate.

[4] In comparing the estimated level of offences in Scotland revealed by the BCS with those in *Criminal Statistics*, it was not considered necessary to make adjustments in order to account for the fact that incidents coded as one offence in the BCS may have generated more than one offence in police records. Although provision was made at the coding stage for Scottish offences to be classified in the way operated by Scottish police forces (*i.e.* different offences in any one incident being separately coded), *and* in the same way as for England and Wales offences (*i.e.* one offence per incident), examination of the results indicated that almost 90 per cent. of victimisations were single offence incidents. Of the remainder, nearly all the secondary offences which could have been recorded were ciminal damage. This makes any comparison beween the BCS estimate for this offence and Scottish *Criminal Statistics* rather hazardous.

The fact that BCS coding did not reveal that multiple counting of offences was relevant to many incidents suggests, on the face of it, that multiple coding may not be very important in explaining the higher rate of recorded crime in Scotland. This conclusion, however, can only be very tentative; how BCS coders interpreted multiplicity of offences in the reports they were working on may have been different from the way in which Scottish police officers operate.

[5] This is no doubt due to the many sources of errors (see footnote 6) attached to BCS estimates.

[6] Hough and Mayhew (1983, p. 12) point to several reasons for caution: sampling error in estimating the incidence of offences; sampling error in estimating the proportion of these reported to the police; non-sampling error in both estimates (for example, have all offences actually reported to the police been recalled in interview?); and errors in the adjustments made to *Criminal Statistics* figures. Other uncertainties are mentioned too, such as whether incidents recorded in the BCS as meeting the criteria of notifiable offences are in practice dealt with as such, and whether some incidents go unrecorded because they have been resolved or because the complainant wanted no action taken.

PAT MAYHEW AND LORNA J. F. SMITH

In summary, this article has shown that evidence from the 1982 BCS is at odds with the picture from offences recorded by the police that there is more crime in Scotland than in England and Wales. Out of a selected 13 offence categories, the BCS showed that for two (wounding and theft in a dwelling) a greater proportion of people in England and Wales were victimised in 1981. The higher rate of wounding is consistent with figures of crimes of violence recorded by the police, although there is reason to be suspicious about the validity of both measures. For the remaining 11 types of offence, there was no significant difference in the rates, though thefts from vehicles posed a bigger risk in Scotland for the smaller number of vehicle-owners there. The BCS suggests that the higher level of recorded crime in Scotland may be at least partly due to a greater tendency for Scots to say that they had reported more offences to the police, though it is not clear why this is so. At least on the basis of BCS questions, there was little difference in the way in which the police in the two countries were viewed, while the suggestion that reporting in Scotland is encouraged by higher levels of household insurance needs firmer confirmation. The greater number of police per capita in Scotland may possibly be implicated in higher reporting (and recording), though the differences in establishment are not great. Nor is it easy to ascertain the importance of differences in recording procedure of the sort Smith's (1983) comparison draws attention to, particularly in view of the fact (see footnote 4) that the BCS revealed that the vast majority of offences in Scotland involved only one type of incident. On the question of whether more reported offences are recorded by the police in Scotland than in England and Wales, the BCS offers no persuasive evidence, albeit on the basis of rather problematic data.

Discussion

In broader terms, this article has shown that comparing levels of victimisation risks in different countries on the basis of crime survey data can yield a different picture from that given by official statistics. It has also shown that the level at which crimes are reported to the police (information routinely collected in crime surveys) might explain differences between countries in recorded crime. It is timely to ask, then, how energetically criminologists should pursue further crime survey comparisons.

A strong case for more work comes from the deficiencies of official statistics as tools for comparison. These, of course, are an important index of the workload of the police, and they can document a wider range of offences than are typically uncovered by crime surveys based on household or population samples. (Official figures give a poor picture of white-collar, business and corporate crime, etc., but crime surveys are even more deficient in this respect.) Nevertheless, even for assessing crime trends within particular jurisdictions, the value of official figures can be severely undermined by changes in reporting, recording and enforcement practices. And for comparing levels of crime in different countries, many problems are posed by differences in the processes by which official statistics are

CRIME IN ENGLAND AND WALES AND SCOTLAND: A B.C.S. COMPARISON

derived—as indeed has been evidenced by the disappointingly inconclusive findings of comparative studies which have used them to date.

In view of this, the use of crime survey information to assess how much crime different countries face is attractive, particularly as national survey results (and there are also additional city-level ones) are already available for a number of countries, as well as England and Wales and Scotland. The problems involved, however, should not be underestimated. By and large, crime surveys to date have been independently conceived and organised, resulting in differences in sampling, field procedures, response rates, "screening" methods, offence coverage and definitions, etc., which can be as tricky to handle as the differences underlying official statistics. So far only a handful of criminologists have tackled the problems involved, though with some illuminating results (see, for example, Clinard, 1978; Braithwaite and Biles, 1979; Sveri, 1982; van Dijk and Steinmetz, 1983; Hough, 1983; Skogan, 1984; and Block (Ed.), in press). A few examples of the difficulties they have had to deal with may be given here.

In the first place, it is critical that samples should be drawn in the same way. The Canadian and Australian national surveys, for instance, exclude rural areas where victimisation rates are known to be lower, so that any comparison with the results from other countries would need to control for urbanisation. Different lower age limits for inclusion in a sample will also confound results. Secondly, the accuracy with which interviewees report offences experienced over a given "recall" period will vary according to methodology. Known sources of variation here are the duration of the "recall" period itself, whether or not a panel design is used, and whether or not respondents are asked to report on victimisations experienced by other household members as well as themselves ("proxy" interviewing produces fewer victimisations). It is particularly important, too, that methodological considerations (*e.g.* the number of "screening" questions used) can greatly influence the number of multiple victimisations which a survey produces. These can so substantially affect measured *rates* when total numbers of offences are expressed over a base of those at risk, that indeed *prevalence* measures (*i.e.* numbers victimised once or more) may need to be considered as an alternative. Difficulties also arise from the various methods that have been used for counting so-called "series" incidents (incidents experienced so repeatedly that the respondent cannot distinguish between them): different "series" counting rules seriously jeopardise sound comparisons, in particular of rates of personal offences. Thirdly, surveys do not cover the same crimes, with attempted offences being particularly subject to different rules. And even when similar crimes appear to be covered, small differences in the wording of "screening" questions render comparison difficult. Finally, there are specific problems if any attempt is made to compare (within as well as between countries) crime survey estimates of victimisation with other official statistics. Only certain official offence categories will match with survey ones, and various adjustments to official figures will need to be made to allow, for instance, for the fact that police statistics include commercial crimes, offences involving non-residents, and

PAT MAYHEW AND LORNA J. F. SMITH

those committed against people younger than crime survey respondents. Even then (*cf.* footnote 6), the shortfall between survey-measured crime and official levels cannot be attributed with any precision to non-reporting versus non-recording.

These examples give an indication of the difficulties involved (the issue of sampling error is as problematic as any other). Nevertheless, they should not rule out the use of crime surveys for comparative work. Even if they eventually prove limited in documenting the epidemiology of crime, they have much theoretical value in showing how risks of victimisation are distributed across countries in relation to the variables which crime surveys can accommodate (*cf.* van Dijk and Steinmetz, 1983; Block and Block, 1984). Already, it is emerging that risks relate to most demographic and "life-style" factors in similar ways across countries (in both Scotland and England and Wales, for instance, variables such as age, sex, urbanisation, levels of drinking and evening activity patterns were all very similarly implicated in risks). And where risks do vary, measurable cultural differences (*e.g.* in the proportion of women who work or the use of public transportation) can provide some of the explanation.

If their potential is to be maximised, a number of steps need to be taken by those responsible for initiating and administering crime surveys. Ideally, sampling design and questionnaire construction should be standardised, though it is probably more realistic to hope for more uniformity of questioning, particularly in relation to crime definitions and coverage. For the present, data from existing and forthcoming surveys (together with adequate technical documentation) should be made freely available so as to facilitate the reworking of results taking methodological differences into account.

REFERENCES

BLOCK, R. (Ed.). (In press). *Victimisation and Fear of Crime around the World*. Bureau of Justice Statistics, US Department of Justice. Washington DC: Government Printing Office.

BLOCK, R. L. and BLOCK, C. R. (1984). "Crime definition, crime measurement and victim surveys". *Journal of Social Issues*, **40,** 137–160.

BOTTOMLEY, A. K. and COLEMAN, C. (1981). *Understanding Crime Rates*. Farnborough: Gower.

BRAITHWAITE, J. and BILES, D. (1979). "Crime victimisation and reportability rates: a comparison of the United States and Australia". Canberra ACT: Australian Institute of Criminology.

CHAMBERS, G. and TOMBS, J. (Eds.). (1984). *The British Crime Survey: Scotland*. A Scottish Office Social Research Study. Edinburgh: HMSO.

CLINARD, M. B. (1978). "Comparative crime victimization surveys: some problems and results". *International Journal of Criminology and Penology*, **6,** 221–231.

VAN DIJK, J. J. M. and STEINMETZ, C. (1983). "Victimization surveys: beyond measuring the volume of crime". *Victimology: an International Journal*. **8,** 291–309.

CRIME IN ENGLAND AND WALES AND SCOTLAND: A B.C.S. COMPARISON

FARRINGTON, D. P. and Dowds, E. A. (1985). "Disentangling criminal behaviour to crime". In, Farrington, D. P. and Gunn, J. (Eds.), *Reaction to Crime: the public, the police, courts, and prisons*. Chichester: John Wiley.

HOUGH, M. (1983) "Victims of violent crime". Paper presented at the 33rd International Course in Criminology, Vancouver, BC. (March, 1983).

HOUGH, M. and MAYHEW, P. (1983). *The British Crime Survey: first report*. Home Office Research Study No. 76. London: HMSO.

SKOGAN, W. G. (1981). *Issues in the Measurement of Victimization*. Bureau of Justice Statistics, US Department of Justice. Washington, DC: Government Printing Office.

SKOGAN, W. G. (1984). "Reporting crimes to the police: the status of world research". *Journal of Research in Crime and Delinquency*, **21**, 113–137.

SMITH, L. J. F. (1983). *Criminal Justice Comparisons: the case of Scotland and England and Wales*. Research and Planning Unit Paper No. 17. London: Home Office.

SVERI, K. (1982). "Comparative analyses of crime by means of victim surveys: the Scandanavian experience". In, Schneider, H. (Ed.), *The Victim in International Perspective*. Berlin and New York: De Gruyter.

[4]

THE BRITISH JOURNAL

OF

CRIMINOLOGY

Vol. 27   Spring 1987   No. 2

A LOCALISED CRIME SURVEY IN CONTRASTING AREAS OF A CITY

A. E. Bottoms (*Cambridge*)*, R. I. Mawby (*Plymouth*)#, and Monica A. Walker (*Sheffield*)**

A crime survey was conducted in seven small residential areas (pop. 2000–3000) in the city of Sheffield, varying in their housing type and official crime rates. Within each housing type, the survey found that official crime statistics were valid indicators of area crime-rate differences. However, the two high-rise housing areas appeared as more problematic in the crime survey than in official data, with a particularly high ratio of survey offences to recorded offences. Some adjacent small residential areas were found to be demographically very similar but to have very different crime rates (on official or survey measures); this emphasises the importance of the micro-environmental dimension in criminological studies.

CRIME surveys have recently become an important feature of criminological studies in Britain, as in many other countries. In particular, of course, the first two sweeps of the British Crime Survey (Hough and Mayhew 1983, 1985) have provided much data of great value to criminologists, as well as having an impact upon the policy-making process and upon some sections of the wider public.

* Institute of Criminology, University of Cambridge.
\# Department of Social and Political Studies, Plymouth Polytechnic.
** Centre for Criminological and Socio-Legal Studies, University of Sheffield.
  The research reported in this paper was carried out at the Centre for Criminological and Socio-Legal Studies, University of Sheffield. Survey fieldwork was conducted for the University by British Market Research Bureau Ltd. Financial support for the survey was provided by the then Social Science Research Council (now the Economic and Social Research Council).

A. E. BOTTOMS, R. I. MAWBY, AND M. A. WALKER

The British Crime Survey, covering as it does some 11,000 households scattered throughout England and Wales, necessarily cannot concentrate upon the crime pattern in small areas.[1] Some more localised studies have however been attempted. Farrington and Dowds (1985) used a victim survey as a part of their methodology in their successful attempt to disentangle the extent to which Nottinghamshire's traditionally high crime rate (as compared with other Midlands counties) was an "artificial" product of differential public reporting and/or differential police recording of crime. Sparks *et al* (1977), in the pioneering British victim study, included *inter alia* some comparisons between the three London districts of Brixton, Hackney and Kensington, and found that the ratio between survey-reported crime and officially-reported crime varied in the three districts, as did the comparative distribution of different kinds of offence in the areas—though nevertheless the total crime rate was in the same rank order (Kensington, Brixton, Hackney) whether official or survey data were used.[2] Kinsey (1984, 1985), in the Merseyside crime survey, included some localised data from five wards in contrasting districts of Merseyside (Granley, Birkenhead, Northwood, Haydock and Ainsdale). Most recently, Jones *et al* (1986) have published a comprehensive crime survey of the London borough of Islington, which includes *inter alia* some data on criminal victimisation in the 20 different wards of the borough (chapter 2).

The size of these "local" areas varies considerably. Nottinghamshire is, of course, a whole county with a total population of about a million; Islington's population is 167,000. Sparks' three areas had adult populations of between 45,000 and 62,000 (p.152). The wards considered in the Merseyside and Islington surveys are a good deal smaller (total populations 8,000–15,000), but in neither study were small-area differences the main focus of the research, nor were comparisons made on a small-area basis between survey crime rates and officially recorded crime rates.

The present paper reports the results of a rather more truly localised crime survey, carried out in seven areas of the city of Sheffield. The total population (all ages) of each area was very small (2,000–3,000), systematic comparisons between survey data and official crime data were made, and area differences were the main focus of the research. Moreover, the areas were carefully selected, on the basis of previous research (see Baldwin and Bottoms 1976, Mawby 1979a), to reflect *first*, differences in housing tenures (public housing/privately rented housing/owner-occupied housing); *secondly*, differences in housing design within the public housing sector (high-rise flats or more conventional housing); and *thirdly*, whether the

---

[1] The British Crime Survey does, however, attempt to classify households in different parts of the country according to their neighbourhood type: in the second sweep of the survey this was done using the 'ACORN' system of area classification (Hough and Mayhew 1985, Appendix F). See also the final paragraph of this paper.

[2] The ratio of survey-reported crime to official crime was 14·6 in Hackney, 12·5 in Brixton, and 8·6 in Kensington; nevertheless, using both survey and official data, Kensington had the highest crime rate per 100,000 population of the three areas, and Hackney the lowest (Sparks *et al* 1977, data derived from Table IV.4, p.152). Official and survey data *for different types of offence*, however, showed "no more than a moderate agreement in . . . the rank orders" (p.154 and Table VI.5)

A LOCALISED CRIME SURVEY

officially recorded offender and offence rates in the area (as ascertained from data made available by the police) were high or low.[3]

Although the survey is now some years old (it was carried out in 1975), we believe it remains of importance as an illustration of the potential of the crime survey method when applied to systematically chosen contrasting small areas. Moreover, one of the main conclusions of the study is that the official crime statistics constitute, in general, a valid indicator of differences in crime victimisation in small areas of a similar housing type; and this result is different in emphasis from that of much other research and writing on criminal statistics (for a useful recent summary of which see Bottomley and Pease 1986, chapters 1 and 2). Finally, the small scale of the present study enabled some methodological questions to be investigated.

Areas and Methodology

The small areas used for the survey are the same as those considered in some previous research in Sheffield (*e.g.* Mawby 1979a; Bottoms and Xanthos 1981). As in previous research reports, the areas are distinguished by a three-letter code which connotes the systematic differences of housing tenure, housing design and officially recorded offending used as the basis for area selection (see above). The explanation of the three-letter code is as follows:

> *First Letter:* the predominant housing tenure type in the area at the time of the 1971 census (O=owner-occupied; C=rented from the local authority or "council" (public housing); R=rented privately);
> *Second Letter:* whether the area contains predominantly low-rise houses or high-rise blocks of flats (respectively H and F);
> *Third Letter:* whether the official offender rate[4] in 1971 was high or low (respectively H and L).

Although this notation has been retained, it has been found confusing by some readers of previous reports, so fictitious area names are also now introduced to aid area identification.

The seven chosen areas fall naturally into three groups, of different housing types:

Group I: Inter-war council housing estates

1. CHH (Gardenia): a council house area built in the first quarter of this century, with mainly two-storey semi-detached houses, and a "garden city" area plan. Its official offender and offence rates were among the highest in the city for a residential area, and it was well known as having an adverse reputation.

---

[3] The official *offender rate* of an area measures the extent to which officially recorded offenders live there; the official *offence rate* measures the extent to which officially recorded crimes have been committed in the area. See further the Appendix to Bottoms and Wiles (1986).

[4] The official offender rate (as opposed to offence rate) was chosen for this purpose because the main aim of the overall Sheffield research was to explain differential offender rates in residential areas. However, the research also showed that in residential areas there was a strong (though not perfect) correlation between offender and offence rates—this is illustrated by the data in *Table 1.*

A. E. BOTTOMS, R. I. MAWBY, AND M. A. WALKER

2. CHL (Stonewall): a council house area adjacent to CHH (separated only by a main road and some shops). Built a few years later than CHH, but with a similar housing and area type. Official offender and offence rates were much lower than CHH.

Group II: Post-war high-rise council estates

3. CFH (Skyhigh): a high-rise deck-access council development close to the city centre, built in the 1960s with one large high-rise block and other smaller blocks. Official offender rate was high (though not as high as CHH); official offence rate rather lower.
4. CFL (Lowtowers): another high-rise deck-access council development, adjacent to CFH. It was, however, built a few years earlier than CFH, and to a rather different design only six storeys high, strung out along a hillside. Low official offender and offence rates.

Group III: Non-council ("private") areas

5. RHH (Redlight): a small inner-city area with mixed types of terraced housing, including some very large houses now given over to multi-occupation. Predominantly privately rented. The area lies close to the University and the Polytechnic and provides attractive cheap accomodation for some students. At the time of the survey it had the highest official offender and offence rates in the city, and was notorious as the city's main prostitution area. Three years after the survey it was designated as a Housing Action Area (for aspects of the subsequent history of the area see Bottom and Wiles 1986).
6. RHL (Graybridge)[5]: This was an area of two rather distinct parts. To the east, the area contained mostly semi-detached and terraced houses, mainly owner-occupied but at the bottom end of the price-range for owner-occupied housing. To the west, there was a smaller area of mainly rented terraced houses (mostly privately rented, but some taken over by the council). This second part was designated as a slum clearance area, and was awaiting demolition at the time of the survey; a year or two later it was bulldozed. The area as a whole had low official offender and offence rates. Because the survey analysis has shown that the two parts of this area were very distinct, they have mostly been kept separate in this paper, and designated: (i) RHL (O): the still remaining, now mainly owner-occupied, area; and (ii) RHL (D): the demolished area.
7. OHL (Middleway): This was an area of predominantly middle-class semi-detached owner-occupied housing in the favoured south-western sector of the city; it was the only one of these seven areas to be predominantly middle-class. However, it was among the least expensive of the middle-

[5] In some previous publications from the Sheffield research project, especially Mawby (1979a), there were *two* privately rented low offender rate areas, known as RHL and R'HL. "Graybridge", in those publications, was R'HL, but as the other area was not used in this survey, Graybridge has been redesignated RHL.

A LOCALISED CRIME SURVEY

class housing areas of the city, so could not be described as an affluent area.

In general, results for the survey areas will be analysed in the three housing-based groups as set out above: that is, first the inter-war council housing pair, one with a high and one with a low official offender rate; next, the post-war high-rise council pair, one with a high and one with a low official offender rate; and finally the private areas, with the very high official offender rate RHH (Redlight) being analysed against the two parts of RHL (Graybridge), and with OHL (Middleway) acting as a middle-class comparison area.

The samples used for the survey were selected by the survey research agency conducting the survey (British Market Research Bureau) as statistically random samples of the adult population of each area.[6] A simple electoral register sample was not used because it was believed that in an area of high population turnover (such as RHH (Redlight) was known to be) the register could be seriously faulty as a sampling frame for a population survey. Accordingly the so-called Marchant-Blyth sampling method, originally developed within BMRB for use in the National Readership Survey, was employed. This method is claimed to give non-electors the same probability of selection as electors, and, because it is based on addresses rather than households, should not under-represent people such as those who live in bedsitters (see Blyth and Marchant 1973).

A potential difficulty of method in sampling in such small areas was the possibility of adverse local reactions among residents owing to the sensitive nature of the subjects and the high sampling fraction (on average, about one in 15 adults in the areas was part of the intended sample). This was overcome by using an "area blitz" technique, sending interviewers into each area sequentially and with instructions to complete interviewing in the area as rapidly as possible.

The overall response rate for the survey was 78 per cent. Individual areas did not differ significantly in response rate, and the range was from 73 per cent. in CHH (Gardenia) to 84 per cent. in RHL (Graybridge). The final sample consisted of 806 respondents from 762 addresses (the Marchant-Blyth technique allows sampling of more than one respondent from an address, and from a household, in certain circumstances).[7]

The interview schedule used for the survey covered a number of topics besides recent crime victimisation—notably residents' general perceptions of the areas where they lived; their general perception of crime in their areas; a self-report study; and some social characteristics of the respondent and his/her household. Only the victim survey and population characteristics section of the survey will be reported in detail here, but some results on other topics are considered briefly at the end of the paper.

---

[6] "Adult population" in this survey was defined as aged 17 or over; the British Crime Survey includes those aged 16 or over.
[7] One household consisting of three students in RHL, each of whom was selected by the Marchant-Blyth technique, was excluded from the analysis as being atypical, especially as the students had only lived there for five weeks.

A. E. BOTTOMS, R. I. MAWBY, AND M. A. WALKER

Characteristics of the Areas

Table 1, which is based on previous research, shows in some detail various measures of recorded offences, offenders and other incidents in the seven areas. All these indices were derived in one way or another from official records: police data of various kinds; post office data concerning telephone kiosk vandalism and television licence evasion; and housing department data concerning rent arrears. It should be noted that, according to these data, the three "high crime" areas (CHH, CFH and RHH) are in almost every instance the areas with the three highest rates, despite the very different data sources and different kinds of behaviour characterised in the table (for a much fuller discussion see Mawby 1979a).

Table 2 gives details, from the present survey, of selected characteristics of households and survey respondents in the studied areas (in this and subsequent tables, the student population of RHH (Redlight) is shown separately from the ordinary residents of that area). In *Table 2a* the tenure of the areas is shown on a household basis: not surprisingly, the four council areas had overwhelmingly council properties within them. Of the

TABLE 1

Officially recorded data for the areas concerning offences, offenders, minor incidents and rent arrears (Rates per 1000 households)

		CHH	CHL	CFH	CFL	RHH	RHL	OHL
A.	*Offence/Incident Data*							
1.	Indictable offence rate for offences against residents (1971) [excluding shops etc]	85·1	23·7	31·2	20·2	113·8	18·2	9·5
2.	Non-indictable offences							
	a. Soliciting (1973)	0·0	0·0	0·0	0·0	73·8	0·0	0·0
	b. Other non-indictables recorded by police (1973)	37·5	3·7	6·1	9·1	29·2	3·6	0·0
	c. 'Phone box vandalism* (Post office data: 1973–74)	23·3	15·5	32·7	20·0	8·5	11·0	9·0
3.	Incidents to which police were called (1974) [nuisance, damage, disputes, other than recorded offences]	73·6	23·7	47·1	23·2	101·5	19·4	13·8
B.	*Offender/Personal Data*							
1.	Indictable offender rate (1971)	96·7	32·4	76·7	22·2	141·5	23·1	5·2
2.	Non-indictable							
	a. Soliciting (1973)	0·0	0·0	0·0	0·0	15·4	0·0	0·0
	b. Drugs (1974–76)	4·3	0·0	1·5	1·0	21·5	0·0	0·9
	c. Other public order (1973)	33·2	5·0	14·4	7·1	40·0	4·9	1·7
	d. TV licence evasion (Post office data: prosecution file 1971–73)	62·0	10·0	44·0	19·2	36·9	20·7	1·7
3.	Persons in rent arrears (Council areas only — Housing Dept data 1975)	159·1	68·1	246·8	126·1	—	—	—

* Rates per kiosk

Source (other than B3): Mawby 1979a, Table 2·12, p.62. All data were derived from police records except A2(c), B2(d) and B3.

A LOCALISED CRIME SURVEY

"private sector" districts OHL (Middleway) was almost all owner-occupied; RHH (Redlight) was predominantly privately rented (especially if the students are included), but with a fair proportion of owner-occupied houses; within Graybridge, RHL (O) was mainly owner-occupied, and RHL (D) was divided fairly evenly between the privately rented and owner-occupied tenures, with a minority of houses owned by the council (these were short-life council tenures bought up by the council to offer temporary accommodation to some tenants pending demolition of the site).

Table 2b shows the social class of heads of household according to the Registrar-General's classification. It can be seen that the social class composition within each of the two pairs of council estates is remarkably similar, a point which is particularly striking when one recalls the very great differences in recorded crime (*Table 1*). For example, CHH (Gardenia) and CHL (Stonewall) have very little difference in social class composition, but *threefold* differences in indictable offender and offence rates. RHH (Redlight), which has an interesting minority of social class I and II (mostly young professional people) despite its predominantly working class character,[8] is generally similar in social class composition to the due-for-demolition part of RHL (Graybridge), but the other half of Graybridge, RHL (O), has a significantly greater proportion of residents in social class III. OHL (Middleway) stands out as strikingly different from the other areas with its high proportion of social classes I and II.

Table 2c shows the age of termination of full-time education by survey respondents: in all areas except OHL (Middleway), and RHH (Redlight) with its young professional group, 89 per cent. or over had ceased full-time education by the age of 16.

Table 2d shows that RHH (Redlight) had, not surprisingly for an area of this type, a higher proportion of single people than other areas, which were otherwise generally similar.

Table 2e shows the survey respondents' length of stay in the dwelling. There was no significant difference between the two estates in the inter-war council pair, though CHH (Gardenia) had slightly more recent residents. A striking feature of both areas was their social stability: about 60 per cent. had lived in their house for at least 10 years. In the post-war council pair, however, there was a statistically significant difference between the two areas with CFH (Skyhigh) residents having a shorter average residence than those of CFL (Lowtowers). (CFH was built less than 15 years before the survey, so no responses of "15 years or more" were possible). RHH (Redlight) had, with CFH (Skyhigh), the highest proportions of short-stay residents; it differed significantly on this variable from RHL (O), though not from RHL (D).

Finally, *Table 2f* shows birthplace of sample respondents. The overwhelming majority were born in Britain. Only RHH (Redlight) had a

[8] The exact area chosen for RHH (Redlight) followed the boundaries of the 1966 10 per cent. census enumeration district (the basis of earlier work in the Sheffield crime study: Baldwin and Bottoms 1976). This area boundary also included a very small part of a neighbouring "conservation area", and this fact has also helped to swell the proportion of households of social classes I and II in this survey.

A. E. BOTTOMS, R. I. MAWBY, AND M. A. WALKER

TABLE 2

Characteristics of Households and of Survey Respondents (%)

	CHH	CHL	CFH	CFL	RHH	RHH(ST)	RHL(O)	RHL(D)	OHL
(a) Tenure (Households)									
Owner Occupied	9	0	0	0	44	0	72	46	97
Rented from Council	88	100	100	100	3	0	0	9	0
Rented Privately	3	0	0	0	53	100	28	46	3
n=100%	104	116	99	101	91	30	64	46	111
(b) Social Class (Households) (Registrar-General's classification)									
I, II	3	9	2	4	19		13	14	54
III	57	53	47	49	42		64	40	37
IV, V	39	37	50	46	39		23	45	9
n=100% (excluding unknown)	103	112	99	99	89	30*	63	42	111
			*=all students						
(c) Age when full-time education finished (Respondents)									
14, 15, 16	95	96	99	98	69		89	90	67
17, 18	2	1	1	2	9		8	0	13
19 or over	1	0	0	0	19		0	4	16
Still Studying	2	3	0	0	3	100	3	6	3
n=100%	108	122	104	107	96	40	67	49	113
(d) % single (Respondents)									
	16	25	17	19	45	42	18	6	14
(e) Length of stay in dwelling (Respondents)									
<2 years	19	8	27	10	28	88	12	18	12
2–5 years	7	15	17	14	17	8	9	14	13
5–10 years	14	18	26	20	12	2	21	14	25
10–15 years	11	9	30	21	12	0	10	8	11
>15 years	49	50	0	35	31	2	48	45	38
n=100%	108	122	104	107	96	40	67	49	113
(f) Country of Origin (Respondents)									
Great Britain	98	98	94	97	78	70	97	97	92
Ireland	1	3	0	1	6	0	3	0	1
New Commonwealth & Pakistan	0	0	6	2	12	27	0	2	3
Other (N. America, Europe etc)	2	0	0	0	3	3	1	0	5
n=100%	108	122	104	107	96	40	67	49	113

significant minority born elsewhere, reflecting this area's multi-racial character, with groups of Asian, West Indian, and Irish origin living in the area. Apart from RHH, only CFH (Skyhigh) had any noticeable number of black residents at the time of the survey, and even here the number was very small.

Table 3 gives some further details of population characteristics, this time counting all persons in households contacted in the survey (as opposed to respondents only). There was no significant age difference between the two inter-war council housing estates, but in the post-war pair CFH (Skyhigh) had significantly more young children, and fewer residents over 55. In the private sector, RHH (Redlight) had a particularly high proportion of young persons aged 17–24. Male-female ratios did not differ significantly

A LOCALISED CRIME SURVEY

between areas, though RHH (Redlight) had the highest proportion of males.[9]

Table 3(c) gives data on mean household size, counting both all residents and, separately, all residents aged over 10 (*i.e.* those legally capable of being convicted of crime). On the first index there was a slight tendency (not statistically significant) for the three high crime rate areas to have higher mean household size than their paired areas. This slight difference almost wholly disappeared when the second index was taken.

If we now re-consider the results of the area characteristics as a whole, considering the areas in their three groups, the following picture has emerged:

(i) *Inter-war council house pair* Despite a few slight variations, there were no significant differences between these two areas on any variable. This is particularly remarkable given their very different official offence and offender rates.

(ii) *Post-war high-rise council pair* There were few differences, but CFH (Skyhigh) did have significantly more recent residents and a significantly younger population. Again, the general similarities are notable given the different crime indices.

(iii) *Private areas* RHH (Redlight) had some social class differences from one part of Graybridge, RHL (O)—and also of course from OHL (Middle-way). RHH (Redlight) also had more single people, more people aged 17–24, more people from ethnic minority groups, and the highest proportion of males in any area—in fact, all the classic indicators of a transitional area, though it also had a minority of young professional people. RHL (O) and RHL (D) differed in the way that one might expect for areas respectively (i) moving from privately rented to owner-occupied, and (ii) awaiting the imminent arrival of the demolition firm.

TABLE 3

Characteristics of all residents in households included in Survey

	CHH	CHL	CFH	CFL	RHH	RHH(ST)	RHL(O)	RHL(D)	OHL
(a) *Age group (percentage)*									
Under 10	16	10	23	9	16	4	16	18	10
10–16	14	12	13	12	12	0	13	11	13
17–24	14	14	17	13	20	74	14	10	11
25–54	33	35	33	36	34	21	40	40	40
55+	22	28	13	29	18	1	18	22	25
n=100%	344	362	330	292	328	78	184	137	328
(b) % *Males*	52	49	50	51	57	60	52	51	46
Females	48	51	50	49	43	40	48	49	54
(c) *Mean household size*									
All residents	3·3	3·1	3·3	2·9	3·5	2·7	2·9	3·0	3·0
All aged 10 or over	2·7	2·8	2·5	2·6	2·8	2·6	2·4	2·5	2·7

[9] Although the overall proportions of males and females in CHL (Stonewall) were evenly matched, the sampling procedure produced an over-representation of females among the intended sample, and among the respondents, in that area. Where appropriate we have adjusted the survey results to correct for this error.

A. E. BOTTOMS, R. I. MAWBY, AND M. A. WALKER

OHL (Middleway) stood out from all the other areas as very distinct on tenure, social class, and age of termination of fulltime education.

The Victim Survey: Approach and Methodological Problems

The victim survey section of the present survey was located towards the end of the interview schedule, and closely followed the methodology of Sparks *et al* (1977)[10]—*i.e.* a discussion of the preceding 12 months to aid recall; a series of "screening" questions asking how many times particular kinds of crimes had occurred in the last year (see Appendix); and finally, but only after completion of the screening questions, completion of an "incident sheet" concerning each incident mentioned in the screening (up to a maximum of three incidents per offence type, or nine incidents in all).

Before turning to the results of the survey, certain methodological points may be mentioned. It is not appropriate here to discuss victim survey methodology in general (see, *e.g.* the excellent discussion in Sparks 1981), but this survey is able to throw some light on two issues in particular.

The first is that of the *counting of offences*, often mentioned only in passing by other researchers. Our screening sheet asked, for each offence, "how many times" it had happened in the last year; a maximum of 9 was allowed, with estimates of more than 9 being coded as 9. (The British Crime Survey uses a maximum of 5). The difficulty is that for some respondents certain crimes happen so frequently that any precise estimation of numbers is impossible. Particular crimes where this was so in this survey were *first*, theft of milk bottles and/or milk tokens[11] in the two post-war council developments, which with their deck-access design make such thefts very easy to commit ("it happens all the time," said some); and *secondly*, minor vandalism (*e.g.* garden fence broken "every two or three days"). Two particular respondents occupationally liable to being assaulted (a bouncer in a night club and a warden of a hostel for ex-offenders) also reported multiple victimisation to an unknown extent. Similar issues probably arise in a less spectacular fashion in many other instances, so it is necessary to recognise that any attempted precise estimation of numbers of offences is to a real extent arbitrary. Following Sparks *et al* (1977, p.97) we therefore in this survey distinguish between two measures:

(i) *prevalence, i.e.* the *proportion* of householders or individuals victimised for the given offence in the given time period.

(ii) *incidence, i.e.* the estimated *total number* of crimes in the given offence category occurring in the given period.

The former measure will almost certainly be the more accurate as a survey estimate, though it has to be remembered that it treats in a similar way

[10] The survey was carried out after Sparks's fieldwork, but before publication of his work: we were fortunate in being able to consult Richard Sparks and to benefit from his advice.

[11] "Milk tokens" are used by the Co-operative Societies in Sheffield (and some other cities) as a method of payment for milk: tokens are bought at the Co-operative shop, and then placed on the doorstep as a way of paying for the milk (one token=one pint of milk).

A LOCALISED CRIME SURVEY

someone victimised once and someone victimised many times. Both prevalence and incidence measures are probably necessary to obtain a full picture, and the distinction in indices is perhaps one which the British Crime Survey might consider using in a more prominent way than at present.[12]

The second methodological issue to be raised concerns the validity of estimates of "household" offences. Our survey distinguishes, in a way that has now become common in crime surveys, between: (i) *household offences* (*i.e.* those commited against members of the household as a whole, such as burglary or vehicle theft; or against individual household members' property at the residence, such as theft of toys from the garden): here rates are calculated in relation to the number of households; and (ii) *personal offences* (*i.e.* those committed against individuals such as theft from the person or assault), where rates are calculated in relation to the number of individual respondents. As Sparks (1981, p.29) points out, it has been known since the early victim studies in the U.S.A. in the 1960s that asking one person in a household about other household members' *personal* offences leads to serious under-reporting, "since the proxy respondent may not remember (or even know of) his or her spouse's or child's experience". Sparks goes on to raise the issue, however, whether the common practice of asking one household member about *household* offences may not also lead to under-reporting—an issue of some importance since this has been the practice in the National Crime Surveys in the U.S.A. and in the British Crime Survey. The present survey for the most part followed the same one-per-household practice, but, because of the Marchant-Blyth sampling method used, in a minority of cases more than one respondent in a household was questioned (see above). We have to report that for these households a total of 25 household offences was mentioned by survey respondents, *but only seven of these (or 28 per cent.) were reported by both persons interviewed in the household*. Despite the small numbers, this seems strongly to confirm Sparks's view that there may be serious under-reporting of household offences using the "one member per household" method. The issue seems to warrant close attention in future crime surveys, but in the meantime one should bear it in mind as a limitation of the results of the present research, as of other work such as the British Crime Survey.

The Victim Survey: Overall Results

As with all other victim surveys, this survey produced evidence of a great many more crimes than were officially known to the police in the areas studied. It is important to state at the outset, however, that detailed examination of the incident sheets shows that very many of the offences mentioned are of a rather trivial nature—minor thefts from the garden or

[12] British Crime Survey researchers are well aware of the prevalence/incidence distinction, and of some of the limitations of incidence rates in "series offences" (see Hough 1984, pp.16–17; Hough 1986, p.122; Gottfredson 1984, Appendix B); but the two overview reports on the B.C.S. (Hough and Mayhew 1983, 1985) have not gone into the issue in the interests of simplicity, preferring to use only incidence rates.

A. E. BOTTOMS, R. I. MAWBY, AND M. A. WALKER

doorstep, minor vandalism, and the like. One particularly common crime, especially in the two post-war high-rise council areas, was theft of milk bottles or tokens, and this has been excluded from most of the overall analyses, as in the British Crime Survey. However, it should not be ignored, as it is an unpleasant feature of life especially in the high-rise flats, and is an illustration of the way in which the crime problem can, for many, be best described as an accumulation of nuisances (Mawby and Gill 1987). We report the relevant figures for milk theft in an appropriate table below (see Table 6).

Table 4 shows the overall *prevalence* (not incidence) of victim-reported offences in the areas, distinguishing between household and personal offences. It will be seen that total prevalence varied by area from a low of 22 per cent. to a high of 50 per cent. in the different areas (no overall or "total" figures are given since the seven areas do not as a group constitute any meaningful universe). Prevalence of household offences was in all areas greater than prevalence of personal offences, though the two indices are not directly comparable, one being related to the number of households and the other to the number of respondents. Discussion of area differences is postponed for the time being.

One central task of victim surveys is to act as a method by which to test the validity of official crime indices. *Table 5* provides a summary statement of this comparison for the present survey. In this table, the "survey offence rate" and the "survey victimisation rate" (respectively referring to victim survey offences committed in the areas, and to all victimisations reported by survey respondents whether or not they occurred in the area) are calculated for each area by the following formula:

$$\left[\begin{array}{l}\text{No. of}\\\text{household} +\\\text{offences}\end{array}\left(\begin{array}{ll}\text{Average no.} & \text{Average no. of}\\\text{of personal} \times & \text{people per house-}\\\text{offences} & \text{hold over 16}\end{array}\right)\right] \div \left(\begin{array}{l}\text{No. of}\\\text{households}\end{array}\right)$$

A number of technical points must be made about this table before we can

TABLE 4

Prevalence of Offences[+]

	CHH	CHL	CFH	CFL	RHH	RHH(ST)	RHL(O)	RHL(D)	OHL
% of respondents victims of any offence#§	38*	22	46*	29	50*	33	25	26	25
% of households victims of any household offence#§	34*	21	32	24	43*	23	20	26	19
% of respondents victims of any personal offence	9	5	22*	6	20*	20	7	9	10

[+] In general in the tables of survey results differences of percentages between areas are significant at the 5 per cent level if they exceed 14, and at the 1 per cent level if they exceed 18. Larger differences are needed for comparisons involving the RHH(ST), RHL(O) and RHL(D) groups, as these are based on smaller total numbers.
§ For base numbers see Table 2.
# Excluding milk theft.
* Indicates significant difference between high rate area and matched low rate area (RHH compared with RHL (O)).

136

A LOCALISED CRIME SURVEY

TABLE 5

Summary of Official and Survey Crime Results (per 100 households)

	CHH	CHL	CFH	CFL	RHH	RHL	OHL
#Official indictable offender rate (1971)	9·7	3·2	7·7	2·2	14·2	2·3	0·5
#Official indictable offence rate against residents (*crimes within area only*) (1971)	8·5	2·4	3·1	2·0	11·4	1·8	1·0
+Survey offence rate *for offences within area* (1975)	51*	15	84*	51	109*	20	32
§Ratio survey offence rate: official offence rate	6	6	27	26	10	11	32
Survey rate adjusted to constant 2·7 persons per household over 10 in each area	50*	16	99*	45	136*	26	30
#Official indictable offence rate against residents (*offences inside or outside area*) (1971)	11·3	3·2	6·8	3·1	12·9	2·7	1·7
+Survey victimisation rate for offences *inside or outside area* (1975)	65*	25	97*	57	162*	35	46
§Ratio survey victimisation rate: official victimisation rate	6	8	14	18	13	13	27
Survey rate adjusted to constant 2·7 persons per household over 10 in each area	67*	27	118*	66	178*	43	52

\# See Mawby, 1979a, pp.62 and 48.
+ See text for method of calculation. Vandalism and milk thefts are excluded.
§ These ratios should be treated with caution as the data refer to different years.
* Indicates significant difference between high rate area and matched low rate area (RHH is compared with RHL(O)). [Shown for bottom row and third from bottom row in each part of the table only].

interpret it. First, the official crime data are for 1971 and the survey data for 1975, so that exact comparisons of rates are not possible. At the time of the research, official data for the areas could only be extracted by going through individual crime report forms manually at police headquarters, and there was insufficient research manpower to do this for 1975, the exercise having already been completed for the whole of Sheffield for 1966, and for nine small areas in 1971 (Baldwin and Bottoms 1976; Mawby 1979a). However, in these nine small areas (including the seven in the present survey) there had been reasonable stability in the official crime rate data between 1966 and 1971 (see Mawby 1979a, p.35), and some later official indices of non-indictable offences revealed similar rate differentials between the areas (see *Table 1*), so it is very likely that at least the broad features of the comparison are correct.

Secondly, all rates in Table 5 are given "per 100 households" since this is the way that all the official crime and offender data was reported by

A. E. BOTTOMS, R. I. MAWBY, AND M. A. WALKER

Mawby (1979a). In fact household size for persons over 10 does not differ significantly by area (see above), so there is no objection to this index, but for the sake of completeness we have also provided calculations of the survey and victimisation rates on the assumption of a constant 2·7 persons per household over 10 in different areas.

Thirdly, milk thefts and vandalism have been excluded from the table—the former because of its inaccuracy of counting, triviality, and almost total absence in officially reported criminality; and the latter because criminal damage under £20 was not, at the time of the survey, one of the crimes which was recorded by the police in England and Wales, so that minor vandalism has to be excluded from any comparison with officially recorded crime.[13]

Fourthly, it should be noted that in this table no division is made of the Graybridge area as between RHL (O) and RHL (D); this is because official offence rates are not available separately for these different parts of the area, the two having been treated together in Mawby's (1979a) earlier work.

If we turn now to an interpretation of the table, the greatest attention should be paid to *the survey rate for offences within the area, adjusted for size of household* (row 5 in table). If we take the three groups of areas separately, it is seen that *within each group* of areas the relationship of the "paired" areas to each other is the same as in the official crime data. Thus:

(a) CHH (Gardenia) has a survey offence rate three times that of CHL (Stonewall), and both have a similar ratio of survey to official crime (6:1);

(b) CFH (Skyhigh) has a survey offence rate more than twice that of CFL (Lowtowers), and both have a similar ratio of survey to official crime (26:1);

(c) RHH (Redlight) has a survey offence rate more than five times that of RHL (Graybridge), and both have a similar ratio of survey to official crime (10:1). OHL (Middleway) also has a reasonably low rate.

These data provide clear confirmation of the general validity of official crime statistics for comparisons between residential areas of a similar housing type within a city. This conclusion is congruent with the earlier work of Mawby (1979a), carried out in the same small areas of Sheffield, but based on the way the official data themselves were compiled in these areas.

A complicating feature, however, is the presence of very different ratios of survey to official data in the three different groups of areas. In particular, the ratio in both of the high-rise areas is spectacularly greater than in any of the other working-class areas, leading to the overall (adjusted) survey offence rate for CFL (Lowtowers) being only a little lower than the rate for CHH (Gardenia), although on official indices it is usually very much lower (see *Table 1*). This is a matter for which there are various possible

---

[13] Home Office instructions to police forces on this matter were altered in 1976, and from 1977 all criminal damage, including that under £20, has been required to be recorded.

A LOCALISED CRIME SURVEY

explanations, and to which close attention must be paid as we move to consider more detailed results.

Another area with a surprisingly high survey to official offence ratio is OHL (Middleway). Here, bearing in mind the much better average educational attainment of OHL residents in comparison with the other areas (see *Table 2c*), it is likely that this is another example of the previously reported phenomenon of persons with higher educational attainment reporting more offences in surveys (see Sparks 1981, pp.32–5).

The data below the horizontal line in *Table 5* are similar to those above except that they include offences outside the area (*e.g.* a survey respondent might have had a wallet or handbag stolen when in the city centre). These offences are of lesser importance when considering the crime patterns *of residential areas*, and so are not discussed extensively here. However, it should be noted (i) that they display broadly similar results to those when only offences within the area are considered; and (ii) the ratio of the survey to official crime is considerably diminished for both the high-rise flat complexes, but not for OHL (Middleway), in this part of the table. This obviously suggests that it is particularly offences within the areas themselves that are producing the high ratio for the high-rise areas.

The Victim Survey: Detailed Results

In considering the detailed results of the victim survey it is necessary to distinguish between household and personal offences, as previously defined.

(a) *Household Offences*

In the first instance we will consider *prevalence*, and the relevant data are shown in *Table 6*.

TABLE 6

Prevalence of Household Offences[+]

% households victims of	CHH	CHL	CFH	CFL	RHH	RHH(ST)	RHL(O)	RHL(D)	OHL
– burglary	7	2	1	2	10*	0	0	0	0
– theft in dwelling	3	0	0	3	7	13	5	2	2
– theft outside dwelling#	15*	6	12*	5	18*	3	6	2	4
– milk theft	6	3	23	22	6	3	5	4	2
– vehicle theft	2	1	2	4	0	0	5	2	2
– theft from vehicle	3	1	6	5	7	7	5	4	2
– vandalism	17	11	18	13	22*	0	2	15	8
Any household offence#	34*	21	32	24	43*	23	20	26	19
Household offence in area#	33*	19	32	24	42*	23	19	26	15
Base=no. of households	104	116	99	101	91	30	64	46	111

[+] Care should be taken in interpreting data for individual offences. Standard errors for these figures vary from about 1·0 (for percentage of size 1) to 5·0 (for percentage of size 50). [The exact value is $100 \times \sqrt{\frac{p(1-p)}{n}}$, where p is the population value and n is the sample size].

\# Excluding milk theft.

* Indicates significant difference between high rate area and matched low rate area (RHH compared with RHL(O)). See also note to Table 4.

A. E. BOTTOMS, R. I. MAWBY, AND M. A. WALKER

Household offences usually occur, of course, within the area being studied—the only significant exceptions are offences against vehicles. The bottom two lines of Table 6 give respectively the *total prevalence* and the *prevalence within the area* for all household offences except milk thefts; it can be seen that the two rows have very similar figures. Considering the paired areas, these overall totals show a significant difference in prevalence between CHH (Gardenia) and CHL (Stonewall); an absence of significance between the post-war-council pair, though with CFH (Skyhigh) having the higher rate; and RHH (Redlight) having a higher rate than both RHL (O) and RHL (D) (although only the former is statistically significant).

The detailed prevalence rates for each offence are also shown in the table (here including all offences, whether or not in the area). The three offences with highest prevalence rates were milk theft; theft outside the dwelling other than milk theft; and vandalism. Milk theft was mentioned by nearly a quarter of households in both CFH (Skyhigh) and CFL (Lowtowers); this was significantly higher than in the other areas.[14] Theft outside the dwelling was interesting in producing a significant difference as between each of the three high-rate areas (CHH, CFH, RHH) and its matched pair.

Prevalence rates for vandalism did not differ significantly across the four council estates. It might be thought surprising that the rates were no higher in the high-rise areas, in view of previous research suggesting a close link between vandalism and design features, with a clear difference between high-rise apartment blocks and low-rise conventional housing (*e.g.* Coleman, 1985, p.100). However, it has to be remembered that the present survey concerns only vandalism *against the property of members of the respondent's household,* and not more general vandalism in the public spaces of the estate: with regard to public spaces, casual observation at the time of the research, and survey responses to more general questions about areas (see below) confirmed greater problems in the high-rise areas, especially CFH (Skyhigh). Yet it is an important point that despite this vandalism in "the estate outside the dwelling", vandalism against household units in these high-rise areas was not significantly greater than for those living in inter-war council housing developments (for a fuller discussion of this and other aspects of vandalism in the seven areas, see Mawby, 1984). As for vandalism in the private housing sector, prevalence rates were significantly high in both RHH (Redlight) and the due-for-demolition RHL (D) by comparison with the other two areas. The high prevalence for vandalism, as compared with other household offences, in RHL (D) is striking, and almost certainly reflects the problems of an area known to be shortly facing the bulldozer. The absence of vandalism mentions from students in RHH (Redlight) may be due to the fact that they mostly lived in bedsits and had no gardens, or indeed much else to vandalise.

Apart from these three offences, there were no significant differences

[14] This finding clearly shows the influence of design on some crimes: milk bottles and tokens placed outside the front doors of deck-access flats are, in effect, in a public corridor; most of the housing in the other areas in the survey had at least a small front garden, which reduced opportunist theft.

A LOCALISED CRIME SURVEY

between the matched pairs of areas for individual household offences, except between RHH and RHL for burglary. However, when all seven areas were compared, there was significant variation overall for burglary and for theft in dwellings (but not for vehicle theft or thefts from vehicles). The highest burglary rates were in RHH (Redlight) and CHH (Gardenia).

We may now consider the *incidence* of household offences. *Table 7* shows the mean number of all household offences for households in each area, and also the mean number of offences committed within the area (excluding milk thefts in each case). Significance was similar to that for the total prevalence measures when the paired areas were considered. Once again, the dominant offences were theft outside the dwelling and vandalism, the detailed figures for which are given in the table: in each area, these two offences together constituted at least half of all the household offences after milk theft had been excluded. Table 7 also shows the total for household offences inside the area excluding vandalism, to provide a better comparison with the official crime data (see discussion of Table 5, above): but again, the area differences showed the same pattern.

From this analysis, therefore, we find CHH (Gardenia) and RHH (Redlight) confirmed in their status as high crime rate areas, by comparison with their matched pairs. CFH (Skyhigh) also has a high absolute incidence and prevalence rate (on a par with CHH), but does not differ significantly from its matched area, CFL (Lowtowers), which in respect of incidence particularly has a rate closer to the high crime areas (though it has significantly fewer thefts outside the dwelling than CFH (Skyhigh)).

To see how far area differences in household offences could be statistically explained by other factors, a correlation analysis of the household offence *incidence* rate was conducted with several demographic variables, such as length of stay, sex of respondent, age of respondent, number of adults, and household size. Each of the last four variables was

TABLE 7

Incidence of Household Offences[+]

Mean no. of offences per household	CHH	CHL	CFH	CFL	RHH	RHH(ST)	RHL(O)	RHL(D)	OHL
All household offences#	·59*	·31	·67	·51	·95*	·43	·20	·45	·29
Thefts outside dwelling#	·24*	·06	·20*	·05	·23	·03	·08	·02	·05
Vandalism	·20	·22	·32	·25	·41*	·20	·02	·20	·10
All household offences inside area only#	·58*	·29	·67	·51	·94*	·43	·10	·45	·25
All household offences inside area excluding vandalism#	·38*	·07	·35	·26	·53*	·23	·08	·25	·15
Correlation between all offences and household size	·25	NS	·25	·18	NS	NS	NS	NS	·24

[+] See note to Table 6. Standard errors for incidence are slightly higher than for prevalence.
\# Excluding milk theft.
* Indicates significant difference between high rate area and matched low rate area (RHH compared with RHL(O)).

141

A. E. BOTTOMS, R. I. MAWBY, AND M. A. WALKER

significantly related (age negatively so) to the total number of household offences for the council areas CHH (Gardenia), CFH (Skyhigh) and CFL (Lowtowers)—but not for CHL (Stonewall). The largest correlation was with total household size, and after taking this into account the other (partial) correlations were not significant. In the private sector there were no correlations except with age in RHL (O) (negative) and with household size in OHL (Middleway) (positive). The positive association of household size and household offences in the correlation analysis prompted a more detailed examination of this variable, which produced interesting but puzzling results. These are shown in *Table 8* on a prevalence and incidence basis (combining the two groups in RHH and RHL so far as incidence is concerned). It might perhaps be expected that as household size increased the proportion of households with no household offences committed against them would diminish (especially bearing in mind the importance of theft outside the dwelling and vandalism in the total of household offences, and the fact that each household member may have property capable of being stolen or vandalised). Thus, if for one member the chance of no offence is P, one might hypothesise that for two members it might be P^2 and for three P^3, etc. In fact the decrease in proportions (see Table 8a) is not usually as large as this, even in the areas where there is a significant decrease (CHH, CFH, CFL); and in most areas there was no significant decrease.

Why some areas should produce a strong correlation on this variable while others do not is unclear. More important for the present analysis is how far the variable can help to explain statistically different prevalence and incidence rates in the various areas. Here the important points are:

(i) that overall, there was no statistically significant difference in household size between areas, though the high crime rate areas tended to have slightly larger households (Table 3c);

TABLE 8

Household Offences in relation to Household Size

(a) *Prevalence* (percentage with no victims)

	CHH	CHL	CFH	CFL	RHH	RHH(ST)	RHL(O)	RHL(D)	OHL
Number in household									
1, 2	80	80	81	90	66	78	76	80	86
3, 4	71	78	68	61	56	10	83	73	74
5+	32	81	45	71	46	50	(83)	50	(90)
All	66	79	68	76	57	77	80	74	81
Variation between groups	P<·01	NS	P<·05	P<·01	NS	NS	NS	NS	NS

(b) *Incidence* (Mean no. of offences)

	CHH	CHL	CFH	CFL	RHH	RHL	OHL
Number in household							
1, 2	·32	·02	·22	·37	·71	·25	·20
3, 4	·60	·37	·65	·58	·78	·25	·28
5+	1·05	·19	1·45	·79	1·46	(·44)	(1·00)
Correlation with household size	·25	NS	·25	·18	NS	NS	·24

(Figures in brackets are based on 10 or less households)

A LOCALISED CRIME SURVEY

(ii)   there was no significant association between household offences and size of household in one high crime rate area (RHH)—see Table 7.

(iii) there was an association between size of household and household offences in the other two high rate areas (CFH, CHH). However, CFH did not in any case differ significantly from its matched area (CFL) on the total for household offences, even before controlling for household size. In the case of CHH (Gardenia), detailed comparison with CHL (Stonewall) showed that the significant difference in the household offence rate occurred particularly among the larger households, for reasons that are again unclear. However, since these two areas did not differ significantly in mean household size, this variable cannot statistically account for the household crime rate differences between them found in the survey.

(b) *Personal Offences*

The personal offences included in the survey were assault, theft from the person and fraud, of which the first two were numerically much the most important. *Prevalence* figures, calculated on a per person basis, are shown in *Table 9*. Taking all personal offences together, it is clear that the highest prevalence rates are to be found in the two high-crime rate areas CFH (Skyhigh) and RHH (Redlight). This is so whether one counts all offences or only offences occurring within the areas, though in fact RHH (Redlight) residents had a high proportion of their personal offences committed outside the area.

Taking the usual area groups for analysis, CFH (Skyhigh) had significantly higher rates than CFL (Lowtowers), while RHH (Redlight) was also significantly higher than the two halves of RHL (Graybridge) taken together. On this occasion, however, CHH (Gardenia) did not have high rates at all, in some considerable contrast to the situation as regards household offences (see above).

When the individual offences were considered separately, a similar pattern occurred for both personal theft and assault, but for fraud the

TABLE 9

Prevalence of Personal Offences+

% persons victims of	CHH	CHL	CFH	CFL	RHH	RHH(ST)	RHL(O)	RHL(D)	OHL
Personal theft	5	3	12*	3	9	10	5	3	5
Assault	4	2	11	4	12*	15	3	2	2
Fraud	1	1	4	1	1	3	2	2	3
Any personal offence	9	5	22*	6	20*	20	7	9	10
Inside area only	4	2	17*	2	11	1	6	0	3
Base=no. of respondents	108	122	104	107	96	40	67	49	113

+ Care should be taken in interpreting data for individual offences. Standard errors for these figures vary from about 1·0 (for percentage of size 1) to 5·0 (for percentage of size 50). [The exact value is $100 \times \sqrt{\frac{p(1-p)}{n}}$, where p is the population value and n is the sample size].
* Indicates significant difference between high rate area and matched low rate area (RHH is compared with RHL(O)). See also note to Table 4.

A. E. BOTTOMS, R. I. MAWBY, AND M. A. WALKER

prevalence figures were uniformly low and did not differ significantly between areas.

When *incidence* figures are considered, a very similar picture is obtained, except that, because of high multiple victimisations in RHH (Redlight), it stands out clearly as the highest rate area for personal offence incidence; and, in contrast to the prevalence figures, this is sustained when only within-area offences are considered (see *Table 10*).

Overall, therefore, the personal offence analysis within the three housing groups again generally confirms the picture obtained from official crime data, though this time with the exception of the unexpectedly low prevalence and incidence rates for CHH (Gardenia).

As with the household offences, an attempt was made to see how far personal offence victimisation rates in the areas could be explained statistically by demographic variables, this time concentrating upon age and sex. In line with the results of many other victim surveys, males were more likely to be victims of personal offences than females, and young people than older people (see Gottfredson 1984, Mawby 1982). In this case, the gross area results as regards personal offences (given above) particularly reflect the situation for males: for females, victimisation rates were consistently low except, to a limited extent, in RHH (Redlight). As regards age, the most important point concerns the extent to which the high victimisation rates for CFH (Skyhigh) and RHH (Redlight) can be explained by the fact that both areas have relatively high proportions of younger residents (*Table 3*). Detailed analysis of the contrast between CFH (Skyhigh) and CFL (Lowtowers) in the incidence of personal offences showed that the difference between the two was no longer statistically significant when age was controlled for; but this was not the case as regards the contrast between RHH (Redlight) and RHL (Graybridge).

(c) *Overview*

Taking these results together for the three housing groups, we have found:

TABLE 10

Incidence of Personal Offences[+]

Mean number of offences per person[#]	CHH	CHL	CFH	CFL	RHH	RHH(ST)	RHL(O)	RHL(D)	OHL
Males	·17	·18	·43*	·15	·73*	·31	·06	·13	·21
Females	·04	·01	·15	·15	·28	·36	·11	·04	·05
All	·10	·09	·31	·15	·54*	·32	·07	·09	·12
Inside area only (All)	·05	·03	·24	·08	·50*	·15	·06	0	·05
Correlation with age:									
Males	−·31	−·25	−·23	−·41§	−·22	−·20	−·09	−·35	−·41§
Females	−·17	−·13	−·33§	−·33§	·14	·38	·01	−·15	−·22

[+] See note to Table 9. Standard errors for incidence are slightly higher than for prevalence.
[#] Difference between males and females was significant only for CHH and CHL.
* Indicates significant difference between high rate area and matched low rate area (RHH compared with RHL(O)).
§ Indicates significant correlation.

A LOCALISED CRIME SURVEY

(i) *Inter-war council house pair.* There is a statistically significant difference between CHH (Gardenia) and CHL (Stonewall) for household offences, which is not explicable by demographic characteristics. There is no significant difference for personal offences; but taking household and personal offences together (Table 5), there is a clearly significant difference between the areas.

(ii) *Post-war high-rise council pair.* There is no significant difference between CFH (Skyhigh) and CFL (Lowtowers) for household offences, though CFH has the higher rate. There is a significant difference for personal offences, but this appears to be related to the different age structure of the two estates. Taking household and personal offences together, the two areas differ significantly (Table 5). There is a particularly high ratio of survey crime to reported crime in these estates.

(iii) *Private areas.* As in the official crime data, RHH (Redlight) stands out from the other private areas as having a particularly high survey crime rate, both household and personal. OHL (Middleway) has an especially high ratio of survey crime to reported crime, probably because of the higher social class and educational level of the respondents.

The Victim Survey: Reporting Offences to the Police

Taking all areas together, the extent to which all respondents said they had reported the various offences in the survey to the police is shown in *Table 11(a)*.[15] As may be seen, the reporting rates for most offences were low, and indeed generally lower than comparable data for the whole country from the British Crime Survey (Hough and Mayhew 1985, p.21). Just over a half of all respondents who did not report offences to the police gave triviality of the offence as the reason, and looking at the details of the incidents we found this not surprising. Reporting to the police did not differ significantly

TABLE 11

Reporting Survey Offences to the Police

(a) *Offence Variation (all areas together)*

	(% reported)		(% reported)
Theft of vehicle	100%	Milk Theft	16%
Burglary	68%	Fraud	14%
Theft from vehicle	42%	Theft outside dwelling	13%
Theft in dwelling	26%	Vandalism	8%
Assault & threats	22%	Personal theft	6%

(b) *Area Variation*

	CHH	CHL	CFH	CFL	RHH	RHH(ST)	RHL(O)	RHL(D)	OHL
% of victims who reported any offence*	33	27	18	31	39	30	44	33	22
% of offences reported#	27	24	15	25	29	18	35	29	12

* Excludes milk theft.
# Excludes milk theft and vandalism.
(Overall variation between areas is not significant for either row of Table 11(b), and high rate areas do not differ significantly from their matched pairs.)

[15]. The numbers in each area for each offence type were too small to consider separately.

A. E. BOTTOMS, R. I. MAWBY, AND M. A. WALKER

by age or sex of the respondent, household size, or the household's possession or non-possession of a telephone.

For the purposes of this paper, the most interesting issue concerns area differences in reporting offences to the police, the aggregated data for which are given in *Table 11(b)*. As may be seen, rates did not vary greatly between areas, and the overall variation was not statistically significant. It therefore remains unclear, from this analysis, why the ratio of police-recorded offences to survey offences should have been so much greater in the two high-rise areas (CFH and CFL) than in the other areas (see above and Table 5), though possible reasons obviously include an element of differential police recording by area, and a differential escalation in crime in the high-rise areas, as opposed to others, in the years beween 1971 (to which the police data refer) and 1975 (the date of the survey).

The Self-Report Study

The crime survey reported here also included a self-report study, completed by the respondent him/herself at the end of the interview using self-report cards (the remainder of the survey was interviewer-administered). The form of the cards was to ask, for each of 33 offences, whether the respondent had ever committed the offence; then the age when last committed, and whether the offence was committed once or more than once.

Survey interviewers reported to the firm conducting the survey that this part of the interview created more difficulties than other parts, and raised questions about both comprehension and honesty for a minority of respondents. Taking all areas together, 39 per cent. of male respondents and 66 per cent. of female respondents claimed never to have committed *any* of the 33 listed offences. Since these included such items as:

> "travelled by bus, train or tube and deliberately not paid for your journey";
> "taken for yourself anything left lying around, which you thought belonged to someone else";
> "deliberately taken something from a shop without paying for it";
> "filled in income tax forms so as to pay less tax than you should"

—it is in fact difficult to accept the data at face value, bearing in mind the results of self-report studies for juveniles (see, *e.g.* Shapland 1978; for methodological discussions see Brantingham and Brantingham 1984, pp.58–69; Hirschi *et al* 1980). Indeed, as part of the overall programme of research in Sheffield, a self-report study for juveniles was completed for the inter-war council housing areas CHH (Gardenia) and CHL (Stonewall):[16] this showed substantially higher overall admission rates (males 92 per cent., females 80 per cent.) for a list of nineteen offence items (for more

---

[16] This study was carried out in two local schools, and also incorporated children from a third area adjacent to CHH and CHL but with an intermediate official offender rate (CHM). It had been hoped to conduct self-report studies for juveniles in all the main small areas studied in the Sheffield research, but for various reasons access was declined by headmasters of the other relevant schools.

A LOCALISED CRIME SURVEY

detailed discussion see Mawby 1978, chapter 8; see also Mawby 1984, pp.240–241[17]).

For these reasons, the purported finding of the present survey that there were few differences between areas in self-reported offending has not been taken as a true result in this analysis, and has not influenced our general conclusions drawn from the analysis of the victim survey. Some relevant data are however reported in *Table 12*, which further illustrates the methodological difficulties. Thus in the second line of the table, the percentages saying the police knew of some offences are clearly underestimated—for example, only 12 per cent. of respondents in CHH (Gardenia) admitted that the police knew of any offence they had ever committed, yet *Table 1* shows that *in one year* one person in every ten households in CHH (about one person in 27) was identified as an official offender.[18]

Residents' Perception of the Areas

The survey included a number of questions concerning residents' perceptions of their areas, both in a general way and specifically related to crime. We shall deal with these issues briefly.

Table 13 gives some data on social matters connected with the areas. At the start of the interview, a deliberately general question was asked about whether respondents felt a sense of belonging to the areas where they lived. This produced positive responses of 70 per cent. or higher in most groups. The exceptions were:

(i) the students in RHH (Redlight), who of course were transient residents by definition (there were very few female students, so little credence should be attached to the figure for them);

(ii) females in RHH (Redlight), no doubt anxious about the difficulties of living in a notorious red-light district;

TABLE 12

Self-Reported Offences

	CHH	CHL	CFH	CFL	RHH	RHH(ST)	RHL(O)	RHL(D)	OHL
% "didn't do any"	47	65	46	57	49	15	50	52	57
% admitting police knowledge of some offences	12	6	12	10	15	8	7	14	3

(Overall variation between areas is not significant for either row of the table, and high rate areas do not differ significantly from their matched pairs.)

[17] The juvenile self-report study showed significant differences, in the expected direction, in admission rates between those from CHH and CHL, especially among older boys. By contrast, a study of the victimisation of juveniles for personal offences, carried out in the same schools on the same occasion, found no area differences between CHH and CHL (Mawby 1979b, p.108).

[18] British Crime Survey researchers have had similar doubts about self-report studies with adult populations in their own homes. A pilot study of self-reporting for the B.C.S. found that: "People in older age-groups seemed virtuous to an improbable degree; and from checks against C.R.O. it emerged that rather less than half the people with criminal records were prepared to admit these to interviewers. It must be recognised, therefore, that any estimates of the prevalence of offending based upon the B.C.S. data are likely to be considerable underestimates" (Mayhew and Hough 1982).

A. E. BOTTOMS, R. I. MAWBY, AND M. A. WALKER

TABLE 13

Residents' Perception of Areas: General Issues

		CHH	CHL	CFH	CFL	RHH	RHH(ST)	RHL(O)	RHL(D)	OHL
% feel they belong	M	83	90	47*	77	79	36	87	52	98
to area+	F	77	87	44*	77	47*	82	74	62	95
% would like to leave area#		40*	26	73*	47	48	47	48	60	26
Would others like to live in area §										
% many		17*	45	6*	24	20*	25	57	18	82
% none		25*	6	32*	18	41*	25	4	27	1
% mentioning crime or prostitution among area dislikes ++										
% crime		13*	3	42*	18	5	2	2	4	0
% prostitution		0	0	0	0	24*		0	0	0

+ Question asked: "Thinking about the area where you live, do you feel you belong here?"
# Question asked: "Would you like to leave this area and live somewhere else?"
§ Question asked: "How many people living in other parts of Sheffield do you think would like to come and live in this area — very many, some, only a few, or none at all?"
++ In response   "What do you *personally* consider to be the bad things about living round here?"
    to question   (up to three responses coded for each respondent).
* Indicates significant difference between high rate area and matched low rate area (RHH compared with RHL(O)).

     (iii) residents in RHL (D), feeling a sense of insecurity because of the imminent demolition of the area;
     (iv) residents in CFH (Skyhigh).

Of these results, the most striking is the finding for CFH (Skyhigh) where, uniquely for any of the area groups, only a minority of both sexes felt they belonged to the area. This finding is, however, consistent with data we have from elsewhere showing CFH (Skyhigh) as a classic "difficult-to-let" high-rise deck-access estate, with the shortest waiting list of any of the major council estates in Sheffield at that time, very high tenancy turnover, and many unfavourable comments from residents about litter, noise, etc. (see Bottoms and Xanthos, 1981). It is nevertheless remarkable how much worse CFH (Skyhigh) scores on this question than do *either* (i) its "paired area" of CFL (Lowtowers), which as we have seen above produced not dissimilar results to CFH with regard to the household offences section of the victim survey, *or* (ii) the other high-crime rate areas of RHH (Redlight) for males, or CHH (Gardenia), a well-settled estate with something of a criminal subculture (for a fuller discussion, see Bottoms and Xanthos, 1981).

These differences are reflected in the other questions on social perception of the area (see Table 13), where CFH (Skyhigh) scores consistently badly, though RHH (Redlight) does so as well. In general, on these measures the low-crime rate areas score better than the high-rate areas, with RHL (D) and CFL (Lowtowers) scoring worst among the low-rate areas.

Some other questions asked related more directly to the criminality of

A LOCALISED CRIME SURVEY

areas. *Table 14* shows the results of two questions: one asking about the *offender rate* of the area (whether "people who live around here get into trouble with the law more or less often than people who live in other parts of Sheffield"), and one about the *offence rate* (whether "the number of crimes committed here is high or low compared to other areas of Sheffield"—introduced after a specific cue about the offender rate/offence rate distinction).[19] As may be seen, there is in general a striking and consistent resemblance between high or low official offender and offence rates (see *Table 1*), and residents' perception of them; though in no high-rate area was an actual majority of ordinary residents prepared to admit that the area had high rates.

Finally, *Table 15* reports responses to a number of hypothetical incidents in the survey, in which residents were asked, *inter alia*, whether the kind of incident depicted occurred frequently in the area (or, in the

TABLE 14

Residents' Perception of Criminality of Areas

(a) *Offender Rate (%)*

	CHH	CHL	CFH	CFL	RHH	RHH(ST)	RHL(O)	RHL(D)	OHL
Higher than elsewhere	30*	3	38*	11	46*	58	0	18	0
Same	50	55	48*	73	29	20	49	48	81
Less than elsewhere	6*	28	0	7	12*	2	34	22	10
Don't know	14	14	14	9	13	20	17	12	9

(b) *Offence Rate (%)*

	CHH	CHL	CFH	CFL	RHH	RHH(ST)	RHL(O)	RHL(D)	OHL
Higher than elsewhere	17*	3	30*	13	23*	28	1	6	9
Same	33	39	38	35	27	20	30	29	16
Less than elsewhere	31	42	19*	39	28*	20	51	47	65
Don't know	19	16	13	13	22	32	18	18	10

* Indicates significant difference between high rate area and matched low rate area (RHH compared with RHL(O)).

TABLE 15

Residents' Perception of Certain Hypothetical Incidents

(Figures given are % saying the listed kind of incident happens in their area 'very often' or 'quite often')

% households	CHH	CHL	CFH	CFL	RHH	RHH(ST)	RHL(O)	RHL(D)	OHL
(i) Drunk and disorderly man on Saturday night	46*	21	60*	43	58*	67	20	35	0
(ii) Stealing small item from supermarket	37*	21	37*	18	36*	55	8	11	12
(iii) Petty vandalism	86*	39	93*	68	59*	76	29	54	12
(iv) Husband assaulting wife	24*	6	35*	16	39*	44	6	13	0
(v) Television licence evasion	62*	24	72*	54	62*	68	28	47	13

('Don't know' figures for all areas combined: (i) 3%, (ii) 31%, (iii) 3%, (iv) 24%, (v) 32%).
* Indicates significant difference between high rate area and matched low rate area (RHH compared with RHL(O)).

[19] This cue was introduced after the pilot work for the survey revealed that residents, perhaps surprisingly, made little distinction between the two unless prompted.

A. E. BOTTOMS, R. I. MAWBY, AND M. A. WALKER

shoplifting case, whether people from the area did that kind of thing often). Once again there were striking differences between the officially high-rate and officially low-rate areas for most of the incidents (though the number of "don't knows" must be borne in mind in interpreting the figures). However, both here and to an extent in the "offence rate" section of Table 14 it is notable that CFL (Lowtowers) has rates well ahead of most of the low-rate areas except RHL (D). (See particularly the figures for the drunkenness, vandalism and licence evasion questions). This tends to confirm some of the findings from the victim survey questioning the extent to which this area is genuinely a "low crime" rate area, despite its low official crime rate and its well-settled population who feel at home in the area (see *Table 13*).

Concluding Discussion

If we leave aside the methodological issues and the self-report study, five main points can perhaps appropriately be made in concluding this paper:

First, and most importantly, small areas of the same housing type within a city have been shown in a victim survey analysis to reproduce differences based on official offence and offender rates. This suggests that, while extreme caution is necessary when considering time-trends in official crime rates (see Bottomley and Pease 1986, pp.22–24), or when comparing official data for large areas with different police forces (Farrington and Dowds 1985), comparative official data for small areas within a city of the same housing type, and policed by the same police force, may provide a much more valid basis for comparison. These data support and complement the previous analysis by Mawby (1979a) based on the way the official data themselves were compiled in these areas.

Secondly, the first conclusion has had to be qualified by the phrase "of the same housing type" because of the data for the two high-rise areas in this study. A low-official-rate area has been seen to throw up more criminal and social problems than expected from its official offence and offender indices; and a relatively high-rate area is shown to stand out rather more problematically on a number of indices than official data would lead one to suppose (note that CFH (Skyhigh) is the *least serious* of the three high-rate areas on official offence and offender data (*Table 1*) but this position has not been sustained in the victim and residents' perception analyses). In both areas, the ratio of survey crime to official crime was particularly high. This second conclusion clearly points to the problematic nature of certain aspects of high-rise living (see generally Coleman 1985) some facets of which it would seem are not adequately captured in official police statistics.[20]

Thirdly, in some ways the residents' perception of criminality in the areas has provided a clearer differentiation as between officially high and

[20] This should not be read as a general endorsement of Coleman's work, which has a number of serious flaws including an over-emphasis on design as opposed to other social factors, and an over-emphasis on the differences between high-rise flat areas and low-rise housing areas so far as crime is concerned: see generally Hope 1986.

A LOCALISED CRIME SURVEY

officially low rate areas than has the victim survey (especially in its more detailed aspects). This might be because residents' perceptions depend upon stereotypes of the areas, which are less accurate than the reality. Alternatively, it might be linked to faulty recall in response to victim survey questions (see Sparks 1981), so that in fact the more general questions about criminality in the areas (offender and offence rates), or hypothetical questions about possible incidents, give a better picture than victim survey questions, particularly given the trivial and eminently forgettable nature of much of the crime uncovered by the survey. It would be fascinating to explore these issues more fully in future methodologically-orientated research targeted on this specific issue.

Fourthly, it was notable that even in the high crime rate areas (and, according to official statistics, CHH (Gardenia) and RHH (Redlight) were among the residential areas with the highest offender and offence rates in Sheffield) serious crime was not particularly common. Rather, minor crimes which were problematic because of their nuisance value (minor vandalism, thefts outside the dwelling, milk thefts etc.) constituted much of the "crime problem" in these areas. In this context, crimes were one further example of the undesirable features of certain housing areas, to be put alongside lack of facilities, litter, noise, rowdyism, etc. This is a rather different emphasis from the one recently suggested in other research in urban areas such as Merseyside and Inner London (see Kinsey 1984, 1985; Jones *et al* 1986; Kinsey *et al* 1986), where crime is seen, next to unemployment, as a serious social problem in inner-city areas. But in considering this contrast, it has to be remembered that our data refer to 1975, not 1985; and also that they refer to Sheffield, a city famous for its relatively high degree of social cohesion (for a summary, see Baldwin and Bottoms 1976, pp.45–53).

Fifthly and finally, an important result of the present research, whether one considers official crime data or survey data, is that adjacent areas such as neighbouring council housing estates or blocks of flats can appear to the casual observer to be very similar, and can even be almost identical demographically (see Tables 2 and 3), yet they can have very different crime rates, and can be perceived by their residents as presenting very different levels of social problems. Hence, official statistics, or crime surveys produced on a larger-area basis (even on a ward level) can be misleading because they can miss important within-area variations. The same is, *a fortiori*, true of a national neighbourhood classification system such as ACORN (used by the British Crime Survey: see footnote 1), which tries to classify all residential neighbourhoods in Britain into 11 types (and most council estates into just three types). In our justifiable enthusiasm for what can be learned from the large data sets of major crime surveys, it is very important not to neglect the micro-environmental dimension.

REFERENCES

Baldwin, J. and Bottoms, A. E. (1976). *The Urban Criminal*. London: Tavistock.

151

A. E. BOTTOMS, R. I. MAWBY, AND M. A. WALKER

BLYTH, W. G. and MARCHANT, L. J. (1973). "A self-weighting random sampling technique". *Journal of the Market Research Society*, **15**, 157–162.

BOTTOMLEY, A. K. and PEASE, K. (1986). *Crime and Punishment: Interpreting the Data*. Milton Keynes: Open University Press.

BOTTOMS, A. E. and WILES, P. (1986). "Housing tenure and residential community crime careers in Britain". In A. J. Reiss, Jr., and M. Tonry (eds.) *Communities and Crime*. Chicago: University of Chicago Press.

BOTTOMS, A. E. and XANTHOS, P. (1981). "Housing policy and crime in the British public sector". In P. J. Brantingham and P. L. Brantingham (eds.) *Environmental Criminology*. Beverly Hills, Calif.: Sage.

BRANTINGHAM, P. J. and BRANTINGHAM, P. L. (1984). *Patterns in Crime*. New York: Macmillan.

COLEMAN, A. (1985). *Utopia on Trial*. London: Hilary Shipman.

FARRINGTON, D. P. and DOWDS, E. A. (1985). "Disentangling criminal behaviour and police reaction". In D. P. Farrington and J. C. Gunn (eds.). *Reactions to Crime*. Chichester: John Wiley.

GOTTFREDSON, M. R. (1984). *Victims of Crime: The Dimensions of Risk*, Home Office Research Study No. 81. London: H.M.S.O.

HIRSCHI, T., HINDELANG, M. J. and WEIS, J. G. (1980). "The status of self-report measures". In M. W. Klein and K. S. Teilmann (eds.) *Handbook of Criminal Justice Evaluation*. Beverly Hills, Calif.: Sage.

HOPE, T. (1986). "Crime, community and environment". *Journal of Environmental Psychology*, **6**, 65–78.

HOUGH, M. (1984). "Residential burglary: a profile from the British Crime Survey". In R. V. G. Clarke and T. Hope (eds.) *Coping with Burglary*. Boston, Mass.: Kluwer-Nijhoff.

HOUGH, M. (1986). "Victims of violent crime" in *From Crime Policy to Victim Policy* (ed. E. A. Fattah). London: Macmillan.

HOUGH, M. and MAYHEW, P. (1983). *The British Crime Survey*, Home Office Research Study No. 76. London: H.M.S.O.

HOUGH, M. and MAYHEW, P. (1985). *Taking Account of Crime: Key Findings from the 1984 British Crime Survey*, Home Office Research Study No. 85. London: H.M.S.O.

JONES, T., MACLEAN B. and YOUNG, J. (1986). *The Islington Crime Survey*. Aldershot: Gower.

KINSEY, R. (1984). *Merseyside Crime Survey: First Report*. Liverpool: Merseyside County Council.

KINSEY, R. (1985). *Merseyside Crime and Police Surveys: Final Report*. Liverpool: Merseyside County Council.

KINSEY, R., LEA, J. and YOUNG, J. (1986). *Losing the Fight against Crime*. Oxford: Basil Blackwell.

MAWBY, R. I. (1978). "Crime and Law Enforcement in Different Residential Areas of the City of Sheffield". Unpublished Ph. D. thesis, University of Sheffield.

MAWBY, R. I. (1979a). *Policing the City*. Farnborough, Hants: Saxon House.

MAWBY, R. I. (1979b). "The victimization of juveniles". *Journal of Research in Crime and Delinquency*, **16**, 98–113.

A LOCALISED CRIME SURVEY

MAWBY, R I. (1982). "Crime and the elderly: a review of British and American research". *Current Psychological Reviews,* **2,** 301–310.

MAWBY, R. I. (1984). "Vandalism and public perceptions of vandalism in contrasting residential areas". In C. Levy-Leboyer (ed.) *Vandalism: Behaviour and Motivations.* Amsterdam: North-Holland.

MAWBY, R. I. and GILL, M. L. (1987). *Crime Victims: Needs, Service and the Voluntary Sector.* Tavistock: London.

MAYHEW, P. and HOUGH, M. (1982). "The British Crime Survey". *Home Office Research Bulletin,* **14,** 24–27.

SHAPLAND, J. M. (1978)."Self-reported delinquency in boys aged 11 to 14". *Brit J Criminol,* **18,** 255–266.

SPARKS, R. F. (1981). "Surveys of victimization: an optimistic assessment". In M. Tonry and N. Morris (eds.) *Crime and Justice: An Annual Review of Research,* **3.** Chicago: University of Chicago Press.

SPARKS, R. F., GENN, H. G. and DODD, D. H. (1977). *Surveying Victims.* Chichester: John Wiley.

Appendix

The following is the list of questions used to elicit offence data from victims in this survey:

1. Did anyone break into your house/flat in the past year and take something, or try to? Remember, we're talking about the time since last . . . (MONTH). How many times has this happened *since* last . . . (MONTH)?

2. Was anything stolen from inside your house/flat in the last year, even though the house/flat wasn't broken into — for example by a visitor, or someone doing repairs or decorating in the house, or reading a meter. It doesn't matter if they didn't take very *much* — it still counts. And remember, we're talking about the time since last . . . (MONTH), how many times has this happened *since* last . . . (MONTH)?

3. Was anything taken from *outside* your house/flat in the past year? For example from the doorstep, the garage or the garden? I'm even thinking of things like clothes off the line, bicycles, milk tokens, or dustbins. (How many times . . . ?)

4. Did you have anything taken from your pocket or bag, or from your hand, during the past year; for example when you were out shopping or going to work? (How many times . . . ?)

5. Did you have anything taken in the past year which you had temporarily left unguarded; for example, your coat hung up in a pub, or a pram left outside a shop? (How many times . . . ?)

6. Did anyone physically attack you, or assault you, or try to . . . did anyone hit you or use any other kind of violence against you, even perhaps someone you knew? (How many times . . . ?) (DO NOT INCLUDE INCIDENTS INVOLVING CHILDREN IN HOUSEHOLD AGED UNDER 12 YEARS)

7. In the past year, did anyone *threaten* you in any way with violence of any kind so that you were *really frightened* — even someone you knew, for example? (How many times . . . ?)

8. Did you have a car, or any other vehicle like a motor scooter or motorbike, stolen or taken away without your permission, within the last year? (How many times . . . ?)

9. Did anyone in the last year ever tamper with your car or motorbike, so that you thought an attempt had been made to *steal* it? (How many times . . . ?)

10. Did you have anything taken from your car or bike during the past year, like tools, books, goods off the back seat, or *even* the licence? (How many times . . . ?)

11. Did anyone deliberately damage any of your property during the past year — for example, did anyone break a window or door panel, break a fence, or write on the walls? (How many times . . . ?)

A. E. BOTTOMS, R. I. MAWBY, AND M. A. WALKER

12. Did anyone trick you into parting with money or goods under false pretences within the last year: for example, by giving you a valueless cheque, or by promising you goods which you never received? (How many times . . . ?)

13. Can you think of anything else which happened to you within the last 12 months, which might have involved a crime of any kind — anything that might have been against the law? How many times have things like this happened to you in the last 12 months?

14. *Apart* from the things you've already told me about, did any of the sort of incidents I've mentioned happen to *anyone else* in your household in the past year: for example, was anything stolen; did anyone get hurt?

15. Who did it/these things happen to? (WRITE IN RELATIONSHIP TO RESPONDENT BELOW, AND CODE *SEX* AND *AGE*)

    FOR EACH

16. How many different incidents have happened to him/her in the last 12 months, that is since last . . . (MONTH)? (WRITE IN NUMBER OF INCIDENTS BELOW)

[5]

BRIT. J. CRIMINOL. Vol. 22 No. 2 OCTOBER 1982

VICTIMISATION IN THE INNER CITY

A British Case Study

SUSAN J. SMITH (Oxford)*

THIS paper reports some findings of a survey of the victims of crime found amongst 531 randomly sampled residents of an ethnically mixed community in North Central Birmingham (in the Midlands of England).[1] The surveyed zone is part of a ring of late Victorian and Edwardian housing which surrounds the city's re-developed inner core. It nestles between these high-rise public housing projects (which were constructed in the early post-war years) and an encircling band of post-1920 suburbs containing both public and privately owned properties. The study area supports a relatively high proportion of low-income households, high rates of unemployment, and the overcrowding so often associated with nineteenth-century housing which has been subdivided to accommodate two or more families. Traditionally one of the city's main immigrant reception areas, the neighbourhood now exhibits a high degree of spatial mixing amongst ethnically and socially diverse populations at ward and enumeration district level. These include elderly British whites, an Irish community (dating from the late 1930s), and a well-established West Indian population. The West Indians were the largest coloured minority group in the early 1960s, but they have since been joined by comparable numbers of Indian, East African and British-born Asians.

Over a 12-month reference period, 163 (30.7 per cent.) of the 531 respondents said they had been victims of crime, and between them they experienced 281 offences. Table 1 compares the observed frequencies of victimisation with those expected given the Poisson distribution (a formula suggesting that a " random generating process " may be at work).[2] There

TABLE 1

Observed frequencies of victimisation compared with expected numbers based on a Poisson distribution

	0		1		2		3+	
	n	%	n	%	n	%	n	%
Observed	368	(69.3)	110	(20.7)	28	(5.3)	25	(4.7)
Expected	313	(58.9)	166	(31.3)	43	(8.1)	9	(1.7)

$\chi^2 = 62.23$, 3 d.f., $p < 0.0001$

* Research Fellow, St. Peter's College, Oxford.

[1] A simple random sample of 10 per cent. households (based on the electoral registers updated with information from the local authority rating lists) produced a target sample of 690. The response rate was 77 per cent. Amongst 159 non-responses were 62 vacant dwellings, 22 non-contacts and 75 refusals. These form 9, 3 and 11 per cent., respectively, of the target sample. Interviews were conducted with the first household member contacted who was a permanent resident at the address and aged 18 or over.

[2] See *Sparks et al.* (1977, pp. 88–90) for an extended discussion applying this model. Sparks (1981) offers constraints and refinements which could, where appropriate, be built into this formula in an attempt to provide more accurate descriptions of the distribution of victimisation amongst specific sub-populations.

VICTIMISATION IN THE INNER CITY

are more non-victims than expected, and an over-representation of the very
susceptible (those experiencing three or more incidents). Nevertheless, the
skew towards multiple victimisation here (where 26 per cent. of the sample
accounts for 59 per cent. of the incidents) is not as marked as that reported
by Sparks *et al.* (1977) where 60 per cent. of the 582 incidents were directed
against 13 per cent. of the sample.

   The majority of offences recorded in the survey were property crimes
(74 per cent.), comprising thefts (11·7 per cent.) or burglaries from dwellings
(16·7 per cent.), damage to private property (27·4 per cent.) and thefts of or
from vehicles (18·2 per cent.). Personal offences were less common, reflecting the trends both of official statistics and previous victims surveys.
They account for only 15 per cent. of the total: 3·2 per cent. were personal
(direct-contact) theft; 11·8 per cent. were personal violence. The remaining
11 per cent. offences pertain to fraud or deception.

   Overall, only 39·5 per cent. (111) of the 281 incidents recorded in the
survey were reported to the police by respondents (although in a further 21
(7·5 per cent.) cases, the police had already discovered or been notified of
the offence). There were striking differences in the extent to which victims
were likely to report crimes of various kinds. Respondents reported 74·5
per cent. burglaries, 58·8 per cent. thefts of or from vehicles and 55·6
per cent. personal (direct-contact) thefts, but only 33·3 per cent. thefts
from dwellings, 27·3 per cent. personal violence, 23·6 per cent. damage and a
mere 9·7 per cent. cases of fraud or deception. The reasons given for reporting
(or for not reporting) crimes seemed to reflect what the victim regarded as the
likely outcome of informing the police. For the most part, people failed to
report either because the event was not thought serious enough to merit the
attention of the police (48·2 per cent.) or because it was believed that the
police would not be able to do anything about it (27·7 per cent.).

   The Poisson distribution would suggest that offences occurred independently (such that the incidence of any one event did not affect the
probability of a second taking place) and that the probability of victimisation
was the same throughout the sampled population. But in the study area, the
probability of a crime occurring varied both according to crime type and
between population sub-groups. Table 2 shows, for instance, that victims of
criminal damage are more likely to be subjected to that experience again

TABLE 2

Probability of multiple victimisation, by offence

Offence	Probability of falling victim to same offence	Probability of falling victim to at least one other offence type	Probability of falling victim to more than one other offence type
Theft from dwelling	0·192	0·576	0·346
Burglary	0·184	0·395	0·158
Damage	0·283	0·359	0·17
Theft of/from vehicle	0·205	0·308	0·128
Fraud/deception	0·166	0·375	0·25
Personal theft, public place	0·0	0·667	0·222
Personal violence	0·148	0·333	0·222

SUSAN J. SMITH

than are the victims of other kinds of crime. The highest probability (having once been a victim) of becoming the target of at least one other type of offence is associated with personal theft outside the home, while the highest probability of falling victim to *more* than one other offence type affects those vulnerable to theft from their dwelling.

More commonly, these elements of " victim-proneness " are discussed in terms of the demographic, socio-economic and life-style characteristics of known targets. Although the legacy of previous empirical work provides few consistent guidelines here, the temptation was to acknowledge the different axes of susceptibility between cultures and follow the lead of those who propose a series of victim typologies prompted by Von Hentig's (1948) attempt to identify " general classes of victims ". Table 3 shows the categories into which this classification would fall, since only eight of the 16 variables considered bore any significant relationship with the probability of victimisation,[3] and only three had any power to discriminate between one-time and multiple victims.[4]

TABLE 3

*Variables associated with victimisation**

Variable	χ**	d.f.	p$\leqslant$	Cramer's V**
(i) *Discriminating between victims and non-victims*				
Spare-time activites	16·66	5	0·01	0·177
Dwelling rateable value	16·262	4	0·01	0·175
Class***	10·431	3	0·02	0·1402
Dwelling type	6·776	2	0·04	0·113
Age	6·298	3	0·1	0·1099
Area type	5·243	2	0·07	0·0994
Household size	4·859	2	0·1	0·0957
(ii) *Discriminating between single and multiple victims*				
Spare-time activities	16·235	4†	0·005	0·316
Sex	7·889	1	0·007	0·22
Area type	5·5	2	0·07	0·184

* Only statistically significant associations (p$\leqslant$0·1) are listed.
** A non-directional measure of association between categorised nominal variables given by the formula $V = (\phi^2/\min (r-1), (c-1))^{\frac{1}{2}}$ where $\phi = (X^2/N)^{\frac{1}{2}}$ and r=rows, c=columns, N=total count.
*** Amalgamated categories based on the Hope-Goldthorpe occupational scale (cf. Goldthorpe and Hope 1974).
† For statistical purposes, it was necessary to group those participating less than once a week and less than once a month, thus reducing d.f. by 1.

Recognising the need to explain, rather than merely describe, the incidence of victimisation, Gottfredson (1981) has drawn a distinction between the

[3] The eight variables which did not prove important were: race, birthplace, father's birthplace and family background; dwelling tenure (two measures of the latter included a trichotomous distinction between owner-occupied, council and private rental tenancies, together with the more traditional sub-division of rented accommodation into furnished and unfurnished); employment status (employed or unemployed); and class (after Goldthorpe and Hope, 1974) of the resident head of household (where this was not the respondent).
[4] Multivariate techniques did not add to the range or predictive power of these. None of a variety of logit models (with victimisation as a dichotomous dependent variable and the other variables discussed in the text as independent explanatory factors) adequately explained the differential odds of victimisation.

VICTIMISATION IN THE INNER CITY

utility of traditional " typological " approaches to victimisation and the
recently formulated " life-style exposure " models. Elements of both are
discussed below in terms of a conceptual framework proposed by Sparks
(1981). This represents an attempt to categorise differential rates of victimisation on the basis of explanatory rather than descriptive criteria. He collates
several aspects of victims' actions, attributes or social situations which affect
their vulnerability to crime. The six resulting categories range from structural
" vulnerability ", through degrees of " opportunity " and " attractiveness ",
to active " facilitation ", " precipitation ", and finally to the consequences of
" impunity ". The first four are of relevance to this study, although they are
not examined systematically. Rather, they are helpful in illustrating two
broad themes suggested by the associations listed in Table 3. The first of
these documents the relationship between victimisation and inner-city
life-styles, implying that a certain level of crime is contingent on improvements in the quality of life, and so need not carry wholly negative connotations. The second concern is to establish the risk of becoming a victim as
integral to the concept of multiple deprivation, affirming the importance of
victim surveys in formulating some critical areas of public policy. These are
offered as complementary, rather than incompatible, interpretations of
victimisation.

Levine (1978) attempted to link the distribution of victims, as disclosed by
epidemiological research, with a broader set of structural and institutional
variables by way of the notion of victimisation opportunity. " Such opportunities are the unintended and unsanctioned concomitants of basic structural
arrangements including, especially, modes of organisation and technological
developments " (p. 87). The implication is that a certain base rate of
victimisation is to be expected by virtue of the life-styles associated with a
specific mode of production and particular mechanisms of distribution.
If this suggestion is combined with Gottfredson's (1981) distinction between
" absolute " and " relative " exposure to victimisation, a helpful analytical
framework begins to emerge. Absolute victimisation may be taken as the
level of exposure to crime necessitated by different urban activity patterns.
To some extent, this is " given "; and, while undesirable in itself, it may also
be indicative of more positive societal processes working to increase the range
and availability of opportunities for social interaction. Relative exposure
reflects any factor increasing the odds of victimisation above those " normally " expected. Where this type of susceptibility is also distributed non-
randomly, it augurs less favourably for the quality of life. These two facets of
victimisation in the inner city are discussed in turn.

Victimisation, Life-style and Activity Patterns

A certain amount of crime is inevitable whenever behaviour is subject to
societal norms and where material rewards and life chances are differentially
distributed. Its base level at any one time depends on the patterns of socialising
among (and between) potential offenders and potential victims; and on the
amount of time property is left unguarded. Both criteria reflect the day-to-day

SUSAN J. SMITH

routine of urban living. The probability of victimisation attendant on routine behaviour patterns may be conceived in terms primarily of two of Sparks' (1981) risk-related categories. First, " opportunity " relates to the activities associated with potential victims' occupations and to the social contacts to which they give rise; secondly, "facilitation" might denote a failure on the part of the victim to take precautions which could prevent others from taking advantage of such opportunities. Both these aspects of risk will tend to increase as the options for different types of behaviour widen and as life-styles improve. Thus, rising crime, which is usually regarded as an aspect of societal breakdown, could in fact index predominantly beneficial processes.

The implications of establishing a positive relationship between crime trends and changes in the quality of life have been discussed by North American authors. " The opportunity for predatory crime appears to be enmeshed in the opportunity for legitimate activities to such an extent that it might be very difficult to root out substantial amounts of crime without modifying much of our way of life. Rather than assuming that predatory crime is simply an indicator of social breakdown, one might take it as a by-product of the freedom and prosperity as they manifest themselves in the routine activities of everyday life ". (Cohen and Felson, 1979, p. 605).

In their empirical examination of this " routine activity " thesis, Cohen and Cantor (1980) assert the significance of two life-style variables. Size of household constitutes a measure of guardianship (both of persons and property), while employment status provides a surrogate for major activity. It was suggested that single persons are less likely than members of large families to be accompanied out of doors, and less able to ensure that their dwelling is occupied when they themselves are absent. Therefore, they should be more vulnerable to crime. In the study area, differences in the probability of victimisation between one and greater-than-one person families, as considered by Cohen and Cantor (1980), proved negligible. The predictive power of household size increased, however, when the sample was divided into families comprising one or two, three or four, and more than four members. Although this variable is the weakest significant predictor of victimisation, Table 4 provides no support for the assumption that large families are the better " guardians " of persons and property. Rather, there is a greater likelihood of victimisation amongst residents from

TABLE 4

Household size and victimisation

		1 or 2		3 or 4		5+		Total	
		n	%	n	%	n	%	n	%
Non-victims		145	75.1	101	65.6	122	66.3	368	69.3
Victims		48	24.9	53	34.4	62	33.7	163	30.7
Total	n	193	100	154	100	184	100	531	100
	%	36.3		29.0		34.7		100	

$\chi^2 = 4.859$, 2 d.f., $p < 0.1$

VICTIMISATION IN THE INNER CITY

large households than amongst those belonging to small families. It is suggested that because large households imply the frequent entrance and exit of dwellings by family members, and by a large assortment of friends and acquaintances, dwelling security is *decreased* and the range of potentially (if only rarely) risky relationships widened.

Employment status, in the sense of a simple distinction between employed and unemployed respondents was also insignificant as a predictor of victimisation in inner Birmingham. Table 3 suggests rather the salience of a second life-style variable—spare-time activities.[5] Theoretically, this would seem even more important than employment status as a risk indicator. For it captures behaviour patterns at times (evenings and weekends) and in situations (the face-to-face contacts made during the course of different social and recreational engagements) when a notable peak of offending occurs. In fact, as many as one-third of the crimes reported to surveyors were known to have taken place between 6·00 p.m. and midnight.

Table 5 shows that the probability of being a victim was least for those whose spare-time activities are least frequent. Only 60 per cent. of those active between three and seven days per week remained non-victims, compared with 70–90 per cent. of those whose activities take place twice a week or less. Table 6 suggests, further, that variations in susceptibility are influenced by the type of spare-time socialising which is undertaken. Victims were more likely to engage in all types of activity than non-victims, but a considerably larger proportion of those victimised engage in regular visits to the cinema, theatre, dancing or bingo; and respondents who tend to meet with friends in pubs or cafes were also twice as likely to have been victims during the year as those who do not. Voluntary workers, too, seem especially at risk.

Broadly, therefore, the thesis holds. Different life-styles—the characteristic ways in which individuals allocate their time to leisure activities—are differentially related to the probability of being in (or leaving accessible) particular places at particular times, and coming into contact with (or leaving an attractive opportunity for) others, who are potential criminals (*cf.* Hindelang *et al.* 1978; Gottfredson, 1981). A certain level of victimisation might, then, be expected to accompany particular urban life-styles. In the present study, the hitherto neglected activity variable " leisure time socialising " proves to be an appropriate indicator of this. Moving on to consider the correlates of victimisation sustained while adjusting for activity frequency, the main predictors of " relative " victimisation might be isolated.[6]

Controlling for spare-time activity rates, neither age nor dwelling type was related to the probability of victimisation. Much of the North American

---

[5] This was also considered by Sparks *et al.* (1977, p. 104) who modestly attribute their inconsequential results to the crude measures employed. In fact their results do show a significant difference between victims and non-victims (though not between non-victims, single and multiple victims, which is their concern) according to the frequency of leisure time activities ($\chi^2 = 11 \cdot 181$, 5 d.f., p < 0·05).

[6] To this end, activity categories were combined as follows: 5–7 days per week, 1–4 days per week, and less than once per week. This ensured expected cell frequencies appropriate to the χ^2 statistic.

SUSAN J. SMITH

TABLE 5

Victimisation and spare-time activity rates

Days per week	7		5 or 6		3 or 4		1 or 2		1		<1 per month		Total	
	n	%	n	%	n	%	n	%	n	%	n	%	n	%
Non-victims	32	62·7	22	61·1	72	60·5	140	71·1	46	88·5	56	73·7	368	69·3
Victims	19	37·3	14	38·9	47	39·5	57	28·9	6	11·5	20	26·3	163	30·7
Total n	51		36		119		197		52		76		531	
Total %	9·6		6·8		22·4		37·1		9·8		14·3		100	100

$X^2 = 16·66$, 5 d.f., $p < 0.01$.

VICTIMISATION IN THE INNER CITY

TABLE 6

Spare-time activities among victims and non-victims

Type of Activity	Participating non-victims		Participating victims	
	n	% (n=368)	n	% (n=163)
Organised clubs	48	13·0	25	15·3
Religious meetings	159	43·2	75	46·0
Visiting family/friends	224	60·9	107	65·6
Cinema/theatre/dancing/bingo	108	29·4	65	39·9
Voluntary work	12	3·3	18	11·0
Further education	20	5·4	12	7·4
Frequenting pubs/cafes	65	17·7	55	33·7
Other	49	13·3	35	21·5
Total number of activities engaged in	685		392	

$\chi^2 = 33·58$, 7 d.f., p<0·001

literature shows that those population groups which one might intuitively expect to be most vulnerable (such as women and the elderly) actually tend to have the lowest rates of victimisation. The data of the present study account for this by revealing that the low rate of crime against the elderly is a consequence of their limited participation in spare-time activities (though this may, of course, itself be caused by fear). Similarly there was no evidence to suggest that, for any frequency of spare-time activities, the occupants of multi-occupied dwellings are more likely to become victims than people living in other kinds of accommodation.

Amongst other variables, however, the relationship with victimisation increased at some levels of activity frequency. Household size retains some explanatory power amongst those active between five and seven days per week ($\chi^2 = 4·72$, 2 d.f., p<0·1). Employment status is a significant predictor of victimisation at activity rates of between one and four days per week ($\chi^2 = 3·498$, 1 d.f., p<0·07). Socio-economic class, like household size, remains important amongst the most active ($\chi^2 = 7·019$, 3 d.f., p<0·08).

Table 7 suggests that, even when they are very active, members of small families remain less " victim-prone " than respondents from medium-sized families. However, at this intensity of socialising, very large households do seem able to fulfil some protective function. Perhaps, then, it is among the

TABLE 7

*Household size and victimisation amongst the very active**

	Total in Household							
	1 or 2		3 or 4		5+		Total	
	n	%	n	%	n	%	n	%
Non-victims	22	71·0	10	43·5	22	66·7	54	62·1
Victims	9	29·0	13	56·5	11	33·3	33	37·9
Total n	31	100	23	100	33	100	87	100
%	35·6		26·4		37·9		99·9	

$\chi^2 = 4·72$, 2 d.f., p<0·1

* Those participating between five and seven days per week

393

SUSAN J. SMITH

most active sections of the population that the enigmatic notion of "guardianship" (*cf.* Huston *et al.*, 1976; Sheleff, 1974; Sheleff and Schicor, 1980) will prove most appropriate.

No relationship between unemployment and the likelihood of becoming a victim of crime was apparent amongst respondents who reported high or very low levels of spare-time activity. At medium levels of socialising, however, the unemployed prove least susceptible as victims (see Table 8). Where the effect of social activities is least extreme, the increased exposure to risk

TABLE 8

Employment status and victimisation at medium activity rates*

		Unemployed		Employed		Total	
		n	%	n	%	n	%
Non-victims		92	73·6	120	62·8	212	67·1
Victims		33	26·4	71	37·2	104	32·9
Total	n	125	100	191	100	316	100
	%	39·6		60·4		100	

$\chi^2 = 3·498$, 1 d.f., p<0·1

* Those participating between one and four days per week

associated with commitment to regular employment seems instrumental in increasing the likelihood of victimisation. This contention is qualified with reference to Table 9 which shows that, among the very active, it is the higher-class individuals who are most likely to have been victims. It is also

TABLE 9

Class and victimisation amongst the very active*

Socio-economic class**		Upper/lower service		Non-manual		Manual		Unemployed		Total	
		n	%	n	%	n	%	n	%	n	%
Non-victims		3	27·3	9	64·3	19	73·1	23	63·9	54	62·1
Victims		8	72·7	5	35·7	7	26·9	13	36·1	33	37·9
Total	n	11	100	14	100	26	100	36	100	87	100
	%	12·6		16·1		29·9		41·4		100	

$\chi^2 = 7·019$, 3 d.f., p<0·1

* Those participating between five and seven days per week
** After Goldthorpe and Hope (1974)

interesting to note that manual workers (rather than the unemployed) have the lowest probability of becoming victims at this high activity level. Perhaps long hours and below-average wages depress their "opportunity" value below that both of the more affluent non-manual workers and the more "available" or exposed unemployed faction.

In contrast to the variables discussed so far, the association between area type and victimisation is sustained for every level of activity rates. If activity

VICTIMISATION IN THE INNER CITY

frequencies condition the " absolute " odds of victimisation, then area type must be an important indicator of " relative " victimisation, despite its low overall predictive power. The extent and implications of this influence should therefore be examined in more detail.

Victimisation, Location and Multiple Deprivation

To date, little has been written about spatial variations in the distribution of victims. Wolf and Hauge (1975) noted some inter-urban difference in Finland, Denmark, Norway and Sweden, where the risk of falling victims to violent crimes is greatest in the capital city. Similarly, within the United States inter-urban variations in the rates of crimes against households have shown marked fluctuations from a high (in 1973) of 131 larceny incidents per 100 households in Los Angeles to a low of 33 per 100 in New York (U.S. Department of Justice, 1975).[7] Several victim surveys also confirm the impression conveyed in official statistics of a higher incidence of crime in central urban areas than in suburban or rural zones. Among them, Sparks *et al.* (1977, p. 82) provide tentative support from Britain by comparing their inner-London sample with pilot surveys in Peterborough.

Smaller scale intra-urban variations have also been noted. Meurer (1979) collated the results of several victim surveys in the United States which showed that people with the highest probability of victimisation live in the most economically depressed niches of large metropolitan areas. Fishman (1979) also found a marked over-representation of crimes against persons and of multiple victimisation amongst the residents of lower-class areas in Haifa, Israel. Block (1979), however, found crimes of violence to be rife among neighbourhoods where the very poor and the middle classes live in close proximity, while Pope (1979) showed that burglary, larceny and vehicle theft vary with the age and sex structure of urban sub-communities. Despite the exploratory nature of most of these studies, there does appear to be some agreement that place of residence has a significant effect on the likelihood of individuals experiencing crime.

Area type proved to be a significant correlate of victimisation in the present study. It does not have the highest predictive power, but its implications are far-reaching. For the areas concerned are distinguished by their status—Housing Action Area (HAA), General Improvement Area (GIA), and Non-Designated Area (NDA)—with respect to the govenment's environment-orientated urban improvement schemes. The rationale for the area-based policies on whose mandate these zones were declared is most clearly expressed in the Department of the Environment's (1977) *Policy for the Inner Cities.* The assumption is that collective deprivation associated with inner-city residence is distinct from individual deprivation, in that geographical disadvantage is seen as more than the sum of the socio-economic problems which variously beset each household.

The validity of this argument is open to question, and it is debatable

---

[7] The approximate equivalent in North central Birmingham would be 49 cases of burglary and theft from dwellings per 100 households.

SUSAN J. SMITH

whether or not deprived areas have been (or can ever be) isolated accurately for planning purposes. Certainly, areal deprivation cannot be conceived in the final instance in terms of areal causes, since, as Smith (1979) reasons at length, intra-urban locational disadvantage is just one consequence of structural processes operating on a national and international scale. However, given that there are obvious locational variations in well-being, at all spatial scales and under diverse political economies, any corresponding variations in victimisation must be worthy of attention. The designated planning zones of the study area are defined so as to circumscribe differentially deprived areas; and people's experience of crime varies between these same areas. It seems possible, therefore, that victimisation itself can be analysed as an element or indicator of inner-city deprivation.

Lambert's (1970) research in South Birmingham confirms the importance of examining small-scale spatial variations within the inner city. Although he was concerned with the incidence of crime rather than the residential environment of victims, two of his observations are especially pertinent. First, the contrast between small-scale areal variations in crime patterns in the inner city and the relative homogeneity among suburban tracts draws attention to the importance of focusing on even the smallest neighbourhood differences characterising inner-urban areas. Secondly, the association of crime with different housing environments (Lambert, 1970, p. 118) confirms the relevance of assessing victimisation in terms of the mosaic of planning zones with which it seems to be associated in the study area. Moreover, by examining victimisation as integral to the spatial character of urban disadvantage, new aspects of the problem of deprivation itself may be explored —a reply to Norris's (1979) criticism that research on urban deprivation is often constrained by, and biased towards, the most easily accessible or measurable surrogates of inequality. This reflects an extreme operationalism which, he contends, has resulted in many facets of the problem being ignored.

Assuming that the probability of victimisation is increased by the different residential environments of the inner city, the hazards of living there might usefully be assessed in terms of Sparks' (1981) first category of victim-proneness—" vulnerability ". This is conceived as a function of designated positions within the social (and here, spatial) order which render their incumbents less than normally capable of protecting themselves against victimisation. Sparks' notion of " attractiveness " also seems appropriate given the relatively marked socio-economic variations over very short physical distances which are so characteristic of the inner city (*cf.* Smith, 1981).

Table 10 shows in detail the areal differences in victimisation observed in North Central Birmingham. The distinctions pertain to three contiguous GIAs, three HAAs (two are contiguous and separated from the third by one of the GIAs) and several pockets of non-designated residences. Overall, the highest rates of victimisation were experienced by householders in GIAs and NDAs. However, it is in the HAAs that multiple victimisation was most prevalent. HAAs contain 31·3 per cent. victims but 44 per cent. multiple

VICTIMISATION IN THE INNER CITY

TABLE 10

Victimisation and residential zoning

Area type		GIA		HAA		NDA		Total	
		n	%	n	%	n	%	n	%
Non-victims		209	67·4	146	74·1	13	54·2	368	69·3
Victims		101	32·6	51	25·9	11	45·8	163	30·7
Total	n	310	100	197	100	24	100	531	100
	%	58·4		37·1		4·5		100	

$\chi^2 = 5 \cdot 243$, 2 d.f., $p < 0 \cdot 1$

GIA = General improvement areas.
HAA = Housing actions area.
NDA = Non-designated zones.

victims, and while the average victim resident in a GIA experienced 1·5 offences, victims in HAAs averaged 2·1 each.

Controlling for area type, none of the previously established relationships between victimisation and socio-economic or demographic factors was sustained within GIAs or NDAs, and no new correlates appeared. For these areas, the influence of neighbourhood type effectively subsumes a range of factors initially thought to be important either on theoretical grounds, or as a consequence of previous empirical findings. Within the HAAs, however, not only were three of the associations (with class, rateable value of dwelling and age) strengthened, but also a new relationship emerged between victimisation and housing tenure. These regularities are documented in Table 11. Essentially they show that in neighbourhoods (HAAs) where residents are least likely to be victims, but most likely (having experienced one offence) to be multiple victims, the following groups are most susceptible (in order of statistical explanatory power): those whose dwellings have a rateable value above £164·00, private renters, the under-25s, and a group of professional, self-employed, non-manual or skilled manual workers.[8] Least susceptible are the occupants of dwellings with rateable values less than £136·00, council tenants, the over-60s, and the unemployed. Notably, house type, birthplace, racial characteristics and sex remain uncorrelated with victimisation. Though multi-occupation, immigrant status, the current state of race relations and the position of women in society may be attractive in an explanatory capacity, there are only limited grounds in the study area for linking them directly to the experience of crime.

GIAs were designated as a consequence of the 1969 Housing Act. They were to consist of basically sound dwellings (though a significant proportion would lack basic amenities), and planning would focus on environmental enhancement. HAAs were a product of the 1974 Housing Act, and were assigned to those more severely deprived pockets where housing stress combined with social problems in neighbourhoods characterised by low incomes, overcrowding, multi-occupation and a racially mixed population.

---

[8] To some extent, the over-representation of victims amongst private renters and in very high value properties must be attributed to multiple occupation, even though the dwellings concerned were not rated as apartment houses.

SUSAN J. SMITH

TABLE 11

Significant correlates of victimisation within Housing Action Areas

(i) *Rateable Value (£)*

	≤109		110–136		137–163		164–188		≥189		Total	
	n	%	n	%	n	%	n	%	n	%	n	%
Non-victims	61	80·3	34	85·0	20	69·0	11	52·4	20	64·5	146	74·1
Victims	15	19·7	6	15·0	9	31·0	10	47·6	11	35·5	51	25·9
Total n	76	100	40	100	29	100	21	100	31	100	197	100
%	38·6		20·3		14·7		10·7		15·7		100	

$\chi^2 = 11\cdot027$, 4 d.f., $p < 0\cdot03$, Cramer's V $= 0\cdot237$

(ii) *Housing Tenure*

	Private rental		Council		Owner-occupied		Total	
	n	%	n	%	n	%	n	%
Non-victims	28	62·2	27	93·1	91	74·0	146	74·1
Victims	17	37·8	2	6·9	32	26·0	51	25·9
Total n	45	100	29	100	123	100	197	100
%	22·8		14·7		62·4		99·9	

$\chi^2 = 8\cdot768$, 2 d.f., $p < 0\cdot02$, Cramer's V $= 0\cdot211$

(iii) *Age*

	≤25		26–59		≥60		Total	
	n	%	n	%	n	%	n	%
Non-victims	19	63·3	77	72·0	50	83·3	146	74·1
Victims	11	36·7	30	28·0	10	16·7	51	25·9
Total n	30	100	107	100	60	100	197	100
%	15·2		54·3		30·5		100	

$\chi^2 = 4\cdot733$, 2 d.f., $p < 0\cdot1$, Cramer's V $= 0\cdot155$

(iv) *Socio-economic class**

	Unemployed		Manual		Non-Manual		Total	
	n	%	n	%	n	%	n	%
Non-victims	68	81·9	59	72·8	19	57·6	146	74·1
Victims	15	18·1	22	27·2	14	42·4	51	25·9
Total n	83	100	81	100	33	100	197	100
%	42·1		41·1		16·8		100	

$\chi^2 = 7\cdot51$, 2 d.f., $p < 0\cdot05$, Cramer's V $= 0\cdot195$

* After Goldthorpe and Hope (1974)

Paradoxically, in HAAs—the zones where socio-economic and environmental stress is most acute—it is the least individually disadvantaged rather than the ostensibly most vulnerable, who are most prone to victimisation. Those most susceptible are not the old and infirm, but the young and mobile. The higher income groups rather than the unemployed suffer, as do the occupants of higher rather than lower value property.

Property offences are also most over-represented in HAAs. On the whole, such areas may not be attractive to offenders (hence the lower overall victimisation rate than GIAs or NDAs), but within them the prime targets are the *relatively* affluent and the *relatively* advantaged. Nevertheless, the incentives offered by insecure and often insecurable property may well be an important precursor of the higher rates of multiple victimisation experienced by HAA residents. This is particularly true for private renters whose landlords are often unable to maintain their property and who are unable to force improvement themselves without entering into complex legal procedures (*cf.* Paris and Blackaby, 1979, p. 29). It is almost equally, and

VICTIMISATION IN THE INNER CITY

certainly increasingly, true of low-income owner-occupiers who, as Karn's
(1979) penetrating analysis confirms, are often unable or unwilling to
improve given uncertain planning legislation and the high capital outlay
required.[9]

There is some evidence here that the odds of victimisation are associated
with *in situ* deprivation, not merely with personal vulnerability. That the
relatively affluent within an absolutely deprived community should be most
vulnerable to crime indicates that, even though certain disadvantages may
be assessed in terms of the structural position occupied by people living
near each other, multiple deprivation has social consequences which must
often be appreciated in specifically spatial terms.

The same argument may be extended with respect to victims resident in
GIAs and NDAs where the higher overall rate of victimisation may be
attributable to a noticeably more affluent appearance (for the most part)
than the neighbouring HAAs. Steep socio-economic gradients between them
and the adjacent HAAs also exacerbate the problem (*cf.* Winchester, 1978).
Paradoxically, protective landscaping, the narrowing of road entrances and
exits, and general environmental upgrading seem to have had little tangible
impact on the defensibility of space. Yet, in these areas, despite their slightly
higher rateable values, lower unemployment, more youthful population and
higher proportion of owner-occupiers than HAAs, victimisation proved
unrelated to the socio-economic and demographic variables mentioned
earlier. Susceptibility to crime seems rather to be conditioned by one's
neighbourhood of residence. This " neighbourhood effect " may be most
noticeable in the inner city where offenders are known to travel short
distances, and relative affluence is the most significant indicator of
opportunity.

Victimisation and Inner-City Policy

" Absolute " and " relative " odds of victimisation, as discussed above,
bring to mind two aspects of urban disadvantage which Kirby (1981) claims
are too infrequently distinguished. These are deprivation in the market-place,
and deprivation *in situ*: " people poverty " and " place poverty ". On the
one hand there are set odds of victimisation which people differentially
encounter; on the other hand there are certain attributes of individuals and
groups, including their residential location, which independently increase
their probability of becoming victims.

" Absolute " odds of victimisation reflect the broad structural constraints
which condition the routine activity patterns integral to an urban society.
The amount and distribution of leisure time—which renders those who
exploit it particularly susceptible to crime—is to a large extent contingent on
the social, economic and political development of the West. Reduced
working hours and a widening range of leisure pursuits vastly increase the
potential for social mixing. This increases vulnerability to crime; and it is

[9] Of 12000 houses scheduled for retention in Birmingham's HAAs, only 600 had been improved
by May 1978.

SUSAN J. SMITH

doubtful whether it is expedient to reduce the hazards inherent to these processes of social interaction. For depressed activity rates are themselves indicative of social malaise: they contribute disproportionately to mounting levels of fear and to the social isolation now characteristic of many urban residential sub-communities (*cf.* Knight and Hayes, 1981). Moreover, the opportunity and ability to participate in leisure activities is a good indicator of the quality of life, both socially and psychologically. At this level, crime must to some extent be accepted as integral to the very existence of specifically social relations. Its intensity, however, depends fundamentally on processes rooted in the allocative sphere. Ironically, many desirable changes of a structural kind will tend to increase such risk. And it is this which is so neatly accounted for by Cohen and Felson's (1979) " routine activity " hypothesis.

" Relative " victimisation, as examined in the context of the inner city, can be interpreted as an aspect (and a surprisingly neglected one) of locational or *in situ* disadvantage. Even within these deprived areas, *where* people live affects their likelihood of directly experiencing a crime. In view of the argument of the previous paragraph, it is suggested that it is relative rather than absolute risks that realistic and egalitarian crime prevention policies will seek to reduce.

However, the origins of inner-city deprivation are rooted in the prevailing mode of production and mechanisms of distribution, not in individual inadequacies or pathologies. This raises a question as to whether or not the phenomenon of " multiple deprivation ", with which relative victimisation seems to be associated, can be ameliorated by area-based planning policies. The wide differences in opinion about this are neatly encapsulated in the arguments of two contemporary authors. On the one hand, Hamnett (1979) insists that the spatial character of deprivation reflects essentially an allocative problem, rooted in the productive process. He cites Lee (1976) as representative of his position: " an emphasis on spatial reformisim transforms allocational structures into distributional problems and so suggests distributional solutions to structural conditions. But allocational causes are not area based and cannot be cured by spatial reformism. Indeed, the superficial (distributional) inequalities between areas obscure, in an area based approach to reform, fundamental (allocational) class divisions " (p. 43). On the other hand Kirby (1981) argues forcefully for the primacy of localised causes as well as area-specific solutions, protesting that " deprivation needs to be seen as an issue of consumption, locally fostered and consequently only spatially overcome " (p. 180).

Since the scope for large-scale structural change in Britain is currently limited, spatial inequalities engendered by the prevailing political economy are unlikely to be eradicated at this level. However, there *is* scope at the local level to remove some of the more obvious precursors to vulnerability, particularly those associated with a decaying physical environment[10]:

[10] By May 1979, only one of the study area's GIAs had more than half its dwellings classified as being of " acceptable standard ", and the remaining two GIAs had less than 10 per cent. so designated. None of the HAAs had more than one fifth of their dwellings in this condition.

VICTIMISATION IN THE INNER CITY

insecurable dwellings; vacant buildings and broken fences which make access easy for the opportunistic offender; and an under-supply of garage space which prompts high rates of " on-street " parking. Moves implemented at this level may be merely short-term palliatives, but they could substantially increase the quality of life amongst the " victim-prone ". To this end, victimisation in the inner city can be appropriately examined within an area-based framework of multiple deprivation, in line with current thinking by planners and policy-makers (epitomised in the Inner City Partnership Program), sociologists (*cf.* Rex, 1981) and geographers (Jones, 1980; Kirby, 1981).

In conclusion, it is argued that for the practical ends of policy-making, the social distribution of victimisation must be recognised as possessing at least two analytically distinct components. Increases in absolute risk are a function of the development of society itself, while relative risks are contingent on less desirable processes. The suggestion is that social justice—an equitable distribution of the risks of victimisation—rather than a large (probably undesirable, and certainly unattainable) reduction of crime rates overall, is what is required of contemporary crime control strategies in Britain.

REFERENCES

BLOCK, R. (1979). " Community, Environment and Violent Crime ". *Criminology*, **17**, 46–57.

COHEN, L. E. and CANTOR, D. (1980). "The Determinants of Larceny: An Empirical and Theoretical Study ". *Journal of Research in Crime and Delinquency*, **17**, 140–159.

COHEN, L. E. and FELSON, M. (1979). " Social Change and Crime Rate Trends: A Routine Activity Approach ". *American Sociological Review*, **44**, 588–608.

DEPARTMENT OF THE ENVIRONMENT (1977). " *Policy for the Inner Cities* ", Cmnd. 6845. London: H.M.S.O.

DONNISON, D. (1974). " Policies for Priority Areas ". *Journal of Social Policy*, **3**, 127–135.

FISHMAN, G. (1970). " Patterns of Victimisation and Notification ". *British Journal of Criminology*, **19**, 146–157.

GOLDTHORPE, J. H. and HOPE, K. (1974). *The Social Grading of Occupations: A New Approach and Scale.* Oxford: Oxford University Press.

GOTTFREDSON, M. R. (1981). " On the Etiology of Criminal Victimisation ". *Journal of Criminal Law and Criminology*, **12**, 714–726.

HAMNETT, C. (1979). " Area-based Explanations: A Critical Appraisal ". In (ed.) Herbert, D. T. and Smith, D. M. *Social Problems and the City*, 244–260, Oxford: Oxford University Press.

HENTIG, H. VON (1948). *The Criminal and His Victim.* New Haven: Yale University Press.

HINDELANG, M. J., GOTTFREDSON, M., and GAROFALO, J. (1978). *Victims of Personal Crime*, Cambridge, Mass.: Ballinger.

HUSTON, T. L., GEIS, G., WRIGHT, R. and GARRETT, T. (1976). " Good Samaritans as Crime Victims ". *Victimology*, **1**, 284–294.

SUSAN J. SMITH

JONES, P. N. (1980). " Ethnic Segregation, Urban Planning and the Question of Choice: The Birmingham Case ". Paper presented to the Conference on *Ethnic Segregation in Cities*. St. Antony's College, Oxford.

KARN, V. A. (1979). " Low Income Owner-Occupation in the Inner City ". In (ed.) Jones, C. *Urban Deprivation and the Inner City*, 160–190, London: Croom Helm.

KIRBY, A. (1981). " Geographic Contributions to the Inner City Deprivation Debate: a Critical Assessment ". *Area*, **13,** 177–181.

KNIGHT, B. and HAYES, R. (1981). " *Self Help in the Inner City* ". London: London Voluntary Service Committee.

LAMBERT, J. R. (1970). *Crime, Police and Race Relations*. London: Oxford University Press for Institute of Race Relations.

LEE, R. (1976). " Public Finance and Urban Economy: Some Comments on Spatial Reformism ". *Antipode*, **8,** 43–50.

LEVINE. K, (1978). " Empiricism in Victimological Research: A Critique ". *Victimology*, **3,** 77–90.

MEURER, E. M. Jr. (1979). " Violent Crime Losses: Their Impact on the Victim and Society ". *Annals, American Academy of Political and Social Science*, 54–62.

NORRIS, G. (1979). " Defining Urban Deprivation ". In (ed.) Jones, C. *Urban Deprivation and the Inner City*, 17–31, London: Croom Helm.

PARIS, C. and BLACKABY, B. (1979). *Not Much Improvement: Urban Renewal Policy in Birmingham*. London: Heinemann.

POPE, C. E. (1979). " Victimisation Rates and Neighbourhood Characteristics: Some Preliminary Findings ". In (ed.) Parsonage, W. H. *Perspectives on Victimology*, Beverly Hills and London: Sage.

REX, J. (1981). " Urban Segregation and Inner City Policy in Great Britain ". In (ed.) Peach, C., Robinson, V. and Smith, S. *Ethnic Segregation in Cities*, 25–42, London: Croom Helm.

SHELEFF, L. (1974). " The Criminal Triad—Bystander, Victim and Criminal ". *International Journal of Criminology and Penology*, **2,** 159–174.

SHELEFF, L. S. and SCHICOR, D. (1980). " Victimological Aspects of Bystander Involvement ". *Crime and Delinquency*, **26,** 193–201.

SMITH, D. M. (1979). *Where the Grass is Greener*. London: Croom Helm.

SMITH, S. J. (1981). " Negative Interaction: Crime in the Inner City ". In (ed.) Jackson, P. and Smith, S. J. *Social Interaction and Ethnic Segregation*, 35–37, London: Academic Press.

SPARKS, R. F. (1981). " Multiple Victimisation, Evidence, Theory and Future Research ". *Journal of Criminal Law and Criminology*, **72,** 762–778.

SPARKS, R. F., GENN, H. G., and DODD, D. J. (1977). *Surveying Victims*. Chichester: Wiley.

U.S. DEPARTMENT OF JUSTICE (1975). Law Enforcement Assistance Administration: National Criminal Justice Information and Statistics Service. *Criminal Victimisation in the Nation's Five Largest Cities*. Washington D.C.: U.S. Government Printing Office.

WINCHESTER, S. W. C. (1978). " Two Suggestions for Developing the Geographical Study of Crime ". *Area*, **10,** 116–120.

WOLF, P. and HAUGE, R. (1975). " Criminal Violence in Three Scandinavian Countries ". *Scandinavian Studies in Criminology* (Volume 5). London: Tavistock.

[6]

Victimization and
the Fear of Crime

James Garofalo

*The determinants of the fear of crime are examined with special attention
to how the risk and experience of criminal victimization affect that fear. Using data from victimization and attitude surveys in eight American cities, a
model of the determinants of the fear of crime is developed and evaluated in
a preliminary fashion. The major conclusion is that the fear of crime is not
simply a function of the risk of and actual experiences with victimization.*

The public's fear of crime has become the basis for a number of social-
political decisions and programs in the United States. Unfortunately, while
evidence of the fear of crime (e.g., from public opinion polls) is often cited as
a justification for particular measures, assumptions about the sources of the
fear are left unstated. Judging from the frequency with which fear of crime is
cited as a justification for crime-reduction measures, a major assumption appears to be that the fear of crime is strongly and directly related to the risk or
experiences of criminal victimization. Yet this assumption remains virtually
untested; in fact, very little research has been devoted to examining any of the
sources of the fear of crime.

In this paper a rough model of the determinants of the fear of crime will be
presented and discussed. Then, using data from victimization and attitude surveys conducted in 1975, some indicators of the concepts in the model will be
chosen, and the adequacy of the model will be evaluated. Finally, the shortcomings of the model will be discussed, with particular attention given to the
areas in which our knowledge is still incomplete. Before addressing the substantive issues, however, a brief description of the data source for this paper is
necessary.

JAMES GAROFALO: Director, Statistical Analysis Center, Division of Criminal Justice Services, State of New York, Albany, New York.

A slightly different version of this paper was presented at the annual conference of the American
Association for Public Opinion Research, Buck Hill Falls, Pennsylvania, May 19–22, 1977. Parts
of the research on which this paper is based were performed under federal grant #75-SS-99-6029,
awarded to the Criminal Justice Research Center by the Statistics Division of the Law Enforcement Assistance Administration (LEAA). Points of view or opinions expressed in this paper are
those of the author and do not necessarily represent the official position or policies of LEAA.

Victimization and the Fear of Crime   81

THE NATIONAL CRIME SURVEY

In 1972, the Law Enforcement Assistance Administration (LEAA) of the U.S. Department of Justice began sponsoring a series of victimization surveys, known as the National Crime Survey (NCS). In each of the surveys, residents of a representative sample of households are interviewed concerning certain types of criminal victimizations that they may have suffered during some specified period preceding the interviews. Sampling, interviewing, coding, and data tabulations are performed for LEAA by the Bureau of the Census.

The NCS has had two major components: city surveys and national surveys. Because of methodological differences between the two components and because only the city surveys are used in this paper, the national surveys will not be discussed here.[1] In the city component of the NCS, interviews have been conducted in twenty-six major cities in the United States. Although data from all of the cities are used at one point in this paper, most of the information to be presented here is derived from interviews in eight cities—Atlanta, Baltimore, Cleveland, Dallas, Denver, Newark, Portland, and St. Louis—known collectively as the Impact Cities because of a particular federal program in which they participated.

Interviews were conducted in the eight Impact Cities during March, April, and May of 1975.[2] In each city, interviews were conducted in a representative sample of about 10,000 households. Within each household, members twelve years of age and older were eligible to be interviewed about certain criminal victimizations they might have suffered during the twelve months preceding the month of the interview. This resulted in interviews with about 21,000 persons in each city. The personal victimizations covered by the surveys were rape, robbery, assault, and larceny from the person (i.e., purse snatching and pocket picking without force or threat). Also covered were victimizations deemed to have been directed against the household as a unit (burglary, vehicle theft, and larcenies that involved no contact between the victim and the offender).

A supplemental "attitude questionnaire" was administered to a subsample of respondents in each city. A random half of the households selected for victimization interviewing were designated for administration of the supplemental questionnaire. In these households, every member age sixteen or older was interviewed with the supplemental questionnaire. Most of the analysis in this paper focuses on this subsample of about 70,000 respondents.

For each city a weighting scheme was designed to produce population esti-

1. Readers interested in a description of the national surveys should consult Garofalo and Hindelang, 1977.

2. The cities were also surveyed earlier, during July through November 1972. Five other cities in the NCS city component were also surveyed twice, so that data exist from thirty-nine surveys of the twenty-six cities.

mates from the sample data. The numbers reported in this paper are. therefore. estimates of population parameters based on the sample data. Furthermore. the results have been aggregated across the eight cities to take advantage of the large sample size. When the data are aggregated in this way. an average weighting factor of about 45 is applied to each interviewed individual in the attitude subsample.[3] The only point at which unweighted data are used in this paper is in the regression analysis presented in Figure 4.

A WORKING MODEL

As a first step in discussing the fear of crime. it should be noted that we will be working with a less-than-perfect indicator of the concept. Respondents in the NCS attitude subsample were asked: "How safe do you feel or would you feel being out alone in your neighborhood at night?" The four response categories were very safe. reasonably safe. somewhat unsafe. and very unsafe. Obviously. there are a number of problems in using this item as an indicator of the fear of crime. First. crime is not mentioned in the question. However. in the instrument the item was preceded by questions about crime trends. and the series of questions was introduced by the phrase. "Now I'd like to get your opinions about crime in general." so it is difficult to conceive of the respondent thinking about dangers other than crime. Second. the frame of reference for the question is the respondent's neighborhood. yet the meaning of the term *neighborhood* probably varies from respondent to respondent.[4] and some people may find it necessary to spend much of their time in areas that they perceive as more dangerous than their own. Third. the respondent is directed to think about being "alone." but there is probably great variability among people in the amount of time they spend outside unaccompanied.[5] Finally. the "do you feel or would you feel" portion of the question invites a mixing of actual feelings of fear with guesses about hypothetical situations. Despite these shortcomings. however. the item represents the best single indicator of the fear of crime available from the questionnaire.

In the introduction it was pointed out that studying the fear of crime is important because the proponents of many social programs invoke that fear as

3. For further details about sampling. interviewing. weighting. standard errors of the estimates. instruments. and so on. see Garofalo and Hindelang. 1977. and U.S. Bureau of the Census. 1976.

4. NCS interviewers are instructed that the term *neighborhood* "is defined. loosely. as the general area in which a person lives. The boundaries of this area would be whatever each individual feels is his 'neighborhood'" (U.S. Bureau of the Census. 1975:D5–2).

5. Even the term *alone* is ambiguous because some respondents may have interpreted it as meaning not being accompanied by another person or other persons. while other respondents may have assumed that it referred to situations in which there were no other people (even strangers) around.

**Table 1. Limiting of Behavior because of Crime
by Fear of Crime: Eight Impact Cities Aggregate. 1975**

| | Limiting of Behavior | | |
Fear of Crime	No	Yes	Estimated Number*
Very safe	80%	20%	493,947
Reasonably safe	66%	34%	1.253,019
Somewhat unsafe	42%	58%	706,745
Very unsafe	27%	73%	727,441
Total	54%	46%	3,181,152

(Gamma = .56)
*Excludes persons who gave no response to either item.

a justification for their proposals. But the fear of crime is worthy of study in its own right. It is logical to assume that people who are very fearful of crime suffer psychological discomfort. There is also some indication that the fear of crime leads some people to restrict their behavior. For example, respondents in the NCS attitude subsample were asked: "In general, have you limited or changed your activities in the past few years because of crime?" Table 1 shows the relationship between responses to that question and the fear of crime indicator being used here. Overall, 46 percent of the eight-city residents said that they had limited their behavior. But the percentages vary greatly according to the level of fear expressed: from 20 percent for those who felt very safe to 73 percent for those who felt very unsafe.[6] Thus, a better understanding of the fear of crime could lead to action that will have the effect of improving the quality of life for many people.

A working model of the influences on the fear of crime is presented in Figure 1. Five general factors are seen as affecting fear: the actual risk of being victimized by a criminal act, past experiences of being victimized, the content of the socialization processes connected with particular social roles, the content of media presentations about crime and victimization, and the perceived effectiveness of official barriers that are placed between potential offenders and victims. Each of these factors will be discussed separately, and relevant data from the NCS Impact Cities surveys will be examined to determine the extent of empirical support for each factor. Then the model will be evaluated in a more systematic form using indicators that are available in the NCS.

6. Although the data are not presented here, the relationship maintains within age and sex groups, even though responses to both items vary with age and sex.

84

James Garofalo

Figure 1. Working Model of the Influences on the Fear of Crime

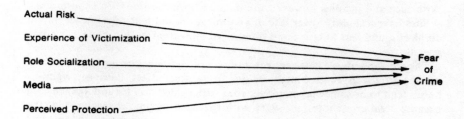

ACTUAL RISK OF VICTIMIZATION

Every person is unique, so it is theoretically possible to assign a unique risk factor (i.e., a probability of being victimized) to everyone in the sample. Our knowledge of the risk of victimization has not reached that stage, even though some work has been done on deriving a typology of persons based on the risk of victimization (Hindelang, Gottfredson, and Garofalo, 1978:ch. 5). Previous analyses of NCS victimization data have shown, however, that several personal characteristics are related more or less strongly to rates of victimization. Four of these characteristics—age, sex, race, and income—are also related to the fear of crime. It is possible, then, to examine how rates of victimization and the fear of crime co-vary among subgroups formed by age, sex, race, and income. The relevant data for the eight Impact Cities are presented in Table 2.

The rates of victimization in Table 2 refer to the personal victimizations of rape, robbery, assault, and larceny involving contact between the victim and offender; these crimes should be most relevant to the fear of crime. The rates are computed per 1,000 persons in the category. The numerator of each rate is the estimated count of the number of *victimizations* suffered by persons in the category, not the number of *persons* victimized. Thus, persons who suffered more than one victimization are counted more than once in the numerator. This provides a measure of risk for the category rather than for any individual within the category. The measure of fear in Table 2 is the summation of the percentages of persons in each category who answered "somewhat unsafe" or "very unsafe" to the question about feeling of safety at night that was described earlier.

Table 2 shows that age has a negative relationship with victimization rates and a positive relationship with the fear of crime. That is, as age goes up, victimization rates decrease (from 125 per 1,000 to 34 per 1,000) and the fear of crime increases (from 37 percent to 63 percent). A similar reversal occurs for

7. The relationships do not change when the percentage who responded "very unsafe" is used as the measure of fear.

males and females: Males show a higher victimization rate (90 per 1,000 vs. 54 per 1,000) while females show a higher level of fear (60 percent vs. 26 percent). With race and income, however, the data are more in line with expectations. Whites have a slightly lower rate of victimization and fear-of-crime level than do blacks, and fear of crime and rates of victimization both decline as income goes up.

The correspondence between fear and risk of victimization among racial and income groups in Table 2 might be due to an areal effect. Because neighborhoods tend to be somewhat homogeneous with respect to race and income, and because areal crime rates also vary with race and income characteristics, the relationship between fear and risk of victimization for racial and income groups in Table 2 may be a reflection of the convergence of these factors in particular geographic locations. The same cannot be said of age and sex be-

**Table 2. Estimated Rates of Victimization and Fear
of Crime among Age, Sex, Race, and Family Income Groups:
Eight Impact Cities Aggregate, 1975**

	Rates of Personal Victimization per 1,000 Persons*	Percent Responding Somewhat Unsafe or Very Unsafe
Age		
16–19	125	37
20–24	105	38
25–34	76	37
35–49	51	43
50–64	42	50
65 or older	34	63
Sex		
Male	90	26
Female	54	60
Race		
White	69	41
Black	72	54
Family income		
Less than $3,000	93	62
$3,000–$7,499	78	53
$7,500–$9,999	70	45
$10,000–$14,999	64	39
$15,000–$24,999	59	34
$25,000 or more	56	30

*Rape, robbery, assault, and larceny with victim/offender contact.

Table 3. Fear of Crime by Dangerousness of Own Neighborhood Compared with Other Neighborhoods in the Metropolitan Area: Eight Impact Cities Aggregate. 1975

Own Neighborhood	Fear of Crime				Estimated Number*
	Very Safe	Reasonably Safe	Somewhat Unsafe	Very Unsafe	
Much less dangerous	36%	39%	15%	10%	315,270
Less dangerous	19%	45%	20%	16%	1,182,990
About average	9%	37%	26%	28%	1,444,880
More dangerous	9%	26%	25%	40%	178,980
Much more dangerous	7%	17%	13%	63%	32,140

(Gamma = .36)

*Excludes persons who gave no response to either item.

cause. in general. neighborhoods are not strongly homogeneous on these fac- tors. There appear to be differences among age and sex groups that override a possible conjunction between fear and risk of victimization; we will return to this issue later.

To specify the relationship between fear and risk for our model. we need some indicator that reflects geographic differences in risk. Unfortunately. the NCS data cannot be broken down by subareas of the cities. mainly because of rules of confidentiality maintained by the Census Bureau. As a proxy variable. we will use the supplemental questionnaire item: "How do you think your

Table 4. Fear of Crime (Proportion Responding "Somewhat Unsafe" or "Very Unsafe") by Total Number of Personal Victimizations during the Twelve Months Preceding the Interview. by Sex and Age: Eight Impact Cities Aggregate. 1975

Number of Personal Victimizations*	Males		Females	
	Less than 35	35 or Older	Less than 35	35 or Older
None	15% (551,974)**	32% (742.920)	54% (681,380)	64% (1,001,074)
One	22% (61,404)	54% (34,753)	63% (48,183)	77% (35,887)
Two or more	26% (15,930)	56% (6,181)	64% (8,196)	78% (3,021)

*Rape. robbery. assault. and larceny with contact between victim and offender.

**Estimated number of person · in category; base on which percentage was computed.

neighborhood compares with others in this metropolitan area in terms of crime?" Responses to this item do vary with race and income, and, as shown in Table 3, the responses are also related to the fear of crime.

Use of the comparative neighborhood danger item as a measure of the actual risk of victimization requires the assumption that, in their replies, the respondents accurately reflect the objective risk of victimization in their neighborhoods. This assumption is probably not justified completely, but without information that is more geographic-specific, it will have to suffice for present purposes.

EXPERIENCE WITH VICTIMIZATION

For every individual interviewed in the NCS attitude subsample, information is available about certain victimizations suffered during the twelve months preceding the interview. Table 4 shows the relationship between the number of personal victimizations suffered during the reference period and the fear of crime expressed; age and sex have also been controlled here.

Table 4 indicates that being victimized is related to the fear of crime: within each age/sex group, nonvictims express less fear than do victims. However, the differences among the age and sex groups remain, regardless of experience with victimization. Furthermore, inspection of the numbers of persons on which the percentages in Table 4 were computed indicates that experience with victimization will not have a major effect in accounting for the total variability in the fear of crime because only a relatively small proportion of respondents were personally victimized during the survey reference period.[8]

Of course, the number of victimizations shown in Table 4 represents personal victimizations that occurred during the twelve months preceding the interview. It is possible that the results could change if information about victimizations were available over a longer period of time. However, it will be assumed here that victimizations that occurred more than twelve months before the interview—unless they were extremely serious—would have little effect on fear of crime at the time of the interview.

ROLE SOCIALIZATION

The findings that fear of crime and risk of victimization are inversely related across age and sex groups (Table 2) and that age and sex have much stronger effects on fear than does actual experience with personal victimization (Table 4) lead to a focus on differences in the life situations of people in the various age and sex groups. The hypothesis here is that sex- and age-specific socialization patterns are responsible for the disjunction between fear and risk.

8. In analysis not presented here, respondents were categorized more finely on victimization experiences: for example, from absolutely no contact with victimization to living in a household in which some *other* person was victimized to suffering a victimization that resulted in serious injury. The results of that analysis did not differ much from those shown in Table 4.

Regardless of the current push for greater equality for women, socialization into the female sex role has traditionally emphasized submissiveness; conversely, assertiveness has been stressed for males. According to some writers (Weis and Borges, 1973), one way submissiveness is achieved is by creating a fear of criminal attack—particularly a fear of rape—in females and thereby teaching them to feel dependent on males for protection. To the extent that these socialization goals are achieved, one would expect females to express more fear than males, regardless of the objective risks of victimization.

For older persons, a number of factors coalesce to produce dependency, isolation, and fear. The shift away from the extended family structure, public and private retirement policies, as well as purely physical changes such as declining health, all operate to place the elderly in positions that maximize feelings of vulnerability. Again, it is not surprising that older people express more fear than younger people, despite their lower risks of victimization.

It is possible that role socialization produces age and sex differences in expressed fear by a different mechanism. Younger people and males might be disinclined to *admit* fear to interviewers—whether or not they *feel* fear—because of the expectations associated with their roles. However, this possibility cannot be tested with the available NCS data, so we will take the fear of crime responses at their face value, as indicating the actual feelings of the respondents.

THE MEDIA

There have been a number of works dealing with the *content* of media treatment of crime and deviance (e.g., Cohen and Young, 1973). However, little has been done to determine the *effects* of the media presentations.[9] Although it would seem self-evident that the media have an influence on the public's fear of crime—if only by way of the pervasiveness of the media's messages—relevant data from the NCS are sparse.

Only one item in the NCS supplemental questionnaire deals directly with the media: "Crime is less (more, about as) serious than (as) the newspapers and TV say." In Table 5, responses to that item are cross-tabulated with the fear of crime. Looking at the row percentages in Table 5, the data show that respondents who thought that crime was actually less serious than portrayed in the media expressed somewhat less fear of crime than did other respondents. However, inspection of the column percentages reveals that, regardless of fear of crime, very few people thought that the media were underestimating the seriousness of crime. Even among those people who felt somewhat unsafe or very unsafe about being out alone in their neighborhoods at night, almost half

9. The exceptions are studies focusing on (a) the effects of violence in the media on attitudes toward violence and violent behavior and (b) the effects of pornography on sex crimes.

Victimization and the Fear of Crime   89

Table 5.   Fear of Crime by Perceived Seriousness of Crime Relative to What the
Newspapers and Television Say: Eight Impact Cities Aggregate, 1975

Seriousness of Crime Relative to What Media Say	Fear of Crime				
	Very Safe	Reasonably Safe	Somewhat Unsafe	Very Unsafe	Estimated Number*
Less serious	28%**	42%	16%	13%	261,623
	15%***	9%	6%	5%	
About the same	15%	42%	23%	20%	1,514,438
	46%	51%	49%	42%	
More serious	13%	36%	23%	28%	1,292,171
	35%	37%	41%	50%	
Estimated number	474,850	1,208,236	683,365	701,781	3,068,232

(Gamma = .19)

  *Excludes persons who gave no response to either item.
 **Row percentages.
***Column percentages.

(49 percent and 42 percent) said that crime was about as serious as portrayed in the media. One can conclude from Table 5 that the media set "minimum standards" concerning perceptions of the seriousness of crime; other factors lead many people to perceive crime as being more serious than media portrayals, but few people believe that crime is actually less serious than depicted by the media.

The effects of the media can also be judged inferentially. The media provide both fictional and nonfictional accounts of crime. For the most part, the nonfictional accounts must be based on crimes that come to the attention of criminal justice officials. This means that media treatments of actual crimes are largely restricted to those crimes that are reported to the police, and the threat of crime communicated by the media will be shaped by those same crimes. Therefore, one would expect the fear of crime to be more strongly related to official measures of crime rates than to victimization survey rates which take into account crimes that are not reported to the police.

In order to test this notion indirectly, data from all the twenty-six cities surveyed in the NCS were used along with *Uniform Crime Reports* (UCR) data (Kelley, 1974 and 1975) from the same cities for the same time periods covered by the surveys. Fear of crime (the percentage of respondents in each city who replied somewhat or very unsafe to the fear of crime item) was regressed first on the personal victimization rate as found in the NCS and then on the UCR

**Figure 2.   Regression of Fear of Crime on NCS Personal Crime Rate:
Twenty-six Cities, 1974–75**

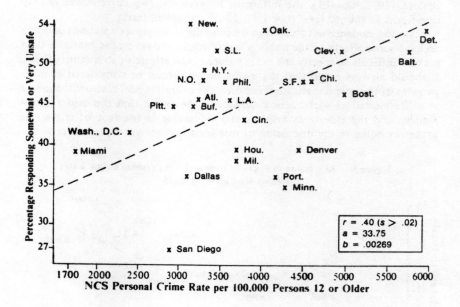

Cities: Atlanta, Baltimore, Boston, Buffalo, Chicago, Cincinnati, Cleveland, Dallas, Denver, Detroit, Houston, Los Angeles, Miami, Milwaukee, Minneapolis, Newark, New Orleans, New York, Oakland, Philadelphia, Pittsburgh, Portland, St. Louis, San Diego, San Francisco, Washington, D.C.

rate. For both crime measures, the crimes of rape, robbery, and aggravated assault were used. The UCR rates were expressed as the number of crimes per 100,000 total population in each city because that is the form in which those rates are communicated officially. The NCS rates were expressed as the number of victimizations per 100,000 persons age twelve years or older. The results are displayed in Figures 2 and 3.

The scattergrams show a much better grouping of the cities around the regression line when fear of crime is regressed on the UCR rate of crime (Figure 3) than on the NCS personal victimization rate (Figure 2). The summary statistics confirm the visual representation: The correlation between fear of crime and the NCS rates is .40, which is not significant at the .02 level, but the

Victimization and the Fear of Crime   **91**

correlation is .66 between the UCR rates and fear of crime, a coefficient that is significant beyond the .01 level. However, using the procedure suggested by Blalock (1972:406–407), the difference between the two correlations is only significant at the .10 level (t = 1.41, 23 df, one-tailed test).

From the evidence in this section we can infer that media depictions of crime do have some effects on the public's fear of crime. However, the available data make it difficult to specify the exact nature of the effects or to quantify them. It should also be noted that the media factor cannot be considered as independent of the role socialization factor in the overall model because the media must be viewed as socialization agents. To the extent that the media depict females and the elderly as helpless and vulnerable in the face of crime, the processes noted in the discussion of role socialization will be reinforced.

Figure 3.   Regression of Fear of Crime on UCR Personal Crime Rate:
Twenty-six Cities. 1974–75

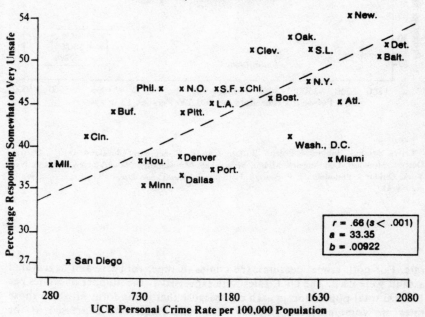

Cities: Atlanta, Baltimore, Boston, Buffalo, Chicago, Cincinnati, Cleveland, Dallas, Denver, Detroit, Houston, Los Angeles, Miami, Milwaukee, Minneapolis, Newark, New Orleans, New York, Oakland, Philadelphia, Pittsburgh, Portland, St. Louis, San Diego, San Francisco, Washington, D.C.

OFFICIAL BARRIERS AGAINST CRIME

If people feel adequately insulated from whatever crimes are occurring, it would seem reasonable to assume that they will not be very fearful of crime. To some extent a degree of insulation comes from knowing and trusting the people with whom one interacts. As a government commission pointed out, the fear of crime is basically a fear of strangers (President's Commission on Law Enforcement and Administration of Justice, 1967:165). In the modern, impersonal urban environment, however, the task of insulating people from crime tends to fall more and more on official government agencies, particularly the police. The confidence that people have in the police, then, should be related to their fear of crime.

Table 6. **Fear of Crime by Evaluation of Police Performance: Eight Impact Cities Aggregate, 1975**

Evaluation of Police Performance	Fear of Crime				
	Very Safe	Reasonably Safe	Somewhat Unsafe	Very Unsafe	Estimated Number*
Good	18%	39%	21%	22%	1,302,350
Average	14%	42%	24%	20%	1,345,100
Poor	14%	33%	21%	32%	394,640

(Gamma = .08)

*Excludes persons who gave no response to either item.

The supplemental NCS questionnaire contains the item: "Would you say, in general, that your local police are doing a good job, an average job, or a poor job?" In Table 6, responses to that item are cross-tabulated with the fear of crime responses. It is obvious from this table that, although the relatively small number of respondents who rated performance of their local police as poor were most likely to feel very unsafe, the relationship between evaluation of police performance and the fear of crime is not very strong (gamma = .08).

SPECIFYING THE MODEL

Each of the five factors in the working model (Figure 1) has been discussed at least briefly. The model can now be presented more systematically, using indicators that are available from the attitude subsample of the NCS Impact Cities surveys. The resulting model is shown in Figure 4.

Respondents' perceptions of the dangerousness of their own neighborhoods as compared with other neighborhoods in the same metropolitan area are used as a proxy measure of the actual risk of victimization. As mentioned earlier,

Victimization and the Fear of Crime   93

Figure 4.   Refinement of the Working Model of the Influences on the Fear of Crime

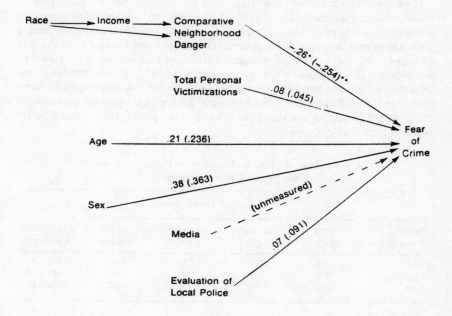

Note: All correlations were computed with unweighted sample cases; *n* = 65,579; cases with missing data on any of the variables were excluded.
  *Simple *r*.
  **Beta weight from multiple regression of fear of crime on comparative neighborhood danger, total personal victimizations, age, sex, and evaluation of local police. In the multiple regression. *R* = .51 and *R*² = .26.

use of this variable requires the assumption that respondents are relatively accurate in assessing the degree of threat present in their immediate environments. Because subcity geographic identifiers are not available in the data, subjective impressions about relative neighborhood dangerousness represent the best available indicator of local risk. Furthermore. it is probably true that respondents more accurately gauge the risk of victimization in their own neighborhoods than in more distant places.

The second component in the model—experience with victimization—is represented by the total number of personal victimizations reported to the interviewer as having occurred to the respondent during the twelve months preceding the interview. This indicator, of course, is not sensitive to victimizations that might have occurred more than one year before the interview.[10] In addition, the variable covers a limited range of victimizations: rape, robbery, assault, and larceny involving contact between the victim and offender. As pointed out earlier, however, the most recent victimizations should have the greatest impact on the fear of crime, and the personal victimizations included in the variable would seem to be the ones most likely to create a fear of crime when they are experienced.

The indicators for role socialization were chosen on theoretical and empirical grounds. Both age and sex are master statuses, in the sense that they have a pervasive effect on all aspects of a person's life. Empirically, it was found that fear and risk were negatively associated across age and sex groups, so role socialization was invoked as a process which can override actual risk in determining the fear of crime in certain cases.

Figure 4 shows the influence of the media on the fear of crime as being unmeasured in this model. In the earlier discussion, some evidence was presented indicating that media presentations of crime do have some effect on the fear of crime. Unfortunately, no variable now exists in the NCS data set to measure the effect of the media adequately.

Finally, official barriers against crime are indicated by respondents' evaluations of how well their local police were performing. A focus on the police rather than on other parts of the criminal justice system in this context seems warranted because the police have more direct contact with the public than does any other criminal justice agency.

DISCUSSION OF THE MODEL

Figure 4 shows the zero-order correlation coefficients between the fear of crime and (1) the actual risk indicator, (2) the experience with victimization indicator, (3) age, (4) sex, and (5) the barrier against crime indicator. Also shown, in parentheses, are the standardized regression coefficients (beta weights) derived from a multiple-linear regression of fear of crime with those same five variables. No attempt has been made to present a complete path diagram of the relationships between all of the variables in this preliminary model.[11]

The beta weights in Figure 4 indicate that the effects of age and sex—the two role socialization variables—on the fear of crime are substantial. It was shown

10. Actually it is sensitive to earlier victimizations in the limited sense that once a person has been victimized, the probability of a subsequent victimization is higher than a simple multiplicative function of the probability of initial victimization; that is, some people are "victimization prone" (see Hindelang, Gottfredson, and Garofalo, 1978:ch. 6). We would expect, then, that people who had been victimized more than one year before the interview would be overrepresented among those who were victimized during the past year.

11. A correlation matrix of all of the variables is available in Garofalo, 1977:app. D.

Victimization and the Fear of Crime   **95**

earlier that the relationship of age and sex to fear cannot be accounted for by the risk of personal victimization, at least when risk is defined as the rates of personal victimization for sex and age subgroups in the sample. Actual experience with victimization cannot account for the relationships either, because females and older respondents, who express the highest levels of fear, have proportionately fewer encounters with victimization than do their male and younger counterparts. However, the possibility remains that females and older persons have low rates of victimization *because* of their fear of crime. That is, feelings of vulnerability lead them to stay indoors or to take other actions which insulate them from victimization. Role socialization can then be invoked as an explanation for the *initial* feelings of vulnerability and for the maintenance of those feelings in the face of risks of victimization that are lower than those faced by other segments of the population.

Figure 4 also shows that perceptions of the relative dangerousness of one's neighborhood also have a strong effect on the fear of crime. In the model, those perceptions are used as an indicator of actual risk, under the tenuous assumptions that respondents can make fairly accurate estimates about the dangerousness of their immediate surroundings and that those estimates are not influenced by the respondents' fear of crime. Geographic-specific data are needed for a more accurate measure of actual risk.

The effect of total personal victimizations suffered during the reference period is quite small in Figure 4. This is not surprising because of the relatively small numbers of persons who reported such victimizations during the interviews. Being victimized does appear to increase the fear of crime (see Table 4), but the number of victims in the population is so relatively small that their higher level of fear does not have a great effect on the overall level of fear in the population. Of course, a larger proportion of the population would be classified as having suffered victimizations if data were available for more than one year preceding the interviews. But even if such data were available, it is doubtful that victimizations suffered two, three, or more years before the interviews would have as much effect on the fear of crime as more recent victimizations.

A small effect is shown in Figure 4 for respondents' evaluations of their local police. There is a real measurement problem here. It is not unlikely that respondents have a low opinion of the criminal justice system's ability to protect them from crime yet believe that their local police are performing well; opinions about police officers already on the street do not have a necessary connection with opinions about overall criminal justice effectiveness. Further research is needed to determine the public's perception of how well the criminal justice system is protecting them from crime and whether variations in such perceptions are related to the fear of crime.

The effect of the fifth element of the model—the media—could not be estimated with any indicators available in the NCS, and it is left unmeasured in Figure 4.

Regression of fear of crime on the indicators that were available in the NCS produced an R^2 of .26, so there is a great deal of the variation in the fear of crime left unexplained. Some of the unexplained variation is probably due to measurement error: The variables used are imperfect indicators of the concepts in the model. In addition, one major factor—the effect of the media—remains unmeasured.

CONCLUSION

A model of the determinants of the fear of crime has been presented, discussed, and partially evaluated using data from victimization surveys conducted in eight American cities. Perhaps the major conclusion that can be drawn from this study is that the fear of crime is not a simple reflection of the risk or experience of being victimized. Social role expectations, in particular, are related to the fear of crime, regardless of—and even contrary to—the objective risk of and experience with personal victimization. Thus, policy makers should not necessarily expect a major decrease in the amount of fear if crime is successfully reduced.

On the other hand, the results do imply that the fear of crime can be reduced without waiting for progress on the difficult task of lowering the level of crime. As Skogan and Klecka (1977:43) note, however, few criminal justice policies "have been aimed specifically at reducing the fear of crime, although there is evidence that this fear is often independent of direct victimization and that it has its own consequences for city life." Programs which accomplish such things as increasing the visibility of the police to citizens, improving street lighting, or educating the public to the very mundane nature of most criminality (as opposed to the sensational portrayals elsewhere) could help to alleviate fear without having any impact on the actual amount of crime. Policies directed specifically at the fear of crime would seem to be justifiable simply in terms of improving the quality of life, especially for segments of the population such as the elderly.

REFERENCES

BLALOCK, H. M., JR.
  1972 *Social Statistics*, 2d ed. New York: McGraw-Hill.
COHEN, S., and J. YOUNG, eds.
  1973 *The Manufacture of News: Social Problems, Deviance and the Mass Media*. London, England: Constable.
GAROFALO, J.
  1977 *The Police and Public Opinion: An Analysis of Victimization and Attitude Data from 13 American Cities*. Analytic Report SD-VAD-3. Law Enforcement As-

Victimization and the Fear of Crime   97

sistance Administration. National Criminal Justice Information and Statistics
Service. Washington. D.C.: Govt. Printing Office.

GAROFALO. J.. and M. J. HINDELANG
   1977   *An Introduction to the National Crime Survey.* Analytic Report SD-VAD-4.
          Law Enforcement Assistance Administration. National Criminal Justice In-
          formation and Statistics Service. Washington. D.C.: Govt. Printing Office.

HINDELANG. M. J.. M. R. GOTTFREDSON. and J. GAROFALO
   1978   *Victims of Personal Crime: An Empirical Foundation for a Theory of Personal
          Victimization.* Cambridge. Mass.: Ballinger.

KELLEY. C.
   1974   *Uniform Crime Reports—1973.* Federal Bureau of Investigation. Washington.
          D.C.: Govt. Printing Office.
   1975   *Uniform Crime Reports—1974.* Federal Bureau of Investigation. Washington.
          D.C.: Govt. Printing Office.

PRESIDENT'S COMMISSION ON LAW ENFORCEMENT AND ADMINIS-
TRATION OF JUSTICE
   1967   *The Challenge of Crime in a Free Society.* Washington. D.C.: Govt. Printing
          Office.

SKOGAN. W. G.. and W. R. KLECKA
   1977   *The Fear of Crime.* rev. ed. Supplementary Empirical Teaching Units in Politi-
          cal Science. Washington. D.C.: American Political Science Association.

U.S. BUREAU OF THE CENSUS
   1976   *Survey Documentation.* National Crime Survey. Central Cities Sample. 1975.
          Washington. D.C.: Govt. Printing Office.
   1975   *Interviewer's Manual.* National Crime Survey. Central Cities Sample. Wash-
          ington. D.C.: Govt. Printing Office.

WEIS. K.. and S. S. BORGES
   1973   "Victimology and Rape: The Case of the Legitimate Victim." *Issues in Crimi-
          nology* 8 (Fall): 71-115.

[7]

The Howard Journal Vol 24 No 1. Feb 85
0265–5527 $2.50/£2.00

Elderly Victims of Crime and Exposure to Risk

RONALD CLARKE, PAUL EKBLOM, MIKE HOUGH and
PAT MAYHEW

*Ronald Clarke (formerly head of the Home Office Research and
Planning Unit) is Professor of Criminal Justice, Temple University,
Philadelphia
Paul Ekblom is Senior Research Officer and Mike Hough and Pat
Mayhew are Principal Research Officers at the Home Office
Research and Planning Unit*

*Abstract: It has been debated for some time whether lower rates of personal victimisation among
the elderly are due to the fact that – because of fear or other reasons – they shield themselves from
situations in which they might be victimised. This 'differential exposure' explanation is
examined using data from the 1982 British Crime Survey which provides risks for different age/
sex groups and detailed information about respondents' 'lifestyles'. Looking at evening 'street'
offences, differences in risks between the age groups change very little when account is taken of
different patterns of going out: irrespective of frequency, means of travel, destination and
activity, the elderly are still less frequently victimised. Some theoretical and practical
implications of the findings are discussed.*

It has been shown in numerous victimisation surveys (see for example,
Hough and Mayhew 1983; Ministry of the Solicitor General 1983; van
Dijk and Steinmetz 1983; Smith 1983; U.S. Department of Justice 1984)
that the elderly are less at risk of most crimes than others are. In the first
report on the 1982 British Crime Survey (B.C.S.), for example, Hough
and Mayhew (1983) showed that older people (aged 61 or over) were
much less likely to be the victims of 'street crime' than the 'middle-aged'
(31–60) or the 'young' (16–30); rates of victimisation for the young were
nearly six times greater than those for older people.

Despite being much less at risk, the elderly are more fearful of crime
than others are (see for example, Maxfield 1984) and it is not clear
whether this is because they misperceive their risks or because the
consequences of victimisation may generally be more severe for them –
they may be more likely to be injured, upset or seriously inconvenienced
by crime than younger people. What is known, however, is that the elderly
go out much less often and are more likely to give fear of attack as a
reason. This leaves open the disquieting possibility (cf. Balkin 1979;
Lindquist and Duke 1982; Stafford and Galle 1984) that if the elderly were
to go out as much as younger people they would indeed be the most
frequently victimised age group. This hypothesis – which underlies the

1

'differential exposure' explanation of low risks among the elderly – is examined in the present paper using data from the 1982 B.C.S. Some other relevant findings from the same source about the consequences of victimisation for the elderly and the characteristics of whose who victimise them are presented *en passant*.

This is not entirely new territory. Corrado *et al.* (1980) present data from a survey undertaken in Greater Vancouver which shows that even those older people (aged 40 or over) who go out more than average in the evenings are less likely to be victims of violent victimisation than the young. Victim survey results from Holland also show the same pattern (van Dijk and Steinmetz 1983). More directly relevant are Hough and Mayhew's B.C.S. figures which show that, taking only those who said they went out four or more evenings during the week preceeding the interview, the elderly (aged 61 or over) faced a risk of 'street crime' three times lower than that of younger people going out as often. But these B.C.S. data, valuable as they are, do not settle the question. In the first place, Hough and Mayhew's definition of 'street crime' includes offences committed by people known to the victims, whereas attack by strangers is probably the main source of concern. Secondly, Hough and Mayhew's data about victimisation relate to the 24 hours of the day, whereas their measure of 'exposure' to risk related only to the evenings (6.00 to 12.00 p.m.). Finally, their measure of exposure included no information about the riskiness of the activities pursued when out in the evening: even those elderly people who go out frequently may avoid more risky places such as clubs and pubs, and they may avoid the more risky means of travel. These various deficiencies are remedied in the current study, by taking advantage of the unusually detailed information about respondents' routine activities and 'lifestyles' collected in the course of the 1982 B.C.S. (see Gottfredson 1984, for further analysis of B.C.S. 'lifestyle' data).

Data

The data derive from the first sweep of the B.C.S., a national victimisation survey mounted by the Home Office Research and Planning Unit. One person aged 16 or over was interviewed at home in each of about 11,000 households in England and Wales; some 6,300 of these completed a follow-up questionnaire in which the lifestyle questions were included. The survey was conducted in parallel in Scotland by the Scottish Home and Health Department, with a sample of about 5,000, of whom 2,800 completed the follow-up questionnaire. Respondents were selected in both countries using the Electoral Register as a sampling frame and interviews were conducted in 80% of eligible households (which excluded institutions). Fieldwork was conducted in the first quarter of 1982, and all respondents were asked about crimes – whether or not reported to the police – that they had experienced since the beginning of 1981. Further details about the survey design are to be found in Hough and Mayhew (1983) and Wood (1984).

All those completing the follow-up questionnaire from the combined England and Wales and Scotland samples were used for the present analysis, yielding a sample of 9,150; 30% of these were 'young' (aged 16–30), 49% middle-aged (31–60), and 21% old (60+). The data were weighted to restore national representativeness, correcting for certain features of the interview design (for example, over-representation of inner-city residents, and the fact that while all victims completed the follow-up questionnaire only 40% of non-victims did so).

Definition of Victimisation

This paper is concerned with 'street' offences which: (i) involve contact (though not necessarily confrontation) between offender and victim; (ii) do not take place inside the victim's home (or those of friends and relatives) or inside the workplace, and (iii) are committed by offenders who are strangers to the victims, or known only by sight. Offences meeting these conditions included: serious woundings, assaults and attempted assaults; attempted rape; indecent assault; robberies and attempts; thefts and attempted theft from the person (snatch thefts and pickpocketings). Offences classified as threats were excluded. 'Victims' are those who had been victimised once or more by any of the specified 'street' offences between the start of 1981 and the time of interview (Feb/March 1982). The prevalence rates presented here, expressed per 1,000 people, are thus slightly higher than annual ones would be. The present definitions yielded a total of 554 victims of whom 303 were victimised during the evening hours (6.00–12.00 p.m.). These are unweighted figures; all rates in the tables are based on weighted data.

Findings

In keeping with previous results, the old were found to be less frequently the victims of 'street' crime as defined. This holds for the 24-hour (*Table 1*) and evening (*Table 2*) periods, though it is particularly marked for the latter. It also holds for both men and women though the age trend is more marked for men; for example, young men are about 25 times as likely to be victimised in the evening as are the old, whereas for women the corresponding multiple is only six. Overall, women are less victimised than men, but during the 24 hours of the day elderly women are more at risk than elderly men – apparently because of a greater risk of snatch thefts and pickpocketing. (The slightly higher rate for women than men in the middle-aged category is too small to be statistically significant).

As the elderly are known to go out less than the young (particularly in the evenings) and women less than men, these victimisation patterns are on the face of it consistent with a differential exposure hypothesis. In the remainder of the analysis the hypothesis is tested more directly by using measures of the frequency and riskiness of going out; as these measures relate only to the evening period, evening victimisation is considered alone.

3

TABLE 1

Risk per 1,000 of 24-hour 'Street Crime' Victimisation, by Age and Sex

| | | AGE | | |
	Young	Middle	Old	Total
		Risk per 1,000		
Men	99	22	8	42
Women	38	24	20	26
Total	69	23	15	33
		Unweighted nos.		
Sample	2738	4460	1952	9150
Victims	293	192	69	554

TABLE 2

Risk per 1,000 of Evening 'Street Crime' Victimisation, by Age and Sex

| | | AGE | | |
	Young	Middle	Old	Total
		Risk per 1,000		
Men	74	14	3	30
Women	19	7	3	9
Total	48	10	3	19
		Unweighted nos.		
Sample	2738	4460	1952	9150
Victims	196	94	13	303

Table 3 shows the relationship between victimisation and evenings out of the house for the week immediately preceeding the interview. For whatever frequency of going out (no evenings, 1 or 2 evenings, and 3+ evenings), the young were much more likely to be victimised than were the middle-aged and especially more likely than were the old. Once again, the pattern was much less marked for women: for instance, risks among women who went out 3 evenings a week do not show a clear decline with age, although women aged 16–30 were about half as likely again to be victimised as were all those over 30. (The corresponding difference for men was about seven times as likely). Despite this it is clear

4

that the elderly's lower rate of victimisation cannot be explained by less exposure to risk and a simple 'differential exposure' hypothesis must be rejected – at least when exposure is measured only by evenings out.

TABLE 3

Risk per 1,000 of Evening 'Street Crime' Victimisation, by Age, Sex and Evenings Out Last Week

		EVENINGS OUT							
	None				1,2			3+	
	Yng	Middle	Old	Yng	Middle	Old	Yng	Middle	Old
Risk per 1,000									
Men	68	16	2	63	11	4	85	16	4
Women	18	5	2	17	6	1	23	13	20
Total	39	10	2	38	8	2	62	14	11
Unweighted nos.									
Sample	563	1572	1117	1056	2004	635	1119	884	200
Victims	25	30	4	65	44	4	106	20	4

In fact, when the measure of going out is further refined to take into account the 'riskiness' of the places visited when out in the evening, or the 'riskiness' of the means of travel, the picture remains substantially unchanged, though within the 'middle-aged' and 'old' age groups there are some exceptions probably due to small victim numbers. The relevant data are presented in *Tables 4* and *5*. In *Table 4* risky places were defined – following inspection of the data – as pubs, dances, discos or parties. In *Table 5* risky means of travel are defined as by public transport or on foot. The main anomaly relates once again to elderly women who are more at risk than younger ones are under certain conditions (when they go out frequently to 'non-risky' places and when they go out frequently by risky means of travel); but numbers are very small and these differences may well be unreliable. It must be concluded therefore that even when riskiness (as well as frequency) of going out is taken into account, the elderly are generally much less at risk of crime than others are.

Implications for Theory

The most noteworthy finding of the analyses presented above is that the differences in rates of victimisation between the age groups change hardly at all when account is taken of different patterns of going out: irrespective of frequency, means of travel, destination and activity the elderly are less

5

TABLE 4

Risk per 1,000 of Evening 'Street Crime' Victimisation, by Age, Sex, and Number of Evenings Out, Comparing Those Who Went to 'Risky' and 'Non-risky' Places

EVENINGS OUT

	1,2			3+		
	Yng	Middle	Old	Yng	Middle	Old
Risks per 1,000						
Men: non-risky	55	7	5	83	3	6
Men: risky	70	17	–	85	23	2
Women: non-risky	12	3	1	7	20	29
Women: risky	23	14	5	29	5	–
Total	38	8	2	62	14	11
Unweighted nos.						
Sample	1056	2004	635	1119	884	200
Victims	65	44	4	106	20	4

Note: 'Non-risky' = people who did not go to pubs, clubs, discos or parties on any night out; 'risky' = all other people

at risk of attack than are the middle-aged or young.[1] Whether this conclusion would be changed by further refining measures of risky activities remains to be seen. Clearly, any research that pursues this will need methods which generate sufficient numbers of elderly victims relative to younger ones, and very detailed measures of the activity dimensions which might be implicated in increasing risks.

As differential exposure (at least as measured at present) appears not to be the explanation, it is worth asking what does protect the elderly from crimes. Perhaps the major competing explanations proposed by other commentators (for example, Skogan and Klecka 1976; Hindelang *et al.* 1978; Mawby 1982; Garofalo 1983) would be the elderly's lesser chances of 'association' with offenders, or their lesser 'attractiveness' as victims. According to the association hypothesis, the elderly may be protected from victimisation simply because they are less likely to come into regular contact with offenders than others. The nub of this idea seems to be that victims are not sought out actively by predatory offenders (as is perhaps more implicit in the exposure hypothesis), but that they are identified in the course of rubbing shoulders with potential offenders as a result, say, of living in the same areas. In fact, the relationship between area of residence and victimisation can be examined using B.C.S. data, and preliminary analysis (cf. Hough and Mayhew 1983) has shown that those living in inner city areas are much more likely than others to be the

6

TABLE 5

Risk per 1,000 of Evening 'Street Crime' Victimisation, by Age, Sex, and Number of Evenings Out, Comparing Those Who Travelled 'Riskily' and 'Non-riskily

	EVENINGS OUT 1,2			3+		
	Yng	Middle	Old	Yng	Middle	Old
Risk per 1,000						
Men: non-risky	42	10	–	71	20	3
Men: risky	107	14	10	104	6	5
Women: non-risky	10	5	–	18	14	–
Women: risky	33	10	4	32	8	35
Total	37	9	2	61	15	11
Unweighted nos.						
Sample	1046	1983	627	1098	871	195
Victims	64	44	4	104	20	4

Note: Respondents were given a score of 2 whenever they went out on foot or by public transport (bus, taxi, train, underground) and a score of 1 when they went out by any other mode of travel. Scores were summed and divided by the number of evenings out, to give a continuous variable ranging from 1 to 2. This was then dichotomised to give an even distribution: 'non-risky' = anyone scoring 1.5 or less; 'risky' = anyone scoring over 1.5

victims of street crimes. Analysis of the present sample showed, however, that there was very little variation across the three age groups in the proportion (rather less than a fifth) who lived in inner cities.

The attractiveness hypothesis would posit that the elderly face lower risks because compared with others they are less desirable sexual targets, or because they are seen as less likely to be carrying valuables. In addition, there will rarely be much cachet in victimising old and defenceless people, and perhaps considerable moral prohibitions against it. The attractiveness hypothesis cannot be tested using B.C.S. data since this would require detailed interviews, not with victims but with offenders. However, the nature of the offences to which old people are particularly vulnerable – snatch thefts and pickpocketings – may throw some indirect light on this: though these are usually fairly low reward offences, they are also low risk when committed against old people, who are unlikely to be able to detain an able-bodied offender. In other words, without causing much harm to the victim and without taking much risk, the offender will get some reward for his effort. The less frequent nature of other offences against the elderly may support the attractiveness explanation, in particular the idea that some offenders refrain from choosing the elderly as target.

Practical Implications

This paper cannot address all of the practical issues concerned with the victimisation of the elderly, but it has produced important results that deserve to be more widely known. It is not the case that the elderly are less vulnerable than others to 'street crimes' simply because – on account of fear or not – they venture out of their homes less frequently; even when they go out often, and expose themselves to risky situations, they are much less likely to be victims of street attacks. Moreover – and this is an incidental finding of the analysis – they are not especially at risk from 'the callous young': 51% of offenders against elderly victims were judged to have been over 25, while for young victims, 79% of offenders were in their late teens or early twenties.

Any offence against an elderly person is of course one offence too many, and clearly the average risks for the elderly presented in this paper conceal greater vulnerability in some areas, particularly inner cities. The elderly who are victimised, too, may well merit special help and support, even though one B.C.S. measure of the objective consequences of victimisation showed that only 23% of the present elderly crime victims reported injury compared with 41% of those younger.

Nevertheless, there is some comfort in these findings for a society concerned with protecting the weak and vulnerable. Wider dissemination of the results might also help to counteract some of the elderly's apparently undue fear at least to the extent that this is based on exaggerated ideas about the possibility of victimisation. A powerful countervailing force, of course, will be the frequent media portrayals of elderly victims, playing on those consequences of victimisation which may weigh heavier in the minds of the elderly than risks. Issues such as these need to be further explored – and they are due to be considered in analysis of the 1984 B.C.S. results – before it will be possible to answer the elderly's fears effectively.

The results also suggest that there is no special need for a national crime prevention effort concerned with the elderly and most 'street crimes', though it is possible that action may be required in particular localities in response to particular problems. Neither, incidentally, does it seem that the risks of burglary for the elderly generally are such as to focus burglarly prevention initiatives on them. The 1982 B.C.S. shows that households headed by young or middle-aged people were about 30% more likely to be the victims of buglary than were older households (cf. Goffredson 1984), though whether their lower risks reflect more time spent at home, lower potential rewards, or inhibition on the part of offenders who realise the elderly are in residence are again factors which need more exploration. Apart from burglary, it may be that older people are at greater risk than others of some other crimes such as being defrauded by confidence tricksters (cf. Jones 1984) and, among street crimes themselves, they are more at risk of snatch thefts and pick-pocketings. However, effective remedies for these problems must await much better information about the circumstances in which they occur.[2]

Notes

[1] Logistic regression analysis produced results essentially consistent with the tabular analyses presented in this paper. It showed that age (and sex) made the largest contribution to predicting victimisation rates. Going out was strongly correlated with age, but still made a small, but significant, independent contribution.

[2] This article is subject to Crown Copyright.

References

Balkin, S. (1979) 'Victimization rates, safety and fear of crime', *Social Problems*, *26*, 343–58.

Corrado, R.R., Roesch, R., Glackman, W., Evans, J.L. and Leger, G.J. (1980) 'Life styles and personal victimization: a test of the model with Canadian survey data', *Journal of Crime and Justice*, *3*, 129–39.

van Dijk, J.J.M. and Steinmetz, C. (1983) 'Victimization surveys: beyond measuring the volume of crime', *Victimology*, *8*, 291–301.

Garofalo, J. (1983) 'Lifestyles and victimization: an update' (Paper presented at the 33rd International Course in Criminology, Vancouver, B.C., Canada, March).

Gottfredson, M.R. (1984) *Victims of Crime: the Dimensions of Risk* (Home Office Research Study No. 81), London: H.M.S.O.

Hindelang, M.J., Gottfredson, M.R. and Garofalo, J. (1978) *Victims of Personal Crime: An Empirical Foundation for a theory of Personal Victimisation*, Cambridge, Mass.: Ballinger.

Hough, M. and Mayhew, P. (1983) *The British Crime Survey: First Report* (Home Office Research Study No. 76), London: H.M.S.O.

Jones, G. (1984) *Elderly People and Domestic Crime*, Lancaster, Department of Social Administration: University of Lancaster.

Lindquist, J.H. and Duke, J.M. (1982) 'The elderly victim at risk', *Criminology*, *20*, 113–26.

Mawby, R.I. (1982) 'Crime and the elderly: a review of British and American research', *Current Psychological Reviews*, *2*, 301–10.

Maxfield, M.G. (1984) *Fear of Crime in England and Wales* (Home Office Research Study No. 78), London: H.M.S.O.

Ministry of the Solicitor General (1983) *Who are the Victims?* (User Report No. 1 on the Canadian Urban Victimization Survey), Ottawa: Research and Statistics Group, Ministry of the Solicitor General.

Skogan, W.G. and Klecka, W.R. (1976) 'The fear of crime' (Paper presented to the American Political Science Association, Washington).

Smith, S.J. (1983) 'Public policy and the effects of crime in the inner city: a British example', *Urban Studies*, *20*, 229–40.

Stafford, M.C. and Galle, O.R. (1984) 'Victimization rates, exposure to risk, and fear of crime', *Criminology*, *22*, 173–85.

U.S. Department of Justice (1984) *Report to the Nation on Crime and Justice: The Data* (Bureau of Justice Statistics Report, NCJ–87068), Washington, D.C.: Government Printing Office.

Wood, D.S. (1983) *British Crime Survey: Technical Report*, London: Social and Community Planning Research.

[8]

SOCIAL CHANGE AND CRIME RATE TRENDS:
A ROUTINE ACTIVITY APPROACH*

LAWRENCE E. COHEN AND MARCUS FELSON

University of Illinois, Urbana

American Sociological Review 1979, Vol. 44 (August):588-608

In this paper we present a "routine activity approach" for analyzing crime rate trends and cycles. Rather than emphasizing the characteristics of offenders, with this approach we concentrate upon the circumstances in which they carry out predatory criminal acts. Most criminal acts require convergence in space and time of *likely offenders, suitable targets* and the *absence of capable guardians* against crime. Human ecological theory facilitates an investigation into the way in which social structure produces this convergence, hence allowing illegal activities to feed upon the legal activities of everyday life. In particular, we hypothesize that the dispersion of activities away from households and families increases the opportunity for crime and thus generates higher crime rates. A variety of data is presented in support of the hypothesis, which helps explain crime rate trends in the United States 1947-1974 as a byproduct of changes in such variables as labor force participation and single-adult households.

INTRODUCTION

In its summary report the National Commission on the Causes and Prevention of Violence (1969: xxxvii) presents an important sociological paradox:

> Why, we must ask, have urban violent crime rates increased substantially during the past decade when the conditions that are supposed to cause violent crime have not worsened—have, indeed, generally improved?

The Bureau of the Census, in its latest report on trends in social and economic conditions in metropolitan areas, states that most "indicators of well-being point toward progress in the cities since 1960." Thus, for example, the proportion of blacks in cities who completed high school rose from 43 percent in 1960 to 61 percent in 1968; unemployment rates dropped significantly between 1959 and 1967 and the median family income of blacks in cities increased from 61 percent to 68 percent of the median white

family income during the same period. Also during the same period the number of persons living below the legally-defined poverty level in cities declined from 11.3 million to 8.3 million.

Despite the general continuation of these trends in social and economic conditions in the United States, the *Uniform Crime Report* (FBI, 1975:49) indicates that between 1960 and 1975 reported rates of robbery, aggravated assault, forcible rape and homicide increased by 263%, 164%, 174%, and 188%, respectively. Similar property crime rate increases reported during this same period[1] (e.g., 200% for burglary rate) suggest that the paradox noted by the Violence Commission applies to nonviolent offenses as well.

---

* Address all communications to: Lawrence E. Cohen; Department of Sociology; University of Illinois; Urbana, IL 61801.

For their comments, we thank David J. Bordua, Ross M. Stolzenberg, Christopher S. Dunn, Kenneth C. Land, Robert Schoen, Amos Hawley, and an anonymous reviewer. Funding for this study was provided by these United States Government grants: National Institute for Mental Health 1-R01-MH31117-01;National Science Foundation, SOC-77-13261; and United States Army RI/DAHC 19-76-G-0016. The authors' name order is purely alphabetical.

[1] Though official data severely underestimate crime, they at least provide a rough indicator of trends over time in the volume of several major felonies. The possibility that these data also reflect trends in rates at which offenses are reported to the police has motivated extensive victimology research (see Nettler, 1974; and Hindelang, 1976, for a review). This work consistently finds that seriousness of offense is the strongest determinant of citizen reporting to law enforcement officials (Skogan, 1976: 145; Hindelang, 1976: 401). Hence the upward trend in official crime rates since 1960 in the U.S. may reflect increases in *both* the volume and seriousness of offenses. Though disaggregating these two components may not be feasible, one may wish to interpret observed trends as generated largely by both.

SOCIAL CHANGE AND CRIME RATE TRENDS   589

In the present paper we consider these paradoxical trends in crime rates in terms of changes in the ''routine activities'' of everyday life. We believe the structure of such activities influences criminal opportunity and therefore affects trends in a class of crimes we refer to as *direct-contact predatory violations*. Predatory violations are defined here as illegal acts in which ''someone definitely and intentionally takes or damages the person or property of another'' (Glaser, 1971:4). Further, this analysis is confined to those predatory violations involving direct physical contact between at least one offender and at least one person or object which that offender attempts to take or damage.

We argue that structural changes in routine activity patterns can influence crime rates by affecting the convergence in space and time of the three minimal elements of direct-contact predatory violations: (1) motivated offenders, (2) suitable targets, and (3) the absence of capable guardians against a violation. We further argue that the lack of any one of these elements is sufficient to prevent the successful completion of a direct-contact predatory crime, and that the convergence in time and space of suitable targets and the absence of capable guardians may even lead to large increases in crime rates without necessarily requiring any increase in the structural conditions that motivate individuals to engage in crime. That is, if the proportion of motivated offenders or even suitable targets were to remain stable in a community, changes in routine activities could nonetheless alter the likelihood of their convergence in space and time, thereby creating more opportunities for crimes to occur. Control therefore becomes critical. If controls through routine activities were to decrease, illegal predatory activities could then be likely to increase. In the process of developing this explanation and evaluating its consistency with existing data, we relate our approach to classical human ecological concepts and to several earlier studies.

The Structure of Criminal Activity

Sociological knowledge of how community structure generates illegal acts has made little progress since Shaw and McKay and their colleagues (1929) published their pathbreaking work, *Delinquency Areas*. Variations in crime rates over space long have been recognized (e.g., see Guerry, 1833; Quètelet, 1842), and current evidence indicates that the pattern of these relationships within metropolitan communities has persisted (Reiss, 1976). Although most spatial research is quite useful for describing crime rate patterns and providing post hoc explanations, these works seldom consider—conceptually or empirically—the fundamental human ecological character of illegal acts as *events* which occur at specific locations in *space* and *time*, involving specific persons and/or objects. These and related concepts can help us to develop an extension of the human ecological analysis to the problem of explaining changes in crime rates over time. Unlike many criminological inquiries, we do not examine why individuals or groups are inclined criminally, but rather we take criminal inclination as given and examine the manner in which the spatio-temporal organization of social activities helps people to translate their criminal inclinations into action. Criminal violations are treated here as routine activities which share many attributes of, and are interdependent with, other routine activities. This interdependence between the structure of illegal activities and the organization of everyday sustenance activities leads us to consider certain concepts from human ecological literature.

Selected Concepts from Hawley's Human Ecological Theory

While criminologists traditionally have concentrated on the *spatial* analysis of crime rates within metropolitan communities, they seldom have considered the *temporal* interdependence of these acts. In his classic theory of human ecology, Amos Hawley (1950) treats the community not simply as a unit of territory but rather as an organization of symbiotic and commensalistic relationships as human activities are performed over both space and time.

Hawley identified three important temporal components of community structure: (1) *rhythm*, the regular periodicity with which events occur, as with the rhythm of travel activity; (2) *tempo*, the number of events per unit of time, such as the number of criminal violations per day on a given street; and (3) *timing*, the coordination among different activities which are more or less interdependent, such as the coordination of an offender's rhythms with those of a victim (Hawley, 1950:289; the examples are ours). These components of temporal organization, often neglected in criminological research, prove useful in analyzing how illegal tasks are performed—a utility which becomes more apparent after noting the spatio-temporal requirements of illegal activities.

The Minimal Elements of Direct-Contact Predatory Violations

As we previously stated, despite their great diversity, direct-contact predatory violations share some important requirements which facilitate analysis of their structure. Each successfully completed violation minimally requires an *offender* with both criminal inclinations and the ability to carry out those inclinations, a person or object providing a *suitable target* for the offender, and *absence of guardians* capable of preventing violations. We emphasize that the lack of any one of these elements normally is sufficient to prevent such violations from occurring.[2] Though guardianship is implicit in everyday life, it usually is marked by the absence of violations; hence it is easy to overlook. While police action is analyzed widely, guardianship by ordinary citizens of one another and of property as they go about routine activities may be one of the most neglected elements in sociological research on crime, especially since it links seemingly unre-

lated social roles and relationships to the occurrence or absence of illegal acts.

The conjunction of these minimal elements can be used to assess how social structure may affect the tempo of each type of violation. That is, the probability that a violation will occur at any specific time and place might be taken as a function of the convergence of likely offenders and suitable targets in the absence of capable guardians. Through consideration of how trends and fluctuations in social conditions affect the frequency of this convergence of criminogenic circumstances, an explanation of temporal trends in crime rates can be constructed.

The Ecological Nature of Illegal Acts

This ecological analysis of direct-contact predatory violations is intended to be more than metaphorical. In the context of such violations, people, gaining and losing sustenance, struggle among themselves for property, safety, territorial hegemony, sexual outlet, physical control, and sometimes for survival itself. The interdependence between offenders and victims can be viewed as a predatory relationship between functionally dissimilar individuals or groups. Since predatory violations fail to yield any net gain in sustenance for the larger community, they can only be sustained by feeding upon other activities. As offenders cooperate to increase their efficiency at predatory violations and as potential victims organize their resistance to these violations, both groups apply the symbiotic principle to improve their sustenance position. On the other hand, potential victims of predatory crime may take evasive actions which encourage offenders to pursue targets other than their own. Since illegal activities must feed upon other activities, the spatial and temporal structure of routine legal activities should play an important role in determining the location, type and quantity of illegal acts occurring in a given community or society. Moreover, one can analyze how the structure of community organization as well as the level of technology in a society provide the circumstances under which crime can thrive. For example, technology and organization

[2] The analytical distinction between target and guardian is not important in those cases where a personal target engages in self-protection from direct-contact predatory violations. We leave open for the present the question of whether a guardian is effective or ineffective in all situations. We also allow that various guardians may primarily supervise offenders, targets or both. These are questions for future examination.

affect the capacity of persons with criminal inclinations to overcome their targets, as well as affecting the ability of guardians to contend with potential offenders by using whatever protective tools, weapons and skills they have at their disposal. Many technological advances designed for legitimate purposes—including the automobile, small power tools, hunting weapons, highways, telephones, etc.— may enable offenders to carry out their own work more effectively or may assist people in protecting their own or someone else's person or property.

Not only do routine legitimate activities often provide the wherewithal to commit offenses or to guard against others who do so, but they also provide offenders with suitable targets. Target suitability is likely to reflect such things as value (i.e., the material or symbolic desirability of a personal or property target for offenders), physical visibility, access, and the inertia of a target against illegal treatment by offenders (including the weight, size, and attached or locked features of property inhibiting its illegal removal and the physical capacity of personal victims to resist attackers with or without weapons). Routine production activities probably affect the suitability of consumer goods for illegal removal by determining their value and weight. Daily activities may affect the location of property and personal targets in visible and accessible places at particular times. These activities also may cause people to have on hand objects that can be used as weapons for criminal acts or self-protection or to be preoccupied with tasks which reduce their capacity to discourage or resist offenders.

While little is known about conditions that affect the convergence of potential offenders, targets and guardians, this is a potentially rich source of propositions about crime rates. For example, daily work activities separate many people from those they trust and the property they value. Routine activities also bring together at various times of day or night persons of different background, sometimes in the presence of facilities, tools or weapons which influence the commission or avoidance of illegal acts. Hence, the timing of work, schooling and leisure may

be of central importance for explaining crime rates.

The ideas presented so far are not new, but they frequently are overlooked in the theoretical literature on crime. Although an investigation of the literature uncovers significant examples of descriptive and practical data related to the routine activities upon which illegal behavior feeds, these data seldom are treated within an analytical framework. The next section reviews some of this literature.

A major advantage of the routine activity approach presented here is that it helps assemble some diverse and previously unconnected criminological analyses into a single substantive framework. This framework also serves to link illegal and legal activities, as illustrated by a few examples of descriptive accounts of criminal activity.

Descriptive Analyses

There are several descriptive analyses of criminal acts in criminological literature. For example, Thomas Reppetto's (1974) study, *Residential Crime*, considers how residents supervise their neighborhoods and streets and limit access of possible offenders. He also considers how distance of households from the central city reduces risks of criminal victimization. Reppetto's evidence—consisting of criminal justice records, observations of comparative features of geographic areas, victimization survey data and offender interviews—indicates that offenders are very likely to use burglary tools and to have at least minimal technical skills, that physical characteristics of dwellings affect their victimization rates, that the rhythms of residential crime rate patterns are marked (often related to travel and work patterns of residents), and that visibility of potential sites of crime affects the risk that crimes will occur there. Similar findings are reported by Pope's (1977a; 1977b) study of burglary in California and by Scarr's (1972) study of burglary in and around the District of Columbia. In addition, many studies report that architectural and environmental design as well as community crime programs serve to decrease target suitability and increase capable guardianship (see, for example, Newman, 1973; Jeffery, 1971; Washnis, 1976), while many biographical or autobiographical descriptions of illegal activities note that lawbreakers take into account the nature of property and/or the structure of human activities as they go about their illegal work (see, e.g., Chambliss, 1972; Klockars, 1974; Sutherland, 1937; Letkemann, 1973; Jackson, 1969; Martin, 1952; Maurer, 1964; Cameron, 1964; Williamson, 1968).

Evidence that the spatio-temporal organization of society affects patterns of crime can be found in several sources. Strong variations in specific predatory crime rates from hour to hour, day to day, and month to month are reported often (e.g., Wolfgang, 1958; Amir, 1971; Reppetto, 1974; Scarr, 1972; FBI, 1975; 1976), and these variations appear to correspond to the various tempos of the related legitimate activities upon which they feed. Also at a microsociological level, Short and Strodtbeck (1965: chaps. 5 and 11) describe opportunities for violent confrontations of gang boys and other community residents which arise in the context of community leisure patterns, such as "quarter parties" in black communities, and the importance, in the calculus of decision making employed by participants in such episodes, of low probabilities of legal intervention. In addition, a wealth of empirical evidence indicates strong spatial variations over community areas in crime and delinquency rates[3] (for an excellent discussion and re-

view of the literature on ecological studies of crimes, see Wilks, 1967). Recently, Albert Reiss (1976) has argued convincingly that these spatial variations (despite some claims to the contrary) have been supported consistently by both official and unofficial sources of data. Reiss further cites victimization studies which indicate that offenders are very likely to select targets not far from their own residence (see USDJ, 1974a; 1974b; 1974c).

Macrolevel Analyses of Crime Trends and Cycles

Although details about how crime occurs are intrinsically interesting, the important analytical task is to learn from these details how illegal activities carve their niche within the larger system of activities. This task is not an easy one. For example, attempts by Bonger (1916), Durkheim (1951; 1966), Henry and Short (1954), and Fleisher (1966) to link the rate of illegal activities to the economic condition of a society have not been completely successful. Empirical tests of the relationships postulated in the above studies have produced inconsistent results which some observers view as an indication that the level of crime is not related systematically to the economic conditions of a society (Mansfield et al., 1974: 463; Cohen and Felson, 1979).

It is possible that the wrong economic and social factors have been employed in these macro studies of crime. Other researchers have provided stimulating alternative descriptions of how social change affects the criminal opportunity structure, thereby influencing crime rates in particular societies. For example, at the beginning of the nineteenth century, Patrick Colquhoun (1800) presented a detailed, lucid description and analysis of crime in the London metropolitan area and suggestions for its control. He assembled substantial evidence that London was experiencing a massive crime wave attributable to a great increment in the assemblage and

---

[3] One such ecological study by Sarah Boggs (1965) presents some similar ideas in distinguishing *familiarity* of offenders with their targets and *profitability* of targets as two elements of crime occurrence. Boggs's work stands apart from much research on the ecology of crime in its consideration of crime occurrence rates separately from offender rates. The former consist of the number of offenses committed in a given area per number of suitable targets within that area (as estimated by various indicators). The latter considers the residence of offenders in computing the number of offenders per unit of population. Boggs examines the correlations between crime occurrence rates and offender rates for several of-

fenses in St. Louis and shows that the two are often independent. It appears from her analysis that *both* target and offender characteristics play a central role in the location of illegal activity.

SOCIAL CHANGE AND CRIME RATE TRENDS   593

movement of valuable goods through its ports and terminals.

A similar examination of crime in the period of the English industrial expansion was carried out by a modern historian, J. J. Tobias (1967), whose work on the history of crime in nineteenth century England is perhaps the most comprehensive effort to isolate those elements of social change affecting crime in an expanding industrial nation. Tobias details how far-reaching changes in transportation, currency, technology, commerce, merchandising, poverty, housing, and the like, had tremendous repercussions on the amount and type of illegal activities committed in the nineteenth century. His thesis is that structural transformations either facilitated or impeded the opportunities to engage in illegal activities. In one of the few empirical studies of how recent social change affects the opportunity structure for crime in the United States, Leroy Gould (1969) demonstrated that the increase in the circulation of money and the availability of automobiles between 1921 and 1965 apparently led to an increase in the rate of bank robberies and auto thefts, respectively. Gould's data suggest that these relationships are due more to the abundance of opportunities to perpetrate the crimes than to short-term fluctuations in economic activities.

Although the sociological and historical studies cited in this section have provided some useful *empirical* generalizations and important insights into the incidence of crime, it is fair to say that they have not articulated systematically the *theoretical* linkages between routine legal activities and illegal endeavors. Thus, these studies cannot explain how changes in the larger social structure generate changes in the opportunity to engage in predatory crime and hence account for crime rate trends.[4]

To do so requires a conceptual framework such as that sketched in the preceding section. Before attempting to demonstrate the feasibility of this approach with macrolevel data, we examine available microlevel data for its consistency with the major assumptions of this approach.

Microlevel Assumptions of the Routine Activity Approach

The theoretical approach taken here specifies that crime rate trends in the post-World War II United States are related to patterns of what we have called routine activities. We define these as any recurrent and prevalent activities which provide for basic population and individual needs, whatever their biological or cultural origins. Thus routine activities would include formalized work, as well as the provision of standard food, shelter, sexual outlet, leisure, social interaction, learning and childrearing. These activities may go well beyond the minimal levels needed to prevent a population's extinction, so long as their prevalence and recurrence makes them a part of everyday life.

Routine activities may occur (1) at home, (2) in jobs away from home, and (3) in other activities away from home. The latter may involve primarily household members or others. We shall argue that, since World War II, the United States has experienced a major shift of routine activities away from the first category into the remaining ones, especially those nonhousehold activities involving nonhousehold members. In particular, we shall argue that this shift in the structure of routine activities increases the probability that motivated offenders will converge in space and time with suitable targets in the absence of capable guardians, hence contributing to significant increases in the

---

[4] The concept of the opportunity for crime contained in the above research and in this study differs considerably from the traditional sociological usage of the *differential opportunity* concept. For example, Cloward and Ohlin (1960) employed this term in discussing how legitimate and illegitimate opportunities affect the resolution of adjustment problems leading to gang delinquency. From their viewpoint, this resolution depends upon the kind of social support for one or another type of illegitimate activity that is

given at different points in the social structure (Cloward and Ohlin, 1960: 151). Rather than circumstantial determinants of crime, they use differential opportunity to emphasize structural features which motivate offenders to perpetrate certain types of crimes. Cloward and Ohlin are largely silent on the interaction of this motivation with target suitability and guardianship as this interaction influences crime rates.

594   AMERICAN SOCIOLOGICAL REVIEW

direct-contact predatory crime rates over these years.

If the routine activity approach is valid, then we should expect to find evidence for a number of empirical relationships regarding the nature and distribution of predatory violations. For example, we would expect routine activities performed within or near the home and among family or other primary groups to entail lower risk of criminal victimization because they enhance guardianship capabilities. We should also expect that routine daily activities affect the location of property and personal targets in visible and accessible places at particular times, thereby influencing their risk of victimization. Furthermore, by determining their size and weight and in some cases their value, routine production activities should affect the suitability of consumer goods for illegal removal. Finally, if the routine activity approach is useful for explaining the paradox presented earlier, we should find that the circulation of people and property, the size and weight of consumer items etc., will parallel changes in crime rate trends for the post-World War II United States.

The veracity of the routine activity approach can be assessed by analyses of both microlevel and macrolevel interdependencies of human activities. While consistency at the former level may appear noncontroversial, or even obvious, one nonetheless needs to show that the approach does not contradict existing data before proceeding to investigate the latter level.

EMPIRICAL ASSESSMENT

Circumstances and Location of Offenses

The routine activity approach specifies that household and family activities entail lower risk of criminal victimization than nonhousehold-nonfamily activities, despite the problems in measuring the former.[5]

National estimates from large-scale government victimization surveys in 1973 and 1974 support this generalization (see methodological information in Hindelang et al., 1976: Appendix 6). Table 1 presents several incident-victimization rates per 100,000 population ages 12 and older. Clearly, the rates in Panels A and B are far lower at or near home than elsewhere and far lower among relatives than others. The data indicate that risk of victimization varies directly with social distance between offender and victim. Panel C of this table indicates, furthermore, that risk of lone victimization far exceeds the risk of victimization for groups. These relationships are strengthened by considering time budget evidence that, on the average, Americans spend 16.26 hours per day at home, 1.38 hours on streets, in parks, etc., and 6.36 hours in other places (Szalai, 1972:795). Panel D of Table 1 presents our estimates of victimization per billion person-hours spent in such locations.[6] For example, personal larceny

---

[5] Recent research indicates the existence of substantial quantities of family violence which remains outside of UCR data (see annotated bibliography of family violence in Lystad, 1974). While we cannot rule out the likelihood that much family violence is concealed from victimization surveys, the latter capture information absent from police data and still

indicate that nonfamily members are usually much more dangerous than family members are to each other (see text). Also, when family violence leads to death, its suppression becomes quite difficult. The murder circumstances data indicate that about two-thirds of killings involve nonrelatives. Without denying the evidence that the level of family violence is far greater than police reports would indicate, available data also suggest that time spent in family activities within households incurs less risk of victimization than many alternative activities in other places. In addition, many of the most *common* offenses (such as robbery and burglary) always have been recognized as usually involving nonfamily members.

[6] Billion person-hours can easily be conceptualized as 1,000,000 persons spending 1,000 hours each (or about 42 days) in a given location (Szalai, 1972:795). Fox obtained these data from a 1966 time budget study in 44 American cities. The study was carried out by the Survey Research Center, the University of Michigan. We combined four subsamples in computing our figures. We combined activities into three locations, as follows: (1) at or just outside home; (2) at another's home, restaurants or bars, or indoor leisure; (3) in streets, parks, or outdoor leisure. Our computing formula was

$$Q = [(R \div 10^5) \div (A \cdot 365)] \cdot 10^9,$$

where Q is the risk per billion person-hours; R is the victimization rate, reported per 10^5 persons in Hindelang et al. (1976: Table 318); A is the hours spent per location calculated from Szalai (1972: 795); 365 is the multiplier to cover a year's exposure to risk; and 10^9 converts risk per person-hour to billion person-hours.

SOCIAL CHANGE AND CRIME RATE TRENDS   595

Table 1. Incident-Specific Risk Rates for Rape, Robbery, Assault and Personal Larceny with Contact, United States, 1974

A.*		Rape	Robbery	Assault	Personal Larceny with Contact	Total
PLACE OF	In or near home	63	129	572	75	839
RESIDENCE	Elsewhere	119	584	1,897	1,010	3,610
B. *						
VICTIM-	(Lone Offender)					
OFFENDER	Relative	7	13	158	5	183
RELATIONSHIP	Well Known	23	30	333	30	416
	Casual Acquaintance	11	26	308	25	370
	Don't Know/Sight Only	106	227	888	616	1,837
	(Multiple Offender)					
	Any known	10***	68	252	43	373
	All strangers	25***	349	530	366	1,270
C. *						
NUMBER	one	179	647	2,116	1,062	4,004
OF	Two	3	47	257	19	326
VICTIMS	Three	0	13	53	3	09
	Four Plus	0	6	43	1	50
D. **						
LOCATION AND	Home, Stranger	61	147	345	103	654
RELATIONSHIP	Home, Nonstranger	45	74	620	22	761
(sole	Street, Stranger	1,370	7,743	15,684	7,802	32,460
offender	Street, Nonstranger	179	735	5,777	496	7,167
only)	Elsewhere, Stranger	129	513	1,934	2,455	4,988
	Elsewhere, Nonstranger	47	155	1,544	99	1,874

   * Calculated from Handelang et al., 1977: Tables 3.16, 3.18, 3.27, 3.28. Rates are per 100,000 persons ages 12 and over.
   ** See fn. 6 for source. Rates are per billion person-hours in stated locations.
   *** Based on white data only due to lack of suitable sample size for nonwhites as victims of rape with multiple offenders.

rates (with contact) are 350 times higher at the hands of strangers in streets than at the hands of nonstrangers at home. Separate computations from 1973 victimization data (USDJ, 1976: Table 48) indicate that there were two motor vehicle thefts per million vehicle-hours parked at or near home, 55 per million vehicle-hours in streets, parks, playgrounds, school grounds or parking lots, and 12 per million vehicle-hours elsewhere. While the direction of these relationships is not surprising, their magnitudes should be noted. It appears that risk of criminal victimization varies dramatically among the circumstances and locations in which people place themselves and their property.

Target Suitability

Another assumption of the routine activity approach is that target suitability influences the occurrence of direct-contact predatory violations. Though we lack data to disaggregate all major components of target suitability (i.e., value, visibility, accessibility and inertia), together they imply that expensive and movable durables, such as vehicles and electronic appliances, have the highest risk of illegal removal.

As a specific case in point, we compared the 1975 composition of stolen property reported in the Uniform Crime Report (FBI, 1976: Tables 26–7) with national data on personal consumer expenditures for goods (CEA, 1976: Tables 13–16) and to appliance industry estimates of the value of shipments the same year (*Merchandising Week*, 1976). We calculated that $26.44 in motor vehicles and parts were stolen for each $100 of these goods consumed in 1975, while $6.82 worth of electronic appliances were stolen per $100 consumed. Though these estimates are subject to error in citizen and police estimation, what is important here is their size relative to other rates. For example, only

8¢ worth of nondurables and 12¢ worth of furniture and nonelectronic household durables were stolen per $100 of each category consumed, the motor vehicle risk being, respectively, 330 and 220 times as great. Though we lack data on the "stocks" of goods subject to risk, these "flow" data clearly support our assumption that vehicles and electronic appliances are greatly overrepresented in thefts.

The 1976 Buying Guide issue of *Consumer Reports* (1975) indicates why electronic appliances are an excellent retail value for a thief. For example, a Panasonic car tape player is worth $30 per lb., and a Phillips phonograph cartridge is valued at over $5,000 per lb., while large appliances such as refrigerators and washing machines are only worth $1 to $3 per lb. Not surprisingly, burglary data for the District of Columbia in 1969 (Scarr, 1972: Table 9) indicate that home entertainment items alone constituted nearly four times as many stolen items as clothing, food, drugs, liquor, and tobacco combined and nearly eight times as many stolen items as office supplies and equipment. In addition, 69% of national thefts classified in 1975 (FBI, 1976: Tables 1, 26) involve automobiles, their parts or accessories, and thefts from automobiles or thefts of bicycles. Yet radio and television sets plus electronic components and accessories totaled only 0.10% of the total truckload tonnage terminated in 1973 by intercity motor carriers, while passenger cars, motor vehicle parts and accessories, motorcycles, bicycles, and their parts, totaled only 5.5% of the 410 million truckload tons terminated (ICC, 1974). Clearly, portable and movable durables are reported stolen in great disproportion to their share of the value and weight of goods circulating in the United States.

Family Activities and Crime Rates

One would expect that persons living in single-adult households and those employed outside the home are less obligated to confine their time to family activities within households. From a routine activity perspective, these persons and their households should have higher rates of predatory criminal victimization. We also expect that adolescents and young adults who are perhaps more likely to engage in peer group activities rather than family activities will have higher rates of criminal victimization. Finally, married persons should have lower rates than others. Tables 2 and 3 largely confirm these expectations (with the exception of personal larceny with contact). Examining these tables, we note that victimization rates appear to be related inversely to age and are lower for persons in "less active" statuses (e.g., keeping house, unable to work, retired) and persons in intact marriages. A notable exception is indicated in Table 2, where persons unable to work appear more likely to be victimized by rape, robbery and personal larceny with contact than are other "inactive persons." Unemployed persons also have unusually high rates of victimization. However, these rates are consistent with the routine activity approach offered here: the high rates of victimization suffered by the unemployed may reflect their residential proximity to high concentrations of potential offenders as well as their age and racial composition, while handicapped persons have high risk of personal victimization because they are less able to resist motivated offenders. Nonetheless, persons who keep house have noticeably lower rates of victimization than those who are employed, unemployed, in school or in the armed forces.

As Table 3 indicates, burglary and robbery victimization rates are about twice as high for persons living in single-adult households as for other persons in each age group examined. Other victimization data (USDJ, 1976: Table 21) indicate that, while household victimization rates tend to vary directly with household size, larger households have lower rates per person. For example, the total household victimization rates (including burglary, household larceny, and motor vehicle theft) per 1,000 households were 168 for single-person households and 326 for households containing six or more persons. Hence, six people distributed over six single-person households experience an average of 1,008 household victimizations, more than three times as many as

SOCIAL CHANGE AND CRIME RATE TRENDS   597

Table 2. Selected Status-Specific Personal Victimization Rates for the United States (per 100,000 Persons in Each Category)

Variables and Sources	Victim Category	Rape	Robbery	Assault	Personal Larceny with Contact	Personal Larceny without Contact
A. AGE	12–15	147	1,267	3,848	311	16,355
(Source:	16–19	248	1,127	5,411	370	15,606
Hindelang, et al., 1977:	20–24	209	1,072	4,829	337	14,295
Table 310, 1974	25–34	135	703	3,023	263	10,354
rates	35–49	21	547	1,515	256	7,667
	50–64	33	411	731	347	4,588
	65+	20	388	492	344	1,845
B. MAJOR	(Male 16+)					
ACTIVITY OF	Armed Forces	—	1,388	4,153	118	16,274
VICTIM	Employed	—	807	3,285	252	10,318
(Source:	Unemployed	—	2,179	7,984	594	15,905
Hindelang, et al., 1977:	Keep house	—	0	2,475	463	3,998
Table 313, 1974	In school	—	1,362	5,984	493	17,133
rates)	Unable to work	—	1,520	2,556	623	3,648
	Retired	—	578	662	205	2,080
	(Female 16+					
	Keep house	116	271	978	285	4,433
	Employed	156	529	1,576	355	9,419
	Unemployed	798	772	5,065	461	12,338
	In School	417	430	2,035	298	12,810
	Unable to work	287	842	741	326	1,003
	Retired	120	172	438	831	1,571
C. MARITAL STATUS	(Male 12+)					
(Source:USDJ:	Never Married	—	1,800	5,870	450	16,450
1977, Table 5,	Married	—	550	2,170	170	7,660
1973 rates)	Separated/Divorced	—	2,270	5,640	1,040	12,960
	Widowed	—	1,150	1,500	—	4,120
	(Female 12+)					
	Never Married	360	580	2,560	400	12,880
	Married	70	270	910	220	6,570
	Separated/Divorced	540	1,090	4,560	640	9,130
	Widowed	—	450	590	480	2,460

Line indicates too few offenses for accurate estimates of rate. However, rates in these cells are usually small.

one six-person household. Moreover, age of household head has a strong relationship to a household's victimization rate for these crimes. For households headed

Table 3. Robbery-Burglary Victimization Rates by Ages and Number of Adults in Household, 1974 and 1976 General Social Survey

	Number of Adults in Household			
Age	One		Two or More	Ratio
18–35	0.200	(140)	0.095 (985)	2.11
36–55	0.161	(112)	0.079 (826)	2.04
56 and over	0.107	(262)	0.061 (640)	1.76
All Ages	0.144	(514)	0.081 (2451)	1.78

(Numbers in parentheses are the base for computing risk rates.)
Source: Calculated from 1974 and 1976 General Social Survey, National Opinion Research Center, University of Chicago.

by persons under 20, the motor vehicle theft rate is nine times as high, and the burglary and household larceny rates four times as high as those for households headed by persons 65 and over (USDJ, 1976: Table 9).

While the data presented in this section were not collected originally for the purpose of testing the routine activity approach, our efforts to rework them for these purposes have proven fruitful. The routine activity approach is consistent with the data examined and, in addition, helps to accommodate within a rather simple and coherent analytical framework certain findings which, though not necessarily new, might otherwise be attributed only "descriptive" significance. In the next section, we examine macrosocial

AMERICAN SOCIOLOGICAL REVIEW

trends as they relate to trends in crime rates.

CHANGING TRENDS IN ROUTINE ACTIVITY STRUCTURE AND PARALLEL TRENDS IN CRIME RATES

The main thesis presented here is that the dramatic increase in the reported crime rates in the U.S. since 1960 is linked to changes in the routine activity structure of American society and to a corresponding increase in target suitability and decrease in guardian presence. If such a thesis has validity, then we should be able to identify these social trends and show how they relate to predatory criminal victimization rates.

Trends in Human Activity Patterns

The decade 1960–1970 experienced noteworthy trends in the activities of the American population. For example, the percent of the population consisting of female college students increased 118% (USBC, 1975: Table 225). Married female labor force participant rates increased 31% (USBC, 1975: Table 563), while the percent of the population living as primary individuals increased by 34% (USBC, 1975: Table 51; see also Kobrin, 1976). We gain some further insight into changing routine activity patterns by comparing hourly data for 1960 and 1971 on households *unattended* by persons ages 14 or over when U.S. census interviewers first called (see Table 4). These data suggest that the proportion of households unattended at 8 A.M. increased by almost half between 1960 and 1971. One also finds increases in rates of out-of-town travel, which provides greater opportunity for both daytime and nighttime burglary of residences. Between 1960 and 1970, there was a 72% increase in state and national park visits per capita (USBC, 1975), an 144% increase in the percent of plant workers eligible for three weeks vacation (BLS, 1975: Table 116), and an 184% increase in overseas travellers per 100,000 population (USBC, 1975: Table 366). The National Travel Survey, conducted as part of the U.S. Census Bureau's Census of Transportation, confirms the general

Table 4. Proportion of Households Unattended by Anyone 14 Years Old or Over by Time of Day during First Visit by Census Bureau Interviewer, 1960 and 1971

Time of day	1960 Census	November, 1971 Current Pop. Survey	Percent Change
8:00– 8:59 a.m.	29%	43	+48.9%
9:00– 9:59 a.m.	29	44	+58
10:00–10:59 a.m.	31	42	+36
11:00–11:59 a.m.	32	41	+28
12:00–12:59 p.m.	32	41	+28
1:00– 1:59 p.m.	31	43	+39
2:00– 2:59 p.m.	33	43	+30
3:00– 3:59 p.m.	30	33	+10
4:00– 4:59 p.m.	28	30	+ 7
5:00– 5:59 p.m.	22	26	+18
6:00– 6:59 p.m.	22	25	+14
7:00– 7:50 p.m.	20	29	+45
8:00– 8:59 p.m.	24	22	– 8

Source: Calculated from USBC (1973b: Table A).

trends, tallying an 81% increase in the number of vacations taken by Americans from 1967 to 1972, a five-year period (USBC, 1973a: Introduction).

The dispersion of activities away from households appears to be a major recent social change. Although this decade also experienced an important 31% increase in the percent of the population ages 15–24, age structure change was only one of many social trends occurring during the period, especially trends in the circulation of people and property in American society.[7]

The importance of the changing activity structure is underscored by taking a brief look at demographic changes between the years 1970 and 1975, a period of continuing crime rate increments. Most of the recent changes in age structure relevant to crime rates already had occurred by 1970; indeed, the proportion of the population ages 15–24 increased by only 6% between 1970 and 1975, compared with a 15% increase during the five years 1965 to 1970. On the other hand, major changes in the structure of routine activities continued

---

[7] While the more sophisticated treatments of the topic have varied somewhat in their findings, most recent studies attempting to link crime rate increases to the changing age structure of the American population have found that the latter account for a relatively limited proportion of the general crime trend (see, for example, Sagi and Wellford, 1968; Ferdinand, 1970; and Wellford, 1973).

SOCIAL CHANGE AND CRIME RATE TRENDS   599

during these years. For example, in only five years, the estimated proportion of the population consisting of husband-present, married women in the labor force households increased by 11%, while the estimated number of non-husband-wife households per 100,000 population increased from 9,150 to 11,420, a 25% increase (USBC, 1976: Tables 50, 276; USBC, 1970–1975). At the same time, the percent of population enrolled in higher education increased 16% between 1970 and 1975.

Related Property Trends and Their Relation to Human Activity Patterns

Many of the activity trends mentioned above normally involve significant investments in durable goods. For example, the dispersion of population across relatively more households (especially non-husband-wife households) enlarges the market for durable goods such as television sets and automobiles. Women participating in the labor force and both men and women enrolled in college provide a market for automobiles. Both work and travel often involve the purchase of major movable or portable durables and their use away from home.

Considerable data are available which indicate that sales of consumer goods changed dramatically between 1960 and 1970 (as did their size and weight), hence providing more suitable property available for theft. For example, during this decade, constant-dollar personal consumer expenditures in the United States for motor vehicles and parts increased by 71%, while constant-dollar expenditures for other durables increased by 105% (calculated from CEA, 1976: Table B-16). In addition, electronic household appliances and small houseware shipments increased from 56.2 to 119.7 million units (*Electrical Merchandising Week,* 1964; *Merchandising Week,* 1973). During the same decade, appliance imports increased in value by 681% (USBC, 1975: Table 1368).

This same period appears to have spawned a revolution in small durable product design which further feeds the opportunity for crime to occur. Relevant data from the 1960 and 1970 Sears catalogs

on the weight of many consumer durable goods were examined. Sears is the nation's largest retailer and its policy of purchasing and relabeling standard manufactured goods makes its catalogs a good source of data on widely merchandised consumer goods. The lightest television listed for sale in 1960 weighed 38 lbs., compared with 15 lbs. for 1970. Thus, the lightest televisions were 2½ times as heavy in 1960 as 1970. Similar trends are observed for dozens of other goods listed in the Sears catalog. Data from *Consumer Reports Buying Guide,* published in December of 1959 and 1969, show similar changes for radios, record players, slide projectors, tape recorders, televisions, toasters and many other goods. Hence, major declines in weight between 1960 and 1970 were quite significant for these and other goods, which suggests that the consumer goods market may be producing many more targets suitable for theft. In general, one finds rapid growth in property suitable for illegal removal and in household and individual exposure to attack during the years 1960–1975.

Related Trends in Business Establishments

Of course, as households and individuals increased their ownership of small durables, businesses also increased the value of the merchandise which they transport and sell as well as the money involved in these transactions. Yet the Census of Business conducted in 1958, 1963, 1967, and 1972 indicate that the number of wholesale, retail, service, and public warehouse establishments (including establishments owned by large organizations) was a nearly constant ratio of one for every 16 persons in the United States. Since more goods and money were distributed over a relatively fixed number of business establishments, the tempo of business activity per establishment apparently was increasing. At the same time, the percent of the population employed as sales clerks or salesmen in retail trade declined from 1.48% to 1.27%, between 1960 and 1970, a 14.7% decline (USBC, 1975: Table 589).

Though both business and personal

property increased, the changing pace of activities appears to have exposed the latter to greater relative risk of attack, whether at home or elsewhere, due to the dispersion of goods among many more households, while concentrating goods in business establishments. However, merchandise in retail establishments with heavy volume and few employees to guard it probably is exposed to major increments in risk of illegal removal than is most other business property.

Composition of Crime Trends

If these changes in the circulation of people and property are in fact related to crime trends, the *composition* of the latter should reflect this. We expect relatively greater increases in personal and household victimization as compared with most business victimizations, while shoplifting should increase more rapidly than other types of thefts from businesses. We expect personal offenses at the hands of strangers to manifest greater increases than such offenses at the hands of nonstrangers. Finally, residential burglary rates should increase more in daytime than nighttime.

The available time series on the composition of offenses confirm these expectations. For example, Table 5 shows that commercial burglaries declined from 60% to 36% of the total, while daytime residential burglaries increased from 16% to 33%. Unlike the other crimes against business, shoplifting increased its share. Though we lack trend data on the circumstances of other violent offenses, murder data confirm our expectations. Between 1963 and 1975, felon-type murders increased from 17% to 32% of the total. Compared with a 47% increase in the rate of relative killings in this period, we calculated a 294% increase in the murder rate at the hands of known or suspected felon types.

Thus the trends in the composition of recorded crime rates appear to be highly consistent with the activity structure trends noted earlier. In the next section we apply the routine activity approach in order to model crime rate trends and social change in the post-World War II United States.

Table 5. Offense Analysis Trends for Robbery, Burglary, Larceny and Murder; United States, 1960–1975

A. ROBBERIES[a]	1960	1965	1970	
Highway Robbery	52.6	57.0	59.8	
Residential Robbery	8.0	10.1	13.1	
Commercial Robbery	39.4	32.9	27.1	
Totals	100.0	100.0	100.0	
B. BURGLARIES	1960	1965	1970	1975
Residential	15.6	24.5	31.7	33.2
Residential Nightime	24.4	25.2	25.8	30.5
Commercial	60.0	50.2	42.5	36.3
Totals	100.0	99.9	100.0	100.0
C. LARCENIES	1960	1965	1970	1975
Shoplifting	6.0	7.8	9.2	11.3
Other	94.0	92.2	90.8	88.7
Totals	100.0	100.0	100.0	100.0
D. MURDERS	1963	1965	1970	1975
Relative Killings	31.0	31.0	23.3	22.4
Romance, Arguments[b]	51.0	48.0	47.9	45.2
Felon Types[c]	17.0	21.0	28.8	32.4
Totals	100.0	100.0	100.0	100.0

Source: Offense Analysis from UCR, various years.

[a] Excluding miscellaneous robberies. The 1975 distribution omitted due to apparent instability of post-1970 data.

[b] Includes romantic triangles, lovers' quarrels and arguments.

[c] Includes both known and suspected felon types.

THE RELATIONSHIP OF THE HOUSEHOLD ACTIVITY RATIO TO FIVE ANNUAL OFFICIAL INDEX CRIME RATES IN THE UNITED STATES, 1947–1974

In this section, we test the hypothesis that aggregate official crime rate trends in the United States vary directly over time with the dispersion of activities away from family and household. The limitations of annual time series data do not allow construction of direct measures of changes in hourly activity patterns, or quantities, qualities and movements of exact stocks of household durable goods, but the Current Population Survey does provide related time series on labor force and household structure. From these data, we calculate annually (beginning in 1947) a household activity ratio by adding the number of married, husband-present female labor force participants (source: BLS, 1975: Table 5) to the number of non-husband-wife households (source: USBC, 1947–1976), dividing this sum by

SOCIAL CHANGE AND CRIME RATE TRENDS   601

the total number of households in the U.S. (source: USBC, 1947–1976). This calculation provides an estimate of the proportion of American households in year t expected to be most highly exposed to risk of personal and property victimization due to the dispersion of their activities away from family and household and/or their likelihood of owning extra sets of durables subject to high risk of attack. Hence, the household activity ratio should vary directly with official index crime rates.

Our empirical goal in this section is to test this relationship, with controls for those variables which other researchers have linked empirically to crime rate trends in the United States. Since various researchers have found such trends to increase with the proportion of the population in teen and young adult years (Fox, 1976; Land and Felson, 1976; Sagi and Wellford, 1968; Wellford, 1973), we include the population ages 15–24 per 100,000 resident population in year t as our first control variable (source: USBC, various years). Others (e.g., Brenner, 1976a; 1976b) have found unemployment rates to vary directly with official crime rates over time, although this relationship elsewhere has been shown to be empirically questionable (see Mansfield et al., 1974: 463; Cohen and Felson, 1979). Thus, as our second, control variable, we take the standard annual unemployment rate (per 100 persons ages 16 and over) as a measure of the business cycle (source: BLS, 1975).

Four of the five crime rates that we utilize here (forcible rape, aggravated assault, robbery and burglary) are taken from FBI estimates of offenses per 100,000 U.S. population (as revised and reported in OMB, 1973). We exclude larceny-theft due to a major definitional change in 1960 and auto theft due to excessive multicollinearity in the analysis.[8] For our homicide indicator we employ the

homicide mortality rate taken from the vital statistics data collected by the Bureau of the Census (various years). The latter rate has the advantage of being collected separately from the standard crime reporting system and is thought to contain less measurement error (see Bowers and Pierce, 1975). Hence, this analysis of official index crime rates includes three violent offenses (homicide, forcible rape, and aggravated assault), one property offense (burglary), and one offense which involves both the removal of property and the threat of violence (robbery). The analysis thus includes one offense thought to have relatively low reporting reliability (forcible rape), one thought to have relatively high reliability (homicide), and three others having relatively intermediate levels of reporting quality (Ennis, 1967).

Since official crime rates in year t are likely to reflect some accumulation of criminal opportunity and inclinations over several years, one should not expect these rates to respond solely to the level of the independent variables for year t. A useful model of cumulative social change in circumstances such as this is the difference equation, which can be estimated in two forms (see Goldberg, 1958). One form takes the first difference $(y_t - y_{t-1})$ as the dependent variable—in this case, the change in the official crime rate per 100,000 population between year $t-1$ and year t. Alternatively, one can estimate the difference equation in autoregressive form by taking the official crime rate in year t as a function of the exogenous predictors plus the official crime rate in year $t - 1$ on the right-hand side of the equation. (See Land, 1978, for a review of these and other methods and for references to related literature.) Both forms are estimable with ordinary least squares methods, which we employ for the years 1947 through 1974. The N is 28 years for all but the homicide rate, for which publication lags reduce our N to 26.

Even if a positive relationship between the household activity ratio and the official crime rates is observed, with controls for age and unemployment, we are open to the charge that this may be a spurious consequence of autocorrelation of disturbances, that is, the possibility that residu-

---

[8] The auto theft rate lagged one year correlated quite strongly with the predictor variables. This multicollinearity impaired our difference equation analysis, although we again found consistently positive coefficients for the household activity ratio. We were able to remove autocorrelation by logging all variables and including the unemployment as a control, but do not report these equations.

als are systematically related for nearby time points. While spurious relationships are a risk one also takes in cross-sectional regression analysis, time-series analysts have devised a variety of methods for monitoring and adjusting for spuriousness due to this autocorrelation, including the Durbin and Watson (1951) statistic, Durbin's h statistic (Durbin, 1970), the Griliches (1967) criterion, as well as Cochrane and Orcutt (1949) corrections. We employ (but do not report in detail) these methods to check for the likelihood that the observed relationship is spurious. (See Land, 1978, for a review of such tests and the related literature on their applicability and robustness; see Theil, 1971, for a methodological review.)

Findings

Our time-series analysis for the years 1947–1974 consistently revealed positive and statistically significant relationships between the household activity ratio and each official crime rate change. Whichever official crime rate is employed, this finding occurs—whether we take the first difference for each crime rate as exogenous or estimate the equation in autoregressive form (with the lagged dependent variable on the right-hand side of the equation); whether we include or exclude the unemployment variable; whether we take the current scales of variables or convert them to natural log values; whether we employ the age structure variable as described or alter the ages examined (e.g., 14–24, 15–19, etc.). In short, the relationship is positive and significant in each case.

Before calculating the difference equations, we regressed each crime rate in year t on the three independent variables for year t. This ordinary structural equation also produced consistent positive and significant coefficients for the routine activity coefficient, the total variance explained ranges from 84% to 97%. However, the Durbin-Watson statistics for these equations indicated high risk of autocorrelation, which is hardly surprising since they ignore lagged effects. Reestimated equations taking first differences as endogenous reduced the risk of autocorre-

lation significantly (and also reduced variance explained to between 35% and 77%). These equations also consistently produce significant positive coefficients for the household activity variable. When unemployment is included in these equations, its coefficients are all negative and near zero.

The top panel of Table 6 presents regression estimates of first differences for five official crime rates, with the age structure and household activity variables in year t as the only predictors. Again, the household activity coefficients are consistently positive, with t ratios always significant with a one-tailed test. Except for the aggravated assault equation, the household activity variable has a t ratio and standardized coefficient greater than that of the age structure variable. The standardized coefficients for the household activity variable range from .42 to .72, while the age structure coefficients are consistently positive. In general, the household activity variable is a stronger predictor of official crime rate trends than the age structure.

The equations in the top panel of Table 6 generally have lower variance explained but also lower risk of autocorrelation of disturbances than those reported above. For all five equations, the Durbin-Watson statistic allows acceptance of the null hypothesis that autocorrelation is absent at the 1% level. A 5% level (which *increases* the likelihood of proving the statistic nonzero) allows us neither to accept nor reject the null hypothesis that autocorrelation is absent in the homicide and robbery equations.

Though autocorrelation has not been proven to exist in these five equations, its risk may be sufficient in two to motivate further efforts at equation estimation (see bottom panel of Table 6). We estimated the equations in autoregressive form to see if the risk abates. Since the Durbin-Watson statistic was not designed for evaluating autocorrelation in these equations, we calculated Durbin's h, a statistic specifically designed for equations estimated with a lagged dependent variable (Durbin, 1970), and recently found to be robust for small samples (Maddala and Rao, 1973). This statistic allows ac-

Table 6. Regression Equations for First Differences in Five Index Crime Rates and Sensitivity Analyses, the United States, 1947–1974

FIRST DIFFERENCE FORM	(1) Nonnegligent Homicide	(2) Forcible Rape	(3) Aggravated Assault	(4) Robbery	(5) Burglary
Constant	−2.3632	−4.8591	−32.0507	−43.8838	−221.2303
t ratio	.3502	5.3679	7.6567	3.4497	3.7229
Proportion 15–24 (t)					
Standardized	.1667	.1425	.4941	.2320	.1952
Unstandardized	3.2190	6.4685	132.1072	116.7742	486.0806
t ratio	1.0695	.7505	3.3147	.9642	.8591
Household Activity Ratio (t)					
Standardized	.7162	.6713	.4377	.4242	.5106
Unstandardized	4.0676	8.9743	34.4658	62.8834	374.4746
t ratio	4.5959	3.5356	2.9364	1.7629	2.2474
Multiple R² Adjusted	.6791	.5850	.7442	.3335	.4058
Degrees of Freedom	23	25	25	25	25
Durbin-Watson Value	2.5455	2.3388	2.3446	1.4548	1.7641
1% test	Accept	Accept	Accept	Accept	Accept
5% test	Uncertain	Accept	Accept	Uncertain	Accept
AUTOREGRESSIVE FORM					
Multiple R² Adjusted	.9823	.9888	.9961	.9768	.9859
Durbin's h	−1.3751	−.7487	.9709	1.5490	1.1445
−1% test	Accept	Accept	Accept	Accept	Accept
−5% test	Accept	Accept	Accept	Accept	Accept
Griliches Criterion	Accept	Accept	Accept	Accept	Accept
Cochrane-Orcutt Correction.					
Effect upon Household Activity	Minimal	Minimal	Minimal	Minimal	Minimal
Unemployment Rate as Control.					
Effect Upon Household Activity	Minimal	Minimal	Minimal	Minimal	Minimal

ceptance of the null hypothesis (at both 1% and 5% levels) that autocorrelation is absent for all five equations. Application of the Griliches (1967) criterion further allows acceptance of each equation as manifesting distributing lags rather than serial correlation. We also employed the Cochrane-Orcutt (1949) iterative procedure to calculate a correction estimate for any autocorrelation present. The resulting correction for the household activity coefficient proves minimal in all five cases. Finally, we calculated each of the above equations for natural log values of the relevant variables, finding again that the household activity coefficient was consistently positive and statistically significant and the risk of autocorrelation reduced still further.

The positive and significant relationship between the household activity variable and the official crime rates is robust and appears to hold for both macro- and microlevel data; it explains five crime rate trends, as well as the changing composition of official crime rates reported in Table 5. These results suggest that routine activities may indeed provide the opportunity for many illegal activities to occur.

DISCUSSION

In our judgment many conventional theories of crime (the adequacy of which usually is evaluated by cross-sectional data, or no data at all) have difficulty accounting for the annual changes in crime rate trends in the post-World War II United States. These theories may prove useful in explaining crime trends during other periods, within specific communities, or in particular subgroups of the population. Longitudinal aggregate data for the United States, however, indicate that the trends for many of the presumed causal variables in these theoretical structures are in a direction opposite to those hypothesized to be the causes of crime. For example, during the decade 1960–1970, the percent of the population below the low-income level declined 44% and the unemployment rate declined 186%. Central city population as a share of the whole population declined slightly, while the

percent of foreign stock declined 0.1%, etc. (see USBC, 1975: 654, 19, 39).

On the other hand, the convergence in time and space of three elements (motivated offenders, suitable targets, and the absence of capable guardians) appears useful for understanding crime rate trends. The lack of any of these elements is sufficient to prevent the occurrence of a successful direct-contact predatory crime. The convergence in time and space of suitable targets and the absence of capable guardians can lead to large increases in crime rates without any increase or change in the structural conditions that motivate individuals to engage in crime. Presumably, had the social indicators of the variables hypothesized to be the causes of crime in conventional theories changed in the direction of favoring increased crime in the post-World War II United States, the increases in crime rates likely would have been even more staggering than those which were observed. In any event, it is our belief that criminologists have underemphasized the importance of the convergence of suitable targets and the absence of capable guardians in explaining recent increases in the crime rate. Furthermore, the effects of the convergence in time and space of these elements may be multiplicative rather than additive. That is, their convergence by a fixed percentage may produce increases in crime rates far greater than that fixed percentage, demonstrating how some relatively modest social trends can contribute to some relatively large changes in crime rate trends. The fact that logged variables improved our equations (moving Durbin-Watson values closer to "ideal" levels) lends support to the argument that such an interaction occurs.

Those few investigations of cross-sectional data which include household indicators produce results similar to ours. For example, Roncek (1975) and Choldin and Roncek (1976) report on block-level data for San Diego, Cleveland and Peoria and indicate that the proportion of a block's households which are primary individual households consistently offers the best or nearly the best predictor of a block's crime rate. This relationship persisted after they controlled for numerous

SOCIAL CHANGE AND CRIME RATE TRENDS   605

social variables, including race, density, age and poverty. Thus the association between household structure and risk of criminal victimization has been observed in individual-level and block-level cross-sectional data, as well as aggregate national time-series data.

Without denying the importance of factors motivating offenders to engage in crime, we have focused specific attention upon violations themselves and the prerequisites for their occurrence. However, the routine activity approach might in the future be applied to the analysis of offenders and their inclinations as well. For example, the structure of primary group activity may affect the likelihood that cultural transmission or social control of criminal inclinations will occur, while the structure of the community may affect the tempo of criminogenic peer group activity. We also may expect that circumstances favorable for carrying out violations contribute to criminal inclinations in the long run by rewarding these inclinations.

We further suggest that the routine activity framework may prove useful in explaining why the criminal justice system, the community and the family have appeared so ineffective in exerting social control since 1960. Substantial increases in the opportunity to carry out predatory violations may have undermined society's mechanisms for social control. For example, it may be difficult for institutions seeking to increase the certainty, celerity and severity of punishment to compete with structural changes resulting in vast increases in the certainty, celerity and value of rewards to be gained from illegal predatory acts.

It is ironic that the very factors which increase the opportunity to enjoy the benefits of life also may increase the opportunity for predatory violations. For example, automobiles provide freedom of movement to offenders as well as average citizens and offer vulnerable targets for theft. College enrollment, female labor force participation, urbanization, suburbanization, vacations and new electronic durables provide various opportunities to escape the confines of the household while they increase the risk of predatory victimization. Indeed, the opportunity for predatory crime appears to be enmeshed in the opportunity structure for legitimate activities to such an extent that it might be very difficult to root out substantial amounts of crime without modifying much of our way of life. Rather than assuming that predatory crime is simply an indicator of social breakdown, one might take it as a byproduct of freedom and prosperity as they manifest themselves in the routine activities of everyday life.

REFERENCES

Amir, Menachem
  1971 Patterns of Forcible Rape. Chicago: University of Chicago Press.
Boggs, Sarah
  1965 "Urban crime patterns." American Sociological Review 30:899–905.
Bonger, W. A.
  1916 Criminality and Economic Conditions. Boston: Little, Brown.
Bowers, W. J. and Glen L. Pierce
  1975 "The illusion of deterrence of Isaac Ehrlich's research on capital punishment." Yale Law Journal 85:187–208.
Brenner, Harvey
  1976a Estimating the Social Costs of National Economic Policy: Implications for Mental and Physical Health and Criminal Aggression. Paper no. 5, Joint Economic Committee, Congress of the United States. Washington, D.C.: U.S. Government Printing Office.
  1976b Effects of the National Economy on Criminal Aggression II. Final Report to National Institute of Mental Health. Contract #282-76-0355FS.
Bureau of Labor Statistics (BLS)
  1975 Handbook of Labor Statistics 1975—Reference Edition. Washington, D.C.: U.S. Government Printing Office.
Cameron, Mary Owen
  1964 The Booster and the Snitch. New York: Free Press.
Chambliss, William J.
  1972 Boxman: A Professional Thief's Journey. New York: Harper and Row.
Choldin, Harvey M. and Dennis W. Roncek
  1976 "Density, population potential and pathology: a block-level analysis." Public Data Use 4:19–30.
Cloward, Richard and Lloyd Ohlin
  1960 Delinquency and Opportunity. New York: Free Press.
Cochrane, D., and G. H. Orcutt
  1949 "Application of least squares regression to relationships containing autocorrelated error terms." Journal of the American Statistical Association 44:32–61.

AMERICAN SOCIOLOGICAL REVIEW

Cohen, Lawrence E. and Marcus Felson
1979 "On estimating the social costs of national economic policy: a critical examination of the Brenner study." Social Indicators Research. In press.
Colquhoun, Patrick
1800 Treatise on the Police of the Metropolis. London: Baldwin.
Consumer Reports Buying Guide
1959 Consumer Reports (December). Mt. Vernon: Consumers Union.
1969 Consumer Reports (December). Mt. Vernon: Consumers Union.
1975 Consumer Reports (December). Mt. Vernon: Consumers Union.
Council of Economic Advisors (CEA)
1976 The Economic Report of the President. Washington, D.C.: U.S. Government Printing Office.
Durbin, J.
1970 Testing for serial correlation when least squares regressors are lagged dependent variables." Econometrica 38:410–21.
Durbin, J., and G. S. Watson
1951 "Testing for serial correlation in least squares regression, II." Biometrika 38:159–78.
Durkheim, Emile
1951 Suicide: A Study in Sociology. New York: Free Press.
1966 The Division of Labor in Society. New York: Free Press.
Electrical Merchandising Week
1964 Statistical and Marketing Report (January). New York: Billboard Publications.
Ennis, Philip H.
1967 "Criminal victimization in the U.S.: a report of a national survey, field surveys II." The President's Commission on Law Enforcement and the Administration of Justice. Washington, D.C.: U.S. Government Printing Office.
Federal Bureau of Investigation (FBI)
1975 Crime in the U.S.: Uniform Crime Report. Washington, D.C.: U.S. Government Printing Office.
1976 Crime in the U.S.: Uniform Crime Report. Washington, D.C.: U.S. Government Printing Office.
Ferdinand, Theodore N.
1970 "Demographic shifts and criminality." British Journal of Criminology 10:169–75.
Fleisher, Belton M.
1966 The Economics of Delinquency. Chicago: Quadrangle.
Fox, James A.
1976 An Econometric Analysis of Crime Data. Ph.D. dissertation, Department of Sociology, University of Pennsylvania. Ann Arbor: University Microfilms.
Glaser, Daniel
1971 Social Deviance. Chicago: Markham.
Goldberg, Samuel
1958 Introduction to Difference Equations. New York: Wiley.

Gould, Leroy
1969 "The changing structure of property crime in an affluent society." Social Forces 48:50–9.
Griliches, Z.
1967 "Distributed lags: a survey." Econometrica 35:16–49.
Guerry, A. M.
1833 "Essai sur la statistique morale de la France." Westminister Review 18:357.
Hawley, Amos
1950 Human Ecology: A Theory of Community Structure. New York: Ronald.
Henry, A. F., and J. F. Short
1954 Suicide and Homicide. New York: Free Press.
Hindelang, Michael J.
1976 Criminal Victimization in Eight American Cities: A Descriptive Analysis of Common Theft and Assault. Cambridge: Ballinger.
Hindelang, Michael J., Christopher S. Dunn, Paul Sutton and Alison L. Aumick
1976 Sourcebook of Criminal Justice Statistics—1975. U.S. Dept. of Justice, Law Enforcement Assistance Administration. Washington, D.C.: U.S. Government Printing Office.
1977 Sourcebook of Criminal Justice Statistics—1976. U.S. Dept. of Justice, Law Enforcement Assistance Administration. Washington, D.C.: U.S. Government Printing Office.
Interstate Commerce Commission (ICC)
1974 Annual Report: Freight Commodity Statistics of Class I Motor Carriers of Property Operative in Intercity Service. Washington, D.C.: U.S. Government Printing Office.
Jackson, Bruce
1969 A Thief's Primer. New York: Macmillan.
Jeffery, C. R.
1971 Crime Prevention Through Environmental Design. Beverly Hills: Sage.
Klockars, Carl B.
1974 The Professional Fence. New York: Free Press.
Kobrin, Frances E.
1976 "The primary individual and the family: changes in living arrangements in the U.S. since 1940." Journal of Marriage and the Family 38:233–9.
Land, Kenneth C.
1978 "Modelling macro social change." Paper presented at annual meeting of the American Sociological Association, San Francisco.
Land, Kenneth C. and Marcus Felson
1976 "A general framework for building dynamic macro social indicator models: including an analysis of changes in crime rates and police expenditures." American Journal of Sociology 82:565–604.
Letkemann, Peter
1973 Crime As Work. Englewood Cliffs: Prentice-Hall.
Lystad, Mary
1974 An Annotated Bibliography: Violence at Home. DHEW Publication No. (ADM 75–

SOCIAL CHANGE AND CRIME RATE TRENDS   607

136). Washington, D.C.: U.S. Government
Printing Office.

Maddala, G. S., and A. S. Rao
1973 "Tests for serial correlation in regression
models with lagged dependent variables and
serially correlated errors." Econometrica
41:761–74.

Mansfield, Roger, Leroy Gould, and J. Zvi Namen-
wirth
1974 "A socioeconomic model for the prediction
of societal rates of property theft." Social
Forces 52:462–72.

Martin, John Bower
1952 My Life in Crime. New York: Harper.

Maurer, David W.
1964 Whiz Mob. New Haven: College and University Press.

Merchandising Week
1973 Statistical and Marketing Report (February). New York: Billboard Publications.
1976 Statistical and Marketing Report (March).
New York: Billboard Publications.

National Commission on the Causes and Prevention
of Violence
1969 Crimes of Violence. Vol. 13. Washington,
D.C.: U.S. Government Printing Office.

Nettler, Gwynn
1974 Explaining Crime. New York: McGraw-
Hill.

Newman, Oscar
1973 Defensible Space: Crime Prevention
Through Urban Design. New York: Macmillan.

Office of Management and the Budget (OMB)
1973 Social Indicators 1973. Washington, D.C.:
U.S. Government Printing Office.

Pope, Carl E.
1977a Crime-Specific Analysis: The Characteristics of Burglary Incidents. U.S.
Dept. of Justice, Law Enforcement Assistance Administration. Analytic Report 10.
Washington, D.C.: U.S. Government Printing Office.
1977b Crime-Specific Analysis: An Empirical
Examination of Burglary Offense and Offender Characteristics. U.S. Dept. of Justice, Law Enforcement Assistance Administration. Analytical Report 12. Washington, D.C.: U.S. Government Printing
Office.

Quètelet, Adolphe
1842 A Treatise on Man. Edinburgh: Chambers.

Reiss, Albert J.
1976 "Settling the frontiers of a pioneer in
American criminology: Henry McKay."
Pp. 64–88 in James F. Short, Jr. (ed.), De-
linquency, Crime, and Society. Chicago:
University of Chicago Press.

Reppetto, Thomas J.
1974 Residential Crime. Cambridge: Ballinger.

Roncek, Dennis
1975 Crime Rates and Residential Densities in
Two Large Cities. Ph.D. dissertation, Department of Sociology, University of Illinois, Urbana.

Sagi, Phillip C. and Charles E. Wellford
1968 "Age composition and patterns of change in

criminal statistics." Journal of Criminal
Law, Criminology and Police Science
59:29–36.

Scarr, Harry A.
1972 Patterns of Burglary. U.S. Dept. of Justice,
Law Enforcement Assistance Administration. Washington, D.C.: U.S. Government
Printing Office.

Sears Catalogue
1960 Chicago: Sears.
1970 Chicago: Sears.

Shaw, Clifford R., Henry D. McKay, Frederick Zor-
baugh and Leonard S. Cottrell
1929 Delinquency Areas. Chicago: University of
Chicago Press.

Short, James F., and Fred Strodtbeck
1965 Group Process and Gang Delinquency.
Chicago: University of Chicago Press.

Skogan, Wesley G.
1976 "The victims of crime: some material findings." Pp. 131–48 in Anthony L. Guenther
(ed.), Criminal Behavior in Social Systems.
Chicago: Rand McNally.

Sutherland, Edwin H.
1937 The Professional Thief. Chicago: University of Chicago Press.

Szalai, Alexander (ed.)
1972 The Use of Time: Daily Activities of Urban
and Suburban Populations in Twelve Countries. The Hague: Mouton.

Theil, Henri
1971 Principles of Econometrics. New York:
Wiley.

Tobias, J. J.
1967 Crime and Industrial Society in the
Nineteenth Century. New York: Schocken
Books.

U.S. Bureau of the Census (USBC)
1973a Census of Transportation, 1972. U.S.
Summary. Washington, D.C.: U.S. Government Printing Office.
1973b Who's Home When. Working Paper 37.
Washington, D.C.: U.S. Government Printing Office.
1975– Statistical Abstract of the U.S. Washing-
1976   ton, D.C.: U.S. Government Printing
Office.
1947– Current Population Studies. P-25 Ser.
1976   Washington, D.C.: U.S. Government Printing Office.

U.S. Department of Justice (USDJ)
1974a Preliminary Report of the Impact Cities,
Crime Survey Results. Washington, D.C.:
Law Enforcement Assistance Administra-
tion (NCJISS).
1974b Crime in the Nation's Five Largest Cities:
Advance Report. Washington, D.C.: Law
Enforcement Assistance Administration
(NCJISS).
1974c Crimes and Victims: A Report on the
Dayton-San Jose Pilot Survey of Victimiza-
tion. Washington, D.C.: Law Enforcement
Assistance Administration.
1976 Criminal Victimizations in the U.S., 1973.
Washington, D.C.: Law Enforcement
Assistance Administration (NCJISS).
1977 Criminal Victimizations in the U.S.: A

608   AMERICAN SOCIOLOGICAL REVIEW

Comparison of 1974 and 1975 Findings. Washington, D.C.: Law Enforcement Assistance Administration (NCJISS).

Washnis, George J.
1976   Citizen Involvement in Crime Prevention. Lexington: Heath.

Wellford, Charles F.
1973   "Age composition and the increase in recorded crime." Criminology 11:61–70.

Wilks, Judith A.
1967   "Ecological correlates of crime and delin-

quency." Pp. 138–56 in President's Commission on Law Enforcement and the Administration of Justice Task Force Report: Crime and Its Impact—An Assessment. Appendix A. Washington, D.C.: U.S. Government Printing Office.

Williamson, Henry
1968   Hustler! New York: Doubleday.

Wolfgang, Marvin E.
1958   Patterns of Criminal Homicide. Philadelphia: University of Pennsylvania Press.

Part III
Patterns and Representations
of Victimization

[9]

BRIT. J. CRIMINOL. VOL. 31 NO. 4 AUTUMN 1991

THE TIME COURSE OF REPEAT BURGLARY VICTIMIZATION

Natalie Polvi,* Terah Looman,* Charlie Humphries,† and Ken Pease*

Research has demonstrated that the probability of repeat victimization is greater than the probability of an independent offence. The time course of elevated risk has important implications for crime prevention. For burglaries, the current received wisdom is that the characteristics of homes which make burglary more probable persist over the medium and long term. Addressing the time course question, previous research by the authors examined the change in risk of repeat burglary victimization for up to twelve months after the initial offence (Polvi et al. 1990). The study is here extended to the analysis of a four-year time period (1984 to 1987). It was found that the elevated risk of repeat burglary does not last over long time periods. Based on the present data, the risk becomes average once six months has passed and remains so subsequently. It is contended that the work should be replicated, given its surprising results. One implication of this research is that preventative action should be taken as soon as possible after a burglary.

One of the criminological legacies of the late Richard Sparks was his recognition of the importance of the phenomenon of repeat crime victimization (see Sparks 1981). In essence, the probability of being victimized a second or subsequent time is several times the rate that would be expected if offences were independent events. This seems to be true across a wide range of offence types. Sparks (1981) reviews possible reasons for this phenomenon with typical wit and lucidity. The fact is usable in crime prevention terms, since concentration of preventative effort on prior victims will be more cost-effective than concentration on a different group of similar size. This was the cornerstone of a recent, apparently successful, burglary prevention programme in Rochdale (Forrester *et al.* 1988).

Put generally, we should think in terms of a continuum of crime predictability. The more exactly a crime location can be specified in advance, the greater the opportunity for prevention or detection. At one extreme, entrapment is a seductive technique because it locates a crime precisely in place and time. At the other extreme, random distribution of crime makes the allocation of prevention and detection effort maximally difficult. The heightened probability of repeat victimization serves to move the situation towards the predictable end of the continuum. To be useful, predictability has to apply in terms of both place (target) and time. Research on multiple victimization has hitherto neglected time, tending to look at elevated risk over a standard period, typically a year, rather than at any changes in risk across time. Yet the time course of elevated risk is of crucial importance to preventative effort. Specifically, over what

* Neuropsychiatric Research Unit, Dept of Psychiatry, University of Saskatchewan and Regional Psychiatric Centre (Prairies), Correctional Service of Canada.

† Saskatoon City Police.

We wish to thank Chief Joe Penkala, Saskatoon City Police, for his co-operation and support. We also wish to thank Frank B. Garland, City Assessor, City of Saskatoon, and his associates. We thank Joanna Shapland, Gerry Rose, and Ron Templeman for helpful comments on an earlier version of this note.

NATALIE POLVI *ET AL.*

period does the elevated risk persist? When is it sensible to stop investing special effort to prevent further offending?

Analysis of burglaries in the City of Saskatoon, Saskatchewan, in 1987 showed that, in line with British data (see Forrester *et al.* 1988), the chance of a repeat burglary over the period of one year was around four times the rate to be expected if the events were independent. However, this masked a dramatic reduction within the year (Polvi *et al.* 1990). The likelihood of a repeat burglary within one month was over twelve times the expected rate, but this declined to less than twice the expected rate when burglaries six months apart were considered. Analysis of the repeat burglaries within one month showed that half of the second victimizations occurred within seven days of the first. The present note extends the analysis of Saskatoon burglary data from a single calendar year (1987) to a four-year span, 1984–7.

Burglary data were provided by the Saskatoon City Police (Records Department). The computer generated a month-by-month list of all residential burglaries in the city during 1987. For each address burgled in 1987, it listed the record of all previous burglaries from 1 January 1984 to 31 December 1986.

Because calculations involved the assumption that each burglary was associated with one dwelling, it was necessary to determine whether each address was a single unit or a multiple unit. This was accomplished with the help of the City of Saskatoon's Assessment Department.

While our 1987 data constitute a complete record of residential burglaries in that year, our 1984–6 data include only those addresses also burgled in 1987. It will be recalled that the problem was to see whether elevated risk of burglary persisted over time. Had our data comprised all burglaries in 1984, and data for subsequent years about total burglaries and repeat burglaries of these dwellings, it is obvious that we could readily calculate the persistence of risk. Limitations in data availability and resources made that impracticable. The problem is how to use retrospective data to address the issue.

For each year from 1984 to 1987 we know the total number of dwellings burgled. For 1987 alone, we know precisely which dwellings they were. We also know which of these had been burgled during the period 1984–6, and when. Intuitively, if the number of such dwellings is higher than expected, that is evidence of elevated risk of repeat victimization. We knew the number of dwellings burgled in 1987 and a specified earlier year. We knew the number of dwellings burgled in 1987 but not in the earlier year. We knew the total number of dwellings in the city in all years. We calculated the number of dwellings burgled in the earlier year but not in 1987, on the basis of the total number of dwellings in the city, the total number of burglaries in that year, and the number of dwellings burgled both in the year in question and in 1987. The only concern we were unable to resolve was whether the total number of dwellings we used in our calculations should be the number available at the end of the first or the second year of the pair, so we calculated both. They were only trivially different, and only one set (based on the number of dwellings in 1987) is presented. While the approach we took is counter-intuitive (estimating the number of dwellings burgled in 1986 which were burgled 'again' in 1984!), the series we end up with is equivalent to a prospective series.

For each pair of years (1984/1987, 1985/1987, 1986/1987) the number of dwellings burgled in neither year, in one year but not both, and in both years, was calculated and a Poisson distribution fitted. For example, 3,781 different dwellings were burgled in

TIME COURSE OF REPEAT BURGLARY VICTIMIZATION

1985 and/or 1987. In a housing stock of 70,343 dwellings, the probability of a house being burgled in neither year is 0.9460, and that of a house being burgled in both years is 0.00146, equivalent to an expected number of burgled dwellings of 103. The actual number of houses burgled in both years is 124. Thus the ratio of observed to expected is 1.21. The data are presented in Fig. 1.

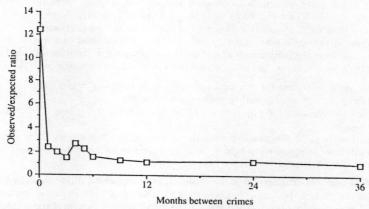

FIG. 1   Ratio of observed to expected repeat burglaries, Saskatoon, by months between crimes

At the one-year point, the ratio is 1.17; at the two-year point, it is 1.21; and at the three-year point, it is 1.02. Figure 1 includes the data points in the range up to one year first published in Polvi *et al.* (1989), so as to enable the whole picture to be seen. (It is important for readers interested in the time course up to one year to read the method section of the earlier paper.) In summary, Fig. 1 reveals that the elevated risk of repeat burglary extends over only a short period, at least for burglary in Saskatoon. After around six months, it ceases to exist for all practical purposes. One would have expected a higher ratio to have persisted over a longer time, if only because houses in the worst areas would retain a higher risk of being burgled, by dint of their location in the area, rather than by reason of their prior victimization. Also, characteristics which distinguish between burgled and non-burgled dwellings (see Winchester and Jackson 1982) are likely to persist over time, thus making for a continued high risk of burglary. Certainly our study should be repeated in other cities in Canada and in other countries before its conclusions are translated into crime prevention practice. Saskatoon could be distinctive in the relative homogeneity of its housing. This could mean that, while short-term repeat victimization by the same offenders remains significant, the burglary opportunities are spread so evenly throughout the city that target selection by different burglars does not identify the same dwellings.

One feature of the data which deserves passing mention is the apparent elevation of risk four to five months after a burglary, compared with three months afterwards. The most likely explanation of this is chance fluctuation in the data; but another possibility which should be kept in mind is that this represents the period after which replacement

413

NATALIE POLVI *ET AL.*

of goods through insurance is virtually certain to have occurred, and thus when a repeat burglary will offer pickings as rich as on the first visit. This possibility should be tested by further research in other places.

The implications of the finding that dramatically enhanced risk of repeat burglaries persists for only a short period after the first burglary are substantial. If confirmed elsewhere, this means that special preventative measures (leafletting neighbours, advising victims, perhaps the loan of silent alarms) are realistic, since they need only endure for a month or so to have their major effect. However, they clearly need to occur very promptly, certainly no later than the day after the first offence.

Assuming that the data are not an artefact of the method used in some unsuspected way, we have to make conjectures about what is happening. Heightened probability of repeat crime victimization may be considered as occurring for three possible reasons:

1. The same offenders return, perhaps upon recognition of neglected crime opportunities, or the anticipated reinstatement of goods.
2. The first offenders tell others of the house and what it still offers. The others then burgle it.
3. Features of the house are such as to mark it out as a compellingly attractive target to all those tempted to burgle it, leading to repeat victimizations linked only by the seductiveness of the target.

The first and second alternatives are difficult to distinguish (although we regard the second as not likely to be a frequent occurrence). The proportion of re-victimizations of the third type will be high to the extent that dwellings vary in their seductiveness as targets. It is difficult to think of a city with less such variation than Saskatoon. It may be that what is shown here is the limiting case, where repeat victimization is as near exclusively of type (1) as is anywhere to be found. This makes it particularly important that the analysis should be repeated elsewhere, since the notion of area or dwelling characteristics as long-term determinants of risk of victimization stems from studies which neglect the phenomenon of repeat victimization. It is conceivable that while these characteristics determine a first victimization, it is more what is found inside which induces an offender to return.

REFERENCES

FORRESTER, D., CHATTERTON, M. R., and PEASE, K. (1988), *The Kirkholt Burglary Prevention Project, Rochdale*, Crime Prevention Paper no. 13. London: Home Office.

POLVI, N., LOOMAN, T., HUMPHRIES, C., and PEASE, K. (1990), 'Repeat Break and Enter Victimization: Time Course and Crime Prevention Opportunity', *Journal of Police Science and Administration*.

SPARKS, R. F. (1981), 'Multiple Victimisation: Evidence, Theory and Future Research', *Journal of Criminal Law and Criminology*, 72: 762–78.

WINCHESTER, S., and JACKSON, H. (1982), *Residential Burglary: The Limits of Prevention*, Home Office Research Study no. 74. London: HMSO.

[10]

BRIT. J. CRIMINOL. Vol. 20 No. 3 JULY 1980

THE IMPACT OF BURGLARY UPON VICTIMS

MIKE MAGUIRE (*Oxford*)*

A CONSIDERABLE body of literature has built up over the past few years emphasising the problems of the victims of sexual and violent offences and suggesting improvements in the way they are treated and compensated (see, for example, McDonald, 1976; Bryant and Cirel, 1977; Knudten *et al.*, 1977; Halpern, 1978; Holmstrom and Burgess, 1978; Miers, 1978). By contrast, victims of property crime have aroused little interest, although it is common knowledge that residential burglary, in particular, can have a serious psychological impact upon the householder. This impact has previously been described only in general terms. For example, Reppetto (1974) reported that 73 per cent. of burglary victims expressed " considerable fear " of a repeat, Waller and Okihiro (1978) that over 40 per cent. of female victims were afraid to be alone in their houses for some weeks, and Haward (1979) that 70 per cent. of victims of a selection of mainly property crimes were " very distressed ". Meanwhile, the only systematic help offered in England has come from a handful of voluntary " Victims Support Schemes ", pioneered in Bristol in 1974 and backed by N.A.C.R.O. (B.V.S.S., 1975; N.A.C.R.O., 1977).[1]

The object of this paper is to provide a more detailed account of people's reactions to becoming the victim of a burglary and to consider some of the ways in which these effects might be alleviated. It is based upon interviews with 322 victims of burglary in a dwelling, carried out in the Thames Valley police force area between 1977 and 1979. The majority of these interviews took place between four and 10 weeks after the burglary was reported [2] and the victims were asked to recall the initial impact as well as the effect upon their lives during the intervening period. The interviewees were drawn from three separate police sectors, one containing a medium-sized market town and surrounding villages, one a town of 130,000 inhabitants and one a wealthy commuter area on the outskirts of London. Although representative of victims reporting burglaries in these areas,[3] they are not necessarily representative of burglary victims as a whole; for example, the third area mentioned has very few working-class residents, which affects the overall class balance of the sample. To counteract this bias,

* Research officer, Centre for Criminological Research, University of Oxford. The writer recently completed a comprehensive survey of the incidence and effects of burglary in dwellings in the Thames Valley area, 1975–79, and hopes to publish the results in book form in due course. The study was carried out by himself and a research assistant, Dr. Trevor Bennett, now a senior research officer at the Institute of Criminology, Cambridge.

[1] The Bristol group also conducted an operational study on its first six months of operation, concluding that 7 per cent. of victims contacted (97 per cent. of whom had reported a case of theft or burglary) had suffered a " severe and long-lasting impact, affecting their life-style " and that " approximately one-third of all victims were upset to a degree which called for some help in restoring normal coping ability " (B.V.S.S., 1975).

[2] The interviews, which lasted on average about one hour, were carried out in the victims' homes by Dr. Bennett and myself.

[3] The response rate was 62 per cent. and there were no significant differences in terms of class, value stolen, method of entry or untidiness of search between respondents and non-respondents.

MIKE MAGUIRE

care was taken in the analysis to control for factors such as class, sex and age.

It may be of interest to look first at the manner in which people discovered that they had been burgled: 78 per cent. had been out when the burglar entered the house, 16 per cent. had been asleep in bed and the remainder had been present and awake. Only 13 (4 per cent.) came face to face with the intruder, and for the most part such confrontations were brief and non-violent, the offender either giving himself up or running away. Of those who either returned home (most commonly in the early evening) or came downstairs to discover that they had been burgled, the majority first noticed not, as one might expect, drawers turned out and property scattered about the floor but simply one or two minor changes in the appearance of the house. Open or broken windows were the most frequent first signs seen, other typical indications being ornaments dropped or knocked over, cupboard doors or drawers opened, or items moved to different places in the room. The word " ransacking " could be used sensibly in no more than 12 per cent. of cases. About 20 per cent. were in the house for some time (several days in a few cases) before they realised that articles were missing, but even among those who immediately knew that something was wrong it often took a period of ten seconds or more to associate the signs they saw with the word " burglary ". Their first instinct seems to have been to find a more " normal " explanation of what had occurred. For example:

No. 37. I saw everything on the floor and I thought my boys had been having a party. I was halfway up the stairs to tell them off before I did a sort of double take.

No. 100. I looked over where the television should be and it wasn't there. It's funny, it didn't click at all, even then. It was only when I noticed the gloves that the truth began to dawn. It was a horrible sinking feeling in my stomach.

One victim likened the feeling to being in a road accident, with an initial refusal to believe what had happened and a " sense of unreality ", followed about a minute later by " sheer panic " when the truth became clear.

Initial Impact

All victims were asked to describe in their own words their first reaction once they realised what had happened. The answers were fairly easily classifiable into six categories.

TABLE 1

What was your first reaction on discovering the burglary?

	Male %	Female %	All %
Anger/annoyance	41	19	30
Shock	9	29	19
Upset/tears/confusion	13	20	17
Surprise/disbelief	11	6	9
Fear	4	13	9
No strong reaction	21	13	17
TOTAL	100 (N=163)	100 (N=159)	100 (N=322)

THE IMPACT OF BURGLARY UPON VICTIMS

The most common reaction was one of anger or annoyance (30 per cent.); shock and general emotional upset were also relatively frequent, but only 9 per cent. said that fear was their first reaction; 17 per cent. reported feeling calm or unworried. A higher proportion of women than men reacted with shock, fear or upset, while the most frequent male response was one of anger.[4]

Of course, all these categories can include anything from mild to very severe reactions. Those who experienced shock ranged from a woman who " felt the need for a glass of brandy " to one who " shook and shook for several days " Anger ranged from indignation to blind fury and " upset " from mild depression to hysteria. Measurement of the intensity of reactions was difficult, as some victims were inclined to use exaggerated language ("petrified", "flabbergasted", "fuming", etc.) to describe their feelings while others played them down in retrospect. Nevertheless, the researchers' subjective assessment was that at least 20 (6 per cent.) of the 322 victims interviewed had suffered acute distress shortly after discovering the crime. Their reactions included severe shock, trembling, panic and uncontrolled weeping. The following are examples of such cases reported in the victim's own words:

> No. 536. I went to pieces. I just couldn't believe it. I cried so much I couldn't phone the police. I was so frightened. I cried every time someone talked to me.

> No. 825. It was the worst shock of my life. The doctor had to give me an injection. I couldn't speak a word.

> No. 1010. I was hysterical. I ran screaming to my neighbour and hammered on her door. Then I went icy cold and shivered for hours.

One woman said she had been found by neighbours " standing dumbstruck in the middle of the street ", and two others reported being physically sick.

The extent of the emotional impact appeared to vary considerably between different social groups. Of the above 20 victims 18 were female, 11 were working-class and eight were pensioners, all these groups being over-represented. It was also interesting that 12 were widowed, separated or divorced, although only 18 per cent. of the total sample fell into this category —a point that will be discussed later.

In addition to the 20 suffering acute distress, a further 63 victims were identified (19 per cent. of the total) upon whom the initial impact appeared to have been considerable. Female victims were again over-represented among them (although not to such a significant degree), but there was little difference by age or class. A brief selection of cases from this second category is given to illustrate the kinds of feeling experienced.

> No. 142. I was shaken to the core. The idea of someone in my house— somehow I felt violated.

[4] There was also a class difference, although not to a statistically significant degree, working-class respondents of both sexes reporting shock, fear and upset more frequently than middle-class interviewees. " Working-class " was defined as all those households where the main provider of income was employed under Registrar-General's classes III M, IV or V, and " middle-class " those under I, II and III N. Retired and unemployed were classified according to their previous employment.

MIKE MAGUIRE

No. 144.   Everything was unreal. I was in a dream. There was just this feeling that someone had been walking about in my house.

No. 650.   I was really frightened—I was trembling. I thought they could have come upstairs. It never hits you till it happens to you.

No. 762.   It was the most terrible feeling to think that someone's been in your house. I nearly made myself sick with shaking.

No. 861.   I was very shocked at first. It's a feeling that you don't own your own house.

No. 920.   When I saw the window I practically heaved up. I didn't know what to do.

No. 1597.   I turned to jelly for half an hour. I was very shocked and tearful and had to have a few drinks.

No. 1717.   I got the spooks. I went round looking in all the cupboards and under the beds to convince myself they weren't still in the house.

No. 1779.   I am used to crime (a barrister) but it was still a bad shock, much worse than I thought it would be. I felt so unsafe.

Lasting Effects

We have seen that at least one-quarter of victims experienced some very unpleasant moments after discovering that they had been burgled. It is perhaps a matter for more concern that 65 per cent. of victims interviewed four to 10 weeks after the event said it was still having some effect upon their lives. The most common persisting effects were a general feeling of unease or insecurity and a tendency to keep thinking about the burglary.

Once the initial shock had worn off, most victims began to speculate about who had committed the offence. As less than 30 per cent. of burglaries are cleared up by the police, the majority never find the answer to the riddle and the imagination is allowed full rein. While some continued to envisage a frightening stranger (typically employing terms such as " rough ", " scruffy " or " unemployed " when asked to describe their mental picture of him), more than half came to suspect on reflection that the burglar was " somebody local " who knew them or was familiar with their habits.[5] On the whole, the latter conclusion was more likely to prolong the worry caused by the incident. Victims tended to re-interpret small events in the past— arguments with neighbours, visits to the house, " prying " questions, etc.— as related to the burglary. For example, one woman stated that she now " suspected everybody " of being the culprit. She was convinced that " he knew his way around ", having chosen one of the few times when she was not in the house to commit the offence and having quickly found some cash she had thought well hidden. She said she was " racking her brains " as to who could have done it: " You have this awful suspicion about everybody who comes near your house: the milkman, the kids, even people you have known for years." Such feelings had developed in at least three cases

[5] This was more frequently the case in housing estates or in streets close to housing areas perceived as containing " problem families ". Residents of the predominantly middle-class town we looked at were much more likely to believe that the culprit was a travelling stranger.

THE IMPACT OF BURGLARY UPON VICTIMS

into a state approaching paranoia, where the victims were convinced that somebody—they did not know who—held a grudge against them and was " watching " them. Even in less serious cases, people were inclined to search for reasons why their house had been chosen among all the possible targets in the area, and this tendency (which might be dubbed the " why me? " syndrome) seems to have been responsible for a great deal of the anxiety produced by burglaries.

Another common consequence of suspecting acquaintances—one which was named by 7 per cent. of victims as the worst effect of the burglary—was a general sense of disillusionment with humanity. An example is provided by case no. 29, a 40-year-old man living alone who lost a weeks' wages from his jacket. He said that prior to the burglary he regularly invited work-mates back for meals and social evenings and had people to stay overnight. He had always trusted people and welcomed them into his house. When he returned one evening to find his back window broken and the money taken he described his initial reaction as intense anger followed by a " complete loss of faith in people ". As he guessed, the offender was a previous visitor to the house, but even after the latter had been arrested the victim's attitude to others remained radically altered. As he put it, he had changed from an " open " to a " closed " person, and was now reluctant to have anybody in his house.

Fifteen per cent. of victims stated that they were still frightened at times as a result of the burglary. This normally took the form of fear when entering the house or certain rooms in the house or of being alone in their homes during the hours of darkness. Many of these thought that now the burglar knew the " layout " of the property he might return to steal what he had not taken originally.[6] The main physical consequences of such fear were difficulty in sleeping (8 per cent. mentioned this) and the use of tranquillisers or other drugs not previously taken (3 per cent.). In all, 6 per cent. said that their physical health had suffered as a result of the incident.

The most striking long-term psychological effect was experienced almost exclusively by women. About 12 per cent. of all females interviewed used words such as "pollution", "violation" or "a presence in the house". Many made an explicit analogy with a sexual assault, expressing revulsion at the idea of a " dirty " stranger touching their private possessions, and had felt impelled to " clean the house from top to bottom ". Such effects tended to persist for several weeks and were so disturbing in two cases that the victims had decided to move house to escape them. Five others had burnt furniture or clothing touched by the burglar. The following examples show the intensity of feeling that could be aroused:

> No. 539. I shall never forget it because my privacy has been invaded. I have worked hard all my life and had my nose to the grindstone ever since and this happens. Now we can't live in peace. I have a feeling of

---

[6] In fact, only 11 of the 322 interviewed were burgled again during the period of study. We were aware of the interest by victimologists in the phenomenon of multiple victimisation (*e.g.* Sparks *et al.*, 1979, p. 231) but apart from a case where some children had stolen a neighbour's key, which they used to enter her house several times, we found no evidence of burglars deliberately returning to the same house.

MIKE MAGUIRE

" mental rape ". I feel a dislocation and disruption of private concerns. I have destroyed everything they touched. I feel so extreme about it.

No. 629.   I'll never get over the thought that a stranger had been in here while we were in bed . . . the idea that a stranger, who could be one of those horrible revolting creatures, has been mauling my things about.

No. 976.   They had gone through all my clothes. I felt a real repulsion—everything felt dirty. I wanted to move—I had nightmares, and it still comes back even now.

No. 1010.   It's the next worst thing to being bereaved; it's like being raped.

A final common effect upon victims was to change what can be called their " security behaviour ". Of those who had not been insured 43 per cent. took out a policy and 42 per cent. of those who had been under-insured increased their cover; 50 per cent. improved the physical security of their homes by fitting new locks or bolts or an alarm; 80 per cent. of those who admitted they had been careless about locking doors or shutting windows prior to the burglary said that they had become more " security-conscious " as a result (although some were already beginning to lapse). A small minority went to desperate extremes, nailing up windows, putting furniture against doors, or sleeping with makeshift weapons beside the bed. With the possible exception of insurance, most of the above activities seemed to have a greater psychological than practical purpose. Victims generally recognised that it is impossible to create a " thief-proof " house, but the very act of making it more difficult to get in gave them some sense of control. As one man put it, " I felt I was fighting back ". Others simply said they " felt better afterwards ".

In addition to describing their reactions, victims were asked what, looking back, had been the worst thing about the whole event. The question was put twice during the interview, on the second occasion asking them to choose one or more possibilities from a prepared list. Table 2 shows the results of this second exercise.

TABLE 2

What was the worst thing about the burglary?

	Selected as worst	Selected as second worst	TOTAL (*i.e.* mentioned as either first or second choice)
	%	%	%
Intrusion on privacy	41	22	63
Emotional upset	19	25	44
Loss of property	25	20	45
Disarrangement of property	4	4	8
Damage to property	3	2	5
None of these	7	27	—
TOTAL	100 (N=322)	100 (N=322)	

The outcome was that 60 per cent. selected either intrusion on their privacy

THE IMPACT OF BURGLARY UPON VICTIMS

or general emotional upset as the worst element.[7] This finding underlines the point that the emotional impact of burglary is more important to victims than financial loss. While there has been some discussion (Marcus *et al.*, 1975; Miers, 1978) of the feasibility of restitution or compensation, our study suggests that, at least where burglary is concerned, the emphasis would be placed more appropriately upon the alleviation of psychological effects.

Differential Vulnerability

It has already been pointed out that certain categories of victim (female, pensioner, separated or divorced, etc.) appear to suffer disproportionately heavy initial effects. To test relative susceptibility to longer-term effects a panel of volunteers were asked to assess each case. Ten people from a variety of backgrounds were given a copy of every victim's account of the effects the burglary had upon his or her life up to the time of interview, and were instructed to rate each one in terms of the overall impact the burglary had produced, using a scale from 1 (severe) to 5 (little or none). The answers were averaged, cases with an average of 1·5 or below being labelled " serious effects ", those with an average between 1·5 and 2·5 " fairly serious " and so on.

The groups emerged as follows:

			%
Serious	(1 to 1·5)	43	(13)
Fairly serious	(1·5 to 2·5)	71	(22)
Moderate	(2·5 to 3·5)	100	(31)
Slight or nil	(3·5 to 5)	108	(34)
		322	(100)

This exercise confirmed that, as with the initial reaction on discovering a burglary, the most serious lasting effects are largely confined to female victims. Of the 43 deemed to be worst affected 34 were women, although almost equal numbers of males and females were interviewed. For this reason, the remainder of the analysis will be concentrated upon female respondents only, looking for any significant differences between the characteristics of those women who were badly affected and those who were not.

[7] Of course, the low numbers who chose damage or disarrangement of property were to some extent produced by the comparatively few cases in which there was any serious damage or ransacking, and the 14 per cent. who lost no property could not select loss as the worst element. However, even allowing for these factors, victims were still more likely to select an emotional element as the worst: only 16 per cent. of those who had to pay over £15 to repair damage selected damage as the worst thing; 14 per cent. of those whose property was scattered on the floor selected disarrangement as the worst thing; and 29 per cent. of those who lost any property selected loss as the worst. Broadly similar results were obtained from the same question when there was no precoded set of choices, but they provide a little extra insight. It was striking how many victims answered with almost identical words: " *The thought that someone had been in my house* "; 22 per cent. used this phrase or a very close equivalent. The answers also showed that many of those most concerned about the loss of their property were upset by *sentimental* rather than financial value. Other replies included " disillusionment, loss of faith in people "—7 per cent., and " not knowing who had done it "— 4 per cent.

Victimology

MIKE MAGUIRE

The most striking finding was that no less than 21 (62 per cent.) of the 34 worst affected were separated, widowed or divorced, although only 49 (31 per cent.) of the total female population interviewed fell into this category.

TABLE 3

Effects on Female Victims by Marital Status

		Married	Single	Separated/ divorced	Widowed	TOTAL
Number of cases with	serious effects	8	5	10	11	34
	less serious effects	67	30	15	13	125
TOTAL		75	35	25	24	159

($x^2 = 19 \cdot 8$ with 3 df p $>$ 0·001).

Other variables of victim characteristics had very little independent effect. For example, female pensioners were more seriously affected than women under 60, but much of this difference can be explained by the presence of 18 widows among the 35 pensioners.[8] Working-class women were marginally worse affected than middle-class women and women living alone worse than those living with others, but both these groups contained a higher proportion of widows and divorcees. When the figures were controlled for marital status, the differences all but disappeared. (Overall, the category of women emerging as most seriously affected was working-class widows over 60, but once one starts subdividing classifications, the numbers become too small to allow full confidence in the results.[9]) These results find some support in data collected in 1974 for a B.V.S.S. study (see note 1 earlier), where a re-analysis revealed[10] that 10 of the 12 female victims of burglary who had been most upset were separated, widowed or divorced.

Finally, it might be expected that, independent of the characteristics of the victim, the nature of the offence would make a considerable difference to its impact upon the household; for example, that night-time burglaries would create more fear than daylight offences, offences where the victim was present more than those where the house was unoccupied, " break-ins " more than " walk-ins ", and so on. However, none of these factors had any significant effect. Nor, indeed, did the type or value of the property stolen;

[8] While eight of these 18 widows suffered badly, only four of the remaining 17 older women did so. Male pensioners, too, were almost as resilient as younger male victims.

[9] Selected categories of victims interviewed, showing percentage seriously affected:

	No. in sample	Rated as seriously affected No.	%
All victims	322	43	13·4
Women	159	34	21·4
Working-class women	65	16	24·5
Women living alone	60	17	28·3
Women over 60	35	12	34·3
Divorcees	25	10	40·0
Widows	24	11	45·8
Widows living alone	18	9	50·0
Working-class widows	10	6	60·0
Working-class widows over 60	8	5	62·5

[10] Chris Holtom of Bristol University, who directed the study, kindly lent us the original data, from which we selected the 135 cases of burglary.

THE IMPACT OF BURGLARY UPON VICTIMS

people who lost nothing at all were as likely to be badly affected as those losing hundreds of pounds. The one exception was in the case of ransacking. Eight of the 18 women interviewed whose property had been seriously damaged or disarranged were among those most seriously affected.

Explanations and Implications

There is little doubt on the evidence presented here that a burglary is a significant event in the lives of a considerable proportion of victims. Almost all those interviewed had a clear memory of their reactions on discovering that their house had been entered. As many as 25 per cent. (and 40 per cent. of all female victims) were fairly seriously shocked or distressed at the time, and more than a month after the event only one-third of all victims said that they had fully recovered from the experience. Fifteen per cent. were still in some fear, about one in eight women felt " contaminated " or " violated ", and others reported worry, difficulty in sleeping, reluctance to leave the house unoccupied and a distrustful and suspicious attitude to strangers. Above all, the impression was of people struggling to recapture a lost sense of security. The irony is that the event triggering off such responses was often objectively a fairly trivial incident. Most of the victims quoted had lost very little and their houses had not been ransacked; more often than not it was still daylight when they discovered the offence and there was no sign of the offender. Many even suspected local teenagers of whom they would not be physically afraid if confronting them.

Before any remedies for the problem can be suggested, it is important to attempt to understand why it occurs. There seem to be at least three possible explanations, none of which is fully satisfactory, but which at least provide some illumination in a proportion of cases.

The first is simply that those who react badly are often people who are already experiencing a high degree of insecurity in their lives, and that *any* unexpected unpleasant experience might cause a similar reaction. This idea, although not properly testable on our evidence, might be supported by the preponderance of widows and separated and divorced women among those who suffered the worst initial impact. On the other hand, there were also a considerable number of victims to whom the above description clearly did not apply and yet who described strong symptoms of shock. Haward (1979) has also made the point that those he treated for psychiatric conditions following victimisation " were no more vulnerable to psychiatric breakdown than any other random sample of the population ".

A second possibility is that the intensity of feeling aroused is related to the importance people instinctively attach to private territory—a concept explored some time ago by psychologists such as Lorenz (1966). This is supported by the frequent mention of " violation " and disgust at " the idea of someone in my house " and by the fact that the intrusion itself is often considered more disturbing than the loss or damage. However, although many people certainly want to build a secure " nest " in which they can feel safe from outsiders, there is no evidence to show that the greater the degree of emotional investment in a home the greater the distress

MIKE MAGUIRE

will be when it is burgled,[11] nor that those who spend a great deal of their time in a house are worse affected than those who are often away from it (*e.g.* housewives compared with women in employment).

The third explanation is concerned with the public image of burglary. The word conjures up pictures of masked intruders, ransacked rooms and shadowy figures entering the bedroom while people sleep, all images perpetuated in fiction and in sensational media accounts of burglaries [12] but far from the reality of the mass of actual offences committed. Even without such influences, one has only to think back to childhood fears of " noises in the night " to understand why burglary comes high on the list of crimes people fear might happen to them.[13] It thus seems plausible to interpret the initial symptoms of shock so frequently mentioned (shivering, pallor, nausea, etc.) as a result of the combination of the unexpectedness of the event and the imagination of the victim. As previously described, many victims are temporarily unable to understand what has happened. If this state of disorientation is followed by a moment of comprehension in which a word with frightening connotations such as " burglars " suddenly leaps to mind, all sense of perspective can be lost and the victim may react to his or her preconceived image of what burglary entails rather than to the (usually less serious) reality of the situation. Many of those interviewed described their recovery from the initial impact of the burglary in terms of relief that the event had not been " as bad as it could have been ", perhaps a manifestation of the replacement of flights of imagination by a more objective manner of viewing the incident.[14]

These three explanations—which are not mutually exclusive—suggest a variety of possible strategies for reducing the adverse effects of burglary. The first points towards awareness of and action to help types of people particularly susceptible to distress. Victims Support Schemes have already found that the aged and people living alone are likely to require more support than most. Our finding that separated, divorced and widowed women are the most vulnerable groups may provide further insight and help to direct attention where it is most needed. The second implies the importance of restoring victims' sense of safety within the " territory " of the home.

---

[11] Although we found two specific categories of people with short-term homes—students in " digs " and service-men renting houses while stationed at a base—who were almost all unaffected by their burglaries, the numbers were too small to generalise and anyway special cultural factors may explain this. Moreover, it transpired that owner-occupiers, who might be thought to have more emotional attachment to their property than those who rent, were less seriously affected than both tenants of private landlords and council tenants. Waller and Okihiro (1978, p. 37) also found no relationship between length of residence and severity of reaction; neither did it make any difference whether or not people had put extra effort into major alterations or decoration in their home.

[12] Crime prevention literature and films could also be criticised on similar grounds. For example, the sinister silhouette used in the " Watch Out! There's a Thief About " campaign, however effective it may be in encouraging people to lock up their homes, is hardly helpful in fostering a sense of security.

[13] For example, a *New Society* survey (September 29, 1966) found that 26 per cent. of a random sample of the population " worried a great deal " about the possibility of being burgled, while only 16 per cent. worried about being physically assaulted.

[14] Sparks *et al.* (1977, p. 208) have even suggested that the actual experience of victimisation reduces fear of crime by (in most cases!) showing the victim that the reality is not as serious as the imagined event, although this finding is challenged by some Canadian research (Grenier et Manseau 1978).

THE IMPACT OF BURGLARY UPON VICTIMS

Many found it comforting to change locks or to instal new security devices, and the visit of a crime prevention officer or even simple advice from investigating officers was also helpful in this respect. A possible conclusion is that victims should be actively advised and encouraged by the police to make some changes, if only minor, in the way their homes are protected.

The third explanation merits special attention, as it can be used to justify a controversial approach to the problem which has gained some currency in the United States and Canada, but which appears from our research to contain some serious weaknesses. Waller and Okihiro, for example, have used the argument that fear of crime may often be as socially harmful as actual victimisation [15] to advocate a programme of " de-dramaticisation " of burglary, involving fewer prosecutions for minor offences, elimination of fear-producing crime prevention campaigns, and efforts to educate the public " by more frequent publicity of the peaceful nature of residential burglary ". They have also suggested that minor burglaries should be merely recorded over the telephone by civilian employees with an explanation to the public of the scarcity of police resources, so that trained policemen can concentrate upon " more serious offenders " (*ibid.* p. 105).

Unfortunately, Waller and others sometimes seem to confuse the distinction between anxiety that one might become the victim of a burglary and the feelings produced when it actually happens. Although the two are related, there are other elements involved in the latter which may not be affected by general measures to reduce fear. One which deserves special mention is reflected in the following response by McKay (1978): " I would like him [Waller] to be aware that the burglary was neither common nor dull for us. It was in fact an intrusive and psychologically violent act with long-term and enduring consequences. The impact of having our home, privacy and personal belongings violated in a distinctly impersonal fashion was, I can assure him, not dull. . . . If anything, our residual anxiety over the act was heightened by what we perceived as the *lack of reaction* by the local police. Frankly, in the aftermath of such an incident one resents being treated as mundane routine. Contact with the local force reflected less than five minutes of total conversation on the telephone with the investigating officer and with a desk officer at the station." Our results show that this represents a common feeling among victims. About one-third of the sample had some criticism of the manner in which their case had been handled by the police, by far the most frequent complaints being that the latter had displayed a " lack of interest ", had " treated us as unimportant " or had " made us feel as if we were wasting their time ".[16] There was also criticism that once the police had left, no notification was given about the progress (or lack of progress) made in the case.[17] By the same token, those who praised

[15] This is supported by studies such as those by Furstenberg, 1972; Garofalo, 1977; Hindelang *et al.*, 1978; Garofalo and Laub, 1978, which have shown a substantial level of public apprehension and a tendency to over-estimate one's chances of becoming a victim.

[16] 20 per cent. of working-class victims—who were generally more critical than middle-class victims—made remarks of this kind and 5 per cent. were extremely bitter about the way they had been treated.

[17] Only 24 per cent. had heard from the police again after the first two days. One Division had a policy of sending out " progress letters ", but this was not actually carried out in many cases.

MIKE MAGUIRE

the police often did so in terms of " the trouble they took " over the case. Significantly, their satisfaction with the police was not affected by whether or not the burglar was eventually detected.

The clear conclusion to be drawn from the answers to questions about what they wanted from the police was that victims were much less concerned with seeing an offender arrested than with receiving what they regarded as *the appropriate response to the incident*. In a state of considerable emotional upset, they had telephoned the police almost as an instinctive response,[18] with the expectation that the latter would come along and " do something " about the situation. The very routine of investigation—taking fingerprints, recording details, examining the point of entry, questioning neighbours, etc.—if coupled with a sympathetic attitude and a willingness to listen to the victim's fears, was mentioned as having a beneficial effect in helping people to come to terms with what had happened. As both the victim and the police were often well aware that there was little chance of an arrest,[19] these actions can to some extent be regarded as a kind of " ritual ", but this does not mean that they have no value. What they achieve is to " mark " the offence as an experience that others have been through in the past. As Wright (1977) puts it: " A crime is, at the least, a disturbance, at the worst, a disaster in people's lives. It is natural for people to want something to be done, just as they do when there has been an accident. This is partly out of a desire for practical action to put things back to normal, as far as possible, but partly it is because people want recognition of the offence, appropriate to its seriousness, from recording the details of a petty theft which is unlikely to be cleared up, to a full-scale murder-hunt (or, in the case of an accident or natural catastrophe, a visit by a government minister to the disaster area) . . . What offends people's instinctive sense of rightness is that the response is insufficient, rather than that it is insufficiently hurtful to the offender."

For these reasons there need not necessarily be a contradiction between encouraging a less dramatic image of burglary and at the same time taking seriously the psychological impact upon those who become victims. In other words, while it seems sensible to criticise sensational reports which increase public fear, this approach should not be taken to the extreme of making victims feel apologetic or embarrassed to report offences or to ask for attention.

Conclusions

The research outlined in this paper indicates that there are several inter-related factors to be considered if the impact of burglary upon victims is to be alleviated. In the most serious cases the reactions may be related to latent psychological problems which are triggered off by the event. Although these

[18] To the question " Why did you report the burglary? ", 75 per cent. replied that it was a " normal " or " automatic " response. Under 10 per cent. initially mentioned the hope that the offender might be caught.

[19] Victims described the police estimation of the chances of arrest as " optimistic " in only 20 per cent. of cases and they themselves were even less hopeful. Moreover, American research (Greenwood, 1975; Greenberg, 1977) has shown that if there are no immediate indications at the scene of a burglary as to the identity of the perpetrator (generally a witness description or a suspected acqaintance) the chances of an arrest through detective investigation are extremely low.

THE IMPACT OF BURGLARY UPON VICTIMS

are not confined to particular groups, we have identified certain categories of people (particularly women who have been separated from their husbands by death or divorce) who appear to be especially vulnerable. A more general problem is the sense of insecurity that is fostered by the knowledge that unknown persons have entered one's house, which when fuelled by an over-active imagination can result either in suspicion and distrust of acquaintances or in fear of faceless criminals who might return to threaten life and property. Finally, there is the desire for recognition of the offence as a significant event about which " something should be done ".

Although the main objects of this paper have been to describe reactions and to raise questions, some practical conclusions may be drawn. The problem of anxiety caused by exaggeration of the threat posed by burglars can be attacked on two fronts. On the one hand it seems reasonable to attempt to reduce the general fear of crime by the kind of educative pro-gramme recommended by Waller, but on the other the effects on individual victims might be alleviated by the very opposite of another of his recom-mendations—in other words, by *more* rather than less attention to those who have actually suffered a burglary. The latter—which would also deal with the problem of the " recognition " of the offence—could be achieved by changes in police approach or by the extension of Victims Support Schemes, or ideally by both. The burden upon police time would not necessarily be greatly increased if a special effort were made to remind junior officers that what presents itself to a policeman as a trivial, routine offence, holding out little hope of an arrest, may have a vastly different meaning to a person who is experiencing victimisation for the first time. Giving simple advice on security, reassuring victims that the burglar is probably a harmless teenager unlikely to return, carrying out initial investigations in a thorough manner, and later informing people whether or not any progress has been made, although largely unproductive in " thief-catching " terms, are all valuable as aids both to victims' recovery and to police-public relations, and more emphasis could be put upon the simple yet effective technique of talking over the incident with the victim.[20] This kind of help could be augmented by Victims Support Schemes, which also offer practical help and are valuable in identifying people who may eventually need pro-fessional treatment. If these can be developed in more areas, it is important that they be taken seriously by the police and that investigating officers are encouraged to pass on to them all cases in which further help may be needed.[21]

Ultimately, of course, the question of finances and resources may decide

[20] Most of these schemes have found that one or two visits as a sympathetic listener are effective in helping people over the initial effects of burglary. Moreover, it was not uncommon for research interviews to end with the victim saying that our visit had performed a similar function. Having completed the interview we sometimes stayed to continue talking, and in the course of discussion mentioned findings that the majority of arrested burglars are teenagers, that few ever offer violence to householders, and that on average people are victimised only twice in a lifetime, all of which seemed to help people take a more realistic and balanced view of their own burglary.
[21] The Bristol scheme has established a highly successful relationship with the police, being given full access to all reports of offences. However, in other areas volunteers have had to rely on "liaison officers " for the names and addresses of people needing help and lack of enthusiasm by the police has sometimes resulted in very few referrals.

MIKE MAGUIRE

the issue; it is arguable whether or not public funds can be spared to develop support schemes and whether police administrators believe that too much time is already allocated to visits to the scenes of minor crime. Nevertheless, the damage done over the long term by the insecurity and mistrust of others that burglary fosters and by the sense of having been " short-changed " by a casual or unsympathetic response by the police seems, from the results of our study, to deserve some serious consideration.

REFERENCES

BRYANT, G. and CIREL, P. (1977). *Community Response to Rape: Exemplary Project*. Washington, D.C.: L.E.A.A., U.S. Dept. of Justice.

B.V.S.S. (1975). " Summary of First Six Months Work of Bristol Victims Support Scheme ", mimeo.

FURSTENBERG, G. (1972). *Fear of Crime and its Effects on Citizen Behavior*. Washington, D.C.: Bureau of Social Science Research.

GAROFALO, J. (1977). *Public Opinion about Crime*. Washington, D.C.: U.S. Department of Justice.

GAROFALO, J. and LAUB, J. (1978). " The fear of crime: broadening our perspective ", *Victimology: An International Journal*, **3**, 242–253.

GREENBERG, B., ELLIOT, C. V., KRAFT, L. P. and PROCTER, H. S. (1977). *Felony Investigation Decision Model*. Washington, D.C.: L.E.A.A., U.S. Department of Justice.

GREENWOOD, P. W. and PETERSILIA, J. (1975). *The Criminal Investigation Process*. Vol. I. Santa Monica, California: The Rand Corporation.

GRENIER, H. et MANSEAU, H. (1979). " Les petits commercants victimes de vol a main armee en quete de justice ", *Criminologie*, *XII*, 57–65.

HALPERN, S. (1978). *Rape: Helping the Victim*. New Jersey: Medical Economics Company.

HAWARD, L. R. C. (1979). " Psychological Consequences of being the Victim of a Crime ", paper to SSRC Law and Psychology Conference, Trinity College, Oxford, September 1979.

HINDELANG, M., GOTTFREDSON, M. and GAROFALO, J. (1978). *Victims of Personal Crime*. Cambridge, Mass.: Ballinger.

HOLMSTROM, L. L. and BURGESS, A. W. (1978). *The Victim of Rape*. New York: Wiley.

KNUDTEN, R. D., MEADE, A. C., KNUDTEN, M. S. and DOERNER, W. G. (1977). *Victims and Witnesses: their experiences with crime and the criminal justice system*. Washington, D.C.: L.E.A.A., U.S. Department of Justice.

LORENZ, K. (1966). *On Aggression*. London: Methuen.

MARCUS, M., TRUDEL, R. J. and WHEATON, R. J. (1975). *Victim Compensation and Offender Restitution—A Selected Bibliography*. Washington, D.C.: L.E.A.A. U.S. Department of Justice.

McDONALD, W. F. (ed.) (1976). *Criminal Justice and the Victim*. Beverley Hills: Sage.

McKAY, B. (1978). Letter in *Liaison*, Vol. 4, No. 11, p. 4, in reply to an article " Minor Burglary," by Waller, I.

THE IMPACT OF BURGLARY UPON VICTIMS

MIERS, D. (1978). *Responses to Victimization.* Abingdon: Professional Books.

N.A.C.R.O. (1977). *Guidelines for Developing a Victims Support Scheme.* London: N.A.C.R.O.

NEWMAN, O. (1972). *Defensible Space.* New York: Macmillan.

REPPETTO, T. A. (1974). *Residential Crime.* Cambridge, Mass.: Ballinger.

SPARKS, R. F., GENN, H. and DODD, D. (1977). *Surveying Victims.* London: Wiley.

WALLER, I. and OKIHIRO, N. (1978). *Burglary: The Victim and the Public.* Toronto: University of Toronto Press.

WALLER, I. (1979). " Victimisation studies as guides to action: some cautions and suggestions." Paper presented to Third International Symposium on Victimology, Muenster, September 2–8, 1970.

WRIGHT, M. (1977). " Nobody came: criminal justice and the needs of victims," *Howard Journal, XVI,* 22–31.

[11]

ON WITNESSES: A RADICAL CRITIQUE OF CRIMINAL COURT PROCEDURES

Michael Ash*

"I tell you, I didn't see no mugging . . . and I didn't see it, 'cause if you see somethin' you're a witness, and I don't wanna be a witness, so I didn't see nothin'."

Arch, if you saw anything, it's your duty as a citizen to come forward and be a witness.

"That's great for your students and your unemployed, which for you is one and the same. But I'm a working man. I don't get paid if I show up for work absent. . . .

"Lemme tell you somethin'! Do you know what you gotta go through if you're a witness? You gotta put on a shirt and tie, drag myself downtown and hang around till the case comes up, which you never know when. And by the time it does, you forget what you was gonna say, and the other lawyer makes a monkey outta you! And it all goes on your record!"[1]

* * *

"Let's face it. You go down there (as a witness) and you're the one on trial. You get into an accident on 14th and U, and forget it, man, you ain't gonna get no one to go down there for you."[2]

* * *

"Let me get to the fundamental moral issue involved: a legal system should not treat people like this. . . ."[3]

I. Introduction: Some "Previously Identified Goals"

Thirty-three years ago the American Bar Association called attention to the way witnesses were then being treated.[4] Witness fees were described as inadequate and not "commensurate with modern wage standards." Incongruously low fees were said to excite the witness' "ridicule at the methods of justice."[5] Intimidation of witnesses was said to be a problem and, where it existed, "the supreme disgrace of our justice."[6] Courthouse accommodations for witnesses

---

* Member of the Wisconsin Bar. First Assistant District Attorney, Milwaukee County, Wisconsin. B.A., Marquette University, 1962; M.A., Political Science, Harvard University, 1965; J.D., Harvard University, 1967. This article was prepared while the author was on leave to the Law Enforcement Assistance Administration. The views expressed herein are not necessarily those of the L.E.A.A.

1 Archie Bunker (fictional), "Archie Sees a Mugging," *All in the Family,* copyright, Tandem Production. Inc., telecast on CBS-TV, January 29, 1972 (all rights reserved).

2 Unidentified black student. Bell Vocational High School, Washington. D.C. (to the author during question-and-answer period on "Bill of Rights Day"), November 1971.

3 J. FRANK, AMERICAN LAW: THE CASE FOR RADICAL REFORM 9 (1969).

4 RECOMMENDATIONS OF THE COMMITTEE ON IMPROVEMENTS IN THE ADMINISTRATION OF JUSTICE OF THE SECTION OF JUDICIAL ADMINISTRATION OF THE AMERICAN BAR ASSOCIATION (as approved by the Assembly and House of Delegates, July 27, 1938) [hereinafter cited as RECOMMENDATION].

5 *Id.* RECOMMENDATION 11.

6 *Id.* RECOMMENDATION 10.

were portrayed as inadequate and uncomfortable. According to the ABA, "the state owes it to the witness to make the circumstances of his sacrifice as comfortable as possible."[7] Too frequently, it was said, witnesses were being summoned back to court again and again without ever being asked to testify. The committee pointed to an incident involving a burglary case "in a certain city" in which

> there was no real doubt about the accused's guilt; but there were 19 continuances before he was finally tried and convicted. Meanwhile, the witnesses were forced to come ten miles to the court, on 19 occasions, each time being sent home to reflect upon the course of justice.[8]

"Promptness of trial," one of the recommendations concluded, "is essential to the preservation of testimony and to securing the good will and dependable mentality of witnesses."[9]

In 1948 Phillip L. Graham, a non-lawyer, reported on the impressions he gleaned from being part of "the Washington Experiment in judicial administration."[10] Graham wrote that there "seems to be widespread reluctance by many Americans to undergo the ordeal of being a witness."[11] He claimed that witnesses perceived themselves as "being forced into a contest against skillful opponents while knowing none of the rules."[12] He noted that many witnesses were outraged at court delay in the criminal courts and dismayed by the lack of accommodations for their comfort. He concluded that "those individuals among the public who may be called as witnesses need to be assured of fair treatment. . . ."[13]

In 1954 Professor Fannie J. Klein, the noted bibliographer,[14] wrote a short report on witnesses for The Institute of Judicial Administration.[15] In this report she referred to reforms benefiting witnesses as "a neglected area in judicial administration."[16] She wrote:

> In recent years, the distinction of being the "Forgotten Man of the Judicial System" seems to have devolved on the trial witness. Although the literature of the law bursts with erudition concerning methods of examining, cross-examining, impeaching, discrediting his reliability and indeed trying and convicting him, there is an astonishing paucity of material with regard to the attitude of the witness toward the judicial process, his criticisms of it and his suggestions for its improvement. But the trial witness, despite his silence, does have some complaints against the system which deserve review.[17]

---

7   *Id.* RECOMMENDATION 9.
8   *Id.* RECOMMENDATION 8.
9   *Id.* RECOMMENDATION 8.
10   On the program and concept *see* ABA SECTION ON JUDICIAL ADMINISTRATION, CO-OPERATION WITH LAYMEN IN IMPROVING THE ADMINISTRATION OF JUSTICE (1952); Laws, *Participation of Judges and Laymen in Improving the Administration of Justice*, 32 VA. L. REV. 89 (1945); and Laws, *Lay Assistance in Improving Judicial Administration, Symposium on Judicial Administration and the Common Man*, THE ANNALS OF THE AMERICAN ACADEMY OF POLITICAL AND SOCIAL SCIENCE 169 (1952).
11   Graham, *Treatment of Witnesses: Laymen's Suggestions for Better Handling*, 34 A.B.A. J. 23, 24 (1948).
12   *Id.*
13   *Id.* at 23.
14   *See* F. KLEIN, JUDICIAL ADMINISTRATION AND THE LEGAL PROFESSION: A BIBLIOGRAHY (1963).
15   INSTITUTE OF JUDICIAL ADMINISTRATION, TRIAL WITNESSES 1-5 (Unofficial IJA Study 2-066, July 1, 1954).
16   *Id.* at 5.
17   *Id.* at 1.

Indeed, through all these years and to the present, little has been written on the problems, interests, and rights of witnesses.[18] On the basis of the quantity of relevant materials, one would think that the eradication of the problems delineated back in 1938 had proceeded a pace, that the witness is no longer the forgotten man of our criminal justice system, and that we should all be enjoying an orgy of self-congratulation. In fact, the precise opposite is true and the witness, especially the witness in criminal courts,[19] is more abused, more aggrieved, more neglected, and more unfairly treated than ever before. Moreover, the treatment of witnesses in our criminal justice system has a deleterious impact on the prevention and deterrence of crime in at least three ways: First, the exposure to the criminal court process as it actually exists discourages countless numbers of witnesses from ever "getting involved" again, that is, from reporting crime, from cooperating with investigative efforts, and from providing testimony crucial to conviction; second, many crimes are committed by persons who might have been "rehabilitated" by correctional processes or at least "incapacitated" or "neutralized" by prison terms but for convictions that were "lost" because of delay and the "wearing out" of witnesses;[20] third, as Kenneth Lawing Penegar has said:

> [T]hat not only does delay adversely affect the individual's perspective of justice and not only is the habit of keeping people waiting (the accused as

---

18 In 1967 the President's Commission on Law Enforcement and Administration of Justice devoted approximately one third of one page (out of 340 pages) of its report to "jurors and witnesses," lumping the two in the same category. Substantially, the same problems—repeated, unnecessary appearances, poor facilities, inadequate compensation—were alluded to as in the earlier reports mentioned. *See* PRESIDENT'S COMMISSION ON LAW ENFORCEMENT AND CRIMINAL JUSTICE, THE CHALLENGE OF CRIME IN A FREE SOCIETY 156-157 (1967); *but see* Cutler, *Why the Good Citizen Avoids Testifying, Symposium on Judicial Administration and the Common Man,* THE ANNALS OF THE AMERICAN ACADEMY OF POLITICAL AND SOCIAL SCIENCE 103 (1952).

19 For the purpose of this article, a witness may be defined as one who is summoned to testify at a judicial inquiry. This paper will focus on witnesses in criminal cases in state courts. Thus, I leave to the side the problems of witnesses (1) in all civil cases, (2) in federal criminal cases, and (3) in all non-judicial proceedings, including investigative grand juries and legislative hearings.

Obviously, much that is said will be applicable to persons falling within each of the above three categories. For example, for discussion of some very similar problems facing grand jury witnesses and for some suggested solutions similar to the ones advanced in this article, *see* H. EDELHERTZ, THE NATURE, IMPACT, AND PROSECUTION OF WHITE COLLAR CRIME 32-33, 36 (1970).

Testifying before a grand jury will, of course, be considered to the extent that such testimony is part and parcel of state court criminal proceedings, as it often is.

I am excluding witnesses in federal court criminal cases because I have become convinced that state courts and federal courts play two entirely different ball games and that there is very little basis for comparing the operations of the two. In general, United States District Courts are incomparably richer in resources, manpower and facilities than their state counterparts. With respect to "crime" nationwide, federal trial courts have, of course, proportionately only a minor role.

20 In partial support of my "belief," consider the following:

First, when perpetrators of crimes "solved" are apprehended and turned over to the courts, they are quite frequently not convicted of any crime and often convicted only of a lesser charge. According to the *F.B.I.'s Uniform Crime Reports for the United States—1970* (1971) [hereinafter referred to as U.C.R.—1970], of adults prosecuted for "Crime Index" offenses (murder, rape, robbery, aggravated assault, burglary, larceny, and auto theft) in 1970, 61 per cent were found guilty as charged and 10 per cent of a lesser charge. U.C.R.-1970, at 36. Thus, 29 per cent were acquitted or their cases were dismissed. U.C.R.-1970, at 36.

Several things must be noted about these statistics. For one thing, the percentage of "unsuccessful" prosecutions varies considerably with the type of crime charged. U.C.R.-1970, Table 15, at 114. Generally, it appears to be harder to secure convictions on the more violent crimes

well as witnesses, attorneys, policemen, etc.) expensive; more importantly,
it could quite conceivably have detrimental effects on the effectiveness of
the whole system in terms of the goal of deterrence. Seen as a form of communications between the system and the general public, particularly potential violators, the syndrome of delay tells these audiences in effect that crime
and its participants are not really urgent public business, that not much
store is set by it in practical terms however much well meaning judges may

---

than on those less violent ones. U.C.R.-1970, Table 15, at 114. Thus, "[i]n 1970, 41 per cent
of the murder defendants were either acquitted or their cases dismissed at some prosecutive
stage. Forty-six per cent of those charged with forcible rape were acquitted or had their cases
dismissed, and 39 per cent of the persons charged with aggravated assault won their freedom
through acquittal or dismissal." U.C.R.-1970, at 36. When one looks to the percentage of
convictions on the original charge, "[l]arceny, 71 per cent, recorded the highest percentage
for persons found guilty on the original charge in 1970. This was followed by 53 per cent on
the original charge for burglary, 50 per cent for auto theft, 47 per cent for robbery, 44 per
cent for aggravated assault, 44 per cent for murder, and 36 per cent for forcible rape."
U.C.R.-1970, at 36.

Convictions on lesser charges usually mean, in effect, that short prison terms are sub-
stituted for longer ones, probation for short ones, fines for probation, and suspended sentences
for fines. They mean, in other words, that society's capacity to neutralize, rehabilitate, or
simply punish criminals has so much the less chance to operate.

Though this cannot be demonstrated by the FBI statistics that are published, it seems
certain that conviction rates also vary considerably from jurisdiction to jurisdiction. Thus, the
percentage of acquittals may be much higher in certain cities than the average, creating so
much the greater problem. Moreover, there is some impressionistic evidence to suggest that
conviction rates may be lower in larger communities where the crime problem is already
greater.

Obviously, some of those acquitted have in fact not performed any criminal act. However,
I believe that anyone closely associated with the actual operation of the criminal court system,
including defense attorneys and prisoners, in candid moments, would describe the percentage
of truly guiltless defendants to be very small. Many "guilty persons," they would acknowledge,
cannot be convicted solely because of legal reasons or problems of proof beyond a reasonable
doubt.

Thus, in summary, I suggest, first, that substantial numbers of criminals (for reasons good
and bad) "slip through the net," "escape justice," and are left unrehabilitated, unpunished, and
unrestrained to roam the streets and commit crimes.

Second, the likelihood of successful prosecution seems to decrease, generally, with (1) the
length of time between apprehension and disposition, (2) the number of appearances in court
by the defendant, and (3) the number of witness appearances. At least, this is the suggestion
of Banfield & Anderson, *Continuances in the Cook County Criminal Courts,* 35 U. CHI. L. REV.
259, at 287-88 nn. 93 & 94 (1968). Tables 3, 4, and 5, at 300-301, and Table 12, at 303.
Note 32, *infra.* It is also the firmly held belief of most of those closely associated with the operation of criminal courts. In other words, dilatory tactics and the "wearing out of witnesses,"
I suggest, produce results beneficial to accused criminals, but detrimental to anyone victimized
by their future misdeeds.

Third, of those who do commit crimes, amazingly large percentages seem to have been
recently embroiled in criminal court processes. By extrapolating from the analysis of the FBI
in U.C.R.-1970, at 37-38, it can plausibly be suggested that approximately 68 per cent of all
crimes are committed by those who have come before criminal courts sometime in their recent
past. Some of these persons, of course, were convicted. Hence, their recidivism reflects the
failure of prisons and correctional processes rather than courts.

But, fourth, of those brought before criminal courts, the worst recidivists by far seem to
be those who have been acquitted or whose cases have been dismissed. U.C.R.-1970, at 38-42.
The FBI reports that of "offenders released to the community in 1965, 63 per cent had been
rearrested by the end of the fourth calendar year after release. *Of those persons who were
acquitted or had their cases dismissed in 1965, 85 per cent were rearrested for new offenses.*
Of those released on probation, 56 per cent repeated, parole 61 per cent, and mandatory release
after serving prison time 75 per cent. Offenders receiving a sentence of fine and probation in
1965 had the lowest repeating proportion with 37 per cent rearrested." (Emphasis added)
U.C.R.-1970, 38-39.

I emphatically do not intend the above analysis to stand as "proof" of the textual proposition to which this footnote refers. In one or two instances, I have plugged statistical interstices
with what amounts to informed conjecture. Even if this were not so, I am fully aware of the
fact that the reasoning above falls considerably short of what is required for rigorous logical
demonstration. Nevertheless, the above analysis, I believe, at least strongly suggests that there
might be something more than emotion and rhetoric behind the theory I espouse in the text.

huff and puff from the bench when the accused finally comes before it. The English courts have long prided themselves on the practice of providing sure and swift apprehension and trial as one, if not the most effective, way to communicate to its citizenry that the system should really be taken seriously. Whether or not the individual is convicted, regardless of the sentence he receives (whether imprisonment for a short or long period or probation), the most important messages to the individual about society's disapprobation of his conduct will be conveyed to him in the first weeks of apprehension, charging and trial with efficient, deliberate progress throughout.[21]

II. Progress or Regression: Witnesses in Criminal Courts Today

In the typical situation the witness will several times be ordered to appear at some designated place, usually a courtroom, but sometimes a prosecutor's office or grand jury room. Several times he will be made to wait tedious, unconscionably long intervals of time in dingy courthouse corridors or in other grim surroundings. Several times he will suffer the discomfort of being ignored by busy officials and the bewilderment and painful anxiety of not knowing what is going on around him or what is going to happen to him. On most of these occasions he will never be asked to testify or to give anyone any information, often because of a last-minute adjournment granted in a huddled conference at the judge's bench. He will miss many hours from work (or school) and consequently will lose many hours of wages. In most jurisdictions he will receive at best only token payment in the form of ridiculously low witness fees for his time and trouble. In many metropolitan areas he will, in fact, receive no recompense at all because he will be told neither that he is entitled to fees nor how to get them. Through the long months of waiting for the end of a criminal case, he must remain ever on call, reminded of his continuing attachment to the court by sporadic subpoenas. For some, each subpoena and each appearance at court is accompanied by tension and terror prompted by fear of the lawyers, fear of the defendant or his friends, and fear of the unknown. In sum, the experience is dreary, time-wasting, depressing, exhausting, confusing, frustrating, numbing and seemingly endless.

Despite its seriousness, one can find in published materials only tidbits descriptive of the situation.

The Task Force on the Administration of Justice[22] reported:

> In courts in many cities witnesses must come to court each time the case is called and must sit through the entire calendar call, although most cases on the calendar will be settled by a guilty plea. Only a small number of the scheduled cases could possibly be tried that very day because of the shortage of judges. Adjournments are frequently requested and almost routinely granted. Rarely is an attempt made to notify the witnesses that the trial will not proceed as scheduled.[23]

---

21 *See* Penegar, *Appraising the System of Criminal Law, Its Processes and Administration,* 47 N.C.L. REV. 69, 150 (1968).
22 TASK FORCE ON ADMINISTRATION OF JUSTICE, PRESIDENT'S COMMISSION ON LAW ENFORCEMENT AND ADMINISTRATION OF JUSTICE, TASK FORCE REPORT: THE COURTS (1967).
23 *Id.* at 90.

It also quoted from a letter from Edward S. Silver, the former King's County (Brooklyn, New York) District Attorney, to James Vorenberg, the Executive Director of the Commission's staff:

> [I]n my job as District Attorney I frequently received serious complaints from witnesses who were greatly inconvenienced, and at times their jobs were put in jeopardy because of the necessity of coming back again and again when cases appeared on the calendar and were adjourned. In addition to that, there is never proper provision made for their full compensation for loss of time. Of course, I realize some limit must be put on compensation, but today any worthwhile mechanic can earn anywhere from $25.00 to $40.00 a day at his regular job.
>
> [I]n many instances, witnesses . . . develop an attitude that henceforth they will never act as witnesses again. Complainants and witnesses are innocent victims in these situations, and some real thought should be given as to how to minimize the inconvenience to which they are subjected and to make them feel that what they are doing is appreciated by the people and the authorities.[24]

The Task Force, in its report, pointed out that "[f]acilities for witnesses, as a rule, are either inadequate or nonexistent"[25] and that:

> Witnesses and jurors must often spend idle hours in crowded courtrooms or noisy corridors because many of these courts do not provide lounges or other facilities. Telephones for those who could conduct some of their business at the courthouse and reading material for those in forced idleness are lacking almost everywhere.[26]

"Compensation," it was said, "is generally so low that service as a . . . witness is a serious financial burden."[27]

> Repeated court appearances occasioned by adjournment of trials interfere with the private and business lives of witnesses and jurors. This waste of time, compounded by inadequate compensation, cannot be justified.
>
> . . . .
>
> The full impact of these problems does not become apparent until one realizes that a witness may be the victim of the offense and that he is often from the same low stratum of the community as the defendant.[28]

Starting with the week of January 10, 1972, the office of the District Attorney of Wayne County (Detroit and suburbs), Michigan, began collecting weekly statistics on witness appearances in felony and "high misdemeanor" cases in the Recorder's Court, which handles crimes committed within the limits of the city of Detroit.

24 *Id.*
25 *Id.*
26 *Id.* at 91.
27 *Id.* at 90.
28 *Id.*

In Detroit, as in most jurisdictions, each time a case is set for trial, all witnesses are subpoenaed. In some instances, trials are held and witnesses are required to testify. In many other instances, either a plea of guilty is accepted, the trial postponed or the case dismissed for any of a variety of reasons. In none of these events are any of the witnesses subpoenaed asked to testify. In practically all instances they do in fact appear and usually spend between a half day to a day in the court environs.[29]

According to these statistics, between January 10, 1972 and March 17, 1972, a total of 1,360 cases were set for trial, subpoenas were issued for all police and civilian state's witnesses—as well as an undetermined number of defense witnesses. During the same period, only 227 trials were actually held. In the remaining 1,133 instances, nothing happened that required the testimony of any witnesses.

In an average week, although 151.1 cases were set for trial (with witnesses ordered to appear and stand ready) only 25.2 trials were actually held. Thus, between January 10, 1972 and March 17, 1972, 2,055 civilian witnesses and 5,048 police witnesses were ordered into court for trials that were not held. A total of 7,103 witnesses were ordered into court and then, in effect, told to go home. In an average week, 560.8 police and 228.3 civilian witnesses were subpoenaed to no purpose, for an average weekly total of 789.2. These figures do not reflect the number of witnesses who were subpoenaed for trials that were held. An average of 6.3 witnesses per trial were subpoenaed for trials not held. If one makes the reasonable assumption that the average is approximately the same for trials held, then 5.0 witnesses are unproductively subpoenaed for every *one* that is subpoenaed for trial.

This five-to-one ratio of "wasteful" to productive appearances probably understates the situation. It takes no account, for example, of witnesses who were subpoenaed for a trial that was held, but who never actually testified and defense witnesses unnecessarily subpoenaed. Like all statistical representations, it does not capture the anger, anguish, and frustration that such a situation engenders.

If it were atypical there would be little to worry about, but it is not. In February, 1972, the Center for Prosecution Management distributed questionnaires to prosecutors attending an Office Management Seminar sponsored by the National District Attorneys Association. Because the seminar was geared to middle-sized offices, only three or four of the thirty or so largest offices responded. One assumes that larger jurisdictions have greater problems with court delay and witness disaffection than smaller ones. Therefore, the 44 responses to the questionnaire which were received are all the more striking.

The significant question asked the prosecutors to "describe disaffection of prosecution witnesses (*e.g.*, because of court delay, continuances, repeated appearances, etc.) in your jurisdiction." Of the replies, thirty described witness disaffection as being *more* than "a minor problem." Twenty said that in their

---

29   Conversation with James Garber, Chief Assistant to William L. Cahalan, District Attorney of Wayne County, April 20, 1972. I am much indebted to Mr. Garber and Mr. Cahalan for letting me use these statistics.

jurisdictions there was "substantial disaffection" among witnesses. Six acknowledged that the witness situation was a "serious problem affecting overall ability
to prosecute effectively." *None* described witness disaffection as being "nonexistent."

In many, if not most, criminal courts throughout the land, the system
actually works in a manner nicely captured by the authors of *Criminal Justice
Administration*:

> It is standard procedure for the defense counsel . . . to employ every
> means at his disposal to frustrate the efforts of the prosecution in bringing
> the case to trial. Chief dependence is placed upon the continuance, the
> objective being to wear out the state's witnesses.
> The case is routinely continued on the first occasion that it is up for
> trial. This continuance is termed "automatic" by police officers, because
> the request for it is rarely, if ever, turned down by the judge.
>
> . . . .
>
> Among the most common reasons provided by the defense in seeking
> repeated continuances are the claim that the attorney has a commitment in
> another court at the same time (sending a law clerk to offer the explanation
> and request the continuance); that the attorney has not yet received any
> or all of his fee; or that the attorney simply requires more time in which
> to prepare his defense. Attorneys employing this tactic will ask for as many
> continuances as the judge will allow. If the judge refuses additional continu-
> ances, the attorney will request a change of venue so as to start a series of
> hearings on motions or a new string of continuances in another court. As
> witnesses fail to appear, the state is forced into the position of agreeing on
> some occasions to a continuance.
>
> . . . .
>
> Several other methods are employed by defense counsel in frustrating
> the efforts of the state to bring a case to trial: requests for separate trials
> are frequently made in those cases in which multiple defendants are being
> prosecuted; defendants free on bond are not produced in court on the date
> of trial; and a request to stipulate ownership of stolen property is refused,
> thereby requiring the prosecution to produce the owner of the stolen prop-
> erty at each hearing regardless of whether he was a witness to the burglary,
> and even though the ownership may be only formally disputed.
> The results of the several delaying tactics are obvious. Victims or wit-
> nesses are lost—moving out of the state, going on extended vacations, or
> dying. Cooperative victims and witnesses become hostile, refusing to appear
> and, if summoned, unwilling to provide the testimony needed for conviction.
> Some, unfamiliar with the operations of the criminal process, become firmly
> convinced that a conspiracy exists in the particular case to block justice—a
> conspiracy entered into by the presiding judge, the state's attorney, and the
> arresting officer. Even cooperative witnesses find their memories dimmed by
> the passage of time, making them vulnerable to grueling cross-examination
> on the smallest details.[30]

Minor criminal courts, which often have responsibility for conducting pre-

---

30   F. REMINGTON ET AL., CRIMINAL JUSTICE ADMINISTRATION 1325-1326 (1970).

liminary hearings in more serious cases, are probably the most serious offenders. The chaotic atmosphere in one such court was described by Howard James as follows:

> Roughly the time court is scheduled to begin Judge C———— ambles from his office to the desk in the courtroom, sits down, and lights a cigarette. Then he tells those who are interested enough to listen that he will call four cases first—apparently the result of the conversations I had watched in his office.
>
> People still stand around the bench, block the doorways, talk to each other, mill noisily in the hall.
>
> Judge C———— calls the four cases and does not seem surprised when the parties are not present. He tells the witnesses to go home, explaining they will be told when to return again.
>
> . . . .
>
> Another case is called. Nobody is present. Some witnesses ask about their case. They are told it has been rescheduled for 1:30 p.m. and so they go home.
>
> It is 9:15 a.m. and the noise in the hall continues. Two cases "hanging fire since last September" (this was February) will be tried together, the judge announces. Several policemen are sworn together.
>
> The defendant asks for a continuance of two weeks so that he can finish paying off the bad checks, which are "90 percent paid." The policemen leave with the other witnesses. More people come in from the hall and fill up the seats.
>
> . . . .
>
> The next case is called, including a long list of witnesses. One policeman is present, along with the defendant. Judge C———— says that since the witnesses are not present (the case is not described) it will be dismissed— if the defendant agrees to pay court costs.
>
> . . . .
>
> Finally at 9:41 the first witness, a white factory worker, is sworn. He testifies that he was awakened by police "about 6 a.m." one day and was told they had recovered his pink and white '55 Cadillac with a fender smashed.
>
> He is asked if he knows who took it and he points at one of the youngsters and says, "That one." But according to the police, he was not present when the youth was picked up.
>
> The judge calls for the arresting officers to testify. Somebody says, "They called in and said they're on their way." Judge C ———— announces he will "hold the case in abeyance" until they arrive.
>
> . . . .
>
> In the next case the defense attorney tells Judge C ———— his client has been in court "each time the case was called since October," but so far the police officers have not been in court. The judge orders subpoenas issued again, and the case is rescheduled.

Then one of the white youths who arrived in handcuffs is told his case was "set by error" for this day, and that it is being reset for the following Tuesday. The boy is returned to jail.

. . . .

The next case is called and a policeman takes the stand. The case is postponed because the complaining witness has not been subpoenaed.

And so the morning goes: a man charged with using somebody else's credit card; more missing policemen, witnesses, and defendants, the two defense lawyers getting more assignments.[31]

Laura Banfield and C. David Anderson[32] have described Chicago practice:

In both the Criminal Division and the misdemeanor courts, all cases scheduled to be heard on a given day are called for 10 A.M. Since court calls are not staggered, witnesses, defendants, and police officers must all be on hand early in the day regardless of when the case is actually called. Some judges make a practice of calling cases which are to be continued first, or of giving preference as a matter of professional courtesy to those in which retained lawyers are present. In general, however, those required to appear in a case have no way of knowing when it will be called. In the preliminary courts, witnesses come to court on every scheduled court date. In the Criminal Division, the system is somewhat more selective; witnesses are subpoenaed by the state's attorney or by the defense when it is antici- pated that they will be needed. Witnesses are not subpoenaed, and do not attend, court appearances at which testimony is not taken, as, for example, the arraignment or the filing of discovery or other preliminary motions. Even when witnesses are subpoenaed, however, there is no guarantee that the case will go forward as scheduled; if it is continued, the witness will have come to court for nothing unless notified informally in advance of the continuance. Particularly in the crowded misdemeanor courts, the observer's impression is one of great haste and confusion; it is not surprising that wit- nesses sometimes do not realize that the case has been continued, or do not hear the date of the next court appearance. Commentators have criticized these features of the daily rat race in the criminal courts both for their inefficiency and for the burdens which they impose upon witnesses.[33]

Motions for continuance, according to the authors, were handled simply, informally, routinely, and casually, even when witnesses were present and pre- sumably prepared to testify.

Rather than inquire closely into the reasons, many judges say that they apply a standard policy of granting one or two continuances to either party on request; "after that, they'd better have a good reason." Other judges are willing to permit as many "by agreement" continuances as the parties are willing to arrange; close scrutiny is called for, they contend, only when one side is losing its witnesses or otherwise objects to further delay.[34]

---

31 H. James, Crisis in the Courts 39-41 (1967).
32 Banfield & Anderson, *Continuances in the Cook County Criminal Courts*, 35 U. Chi. L. Rev. 259 (1968).
33 *Id.* at 276.
34 *Id.* at 277.

"Wearing down witnesses," said the authors, is an accepted, frequently utilized, and generally successful defense technique.[35] They found that the number of witness appearances set is, in general, directly related to the length of time it takes to dispose of a case[36] and that:

> The most salient relationship between the number of court appearances and convictions is that, with few exceptions, the conviction rate decreases as the case length increases. For the whole sample, the percentage found guilty drops from 92% in cases taking between one and four court appearances to 48% in cases taking 17 or more court appearances.[37]

In reaching its conclusions about the real costs of the Cook County system, the authors report:

> Delay may . . . lessen public willingness to cooperate with the police and court system. Witnesses "worn out" by repeated and, in their eyes, fruitless trips to court become disaffected and unwilling to "get involved" on future occasions.
>
> . . . .
>
> Continuances also impose the burden of fruitless trips to court on witnesses and attorneys. The cost of such trips to the Police Department is measured both in the salaries paid to officers and in time taken away from police work. Private citizens incur these losses as well, since a day in court may often result in lost earnings.
>
> . . . .
>
> These time and money costs to private witnesses and attorneys may eventually be translated into costs to the system of criminal justice when witnesses and attorneys who find trips to court overly burdensome decline to return.
>
> . . . .
>
> Continuances may compromise the fairness of criminal proceedings if a delayed trial has a different, and less just, outcome from a speedy one. Witnesses may die. Their memories may fade. Their testimony may become more vulnerable to cross-examination. They may be "worn out" by repeated trips to court and refuse to appear again, or become less cooperative. A cynic, or a vigilant law enforcement officer, would add that opportunities for intimidating witnesses or bribing officials increase as a function of time. Although these consequences of delay can disadvantage either the prosecution or the defense, observers insist that "staleness" is far more likely to injure the prosecution, which is responsible for the production of most witnesses and has the burden of proving guilt beyond a reasonable doubt. Thus a prosecutor, aware that his case is growing weaker with the passage of time, may be forced to consent to a reduction of the charge or to end prosecution altogether. To those critical of the court system, "lost convictions" are the most significant cost of continuances.[38]

35   *Id.* at 265, 283, 291.
36   *Id.* at 290.
37   *Id.* at 287-288.
38   *Id.* at 261-263.

Victimized by administrative run-around, the witness' lot is not made any easier by the law. For example, he will likely be ordered excluded from the court-room, and he may be subject to penalties for contempt of court if he violates the exclusionary order.[39] He is compelled to testify even if his testimony will bring him into "disgrace."[40] If he refuses to answer he may be punished for contempt. If a witness is once punished for contempt in refusing to answer a question and is then recalled and asked the same or a similar question which he again refuses to answer, he may again be punished without violating the prohibition against double jeopardy.[41]

Certain "testimonial privileges" theoretically preclude testimony emanating from certain confidential relationships; but they are regarded, not as privileges of *witnesses*, but as privileges, waivable and claimable only by parties.[42] A re-calcitrant or uncooperative witness may be held in contempt for any number of reasons.[43] If the judge decides he is lying, not only can he be held and punished for contempt, but he can also, *in addition,* be charged, convicted, and sentenced for the *crime* of perjury.[44]

In certain states he may be liable for the costs of criminal proceedings; "[s]tatutes imposing costs on prosecution witnesses, under certain circumstances, on failure of the prosecution, and authorizing imprisonment until they are paid, generally have been upheld as constitutional."[45] If adjudged to be a "material witness" who cannot be trusted to appear, he may be compelled to post bail to assure his appearance and, in its absence, he may be, and frequently is, jailed until there is no need for his testimony.[46] If he is jailed, he may not be entitled to witness fees.[47] As recently as December 1971, the United States Court of Appeals for the Fifth Circuit issued an opinion reiterating this rule.[48]

In the hallowed halls of the courtroom itself, he may be subjected to verbal abuse without there being much concern for his protection.[49] He may be threatened or assaulted by those concerned with the outcome of the prosecution—perhaps this danger is all the greater in view of the rapid expansion of discovery in criminal cases—especially the practice of early disclosure of the names and ad-

---

39 *See generally* Annot.. 14 A.L.R. 3d 16, 22-23 (1967).
40 Brown v. Walker, 161 U.S. 591 (1896); 25 NOTRE DAME LAWYER 378 (1950).
41 17 AM. JUR. 2d *Contempt* § 29 (1964). *See* Yates v. United States, 355 U.S. 66, 72-75 (1957).
42 *See* Hawkins v. United States, 358 U.S. 74 (1958); Wyatt v. United States, 362 U.S. 525, 528-529 (1960). For anyone interested in following up on the rather subtle point of legal doctrine adverted to in the text, I would suggest referring to the briefs of the parties in the above Supreme Court cases.
43 *See* 3 R. ANDERSON, WHARTON'S CRIMINAL LAW AND PROCEDURE § 1336-1339 (1957).
44 Annot., 89 A.L.R.2d 1258. 1266 (1963). *See* 5 R. ANDERSON, WHARTON'S CRIMINAL LAW AND PROCEDURE § 2027 (1957).
45 20 AM. JUR. 2d *Costs* § 111 (1965).
46 *See* Carlson. *Jailing the Innocent: The Plight of the Material Witness,* 55 IOWA L. REV. 1 (1969); Comment, *Pretrial Detention of Witnesses,* 117 U. PA. L. REV. 700 (1969); and comment, *Witnesses: Imprisonment of the Material Witness for Failure to Give Bond,* 40 NEB. L. REV. 503 (1960).
47 Annot.. 50 A.L.R.2d 1439 (1956).
48 Hurtado v. United States, 452 F.2d 951 (5th Cir. 1971).
49 *E.g.,* "[W]hen the evidence justifies severe and rigorous criticism of a witness, it is not reversible error to allow an attorney to use invective in denouncing him." 5 R. ANDERSON, WHARTON'S CRIMINAL LAW AND PROCEDURE § 2078 (1957).

dresses of witnesses.[50] In some limited circumstances a complaining witness may be ordered to undergo a mental examination.[51] He is deemed to be under a strong obligation to appear at court when summoned and to answer the questions asked.[52] Conversely, he has no general right not to testify. Limitations on his testimonial duty are few and exceptional and, in the words of the leading authority on the law of evidence, "therefore to be discountenanced."[53] At grave financial loss he may be compelled to venture the length of the country should his testimony be thought to be required.[54] *His* interests, *his* convenience will not dictate a change in the location of a trial. In legal terms, "[a] change of venue will not be allowed merely for the convenience of witnesses."[55] In practical terms, he has neither the means of preventing his being subpoenaed unnecessarily or even frivolously, nor the means of obtaining redress for the wrong committed against him.[56] In one remarkable instance in which *167 witnesses,* most of whom knew *nothing whatsoever* about the case, were subpoenaed, it was held that causing the subpoenas to issue was *not* contempt of court.[57]

In criminal cases the witness is often the victim of the crime, that is, the person raped, robbed, beaten, or shot at by the accused. Courthouse contacts (not to mention contacts in the street) with the defendant, especially if he is free on bond or recognizance, are difficult and sometimes traumatic. When courtroom contacts are repeated, the experience may be so much the more unpleasant. Testifying, for the average witness, is terrifying; the more aggressive the cross-examination, the more uncomfortable the witness may be. The more heinous the crime, the more the fear and embarrassment there may be in recounting the details.

For all this, the witness is paid little or nothing. Mileage fees generally range between three cents per mile up to approximately ten cents per mile. Hawaii, Idaho, and Nebraska appear to be the only states offering mileage fees that are in excess (by a few cents) of this range. Typically, five cents per mile, round trip, from home to court is allowed. Out-of-state mileage, if any, is usually not counted. As for daily fees, Alabama, Colorado, Connecticut, Delaware, Kentucky, Maryland, Minnesota, Mississippi, New Jersey, New York, Oklahoma, South Carolina, Tennessee, Texas, Virginia, and West Virginia compensate their criminal court witnesses at two dollars per diem or less; Idaho, Illinois, Michigan, Montana, Nevada, and Wyoming at from eight to twelve dollars and the remaining states between three and six dollars per day.[58]

---

50   21 Am. Jur. 2d *Criminal Law* § 328 (1965).
51   *See* Annot., 20 A.L.R. 2d 684, 691-92 (1968) and Annot., 18 A.L.R. 3d 1433 (1968).
52   *E.g.,* Blair v. United States, 250 U.S. 273, 281-282 (1919) (pertaining to grand juries).
53   8 J. Wigmore, Anglo-American System of Evidence § 2192, at 67 (3d ed. 1940).
54   People v. O'Neill, 359 U.S. 1 (1959).
55   R. Anderson, Wharton's Criminal Law and Procedure § 1517, at 110 (1957).
56   *See generally* Annot., 37 A.L.R. 1112 (1925).
57   *Ex parte* Stroud, 268 S.W. 13, 37 A.L.R. 1111 (1925).
58   "From all of this data on conclusion is obvious: the witness will usually be attending a trial at a financial sacrifice." Comment. *Compensation of a Witness in a Civil Action,* 52 Mich. L. Rev. 112, 115 (1953). *See also* Wisconsin Legislative Reference Bureau, Court Witness Fees and Mileage Allowances in the 50 States (unpublished, 1966).
     The textual material on witness fees is based in small part on the *Michigan Law Review* article cited above and in large part on a survey of the statutory provisions on witness fees, done at my request by Charles N. Clevert, who is at this writing a third-year law student at

Even these are, in some instances, not being paid. The author is aware of two major jurisdictions (and I suspect there are scores of others) where it is very uncommon for witnesses in criminal cases to receive any fees at all. The expedient by which this is accomplished is simple. Witnesses are simply not told that they are entitled to fees. In the unusual instances when they are told or somehow find out, they are required to produce subpoenas or some "proof" of having been present in court. By this time most witnesses have deposited their subpoenas in the trash and find it just too much trouble to scrounge for the paltry sums involved. As a result, few actually collect the sums available.

III. Witnesses: A Pattern of Blindness and Neglect

Nowhere is there hard data on witnesses in criminal cases. This absence is part of a larger pattern of blindness and neglect. In a real sense, our system does not "see" witnesses in their human dimension. Consequently, we are neglectful of their interests and problems.

Illustrative and expressive of the pattern are the references under "witnesses" in any edition of the *Index to Legal Periodicals*. Compared with hundreds of seemingly more arcane headings, the number of articles listed will be few. More-

---

Georgetown University's Law School in Washington, D. C. and a part-time LEAA employee.
    Per diem and mileage compensation rates throughout the country are, respectively, as follows:
28 U.S.C. § 1821 (1970) ($20.00; $.10 per mile). ALA. CODE tit. 11, § 103 (1940) ($0.75; .05 per mile) ARIZ. REV. STAT. ANN. § 12-303 (1956) ($5.00; .20 per mile); ARK. STAT. ANN. § 28.524 (1962) ($3.00); CAL. GOV'T CODE § 68093 (West, 1964) (fees are discretionary and are allowed upon a showing of need; .20 per mile one way); COLO. REV. STAT. § 56-6-2 (1963) ($2.50); CONN. GEN. STAT. § 52.260 (1960) ($0.50; .10 per mile); DEL. CODE ANN. tit. 10, § 8903 (1953) ($2.00; .03 per mile); D.C. CODE ANN. § 15-714 (1967) ($20.00; .10 per mile); FLA. STAT. ANN. tit. 7, § 90.146 (1960) ($3.00; .06 per mile); GA. CODE ANN. § 38-801 (c) (1954) ($4.00; .08 per mile); HAWAII REV. STAT. tit. 32, Ch. 607-12 (1968) ($4.00, $6.00 if inter-island travel is required; .20 per mile); IDAHO CODE ANN. § 9-1601 (1948) ($4.00; .25 per mile); ILL. STAT. ANN. ch. 53, § 65 (Smith-Hurd 1967) ($10.00; .08 per mile); IND. STAT. ANN. § 2-1710 (Burns, 1968) ($5.00; .08 per mile); IOWA CODE ANN. § 622.69 (1950) ($3.00; .07 per mile); KAN. STAT. ANN. § 28.128 (1971 Supp.) ($5.00; .09 per mile); KY. REV. STAT. § 421.010-421.020 (1971) ($1.00; .04 per mile); LA. REV. STAT. § 15:252 (1967) ($3.00; .05 per mile); ME. REV. STAT. ANN. tit. 16, § 251 (1965) ($5.00; .08 per mile); MD. CODE ANN., art. 35, § 18 (1971); ($1.00; .05-.10 per mile); MASS. ANN. LAW., ch. 262, § 29 (1968) ($3.00; .05 per mile); MICH. STAT. ANN., § 27A.2552 (1967) ($12.00; .10 per mile); MINN. STAT. ANN., § 357.22-357.24 (1966) ($1.00; .06 per mile); MISS. CODE ANN., § 3953 (1957) ($1.50; .05 per mile); MO. STAT. ANN., § 491.280 (1952) ($3.00; .07 per mile); MONT. REV. CODE ANN., § 25.404 (1967) ($10.00; .08 per mile); NEB. REV. STAT., § 33.139-33.140 (1968) ($6.00; .08 per mile); NEV. REV. STAT., § 48.290 (1967) ($10.00; .15 per mile); N.H. REV. STAT. ANN., § 516.16 (1971 Supp.) ($5.00; .06 per mile); N.J. STAT. ANN., § 22A:1-4 (1969) ($2.00); N.M. STAT., § 20-1-4 (1953) ($5.00; .08 per mile); N.Y. CIV. PRAC. LAW § 610.50 [C.P.L.R. 8001] (McKinney, 1971) ($2.00; .08 per mile but no mileage for travel wholly within a city); N.C. GEN. STAT., § 6-51-6-63 (1962) (witness is merely entitled to mileage at unspecified rate); N.D. GEN. CODE, § 31-01-16 (1960) ($6.00; .10 per mile); OHIO REV. CODE ANN., § 2335.06 (Page 1954) ($0; .05 per mile); OKLA. STAT. ANN., tit. 28, § 81 et seq. (1955) ($2.00; .05 per mile); ORE. REV. STAT., § 44.410-44.430 (1953) ($5.00; .08 per mile); PENN. STAT., tit. 28, § 416.2-416.4 (Perdon 1955) ($5.00; .07 per mile); R.I. GEN. LAWS § 9-29.7 (1968) ($5.00; .10 per mile); S.C. CODE § 27-611 et seq. (1968) ($0-0.50; .10 per mile); S.D. COMP. LAWS § 19-5-1 (1961) ($4.00; .15 per mile); TENN. CODE ANN. § 24-401 (1955) ($1.00; .10 per mile); TEX. STAT. art. 3708 (Vernons, 1926) ($1.00; .06 per mile); UTAH CODE ANN. § 21-5-4 (1953) ($6.00; .20 per mile); VT. STAT. ANN. tit. 32, § 1552 (1970) ($10.00; .08 per mile); VA. CODE ANN. § 14.1-189-14.1-190 (1950) ($1.00; .07 per mile); WASH. REV. CODE ANN. § 2.40.010 (1961) ($4.00; .10 per mile); W. VA. CODE § 59-1-16 (1966) ($1.00; .05 per mile); WIS STAT. ANN. § 885.05 (1966) ($5.00; .05 per mile); WYO. STAT. ANN. § 1-195 (1957) ($10.00; .10 per mile).

over, there will be practically nothing on the treatment or rights of witnesses. To find what little exists on those subjects, one must search laboriously through a battery of other headings, *e.g.* "administration of justice," "continuances," "victims of crime," which contain much unrelated material. The impression created is that the legal indexing system is simply not geared to finding out about the treatment of witnesses. Like the rest of the system, it is blind to the problems of witnesses.

What one does find under the heading "witnesses" are articles on how to interview witnesses, cross-examine them, subject them to lie-detector tests, prepare them for the "courtroom ordeal," prevent their untruthful testimony from convicting innocent defendants, provide them with immunity so as to extract the information they possess, etc. One finds, in other words, articles on how to handle, manipulate, or exploit witnesses, but little more.

In one especially noteworthy article entitled "Some Things About Witnesses,"[59] attorney E. H. Smith wrote of how the appearance of witnesses may influence a jury and how he used this knowledge in defending a noted bootlegger. It was apparently the custom in his jurisdiction for each side's witnesses to be sworn collectively at the outset of trial, first the prosecution's, then, the defendant's. Attorney Smith relates:

> I knew that when the case was called the witnesses for the prosecution would be called and sworn as a body, and that then the witnesses for the defense would be called and sworn likewise. I also knew that when this was done the appearance of my rough kind of ragamuffins would be a great contrast to the appearance of the prosecution's witnesses and that I would be at a distinct disadvantage; I was fearful of the effect this might have upon the jury.

> To try to remedy this I at once had subpoenas issued for several bankers and professional men, two or three ministers of the gospel, and one or two merchants.

> When the case was called and the witnesses stood up to be sworn I had just as good a looking a bunch of witnesses as the prosecution and in this manner avoided any ill effect from first opinions.

> Incidentally I succeeded in acquitting that client.[60]

To trial attorneys, the author offered this bit of advice:

> To have a witness present in court and not need him is much safer than to permit him to be absent and then to need him.

> In cases where there are many witnesses, witnesses sometimes have to wait hours and sometimes days before being called. Each wants to know of the attorney, if he cannot be excused, stating, "I don't know anything anyway." When this is refused then he wants the attorney to have him called over the telephone when he is needed. If there were only one witness to be called this

---

59   Smith, *Some Things About Witnesses*, 8 KY. S.B.J. 37 (1944).
60   *Id.* at 39-40.

request might be easily complied with, but to have to call each witness over the telephone and wait for him to get into the courtroom would cause unnecessary and expensive delay and furthermore burden the lawyer with the responsibility of remembering to call them. Witnesses are inconvenienced, yes, but there are many inconveniences to be put up with as we travel through life.

A lawyer has to subpoena many witnesses sometimes, to get one he wants [*sic*] he cannot always control the circumstances of his case.[61]

Smith goes on to boast that he once subpoenaed *every single employee* of a hospital to obtain a single scrap of information. "I refused to excuse any of them," he writes "and all remained confined in the witness room throughout the trial."[62] In this room, according to the author,

the witnesses . . . are herded together, closely confined with nothing to do but wait. They are usually uncomfortable, nervous, and restless, [*sic*] after a few hours of this confinement they become miserable.[63]

More startling even than Smith's total obliviousness to the human character of those infinitely manipulable pawns he calls witnesses is the fact that his article made print. Indeed, it made print without provoking any significant comment from the editors of the journal in which it appeared or any reply from the lawyers and judges who read it. The reason for this is that the attitudes toward witnesses reflected are typical of bench and bar. Smith's article, though a bit more blunt and a shade less delicate, is very much like scores of similar pieces that have appeared in bar journals and lawyers' magazines all over the country. Judges and lawyers generally, though more sensitive to the public relations aspects of what they say, share Smith's myopic one-dimensional view of witnesses.

These views are clearly reflected in the substantive law governing witnesses. As we have seen,[64] the law imposes upon witnesses onerous duties for which it provides little or no compensation, and none "of right." In contrast to the proliferating number of protections and defenses the law now accords an accused, it accords to witnesses few and none of real consequence. The very concept of "rights of witnesses" seems foreign to the legal mind. To a most remarkable extent, it is simply not the habit of the law to take account of witnesses.

True, legal writing sometimes *seems* to take explicit account of witnesses (though even this is unusual). For example, in discussing the law relating to the asking of "insulting questions" on cross-examination, one author acknowledged that restrictions on "insulting questions" are necessary "to allay the fears of prospective witnesses that their private lives will be subjected to microscopic scrutiny in the public courtroom."[65] Significantly, the article does *not* support

---

61 *Id.* at 44.
62 *Id.*
63 *Id.* at 38.
64 *See* text accompanying notes 39-58 *supra*.
65 26 CORNELL L. Q. 724, 727 (1941). Triggering the inquiry was a ruling on the question: "Have you ever suffered from venereal disease?" in People v. Kress, 284 N.Y. 452, 31 N.E.2d 898 (1940). The court has stated that the question, asked of a defendant who had taken the stand, was improper.

such restrictions because "microscopic scrutiny" of "private lives" of witnesses in the "public courtroom" should be discouraged, but because "*fears*" of such scrutiny by "*prospective* witnesses" should be allayed. But semantics aside, one might expect that the article's unusual concern for the fears of prospective witnesses might herald the even more unusual espousal of a legal rule truly solicitous of the witness' interest in not being badgered, embarrassed, or psychologically undressed. Instead, he favors the existing rule which requires insulting questions to be answered if it "will assist the jury in finding out whether the witness is telling the truth."[66]

The point is not that this rule is unwise or unjust or even that it burdens significant numbers of witnesses. The point is twofold: First, in a legal system which subordinates fact-finding to a host of other interests (*e.g.*, the right of the accused not to be convicted by "tainted" evidence, regardless of its probative value), this rule entirely subordinates a witness' interest in privacy to fact-finding; second, it is unblinkingly espoused by an article claiming to pay heed to witness interests. Under the rule in question, a witness literally has no right to be free of insulting questions if the judge believes they will assist in testing the witness' veracity.

Similarly, only rarely does legal commentary in general explicitly advert to witness' interests even when they are significantly affected by the topic under discussion. When such reference is made, it is formal and illusory. In the rare instance when witness' interests are considered and weighed on the balance, they are invariably subordinated to what are regarded as "more important interests."[67]

A particularly vivid example of the denigration of witness' interests is the commentary on the question of whether the complaining witness in certain types of sex offense cases should be made to undergo psychiatric examination and whether the results of such an examination should be admissible in evidence. Since this article is not intended to mount elaborate attacks upon particular rules of law, it will suffice to simply state: it is thought that the trend of the law and the tendency of the commentary is that criminal defendants should be afforded some kind of right to have such an examination conducted.[68]

Espousal of such a rule requires the subordination of witness' interests of enormous importance and sympathetic appeal. Is it really fair to a woman who

---

66   *Id.* at 725.
67   Examples illustrative of the tendency to discount witnesses' interests are: Comment, *Right of the Criminal Defendant to the Compelled Testimony of Witnesses,* 67 COL. L. REV. 953, 966-967 (1967), and 15 CHI.-KENT. L. REV. 343, 344, 345 (1936). Hopefully, the reader of this article will become alert to this dismaying tendency and will come to notice similar examples as they appear.
68   *See* Annot., 20 A.L.R 2d 684, 691-92. (1968) and Annot., 18 A.L.R. 3d 1433 (1968). An excellent example, both of the commentary on this question and its tendency to give short shrift to witnesses, is Comment. *Psychiatric Evaluation of the Mentally Abnormal Witness,* 59 YALE L. J. 1325 (1950), a much cited and discussed article which argues for compulsory psychiatric examination of "any witness" who "may be suffering from a 'mental illness' likely to affect his credibility." *Id.* at 1340. I suggest that, in practice, such a rule could only result in massive unfairness and imposition on witnesses. I suggest also that the article in question is typical of much legal writing in that (1) it appears on the surface to reflect reliance on vast quantities of research; (2) it appears on the surface to reach conclusions that are based upon a painstaking, reasoned, explicit consideration of the interests of all concerned; (3) it, in fact, regards the interests of witnesses as being without importance or significance; and (4) it is naive in the extreme about the operation in the real world of the rule it espouses.

has been the victim of a rape, who has been through a horrifying and painful experience of seemingly endless duration, who has been sharply grilled by batteries of police officers, who has been made to look at scores of photographs, who has been summoned to several police line-ups where she finally identified her attacker, who has been interviewed by several assistant prosecutors, who has already recounted the horrifying details of her experience to a grand jury and to the public at a preliminary examination, where she was vigorously cross-examined by her attacker's lawyer, who has made numerous fruitless trips to the courthouse expecting to testify—is it really fair to her to tell her in the end that everyone has doubts about her and that she must divulge her personal and sexual history to a stranger who is said to be a specialist in detecting mental illness? Is the likely result of such examinations such as to justify compelling an innocent human to submit to such an experience?

I think not, but that is not my point. My point is that legal thinking stands so remarkably ready to pour abuse on witnesses in pursuit of some highly fanciful benefits to other components of the system.

The "tunnel vision" afflicting the authors of the previously discussed articles when referring to witnesses is equally apparent in more recent works. Witnesses have been quite neglected and indeed are barely visible in the two major efforts to reappraise the criminal justice system.

In the 1967 report of the President's Commission on Law Enforcement and Administration of Justice, *The Challenge of Crime in a Free Society*, two thirds of one page out of 340 was devoted, not to witnesses, but to "jurors and witnesses."[69] Another two paragraphs were directed to the desirability of "residential facilities" for the comparative handful of witnesses in organized crime cases who might desire special protection.[70] Only two recommendations ("jurors and witnesses" and "residential protection facilities"), out of more than 200, pertained to witnesses.

Similar criticism applies to the American Bar Association's Project on Minimum Standards for Criminal Justice. Among the fourteen volumes published, there is none entitled "Standards Relating to Witnesses in Criminal Cases," though entire volumes were devoted to such comparatively arcane topics as "Electronic Surveillance" and "Appellate Review of Sentences." Scattered here and there are occasional sympathetic remarks, for example, on "repeated impositions on time, energies and talents of judges, jurors, *witnesses*, law enforcement officers, lawyers, and other court personnel [emphasis added]."[71] And admittedly, there are the standard warnings to lawyers about improper interviewing and excessively aggressive cross-examining.[72] Nevertheless, taken *in toto*, the ABA Standards reflect no perception of witnesses as persons, no understanding of

---

69 PRESIDENT'S COMMISSION ON LAW ENFORCEMENT AND ADMINISTRATION OF JUSTICE, THE CHALLENGE OF CRIME IN A FREE SOCIETY 156-157 (1967).

70 *Id.* at 204.

71 ABA STANDARDS, DISCOVERY AND PROCEDURE BEFORE TRIAL 27 (Approved Draft, 1970).

72 ABA STANDARDS, THE PROSECUTION FUNCTION AND THE DEFENSE FUNCTION, Standards 3.2 and 5.7, at 81, 122 (prosecution) and 4.3 and 7.6, at 228 (defense) (Approved Draft, 1971).

404   NOTRE DAME LAWYER   [December, 1972]

how they are affected by participation in the criminal court process, and very
little real concern for their interests.

A few illustrative questions will point up the shortcomings of the Standards.

In spelling out standards for the scheduling of criminal cases and for granting
or denying continuances, why was not the time, expense, and convenience of
witnesses made one factor to be considered?[73]

In warning both prosecutors and defenders about embarrassing or humiliating witnesses on the stand,[74] why were not warnings included about (1) the
summoning of unnecessary witnesses; (2) purposeless insistence on all witnesses
remaining in waiting at the courthouse all through the many tedious days of a
lengthy trial, and (3) lack of maximum diligence in notifying witnesses that a
hearing has been postponed or that their testimony will not be required?

Instead of delicately and circuitously slapping the wrist of an attorney who
engages in "delay for tactical advantage," why did not the Standards condemn
the "wearing out of witnesses" because that, and nothing else, is what "delay for
tactical advantage" is all about.[75]

Finally, other than fairness to defendants, there are few considerations more
important realistically to questions of joinder and severance than the avoidance of
repetitious appearances and repetitious testimony by witnesses; but if so, is the
following introduction to the subject adequate?

> The interests which so often come into conflict in this area are those which
> commonly clash in the field of criminal procedure and which receive con-
> tinued attention throughout the minimum standards: The expeditious han-
> dling of criminal cases without excessive demands on *prosecutorial* and *ju-
> dicial* [but *not* witness'] resources and the protection of defendants from the
> risk of prejudicial and unfair treatment. The traditional rationale for joinder
> of offenses and of defendants is that of conserving the time lost in duplicating
> the efforts of the prosecuting attorney, and *possibly* [!] his witnesses, and of
> judges and court officials[76] [emphasis added].

Likewise, the management-oriented authors of the numerous "court studies"
appear, like judges and lawyers, to be "witness-blind." Generally, "court studies"
are concerned with the following factors: First, the length of time between arrest
and disposition; second, the efficiency with which a judge's time is used, *i.e.*, the
extent to which it is used in adjudicative activities, as opposed to wasteful activities, like waiting for lawyers, or nonactivities, like golf; and third, the efficiency
with which available courtrooms are being utilized. They sometimes contain
generalized expressions of concern about the plight of witnesses, however, there
is, in general, a lack of appreciation of the full significance of the witness' problems and they fail to see him as anything but an object susceptible to virtually
unlimited manipulation and control. No court study makes either the conservation of witness' time or the reduction of "waste appearances" a goal. Not one in

---

73 ABA STANDARDS, SPEEDY TRIAL, Standards 1.1 and 1.3, at 10-13 (Approved Draft,
1968).
74 *See* note 73 *supra.*
75 *See, e.g.,* ABA STANDARDS, THE PROSECUTION FUNCTION AND THE DEFENSE FUNCTION
180 (Approved Draft, 1971).
76 ABA STANDARDS, JOINDER AND SEVERANCE 1 (Approved Draft, 1968).

other words, assesses the operation of courts in terms of the extent to which they protect the interests of witnesses. So concerned are they with "court delay," "valuable judgetime," and "available courtroom space," that they too overlook witnesses and make them, once again, the "forgotten men" of our system.

The United States Supreme Court has not escaped this malady. The revolution in the rights of defendants which the Court has engendered over the past fifteen years has not touched upon the rights of witnesses. And, in certain respects, this "revolution" has had a profound negative impact upon the plight of witnesses.

One of the first and most far-reaching decisions in this field held that indigent defendants were entitled to counsel at the state's expense in serious criminal cases.[77] Another applied the exclusionary rule to the states and thereby precluded the use by governments in criminal trials of any evidence not obtained in accordance with the letter of the law.[78] Using these decisions as a starting point, the Court proceeded to set forth a body of new legal rules and, in effect, to require in all states a whole set of new procedures.

In a series of decisions, the Court made the requirements for both a legal arrest[79] and a valid search warrant more extensive, difficult to meet, complex, and confusing.[80] It imposed a variety of new prerequisites to the use at trial of a defendant's admissions or confession.[81] It required that a *judge,* rather than a jury, determine if these requirements had been met.[82] To discourage unfair line-ups and other suggestive police practices, it ruled that eyewitness identifications "tainted" by suggestiveness or line-ups at which the accused's counsel was not present were inadmissible, thus requiring new types of hearings.[83] In addition, sharp new limits were placed on the practice of trying together two defendants involved in the same crime.[84] Consequently, in many instances, at least two trials must be held to determine the facts of what is substantially one criminal event.

Each series of rulings required new kinds of decisions to be made. Each created a new series of uncertainties that had to be resolved by research and reflection, and, often, by a number of new appeals. Each required new kinds of hearings to be held; many necessitating evidence be taken from witnesses. It is now conceivable that a single witness may be required to testify separately before a magistrate on an application for a search warrant (hearsay testimony is suspect), before a magistrate on an application for an arrest warrant, at a "preliminary examination," before a grand jury, at an evidentiary hearing on a motion to suppress eyewitness identification, at an evidentiary hearing on a motion to suppress

---

77   Gideon v. Wainright. 372 U.S. 335 (1963).
78   Mapp v. Ohio, 367 U.S. 643 (1961).
79   Evidence seized "incident to arrest" is ordinarily considered legally obtained and admissible. If seized pursuant to an arrest later determined to be "without probable cause" and, hence, illegal, it may be considered the "fruit of the poisonous tree" and thereby inadmissible. *See* Wong Sun v. United States, 371 U.S. 471 (1963).
80   *E.g.,* Spinelli v. United States, 393 U.S. 410 (1969).
81   Miranda v. Arizona, 384 U.S. 436 (1966); Escobedo v. Illinois, 378 U.S. 478 (1964).
82   Jackson v. Denno, 378 U.S. 368 (1964).
83   United States v. Wade, 388 U.S. 218 (1967); Gilbert v. California, 388 U.S. 263 (1967); Stovall v. Denno, 388 U.S. 293 (1967); Simmons v. United States, 390 U.S. 377 (1968).
84   Bruton v. United States, 391 U.S. 123 (1968).

a confession or admission, at an evidentiary hearing on a motion to suppress physical evidence, and at trial. Some of these might, in certain circumstances, have to be subdivided into separate hearings which could require additional appearances. Should there be two or more defendants whose cases have been severed, the number of testimonial appearances would have to be increased, possibly by severalfold.

The list above is not exhaustive. Neither, of course, does it take account of the number of "waste" appearances witnesses are usually required to make, nor of the numerous non-testimonial interrogations to which they are required to submit, nor of any witness appearances that may be necessitated either by retrial following appellate court reversal of a lower court's judgment or evidentiary inquiries that may be required by a convicted prisoner's applications for post-conviction relief (which, over the long haul, can be and often are addressed to many different courts, both stat and federal). The point of the list is not that many witnesses are in practice required to go through so many exhausting and repetitive appearances. Probably few are, though no one knows because the statistical work has not been done. The point is rather that each series of rulings has had a massive impact on criminal court processes in every state, notably on the number and frequency of witness appearances and on the dispatch with which an accused person can be brought to trial. And yet, in none of the decisions cited above did any of the opinions—dissenting, concurring, or for the Court—ever devote anything but cursory attention to the interests of witnesses or even to the entire problem of the administration of the criminal court process in light of the ruling. Each of the Justices proved in his opinions that he could write impressive wisdom about the design of the knot, the texture of the ribbon, the color of the wrappings, and the blending of the colors. None of them, however, proved capable of sitting back and taking a reflective look at the overall design of the whole package. Least of all, none of them thought to lift up the package and look underneath where they might have seen little people, witnesses, being crushed.[85]

The result has been "future shock," as Alvin Toffler might say, a "shattering stress and disorientation that we induce in individuals [and institutions] by subjecting them to too much change in too short a time."[86] Our criminal processes have not, as of yet, been adjusted to meet the needs, and protect the rights, of its prime contributors—witnesses. Ironically, court administrators have not even been able to cut back the lengthening time between arrest and trial.

This is not to say that each series of Supreme Court rulings has been unwise. Indeed, in sum, they may have done more good than harm. It is to say that the Court's thinking is out of focus, that its perspective is too narrow, that its reasoning is faulty, and that consequently the decisions have had serious repercussions. To

85 Since this article was completed the United States Supreme Court took an important first step in the direction espoused in this article. In *Argersinger v. Hamlin*, 407 U.S. 25 (1972) the Court guaranteed to all defendants faced with the possibility of prison terms the right to counsel. The noteworthy aspect of this decision is, however, the explicit attention paid by Mr. Justice Douglas, in his Opinion of the Court, to the question of judicial administration. It is difficult to judge the impact, if any, of these considerations, but, perhaps, this is a harbinger of an awakening consciousness.
86 ALVIN TOFFLER, FUTURE SHOCK 2 (1970).

legal thinking, generally, and to Supreme Court reasoning, in particular, can be attributed some part of the blame for court delay and some part of the blame for the abysmal way criminal court witnesses are treated.

What accounts for this pattern of blindness and neglect? What causes our criminal justice system to be so oblivious to witnesses and so neglectful of their problems and interests?

First, as one shrewd observer put it, "Let's face it; the complaining witness is rarely John D. Rockefeller." Typically, he is not well off financially. He has often shared with the defendant the same impoverished background. He lacks knowledge of the system, access to those who man it, and confidence in his ability to deal with it. He remains thoroughly intimidated by the trappings of justice—even if disillusioned by his perception of its actual workings—and by the status and reputations of judges and lawyers. He is short, both in the ability to articulate his grievances and in the social and political "clout" necessary to make his anger felt.

Second, unlike every other class affected by criminal courts, including prisoners, witnesses have no way of helping themselves. They are a class whose members are constantly changing. They do not interact much with one another. They are easily led into believing that the frustrations they experience are atypical rather than a manifestation of a weakness endemic to the system. When they leave the class, they rapidly lose interest in its problems. Indeed, most are so happy at the prospect of no longer having to serve as witnesses that their overwhelming disposition is to leave the whole system as far behind as possible. For these reasons, there is no agency, indeed no forum, legal or otherwise, existing to air their legitimate grievances and effectuate their legitimate demands for reform.

Third, fees paid to witnesses do not begin to reflect the real costs of their services. They do not even compensate for lost time and wages, not to mention the other unpleasantnesses that witnesses bear. In effect, the criminal justice system has passed on some of its costs to the shoulders of its witnesses. If the system ceased extracting this tax from acquiescent witnesses and began paying fairly for their time, it would rapidly be forced to become aware of witnesses and mindful of their problems.

Fourth, our court system exhibits the natural human tendency to favor "insider interests" at the expense of "outsider interests." Wherever minor inconvenience to "insiders" (judges, lawyers, court clerks, etc.) is to be balanced against major inconvenience to outsiders (witnesses, jurors, etc.), and the balancing is to be performed by insiders, insider interests will invariably prevail.

Fifth, legal thinking tends to have an unfortunately narrow focus. It tends in two separate respects to focus excessively on those interests that seem most visibly at stake because tradition puts them in the foreground. First, it focuses on the claims of litigants to the exclusion of those of non-litigants. It tends, therefore, to ignore those in the background whose interests are only indirectly affected by rules developed by litigation. Second, it attends excessively to those whose interests have already received a protective coating by having been defined as "rights." Conversely, it may neglect important interests to which tradition has not attached the word "right" with all its connotations and consequences.

It is essential both to the prevention and deterrence of crime and to the fair and effective working of our criminal courts that this pattern be altered.

IV. Witnesses: What Is To Be Done

If there is one thing that results from this article, it is the author's desire that it be "awareness." If judges, lawyers, court administrators, criminal justice planners, and others become more *aware* of witnesses in their human dimension, if they come to see them as living, breathing, *human* beings, deserving of respect and dignity, improvement will follow. No more will witnesses be treated as objects to be manipulated, as unfeeling pawns to be moved about and discarded as other demands may seem to require. The fair treatment of witnesses will ultimately come to be correctly perceived as an indispensable component of a truly just, effective criminal justice system.

From awareness of witnesses, from understanding the actual workings of our system, from seeing its hidden and hard realities, a number of conclusions about what should be done hopefully will follow.

A. *Criminal Justice Research*

Witnesses are crucial elements of criminal courts but their importance has never been appreciated by researchers or by those who fund criminal justice research projects. As we have seen, hard data need to be gathered about criminal court witnesses, their treatment, their responses to their treatment, their attitudes, and the impact of their attitudes on prosecution, on cooperation with law enforcement, and, in general, on the prevention and deterrence of crime. Research of this nature will produce results that will amaze many, shock some, and persuade most. It will thereby provide the essential first step toward the massive change in consciousness that is required.

1. WITNESS APPEARANCES

The initial subject of inquiry should be witness appearances. Specifically, data should be gathered on the number of times witnesses are summoned to appear, the number of times they actually go to court, the total amount of time (including travel and waiting) they expend on such appearances, the number and proportion of "waste" appearances and the number of times, whether testimonial or nontestimonial, that they are asked to relate what they know.

Although "per case," "per appearance," and "per witness" averages would undoubtedly be useful, it is crucial that the reporting of the data reflect distributions on the extremes. It is more important that large numbers of witness appearances and large expenditures of witness time are required in perhaps fewer criminal cases than that the "average" case required an "average" of so many appearances and so much time. In addition, averages may be misleading because so many cases are resolved by prompt guilty pleas.

2. Witness Costs

Second, inquiry should be commenced concerning the *real* cost of witness appearances and, ultimately, measurements of these costs should be devised. This ought to be relatively easy in the case of police witnesses. In most jurisdictions, policemen are paid at an hourly rate for court appearances. To separate "court time" from "police work time" and compute the cost of "court time" ought to be easy, and in many places has already been done. In the case of civilian witnesses, lost wages should be the starting point. Any adequate measure, however, should take into consideration other factors, such as the cost to employers of lost employee services, the cost of the loss of value created by a witness' uncompensated labor, the cost of lost leisure or family time, and, perhaps, the cost of compensating for some of the unpleasantnesses of being a witness, *e.g.,* disrupted vacations, harrowing cross-examinations, eyeball-to-eyeball confrontations with assailants, or grimy and uncomfortable surroundings.

Cost data should then be correlated with appearance data and reported so as to reflect, for example, costs per case, costs per appearance, total systemic costs, costs of "waste appearances," etc.

3. Witness Attitudes

Third, a study of changes in witness attitudes over the duration of criminal proceedings should be attempted. Included should be components of the clusters of attitudes that determine, for example, the degree of willingness to appear in courts; willingness to cooperate with parties associated with the courtroom proceedings, especially the prosecution; hostility toward the various parties; acquiescence to plea bargains, charge reductions, sentencing concessions, or dismissals; willingness to "get involved," report crime, cooperate with police, and the like; respect for and faith in the criminal justice system; and the relationship between case disposition, promptness of disposition, appearance costs, and these attitudes.

It is essential to avoid testing attitudes by selecting from biased samples of favorably disposed witnesses, for example, from lists of witnesses who have *received* witness fees and who have therefore, presumably, continued to make regular appearances throughout the proceedings. To assure a representative sample, it will be necessary to take into account the attitudes of witnesses who failed to appear and of those who "cannot be found,"[87] possibly by conducting

---

87   For an example of research containing both errors, *see* Committee on the Administration of Justice, Court Management Study: Report for the Use of the Committee on the District of Columbia United States Senate, Part I—Summary, Appendix F (Summary Report of Witness Survey) 169-173 (1970). For some reason, the survey seems also to have relied on interviews with U.S. District Court witnesses whereas the real problems with witnesses in the District of Columbia are in the Superior Court (then the Court of General Sessions). Like federal district courts everywhere, the one in D.C. presents far fewer management or operational problems than harried state courts which perform criminal functions similar to that of the D.C. Superior Court.

Generally, the survey suggests that the experience of the witnesses interviewed was favorable. "The time they spent waiting to see and to speak to various legal officials, however, was a source of irritation to many of them . . . ." In view of the generally high levels of positive

intensive searches for "lost witnesses" interviewing them, and making projections from those interviews. Moreover, an adequate study must measure some fairly subtle attitudinal shadings. For example, it may not be enough to ask a witness, "If subpoenaed, will you appear?" Most witnesses will say, "Yes." It may be necessary to ask about the kinds of alternative events or circumstances (*e.g.,* a death in the family, a flu, a planned one-day trip, a planned birthday party for a small daughter, a cold, etc.) that might prompt nonappearance. Again, researchers must be wary of the fallacy of the average: changes in the attitudes of "the average witness" may be less important than radical changes in the attitudes of comparatively few witnesses.

4. WITNESS DISAFFECTION, UNSUCCESSFUL PROSECUTION, AND CRIME

Fourth, studies should be begun on the relationships between witness disaffection, unsuccessful prosecution, and the commission of crime. One might learn something about these relationships by focusing on, for example, witnesses who fail to appear and asking why they fail to appear; witnesses who "can't remember" or change their stories and asking why; cases that result in dismissals or acquittals and investigating the possible effect of witness attitudes or behavior on the result; cases that are bargained down by the prosecutor below some specified norm and asking why they were so handled; postdispositional criminal behavior by defendants whose cases were bargained down or resulted in acquittals or dismissals; newly apprehended offenders and finding out how many or what percentage had been defendants in prosecutions that had "failed" either by acquittal, dismissal, or excessive bargaining down; and the factors motivating prosecutors to extend concessions in plea bargaining with special reference to witness' attitudes.

It might also be appropriate to scrutinize cases carefully at the outset of proceedings, locate ones in which the alleged offender is "clearly guilty," and then follow these cases through the system to their eventual outcome. Presumably, some would have become "lost conviction" cases which would then provide a fruitful topic for further study, as would the future conduct of the defendants involved.

5. WITNESS' PERSPECTIVES AND PUBLIC ATTITUDES

If technically feasible at this stage of the development of the social sciences, it would be extremely valuable to test the effect of the communication of witness' experiences and attitudes, through individual conversations, by socialization and

---

reports concerning the witnesses' experiences one might expect similar high levels of positive reactions in the respondent's ratings of the court, and the process of law. However, the court was rated as good in handling the specific cases of witness involvement and in handling criminal cases in general, by 58 percent and 53 percent of the respondents, respectively. These are hardly mandate percentages. Moreover, exactly one-half of the respondents were negative about the process and procedures of law, based on what they had seen in their roles as witnesses.

Such data suggests that while the court currently enjoys the confidence of a majority of respondents, this support may be tenuous. *Id.* at 172-173.

group interaction, and through the media, on generalized public attitudes toward crime reporting, "getting involved" with the police, rights of the accused, courts, and the capacity of the government to assure public safety, personal security, and an adequate outlet for retributive impulses. If rigorous scientific inquiry into this last set of questions is impossible, then at least thoughtful reflection seems to be in order. It appears that the "Archie Bunker" and "unidentified black student" quotes at the outset of this article strongly suggest that there are dangerous attitudes abroad in the land which may emanate from the witness experience.

B. *Specific Proposals for Improvement*

To suggest proposals applicable to criminal courts across the land, or even to all "metropolitan" or "urban" criminal courts, requires considerable fortitude. Criminal laws and court procedures vary among the fifty states much more than most observers realize. Even within a single state, criminal court systems differ markedly from one locale to another, reflecting the idiosyncrasies of individual judges.

Hence, these proposals are accompanied with an apology and a request. The apology is that they are not more specific than they are. The request is that the reader stretch his mind a bit, look at my skeletal proposals imaginatively, and try to see how they might be shaped and fitted into a court system with which he is familiar.

1. WITNESS' APPEARANCE-CONTROL PROJECTS

The first suggestion is the establishment of witness' appearance-control projects similar to the one begun by the Vera Institute of Justice and the New York County District Attorney's Office in cooperation with the New York City Criminal Court and the New York City Police Department.[88] These projects would develop, implement, and test devices for reducing the number of unnecessary trips to court required of both police and civilian witnesses and assuring their timely production at court when their presence is in fact required.[89] "The overall goal" of such projects would be "to reduce unnecessary delay in criminal court proceedings while at the same time reducing the inconvenience that often befalls police and citizen witnesses in the scheduling of court appearances."[90]

Among procedures recommended and implemented (on a small scale) by the New York project were:

> (1) excusing witnesses from appearing on a first adjourned date where their testimony was practically never required and then using the date for plea bargaining and schedule setting;

---

88   *See* J. LACEY, THE APPEARANCE CONTROL PROJECT IN THE NEW YORK CITY CRIMINAL COURT: A PROGRESS REPORT AND PROPOSAL (Unpublished Report, February 19, 1971). A final report on this very promising report is expected in June 1972. Mr. Lacey himself is now associated with the Center for Prosecution Management, Washington, D.C.
89   *Id.* at 1.
90   *Id.* at 1-2.

(2) the use of "witness forms" containing complete and accurate information about residence addresses and phone numbers, occupational addresses and phone numbers, working hours, vacation dates, "unavailable" dates, names and telephone numbers of close relatives and friends, and other data facilitating notification and scheduling;

(3) coding witnesses as early as possible according to the ease with which they could be notified by telephone, the probability of their continuing to appear, the likelihood of their appearing promptly, and the time it would take them to travel to court once notified, so as to determine which witness might be summoned by "telephone";

(4) putting selected "reliable" witnesses on telephone alert and then calling them when their presence is required;

(5) giving all civilian witnesses wallet-sized cards containing space for filling in the places and times of scheduled court appearances and a telephone number to be called in the event of questions and directing them to keep the card on their persons at all times; and

(6) using notifications written in two languages.[91]

These specific procedures appear to have produced promising results in the New York context.[92] Similar projects in other jurisdictions could do just as well in developing useful innovations geared to local problems and requirements. Even a modest number of these projects would afford perspective and, hence, a greater likelihood of identifying undesirable practices. They would also provide a vehicle for institutionalizing concern for witnesses and act as an agency for causing procedural alterations. Secondarily, they may provide a much-needed means for airing the complaints of witnesses and voicing their legitimate demands for reform.

The projects should be headed by management-minded lawyers or legally oriented management experts. When so many able private consultants are hungry for new fields into which to expand it would appear that qualified persons would not be too hard to locate. A more difficult problem is getting court administrators, independent-minded judges, prosecutors and court clerks to experiment with new procedures. But this problem will be present until the Millennium, and nothing better can be recommended than to continually apply constructive pressure against those who do not welcome needed reform, especially where a change in their own consciousness is required.

2. WITNESS LIAISON AND SUPPORT SQUADS

The second suggestion is the establishment of Witness Liaison and Support

---

91 *Id.* at 18-33.
92 *Id.* at 34-49.

Squads. In general, these squads would represent the interests of the court system to the witnesses and, more importantly, the interests of the witnesses to the court system. Its members would keep witnesses informed about changes in court dates, court procedures, reasons for postponements and delay, and, in general, about what is going on in the courtroom and courthouse. They would also keep judges, court clerks, and lawyers informed about witness availability, alert them to especially disgruntled witnesses, act as advocates for legitimately aggrieved witnesses who themselves may be too timid or inarticulate to complain and generally just yell "bloody murder" at instances of witness abuse. They might also assist in arranging police protection for witnesses in appropriate cases. The squads might try to pin down attorneys as to their intentions on a scheduled date as far in advance as possible so as to prevent "waste" appearances by witnesses.

They would spend large amounts of time on the telephone trying to locate witnesses, explaining things to them, telling them where to go, conveying reminders, announcing last-minute calendar changes, placating ruffled feelings, and the like. They would often have to work nighttime hours to reach witnesses who could not be reached days. They might frequently provide automobile rides to and from the court, especially for the elderly and handicapped persons. Occasionally, they might even baby-sit or arrange for baby-sitters. They might also meet and greet witnesses at the courthouse, assure their comfort, and provide directions, answers to questions, a smile, and a helping hand.[93]

Squads similar to these already exist in embryonic form in many jurisdictions in the person of "the girl in the subpoena room" or "the girl in the clerk's office." To this extent, what I am suggesting is a massive expansion in the size, importance, and functions of her job.

The members of witness liaison and support squads would have to be mature, responsible, and intelligent individuals, but they would not necessarily have to meet any stringent educational requirements, and they probably would not have to be paid exorbitant sums of money. Indeed, such squads might be made up partly of volunteers, perhaps drawn from the ranks of the retired. In many instances, the perfect person to head such a program at a modest salary, might be found among the ranks of early retirees, notably police officers and military personnel.

This article will not attempt to state which agency or combination of agencies should have administrative responsibility for the squads because court systems, generally, and witness notification responsibility, particularly, vary widely. Conceivably, the witness liaison and support squad could be a police unit, a prosecutor's unit, a judge's unit, a clerk's unit, a unit operated by a board consisting of representatives from several of the above-mentioned agencies, or a unit operated by some independent outside agency. Possibly, they should be completely independent and responsible only to the public.

Both witness appearance-control projects and witness liaison and support

---

93 This idea owes a great deal to the police "community relations units" suggested in Penegar, *Appraising the System of Criminal Law: Its Processes and Administration,* 47 N.C.L. Rev. 59, 140-41 (1968).

squads would also help to reduce court delay. In many jurisdictions, the inability to produce required witnesses at the right time is a substantial cause of adjournments and, thus, of wasted court time and crowded calendars. The two above-mentioned proposals aim at improved two-way communication and notification, and increased attention to witness convenience. To the extent that these aims are realized, witnesses are more likely to appear when needed and therefore adjournments are likely to be fewer, and delay is likely to be less.

3. EARLY SCREENING AND DIVERSIONARY DEVICES

Although the situation varies from jurisdiction to jurisdiction it is clear that many cases that cannot be won come into the criminal courts and wend their way through the court system for a time until they terminate by dismissal. It is also clear that many offenders hauled before criminal courts could better be turned over the rehabilitative or supervisory agencies at the outset of proceedings. The disposition of these cases takes up considerable quantities of court and witness time to little or no benefit. In order to lessen the burden thus created, the third suggestion is "early screening" and increased use of "diversionary devices."

"Early screening" means that an experienced prosecutor should carefully and critically examine each case at the outset of proceedings, determine whether it is likely to be "successful," and not permit "bad" cases to enter the system at all; they should, in other words, "screen out" bad cases early in their history, before they have wasted much court and witness time.

In general, the earlier and more thorough the screening, the better the result. The District Attorney's Office in Philadelphia has experimented with placing prosecutors in police stations at night to screen out "bad" arrests as soon as they are brought in. The District Attorney's Office in Milwaukee seldom lets a felony or a nontraffic misdemeanor get to initial appearance in court without an assistant having interviewed all crucial police and civilian witnesses, including any the defendant can produce. However, the screening practices of these two offices are exceptional. In general, screening either occurs only after several court and witness appearances or consists of a quick look at a police officer's written summary of the evidence, a summary that is likely to be incomplete, self-serving, biased in favor of prosecution, and less than completely candid. My experience in Wisconsin is that the candor and completeness of police reports have tended to diminish with the likelihood of their being discovered and utilized by defense attorneys.

In a few localities, the implementation of thorough early screening might involve statutory changes or massive changes in the thinking of judges, prosecutors, and policemen. In most places, it will require only increases in prosecutorial manpower and the firm belief that the job is worth doing.

Early screening can work smoothly in tandem with the kind of diversionary devices that have been tried in some places, although either can also operate independently to good effect. "Diversionary devices" are methods to "divert" certain types of offenders, especially first offenders, from the criminal courts to more appropriate agencies. Often, the offender is given an option of being

[Vol. 48:386]   A RADICAL CRITIQUE   415

prosecuted for a certain crime or submitting to supervision or treatment by some other person or agency, say, a psychiatrist, a clergyman, a community mental health facility, an alcoholic or narcotics rehabilitation unit, a probation department, and so forth.

Tentative reports on the success of such programs in terms of their impact on offenders tend to be encouraging. Less well recognized is the extent to which they may unclutter our courts and save witnesses time and grief.

4. Formalized Mandatory Pretrial Conferences and "One Shot" "Fish or Cut Bait" Plea Bargaining.

Fourth, it is suggested that within a few weeks of initial appearance, conferences between a prosecutor and the defendant's attorney be scheduled, that appearance be made mandatory for attorneys on both sides, that stipulations be discussed and, if possible, be reached, and that future scheduling be arranged where appropriate.

Further, plea bargaining should be strongly encouraged at these conferences, but prosecutors' offices should make it an iron rule to engage *only* in "one shot" "fish or cut bait" plea bargaining. By "one shot" plea bargaining, it is meant that only one assistant prosecutor per defendant has the authority to extend concessions. Defense attorneys are thereby precluded from shopping for a better deal from another assistant. "Fish or cut bait" plea bargaining means that the *first* concession offered is the *only* one offered. Obviously, this contemplates that the one concession offered be the product of informed and deliberate decision by an experienced and sensitive prosecutor and that it represent the "best deal" the prosecutor can offer. It means also that the accused and his attorney must "fish or cut bait," *i.e.*, take the deal and plead guilty or go to trial in what is often an exercise in futility.

The theory of the above proposal is sound. Mandatory conferences between prosecutors and defense attorneys can do much to iron out difficulties that often consume absurd quantities of court time, cause unnecessary witness appearances, and contribute to court delay. Where quick plea bargains are struck, the savings are all the greater. If the defendant and his counsel know that only one assistant will offer only one deal, and if the deal involves considerable concessions, the likelihood is that they will accept it rather than the comparatively dismal alternatives. When the hope of a "better deal" is eliminated or greatly reduced, it becomes far less advantageous to spend the time and effort required to "bounce the case around." The beneficiaries are the witnesses, the courts, and the public.

In some jurisdictions under certain conditions, notably where the dockets are less crowded, "time bomb" plea bargaining may be combined with the above suggestions to achieve beneficial results. "Time bomb" plea bargaining contains three elements: First, the bargain proposed by the prosecutor must be accepted within some specified length of time, or the offer will terminate and not be renewed; second, the offer is timed to expire several days in advance of the scheduled trial date; and third, it has been made certain as far as possible that on the scheduled trial date, a judge, a prosecutor, a courtroom, jurors, and witnesses will be available for hearing the case. If the offer terminates, the defendant is required on the trial date either to go to trial or to plead guilty to the original, unreduced charge without the comfort of any concessions relating to sentence. Over the long run, the consistent enforcement of "time bomb" plea bargaining will increase the number of guilty pleas, substantially reduce the number of waste appearances, save "court time," and result in speedier trials.

5. JUSTLY COMPENSATORY WITNESS FEES

A fifth suggestion is that witness fees be drastically increased and that they provide witnesses with just compensation. Additionally it is suggested that a start be made toward measuring the cost to the individual witness of his appearances and then providing him with fair reimbursement for those costs. Fees, in other words, would vary, not only with number of appearances and mileage traveled, but also with the amount of wages lost, the amount of time spent waiting around at each appearance, necessary expenditures for meals, transportation, lodgings, and baby-sitters, and perhaps certain more subtle factors. Possibly the victim of a protracted beating by a gang, who might be compelled to relive hours of torture on the witness stand, should be compensated at a higher rate than the passerby. Conversely, the witness using the courts to obtain vengeance for a private grievance should arguably be entitled to less than the bystander who is just doing his duty as a citizen. Merchants pressing bad-check claims as substitutes for more expensive civil collection devices might be entitled to nothing at all.

Simple fairness requires movement in this direction. If the framers of the fifth amendment to the United States Constitution in 1789 could say that "private property"—including time and fruits of labor—should not "be taken for public use, without just compensation"; how can we say otherwise in the Age of Aquarius? In addition, the payment of justly compensatory fees, which will be much higher fees, will prompt painstaking consideration for the witness's time and comfort.

Computation of witness fees could become excessively complicated and could be more trouble than the results are worth. Indeed, the system could wind up paying many witnesses more than they are worth. If that point is ever reached, it will be long after there are sweeping changes in our present crude methods and unjust levels of compensation.

6. COMFORT AND CONVENIENCE

A sixth suggestion is that judges and judicial administrators examine their consciences to find out if they are doing everything possible for the comfort and convenience of witnesses and take any steps necessary to remedy deficiencies in this regard.

Where space is not at too high a premium, courts should provide parking spaces for witnesses. Notifications should include directions to courtrooms in localities where courtrooms are many and hard to find. It does not seem unreasonable that waiting witnesses be provided with reading material, free coffee, access to television, soft chairs, clean rest rooms, and a place to relax. Hearings requiring witnesses should never be postponed in advance of the scheduled time without there being vigorous, thorough, systematic efforts extending beyond normal court working hours to notify witnesses that they need not appear. Witnesses should *always* be kept informed about the status of their case, the reasons for adjournments and the eventual outcome.

Finally, it does not seem unreasonable to think that short courthouse tours might be arranged for groups of witnesses, that outdoor waiting areas might be set up in good weather, and that access to nearby recreational facilities (*e.g.*, the rarely used police gymnasium in a Milwaukee County court facility) be afforded to those few witnesses who might thus find the wait less burdensome.

The point is not that any of the ideas mentioned above is necessarily a good one for any given locality. The point is that things could be done and should be done for witnesses that are not being done. What is needed is not a national blueprint but conscientious self-criticism, imagination and, above all, action on the local level.

7. EVALUATION AND TESTING

Finally, it is suggested that innovations, if at all possible, be systematically tested and evaluated, preferably in connection with the research program outlined earlier. It is best to pinpoint the precise impact of changes on witness appearances, waiting times, attitudes, and absences, conviction rates, speedy trials and the like in order to lay a foundation for exportation of those showing positive results and elimination of those showing little or no promise. Most of these proposals will prove to have merit, but some will undoubtedly have unforeseen undesirable consequences.

C. *Court Management Studies*

Throughout the country, court management studies are proliferating. All of them aim at making courts "better." Most are geared to making the operations of trial court clusters in metropolitan areas more "efficient."

It is suggested that henceforth every such study should sharply focus on the ways in which court operations affect witnesses, and further, that every study should expressly adopt and employ "witness interest" as one yardstick of success. In other words, court operations will have to be pronounced "good" or "efficient" according, in part, to the extent to which they protect the interests of witnesses and the extent to which they treat them well.

The author is *not* suggesting that "witness' interest" become the exclusive or even the primary criterion of evaluation. Certainly, fairness to the accused must remain the central concern of our criminal court system; and a judge's time *is* valuable, should be expended wisely, and valued appropriately. The author is only suggesting that the witness' time is also valuable, though perhaps less so than the judge's, and that fairness to witnesses, as well as to defendants, should be assured. In other words, that the time of witnesses, the comfort of witnesses, and the feelings of witnesses ought to be taken into account. These things must be thrown into the hopper with traditional ingredients. To achieve the right blend may take some mixing and testing. But the soup tastes foul until everything has been put in the pot.

D. *Rethinking of the Approach to Constitutional Questions Involving Criminal Procedure*

Traditionally, and up to the present, appellate courts, notably the United States Supreme Court, have taken a distinctive, fairly well-understood, but never articulated approach to constitutional questions involving criminal procedure. As suggested earlier in this article:

(1) they focus too heavily on the claims and interests of litigants to the virtual exclusion of those of interested non-litigant parties, as witnesses, and thus tend to give the former undue relative importance;

(2) they focus too heavily on those interests previously defined as "rights" to the virtual exclusion of those not so defined and tend, therefore, to give the former too high a priority.

Because of this distinctive approach, they have missed the forest for the trees. In "interpreting" and thereby changing the law, they have ignored overall, systemic, administrative consequences. They have not adequately considered the indirect, collateral effects of their decisions. They have shortchanged peripheral parties like witnesses and victims of crime.

One result has been the multiplication of required hearings and "decision points." The concept of "decision points" may be stated as follows:

> A lawsuit is a unit of court time. That unit in turn is made up of a whole series of subunits, each of which is a decision point. Perhaps, for ease of conception, these subunits or decision points may be regarded as cells within any physical structure. The total time of the case is the time devoted to all of the decision points.[94]

Thus, each time the Supreme Court created a new legal requirement, for example, a new prerequisite for the use of a confession, it "created a decision point and with it the attendant costs in time and dollars."[95] With each new requirement, new types of decisions have to be made and, "because the decisions have to be made, time must be spent in gathering th facts—*i.e.*, presenting the evidence—necessary for their determination."[96] New kinds of hearings, often requiring the presence and testimony of witnesses, must be held. "The case, then," says John P. Frank,

---

94 J. FRANK, AMERICAN LAW: THE CASE FOR RADICAL REFORM 65 (1969).
95 *Id.* at 66.
96 *Id.* at 67.

is a unit of time, which in turn is a collection of subunits of decision
points . . . . [E]very element of the substantive law and every element of
procedure creates decision points that affect costs and affect time . . . .

What is happening in the course of the law is an almost endless increase
in the number of decision points, usually without much regard to the consequences the increase will have on the legal system. If I may use a fanciful
illustration, think of the elephant in a circus, standing with feet close together upon a small supporting pedestal. Let the elephant be the collection
of decision points, and the pedestal be the legal system that has to make the
decisions. What happens is that the elephant grows and grows and grows as
he absorbs more and more decision points . . . . The enlargement comes in
two primary ways. First, the law itself grows. Second, there are more
people presenting matters that need to be decided. The combined effect is
that at some point, the weight of the elephant collapses the pedestal.[97]

"The practical effect of all of this structure," according to Frank, in
another context, but with words fully applicable to criminal procedure, "is
that so many decision points have been created, and so cumbersome a procedure
is necessarily involved in determining them, that for practical purposes we have
put a lawsuit in front of a lawsuit. . . ."[98] In terms of judge and court time, in
terms of witness time and witness exhaustion, in terms of delay in bringing an
accused to trial, "it is *not* two for the price of one."[99] The result, as we have
seen, is "future shock" and a criminal justice system which *sounds* good in theory
and in the rhetoric of Supreme Court opinions, but which functions with dazzling
deficiency in practice.

A second undesirable and unforeseen result has been an increase of great
magnitude in the complexity of criminal procedure. In virtually every criminal
case, a very large number of plausible legal claims can now be made on behalf
of the defendant and, in support of each of these claims, an almost infinite number of arguments and precedents can be cited. Virtually every case, if imaginatively handled by an artful, well-informed defense attorney determined to pull
out all the stops, could easily consume scores of hours of court time.

So great is the law's complexity that it may be literally becoming too complex for its practitioners. As a prosecutor it was the author's experience that few
defense attorneys were aware of all their clients' rights and all the plausible legal
arguments that could be raised in their defense. Frequently, possible attacks on
the legality of proceedings were bypassed under circumstances in which the failure
was clearly neither deliberate nor ethical. It is simply impossible for most practitioners, many of whom do not specialize, to know "everything" that may be done
for an accused criminal.

To a striking degree, the expeditiousness of our court processes, and perhaps
their very functioning, may depend on the extent to which defense counsel are
ignorant of or unconcerned with their clients' rights and on the extent to which
each trial court system has evolved unspoken understandings, rarely visible to
appellate courts, about "punishing" lawyers and clients who assert "too many"

---

97   *Id*. at 68-69.
98   *Id*. at 87.
99   *See id*. at 86-92.

claims. Few are the court systems, where the "troublesome" defendant is not sentenced to more years than his "cooperative" counterpart.

Increasing complexity has another byproduct. It requires increasing expertise among both judges and lawyers. Increased expertise requires more specialization. Specialization tends to reduce the size of the trial bar and to a lesser extent the size of the trial bench. With fewer judges and fewer lawyers to handle more defendants, the problems of scheduling and moving criminal cases on their way become immensely compounded. "Court delay" becomes of increasing concern.

Still another result is great uncertainty about the dictates of the law relating to criminal procedure. It is now quite often impossible to tell in advance of a ruling whether, for example, a search was or would be "reasonable," and the evidence thereby obtained admissible.

The point is that consequences such as uncertainty, complexity, delay, the multiplicity of decision points, increases in hearings, impacts on witnesses and victims were not and are not being given adequate consideration by the Supreme Court and by appellate courts generally.[100] Opinions of these courts in the criminal procedure area illustrate perfectly what has been described as "the lack of consideration by the lawmaking portion of the legal system for the law-administering portion, with the result that the law grows, heedless of its administrative consequences."[101]

Appellate courts must adopt a new approach, a fresh perspective, a different framework of analysis in resolving constitutional questions of criminal procedure. They must deliberately look beyond their traditional concerns, beyond the litigants, beyond the "rights" claimed violated. The appellate courts must consciously focus on projected impacts on those only collaterally involved in the case before the court—on policemen, on attorneys, on victims, and on witnesses. They must always consider and explicitly express themselves on the overall systemic consequences of their decisions. "[T]he administrative consequences of [every] law change," must be "where they belong, in the bright center of our vision."[102]

E. *Rethinking Recent Supreme Court Decisions Affecting Criminal Procedure in Light of Systemic Consequences*

In using this new approach, we must commence the reevaluation and reappraisal of major Supreme Court decisions of the past decade and a half affecting criminal procedure. For the sake of witnesses, we should begin with those that require extra-evidentiary hearings at which witnesses appear. Each decision, each rule, each type of hearing should be seriously and scrupulously evaluated, not only in terms of the purposes the Court thought they would serve, but in terms of their greater consequences for the administration of justice and in terms of their effect on classes of persons, like witnesses, not represented in the original lawsuit. Where complexities prove to be of marginal necessity, they should be eliminated

---

100 *See* note 85 *supra.*
101 J. Frank, *supra* note 94, at 85.
102 *Id.* at 86.

and the law simplified.[103] With respect to each decision, each rule, each type of hearing, we must ask the question posed by Professor Ben Kaplan in another context: "[A]re we in this country simply paying too much in time, effort, and money to pursue the finer lineaments of truth which must in any event elude us?"[104]

F. *Rethinking of Laws and Practices Affecting Witnesses*

Common law systems evolve, not so much by deliberate goal-oriented alteration, as "by piecemeal and expedient tinkering."[105] Both the tinkering and the tinkerers have been witness-blind. Thus, it is not surprising that our entire system of law and practice imposes heavy liabilities on witnesses along with substantially no countervailing rights. Being "invisible," witnesses have been "forgotten." The result is a legal fabric that pervasively disadvantages them in numerous important respects. Therefore the offending system and its legal fabric must be rethought in light of an appropriate concern for the interests of witnesses and subjected to massive reevaluation in terms of the extent to which they are treated with fairness and justice. I do not say that all laws adversely affecting witnesses, once reconsidered, will have to be discarded or modified. Many will prove to have been justified by their service to other important interests. However, nearly every aspect of our present law and practice is eminently challengeable and should be challenged. I am, in other words, recommending the asking of some hard questions, but not necessarily suggesting the answers.

Nationwide, most continuances in state criminal cases are probably granted routinely or automatically upon request without judicial inquiry into the justification for the continuance or its impact on witnesses.[106] Rarely is any but the most perfunctory record made of the decision to continue.[107] Frequently, continuances imposing serious burdens on witnesses are prompted by nothing more substantial than the informal personal relationship between bench and bar.[108] This relationship has resulted in widespread winking at the despicable practice of granting repeated continuances, often with witnesses in the wings, because "my witness, Mr. Green, has not yet appeared," that is, because a lawyer has not yet received his fee.[109] Frequent continuance seems to be the norm rather than the exception. Should not our continuance practices be carefully reappraised?

In some localities, witnesses are routinely required to remain in or near the courtroom, away from work and away from home, all through the many days of a lengthy trial. Should not his practice be reconsidered in light of the advent of the telephone and automobile?

In some jurisdictions it is the practice of police to retain possession of stolen

103 These recommendations parallel and paraphrase John P. Frank's with respect to other areas of the law. *Id.* at 108-110.

104 Kaplan, *Civil Procedure—Reflection on a Comparison of Systems*, 9 Buff. L. Rev. 409, 421 (1960). quoted in Frank, *supra* note 91, at 85.

105 Penegar, *Appraising the System of Criminal Law: Its Processes and Administration*, 46 N.C.L. Rev. 69, 72 (1968).

106 *See, e.g.*, Banfield & Anderson, *Continuances in the Cook County Criminal Courts*, 35 U. Chi. L. Rev. 259 (1968) *passim*.

107 *See id.*

property recovered from an accused person until the termination of all related criminal court proceedings. This means that the already shaken victim is without his television set, record player, stamp collection, wallet, credit cards, power tools, or whatever, for the two-month, six-month, or twelve-month pendency of a criminal prosecution. In some jurisdictions, this practice may be necessitated by existing evidentiary rules. Where this is so, these rules should be reconsidered and probably discarded as unnecessary and hypertechnical. In other jurisdictions the practice is totally unnecessary from the legal standpoint. It provides marginal additional convenience to the prosecutor at the expense of great inconvenience to the victim. Of course, it also provides a club to hold over the victim in the event of his noncooperation. But should such a club be necessary? And should this practice be tolerated?

In many jurisdictions, witnesses, including victims, are routinely excluded from the courtroom at the request of either counsel. Consequently, they are afforded no look at a process which often deeply and intimately concerns them and which they take to reflect upon their veracity and honor. Often, they have no place to go except uncomfortable corridors adjacent to the courtroom. Unlike other practices affecting witnesses, exclusion can have beneficial effects. It may prevent witnesses from coloring their testimony in light of other testimony. But in practice, are the advantages always explicitly measured against the interest of the witness in observing the proceedings of which he is part? If they were, would we not have fewer orders of exclusion? And would not they be applied to fewer witnesses under more limited circumstances? Would not they be limited to parts of the proceedings rather than all the proceedings, *e.g.*, might not a witness be excluded only during the testimony of some witnesses, but not for others?

Should not the devices that keep fees from getting into the hands of witnesses be reconsidered? Should not the prevailing casual attitude toward notifying witnesses of last-minute changes in schedule be revalued? Perhaps the laws having to do with securing the appearance of out-of-state witnesses from distant locations are due for reappraisal? Perhaps also the laws relating to the confinement of material witnesses, which have enormous impact on relatively few lives and which already have been extensively criticized, are now due for immediate change.

In every courtroom of the nation, witnesses are sworn, examined, and cross-examined individually. But does this make sense? As one judge has argued:

> Why hear witnesses only one at a time? If three people saw the accident, why not swear them together and hear their testimony as a group, as is precisely the way the investigating officer originally heard it. That is what the state's attorney, defendant's attorney, and probation officer do when they report the "facts" for a presentence report. That is what a husband and wife do, standing before the court, each asking to be given the child. . .

---

108 Of this relationship (discussing its impact on court delay), one judge has said: "One would hesitate to call it a corrupt bargain, but it is certainly far too often a cozy arrangement." Monroe, *The Urgent Case for American Law Reform: A Judge's Response to a Lawyer's Plea,* 19 De Paul L. Rev. 466, 479-480 (1970).
109 *See* Banfield & Anderson, *supra* note 106, at 265-266.

> If [jurors] can be examined in groups, why not witnesses? . . . Put other-
> wise: if three lawyers can talk at once, why not three witnesses?[110]

In every criminal court, a witness may be required to testify on several
occasions about much the same or similar facts.[111] For example, he is often
required to testify both at a preliminary examination and before a grand jury,
not to mention the trial. Is this necessary?[112] For example, does the requirement
for indictment by grand jury (where it exists) carry with it appreciable benefits
or should it be eliminated as an unnecessary source of repetitive questionings
and appearances? Similarly, should not jurisdictions forbidding the use of hearsay
testimony at preliminary examinations consider whether the repetitive testimony
thus required serves any purposes that could not better be served by devices that
burden witnesses less, say, by expanded rights of discovery? Should duplicate
testimony be the routine? Once a witness testifies at some length on a certain
subject and is once subjected to cross-examination, should he be required to give
essentially the same testimony a second time, absent some special showing of
need? In the ordinary situation (with either party free to show that the situation
was not ordinary), wouldn't it suffice for the witness's earlier testimony simply
to be read into the record?

To what extent should complex proofs and the testimony of hard-to-get
witnesses be required at preliminary stages of prosecution? In Milwaukee, for
example, it is thought that to establish probable cause for crucial elements of
crime at *preliminary examinations,* (1) a county medical examiner's testimony
is necessary to establish "cause of death" in homicide cases, (2) a physician's
testimony is necessary to establish "great bodily harm" in aggravated battery and
certain other similar types of cases, (3) a chemist's testimony is necessary to
establish the identity of "narcotic drugs," "dangerous drugs," and marijuana,
and (4) often, some expert's testimony is necessary to establish "value in excess
of $100" in felony theft or stolen goods cases. Are these proofs really necessary?
Wouldn't it be better overall to tolerate either less rigorous proof or the admission
of letters or other hearsay reports at preliminary stages of inquiry?

Woven into the fabric of criminal law are requirements that the prosecution
prove "elements" of crimes to varying degrees of satisfaction at preliminary
stages and, of course, "beyond a reasonable doubt" at trial. Among such elements
are "nonconsent" elements and "no authority" elements. In burglary cases, for
instance, the prosecution must establish that the burglar entered the building
"without the consent of the owner." Similarly, in forgery cases the prosecution
may be required to show that the forger endorsed another person's name on the
check "without authority to do so." These requirements may necessitate testimony, respectively, by the "owner" and by the purported endorser. Often, these
"nonconsent" or "no-authority" witnesses know nothing about the crime apart
from their nonconsent or nonauthorization. Often, even their nonconsent or
nonauthorization will be fairly obvious from the circumstances. Nevertheless,

---

110   Monroe, *supra* note 108, at 473.
111   *See* Section III *supra.*
112   For the same question in a civil contest, *see* Joiner, *Fog in the Courts and at the Bar:
Archaic Procedures and a Breakdown of Justice,* 47 Tex L. Rev. 968, 975 (1969).

prevailing law and practice in many jurisdictions dictate that their testimony will be required at least once, at trial, and perhaps more often.

Is it necessary that crimes be so defined as to make "nonconsent" and "nonauthorization" elements of crime and therefore part of the state's burden of proof? Should not the definition of burglary, theft, arson, forgery and other crimes involving nonconsent elements be rethought and perhaps changed in light of the burdens they impose on witnesses? In the alternative, could not less rigorous methods of proof suffice to establish such elements at trial? Or could not "presumptions of nonconsent" be applied once certain factual circumstances indicative of nonconsent had been shown? Or could not the prosecution be required to present "allegations of nonconsent" to which the defendant, if he seriously wished to litigate the issue, would have to issue a challenge, perhaps supported by an affidavit alleging facts sufficient to show that the issue was non-frivolous?

Should not "testimonial privileges" be thought of as extending to witnesses as well as to parties? Perhaps a wife should not be required to disclose private communications between herself and her husband even if her husband, the defendant, expressly waives his privilege and permits her to do so? Perhaps a priest should not be required to break the seal of the confessional even if a party-penitent permits him to do so?

Should not a witness be afforded some right not to have to answer some types of questions either because they excessively impinge on his rights or privacy or because they are insulting or abusive or because answering them would damage his reputation and indeed perhaps ruin his life? And ought not this right exist independently of the demands of the parties and the fancied requirements of lawsuits?

And should not our law afford witnesses some practical method of redress for having been frivolously subpoenaed to court, for having been maliciously castigated by judges or lawyers in or out of court, and for having been insufficiently compensated for their time and labor?

But perhaps more important than reevaluating any specific facets of our procedure is reappraising the general statuslessness of witnesses in the eyes of the law.

In a real sense, being a witness means that one's liberty is restricted and that one's property (time and earning capacity) is taken away "for public use." It also means "servitude" to the court that may be "involuntary." When some witnesses are afforded privileges denied to others—as when a doctor awaits a phone call, while a scrubwoman stands by in the corridor—it may raise questions about "the equal protection of the laws." Under extreme cricumstances, it may amount to cruel and unusual punishment. It may entail substantial restriction on the right to interstate travel or massive invasion of privacy. It may involve a person's "being a witness against himself" in ways other than those falling within the "privilege against self-incrimination" as traditionally defined. When the witness' time, a form of property, is taken "for public use," the taking almost always seems to be "without just compensation." Restrictions on his liberty can usually be seen as having been imposed "without due process of law," especially when one considers that "due process is at best a vague concept, one which consists not of a body of precise rules, but rather of the application of general principles of fundamental fairness or ordered liberty to the particular facts of each case."[113]

As most readers will readily observe, the above paragraph applies the language of "the Constitution," notably the Bill of Rights and the 13th and 14th amendments to witnesses in a manner which is neither unreasonable nor outlandish. In this respect it does something that no court has yet done. Is it not perhaps time to apply our fundamental law to persons of that abused class known as witnesses? Is it not time for us to come to regard witnesses, like accused persons, as having "rights"? Is it not time for us to begin to evolve a concept heretofore lacking in our legal tradition, one of *"rights* of witnesses"? If we come to see witnesses as having human dimensions, as being persons worthy of dignity and respect, should we not extend to those persons the kinds of protections we describe as "rights"?

This suggestion, of course, does not mean that witnesses' rights should assume overriding significance with respect to other values. Obviously, the "rights" of witnesses must always be considered along with other values, for example, fairness to an accused, and fairness to a public anxious to secure the neutralization of dangerous persons. When the balance is struck, a witness's rights may have to be sacrificed to other compelling societal or individual interests. Nevertheless, is it not better for legal and administrative decisions to be made with the interests of witnesses explicitly considered? Given the human dimension of witnesses, the extent to which their interests have been ignored in the past, and the substantial respects in which the criminal process can affect their lives, is it not more fair and more likely to produce just results to characterize their interests as "rights"?

It is perhaps unfortunate that our legal system affords so little real opportunity for interests as "trivial" as those of the ordinary witness to be asserted and vindicated by explicit decisions of courts of law. If there had been a history of courtroom confrontations between the interests of witnesses and those of others, perhaps the rights of witnesses would ultimately have become formally enshrined in the American pantheon of values. Even now, perhaps what is needed is a Ralph Nader who would take up the cudgel for witnesses in courts of law, perhaps by making imaginative use of class action provisions, and would compel by litigation the development, definition and elaboration of rights of witnesses.

However, formalization of the rights of witnesses is not the heart of my suggestion. The heart of my suggestion is the need for a massive shift in thinking about witnesses and the need for a vocabulary and framework of analysis attuned to the new thinking. I am suggesting the need for Socrates' and Solomons rather than Naders and Gilberts. I am hoping that our philosophy of witnesses will come to reflect appreciation of their importance and their humanity. I am hoping that our terminology will come to reflect a sounder philosophy. I am suggesting as a first step that a more apt terminology may mold a sounder philosophy. The result, I hope, for witnesses as well as others, will be justice.

With good heart, great faith, and hope for the future, I shall bypass the hemlock and await the fury of the mob.

---

113 Comment, *Right of Criminal Defendant to the Compelled Testimony of Witnesses*, 67 COLUM. L. REV. 953, 957 (1967).

[12]

The Battered-Child Syndrome

C. Henry Kempe, M.D., Denver, Frederic N. Silverman, M.D., Cincinnati, Brandt F. Steele, M.D., William Droegemueller, M.D., and Henry K. Silver, M.D., Denver

The battered-child syndrome, a clinical condition in young children who have received serious physical abuse, is a frequent cause of permanent injury or death. The syndrome should be considered in any child exhibiting evidence of fracture of any bone, subdural hematoma, failure to thrive, soft tissue swellings or skin bruising, in any child who dies suddenly, or where the degree and type of injury is at variance with the history given regarding the occurrence of the trauma. Psychiatric factors are probably of prime importance in the pathogenesis of the disorder, but knowledge of these factors is limited. Physicians have a duty and responsibility to the child to require a full evaluation of the problem and to guarantee that no expected repetition of trauma will be permitted to occur.

THE BATTERED-CHILD SYNDROME is a term used by us to characterize a clinical condition in young children who have received serious physical abuse, generally from a parent or foster parent. The condition has also been described as "unrecognized trauma" by radiologists, orthopedists, pediatricians, and social service workers. It is a significant cause of childhood disability and death. Unfortunately, it is frequently not recognized or, if diagnosed, is inadequately handled by the physician because of hesitation to bring the case to the attention of the proper authorities.

Incidence

In an attempt to collect data on the incidence of this problem, we undertook a nation-wide survey of hospitals which were asked to indicate the in-

cidence of this syndrome in a one-year period. Among 71 hospitals replying, 302 such cases were reported to have occurred; 33 of the children died; and 85 suffered permanent brain injury. In one-third of the cases proper medical diagnosis was followed by some type of legal action. We also surveyed 77 District Attorneys who reported that they had knowledge of 447 cases in a similar one-year period. Of these, 45 died, and 29 suffered permanent brain damage; court action was initiated in 46% of this group. This condition has been a particularly common problem in our hospitals; on a single day, in November, 1961, the Pediatric Service of the Colorado General Hospital was caring for 4 infants suffering from the parent-inflicted battered-child syndrome. Two of the 4 died of their central nervous system trauma; 1 subsequently died suddenly in an unexplained manner 4 weeks after discharge from the hospital while under the care of its parents, while the fourth is still enjoying good health.

Clinical Manifestations

The clinical manifestations of the battered-child syndrome vary widely from those cases in which the trauma is very mild and is often unsuspected and unrecognized, to those who exhibit the most florid evidence of injury to the soft tissues and skeleton. In the former group, the patients' signs and symptoms may be considered to have resulted from failure to thrive from some other cause or to have been produced by a metabolic disorder, an infectious process, or some other disturbance. In these patients specific findings of trauma such as bruises or characteristic roentgenographic changes as described below may be misinterpreted and their significance not recognized.

The battered-child syndrome may occur at any age, but, in general, the affected children are younger than 3 years. In some instances the clinical manifestations are limited to those resulting from a single episode of trauma, but more often the child's general health is below par, and he shows evidence of neglect including poor skin hygiene,

Professor and Chairman (Dr. Kempe) and Professor of Pediatrics (Dr. Silver), Department of Pediatrics; Associate Professor of Psychiatry (Dr. Steele), and Assistant Resident in Obstetrics and Gynecology (Dr. Droegemueller), University of Colorado School of Medicine; and Director, Division of Roentgenology, Children's Hospital (Dr. Silverman).

multiple soft tissue injuries, and malnutrition. One often obtains a history of previous episodes suggestive of parental neglect or trauma. A marked discrepancy between clinical findings and historical data as supplied by the parents is a major diagnostic feature of the battered-child syndrome. The fact that no new lesions, either of the soft tissue or of the bone, occur while the child is in the hospital or in a protected environment lends added weight to the diagnosis and tends to exclude many diseases of the skeletal or hemopoietic systems in which lesions may occur spontaneously or after minor trauma. Subdural hematoma, with or without fracture of the skull, is, in our experience, an extremely frequent finding even in the absence of fractures of the long bones. In an occasional case the parent or parent-substitute may also have assaulted the child by administering an overdose of a drug or by exposing the child to natural gas or other toxic substances. The characteristic distribution of these multiple fractures and the observation that the lesions are in different stages of healing are of additional value in making the diagnosis.

In most instances, the diagnostic bone lesions are observed incidental to examination for purposes other than evaluation for possible abuse. Occasionally, examination following known injury discloses signs of other, unsuspected, skeletal involvement. When parental assault is under consideration, radiologic examination of the entire skeleton may provide objective confirmation. Following diagnosis, radiologic examination can document the healing of lesions and reveal the appearance of new lesions if additional trauma has been inflicted.

The radiologic manifestations of trauma to growing skeletal structures are the same whether or not there is a history of injury. Yet there is reluctance on the part of many physicians to accept the radiologic signs as indications of repetitive trauma and possible abuse. This reluctance stems from the emotional unwillingness of the physician to consider abuse as the cause of the child's difficulty and also because of unfamiliarity with certain aspects of fracture healing so that he is unsure of the significance of the lesions that are present. To the informed physician, the bones tell a story the child is too young or too frightened to tell.

Psychiatric Aspects

Psychiatric knowledge pertaining to the problem of the battered child is meager, and the literature on the subject is almost nonexistent. The type and degree of physical attack varies greatly. At one extreme, there is direct murder of children. This is usually done by a parent or other close relative, and, in these individuals, a frank psychosis is usually readily apparent. At the other extreme are those cases where no overt harm has occurred, and one parent, more often the mother, comes to the psychiatrist for help, filled with anxiety and guilt related to fantasies of hurting the child. Occasionally the disorder has gone beyond the point of fantasy and has resulted in severe slapping or spanking. In such cases the adult is usually responsive to treatment; it is not known whether or not the disturbance in these adults would progress to the point where they would inflict significant trauma on the child.

Between these 2 extremes are a large number of battered children with mild to severe injury which may clear completely or result in permanent damage or even death after repeated attack. Descriptions of such children have been published by numerous investigators including radiologists, orthopedists, and social workers. The latter have reported on their studies of investigations of families in which children have been beaten and of their work in effecting satisfactory placement for the protection of the child. In some of these published reports the parents, or at least the parent who inflicted the abuse, have been found to be of low intelligence. Often, they are described as psychopathic or sociopathic characters. Alcoholism, sexual promiscuity, unstable marriages, and minor criminal activities are reportedly common amongst them. They are immature, impulsive, self-centered, hypersensitive, and quick to react with poorly controlled aggression. Data in some cases indicate that such attacking parents had themselves been subject to some degree of attack from their parents in their own childhood.

Beating of children, however, is not confined to people with a psychopathic personality or of borderline socioeconomic status. It also occurs among people with good education and stable financial and social background. However, from the scant data that are available, it would appear that in these cases, too, there is a defect in character structure which allows aggressive impulses to be expressed too freely. There is also some suggestion that the attacking parent was subjected to similar abuse in childhood. It would appear that one of the most important factors to be found in families where parental assault occurs is "to do unto others as you have been done by." This is not surprising; it has long been recognized by psychologists and social anthropologists that patterns of child rearing, both good and bad, are passed from one generation to the next in relatively unchanged form. Psychologically, one could describe this phenomenon as an identification with the aggressive parent, this identification occurring despite strong wishes of the person to be different. Not infrequently the beaten infant is a product of an unwanted pregnancy, a pregnancy which began before marriage, too soon after marriage, or at some other time felt to be extremely inconvenient. Sometimes several children in one family have been beaten; at other times one child is singled out for attack while others are treated quite lovingly. We have also seen instances in which the sex of the child who is severely attacked is related to very specific factors in the context of the abusive parent's neurosis.

It is often difficult to obtain the information that a child has been attacked by its parent. To be sure, some of the extremely sociopathic characters will say, "Yeah, Johnny would not stop crying so I hit him. So what? He cried harder so I hit him harder." Sometimes one spouse will indicate that the other was the attacking person, but more often there is complete denial of any knowledge of injury to the child and the maintenance of an attitude of complete innocence on the part of both parents. Such attitudes are maintained despite the fact that evidence of physical attack is obvious and that the trauma could not have happened in any other way. Denial by the parents of any involvement in the abusive episode may, at times, be a conscious, protective device, but in other instances it may be a denial based upon psychological repression. Thus, one mother who seemed to have been the one who injured her baby had complete amnesia for the episodes in which her aggression burst forth so strikingly.

In addition to the reluctance of the parents to give information regarding the attacks on their children, there is another factor which is of great importance and extreme interest as it relates to the difficulty in delving into the problem of parental neglect and abuse. This is the fact that physicians have great difficulty both in believing that parents could have attacked their children and in undertaking the essential questioning of parents on this subject. Many physicians find it hard to believe that such an attack could have occurred and they attempt to obliterate such suspicions from their minds, even in the face of obvious circumstantial evidence. The reason for this is not clearly understood. One possibility is that the arousal of the physician's antipathy in response to such situations is so great that it is easier for the physician to deny the possibility of such attack than to have to deal with the excessive anger which surges up in him when he realizes the truth of the situation. Furthermore, the physician's training and personality usually makes it quite difficult for him to assume the role of policeman or district attorney and start questioning patients as if he were investigating a crime. The humanitarian-minded physician finds it most difficult to proceed when he is met with protestations of innocence from the aggressive parent, especially when the battered child was brought to him voluntarily.

Although the technique wherein the physician obtains the necessary information in cases of child beating is not adequately solved, certain routes of questioning have been particularly fruitful in some cases. One spouse may be asked about the other spouse in relation to unusual or curious behavior or for direct description of dealings with the baby. Clues to the parents' character and pattern of response may be obtained by asking questions about sources of worry and tension. Revealing answers may be brought out by questions concerning the baby such as, "Does he cry a lot? Is he stubborn? Does he obey well? Does he eat well? Do you have problems in controlling him?" A few general questions concerning the parents' own ideas of how they themselves were brought up may bring forth illuminating answers; interviews with grandparents or other relatives may elicit additional suggestive data. In some cases, psychological tests may disclose strong aggressive tendencies, impulsive behavior, and lack of adequate mechanisms of controlling impulsive behavior. In other cases only prolonged contact in a psychotherapeutic milieu will lead to a complete understanding of the background and circumstances surrounding the parental attack. Observation by nurses or other ancillary personnel of the behavior of the parents in relation to the hospitalized infant is often extremely valuable.

The following 2 condensed case histories depict some of the problems encountered in dealing with the battered-child syndrome.

Report of Cases

CASE 1.—The patient was brought to the hospital at the age of 3 months because of enlargement of the head, convulsions, and spells of unconsciousness. Examination revealed bilateral subdural hematomas, which were later operated upon with great improvement in physical status. There had been a hospital admission at the age of one month because of a fracture of the right femur, sustained "when the baby turned over in the crib and caught its leg in the slats." There was no history of any head trauma except "when the baby was in the other hospital a child threw a little toy at her and hit her in the head." The father had never been alone with the baby, and the symptoms of difficulty appeared to have begun when the mother had been caring for the baby. Both parents showed concern and requested the best possible care for their infant. The father, a graduate engineer, related instances of impulsive behavior, but these did not appear to be particularly abnormal, and he showed appropriate emotional concern over the baby's appearance and impending operation. The mother, aged 21, a high school graduate, was very warm, friendly, and gave all the appearance of having endeavored to be a good mother. However, it was noted by both nurses and physicians that she did not react as appropriately or seem as upset about the baby's appearance as did her husband. From interviews with the father and later with the mother, it became apparent that she had occasionally shown very impulsive, angry behavior, sometimes acting rather strangely and doing bizarre things which she could not explain nor remember. This was their first child and had resulted from an unwanted pregnancy which had occurred almost immediately after marriage and before the parents were ready for it. Early in pregnancy the mother had made statements about giving the baby away, but by the time of delivery she was apparently delighted with the baby and seemed to be quite fond of it. After many interviews, it became apparent that the mother had identified herself with her own mother who had also been unhappy with her first pregnancy and had frequently beaten her children. Despite very strong conscious wishes to be a kind, good mother, the mother of our patient was evidently repeating the behavior of her own mother toward herself. Although an admission of guilt was not obtained, it seemed likely that the mother was the one responsible for attacking the child; only after several months of treatment did the amnesia for the aggressive outbursts begin to lift. She responded well to treatment, but for a prolonged period after the infant left the hospital the mother was not allowed alone with her.

CASE 2.—This patient was admitted to the hospital at the age of 13 months with signs of central nervous system damage and was found to have a fractured skull. The parents were questioned closely, but no history of trauma could be elicited. After one week in the hospital no further treatment was deemed necessary, so the infant was discharged home in the care of her mother, only to return a few hours later with hemiparesis, a defect in vision, and a new depressed skull fracture on the other side of the head. There was no satisfactory explanation for the new skull fracture, but the mother denied having been involved in causing the injury, even though the history revealed that the child had changed markedly during the hour when the mother had been alone with her. The parents of this child were a young, middle-class couple who, in less than 2 years of marriage, had been separated, divorced, and remarried. Both felt that the infant had been unwanted and had come too soon in the marriage. The mother gave a history of having had a "nervous breakdown" during her teens. She had received psychiatric assistance because she had been markedly upset early in the pregnancy. Following an uneventful delivery, she had been depressed and had received further psychiatric aid and 4 electroshock treatments. The mother tended to gloss over the unhappiness during the pregnancy and stated that she was quite delighted when the baby was born. It is interesting to note that the baby's first symptoms of difficulty began the first day after its first birthday, suggesting an "anniversary reaction." On psychological and neurological examination, this mother showed definite signs of organic brain damage probably of lifelong duration and possibly related to her own prematurity. Apparently her significant intellectual defects had been camouflaged by an attitude of coy, naive, cooperative sweetness which distracted attention from her deficits. It was noteworthy that she had managed to complete a year of college work despite a borderline I.Q. It appeared that the impairment in mental functioning was probably the prime factor associated with poor control of aggressive impulses. It is known that some individuals may react with aggressive attack or psychosis when faced with demands beyond their intellectual capacity. This mother was not allowed to have unsupervised care of her child.

Up to the present time, therapeutic experience with the parents of battered children is minimal. Counseling carried on in social agencies has been far from successful or rewarding. We know of no reports of successful psychotherapy in such cases. In general, psychiatrists feel that treatment of the so-called psychopath or sociopath is rarely successful. Further psychological investigation of the character structure of attacking parents is sorely needed. Hopefully, better understanding of the mechanisms involved in the control and release of aggressive impulses will aid in the earlier diagnosis, prevention of attack, and treatment of parents, as well as give us better ability to predict the likelihood of further attack in the future. At present, there is no safe remedy in the situation except the separation of battered children from their insufficiently protective parents.

Techniques of Evaluation

A physician needs to have a high initial level of suspicion of the diagnosis of the battered-child syndrome in instances of subdural hematoma, multiple unexplained fractures at different stages of healing, failure to thrive, when soft tissue swellings or skin bruising are present, or in any other situation where the degree and type of injury is at variance with the history given regarding its occurrence or in any child who dies suddenly. Where the problem of parental abuse comes up for consideration, the physician should tell the parents that it is his opinion that the injury should not occur if the child were adequately protected, and he should indicate that he would welcome the parents giving him the full story so that he might be able to give greater assistance to them to prevent similar occurrences from taking place in the future. The idea that they can now help the child by giving a very complete history of circumstances surrounding the injury sometimes helps the parents feel that they are atoning for the wrong that they have done. But in many instances, regardless of the approach used in attempting to elicit a full story of the abusive incident(s), the parents will continue to deny that they were guilty of any wrongdoing. In talking with the parents, the physician may sometimes obtain added information by showing that he understands their problem and that he wishes to be of aid to them as well as to the child. He may help them reveal the circumstances of the injuries by pointing out reasons that they may use to explain their action. If it is suggested that "new parents sometimes lose their tempers and are a little too forceful in their actions," the parents may grasp such a statement as the excuse for their actions. Interrogation should not be angry or hostile but should be sympathetic and quiet with the physician indicating his assurance that the diagnosis is well established on the basis of objective findings and that all parties, including the parents, have an obligation to avoid a repetition of the circumstances leading to the trauma. The doctor should recognize that bringing the child for medical attention in itself does not necessarily indicate that the parents were innocent of wrongdoing and are showing proper concern; trauma may have been inflicted during times of uncontrollable temporary rage. Regardless of the physician's personal reluctance to become involved, complete investigation is necessary for the child's protection so that a decision can be made as to the necessity of placing the

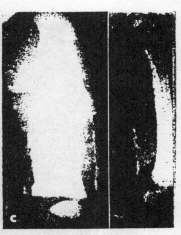

Fig. 1.—Male, 5 months: *a*, Initial films taken 3 to 4 days after onset of knee swelling. Epiphyseal separation shown in lateral projection with small metaphyseal chip shown in frontal projection; *b*, Five days later, there was beginning reparative change; *c*, Twelve days later (16 days after onset), there was extensive reparative change, history of injury unknown, but parents were attempting to teach child to walk at 5 months.

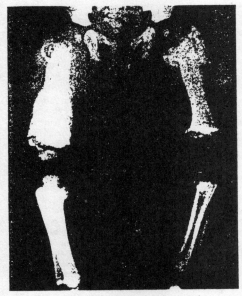

Fig. 2.—Female, 7½ months with a history of recurring abuse, including being shaken while held by legs 4-6 weeks prior to film. Note recent (2-3 weeks) metaphyseal fragmentation, older (4-6 weeks) periosteal reaction, and remote (2-4 months) external cortical thickening. Note also normal osseous structure of uninjured pelvic bones. (By permission of *Amer. J. Roentgenol.*)

child away from the parents until matters are fully clarified.

Often, the guilty parent is the one who gives the impression of being the more normal. In 2 recent instances young physicians have assumed that the mother was at fault because she was unkempt and depressed while the father, in each case a military man with good grooming and polite manners, turned out to be the psychopathic member of the family. In these instances it became apparent that the mother had good reason to be depressed.

Radiologic Features

Radiologic examination plays 2 main roles in the problem of child-abuse. Initially, it is a tool for case finding, and, subsequently, it is useful as a guide in management.

The diagnostic signs result from a combination of circumstances: age of the patient, nature of the injury, the time that has elapsed before the examination is carried out, and whether the traumatic episode was repeated or occurred only once.

Age.—As a general rule, the children are under 3 years of age; most, in fact are infants. In this age group the relative amount of radiolucent cartilage is great; therefore, anatomical disruptions of cartilage without gross deformity are radiologically invisible or difficult to demonstrate (Fig. 1a). Since the periosteum of infants is less securely attached to the underlying bone than in older children and adults, it is more easily and extensively stripped from the shaft by hemorrhage than in older patients. In infancy massive subperiosteal hematomas may follow injury and elevate the active periosteum so that new bone formation can take place around and remote from the parent shaft (Figs. 1c and 2).

Nature of Injury.—The ease and frequency with which a child is seized by his arms or legs make injuries to the appendicular skeleton the most common in this syndrome. Even when bony injuries are present elsewhere, e.g., skull, spine, or

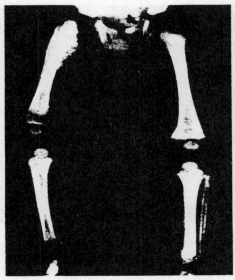

Fig. 3.—Male, 5 months, pulled by legs from collapsing bathinette 6 weeks earlier. Epiphyseal separation, right hip, shown by position of capital ossification center. Healing subperiosteal hematoma adjacent to it. Healing metaphyseal lesions in left knee, healing periosteal reactions (mild) in left tibia. No signs of systemic disease. (By permission of *Amer J Roentgenol.*)

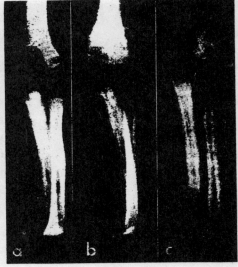

Fig. 4.—Female 7½ months: *a*, Elbow injured 30 hours before, except for thickened cortex from previous healed reactions, no radiologic signs of injury: *b*, Fifteen days after injury, irregular productive reaction, clinically normal joint; *c*, Three weeks after *b*, organization and healing progressing nicely. (By permission of *Amer J Roentgenol.*)

ribs, signs of injuries to the extremities are usually present. The extremities are the "handles" for rough handling, whether the arm is pulled to bring a reluctant child to his feet or to speed his ascent upstairs or whether the legs are held while swinging the tiny body in a punitive way or in an attempt to enforce corrective measures. The forces applied by an adult hand in grasping and seizing usually involve traction and torsion; these are the forces most likely to produce epiphyseal separations and periosteal shearing (Figs. 1 and 3). Shaft fractures result from direct blows or from bending and compression forces.

Time After Injury That the X-Ray Examination Is Made.—This is important in evaluating known or suspected cases of child-abuse. Unless gross fractures, dislocations, or epiphyseal separations were produced, no signs of bone injury are found during the first week after a specific injury. Reparative changes may first become manifest about 12 to 14 days after the injury and can increase over the subsequent weeks depending on the extent of initial injury and the degree of repetition (Fig. 4). Reparative changes are more active in the growing bones of children than in adults and are reflected radiologically in the excessive new bone reaction. Histologically, the reaction has been confused with neoplastic change by those unfamiliar with the vigorous reactions of young growing tissue.

Repetition of Injury.—This is probably the most important factor in producing diagnostic radiologic signs of the syndrome. The findings may depend on diminished immobilization of an injured bone leading to recurring macro- and microtrauma in the area of injury and healing, with accompanying excessive local reaction and hemorrhage, and ultimately, exaggerated repair. Secondly, repetitive injury may produce bone lesions in one area at one time, and in another area at another, producing lesions in several areas and in different stages of healing (Fig. 3).

Thus, the classical radiologic features of the battered-child syndrome are usually found in the appendicular skeleton in very young children. There may be irregularities of mineralization in the metaphyses of some of the major tubular bones with slight malalignment of the adjacent epiphyseal ossification center. An overt fracture may be present in another bone. Elsewhere, there may be abundant and active but well-calcified subperiosteal reaction with widening from the shaft toward one end of the bone. One or more bones may demonstrate distinctly thickened cortices, residuals of previously healed periosteal reactions. In addition, the radiographic features of a subdural hematoma with or without obvious skull fracture may be present.

Differential Diagnosis.—The radiologic features are so distinct that other diseases generally are considered only because of the reluctance to accept the implications of the bony lesions. Unless certain aspects of bone healing are considered, the pertinent findings may be missed. In many cases roentgenographic examination is only undertaken soon after known injury; if a fracture is found, reexamination is done after reduction and immobilization; and, if satisfactory positioning has been obtained, the next examination is usually not carried out for a period of 6 weeks when the cast is removed. Any interval films that may have been taken prior to this time probably would have been unsatisfactory since the fine details of the bony lesions would have been obscured by the cast. If fragmentation and bone production are seen, they are considered to be evidence of repair rather than manifestations of multiple or repetitive trauma. If obvious fracture or the knowledge of injury is absent, the bony changes may be considered to be the result of scurvy, syphilis, infantile cortical hyperostoses, or other conditions. The distribution of lesions in the abused child is unrelated to rates of growth; moreover, an extensive lesion may be present at the slow-growing end of a bone which otherwise is normally mineralized and shows no evidence of metabolic disorder at its rapidly growing end.

Scurvy is commonly suggested as an alternative diagnosis, since it also produces large calcifying subperiosteal hemorrhages due to trauma and local exaggerations most marked in areas of rapid growth. However, scurvy is a systemic disease in which all of the bones show the generalized osteoporosis associated with the disease. The dietary histories of most children with recognized trauma have not been grossly abnormal, and whenever the vitamin C content of the blood has been determined, it has been normal.

In the first months of life *syphilis* can result in metaphyseal and periosteal lesions similar to those under discussion. However, the bone lesions of syphilis tend to be symmetrical and are usually accompanied by other stigmata of the disease. Serological tests should be obtained in questionable cases.

Osteogenesis imperfecta also has bony changes which may be confused with those due to trauma, but it too is a generalized disease, and evidence of the disorder should be present in the bones which are not involved in the disruptive-productive reaction. Even when skull fractures are present, the mosaic ossification pattern of the cranial vault, characteristic of osteogenesis imperfecta, is not seen in the battered-child syndrome. Fractures in osteogenesis imperfecta are commonly of the shafts; they usually occur in the metaphyseal regions in the battered-child syndrome. Blue sclerae,

skeletal deformities, and a family history of similar abnormalities were absent in reported instances of children with unrecognized trauma.

Productive diaphyseal lesions may occur in *infantile cortical hyperostosis*, but the metaphyseal lesions of unrecognized trauma easily serve to differentiate the 2 conditions. The characteristic mandibular involvement of infantile cortical hyperostosis does not occur following trauma although obvious mandibular fracture may be produced.

Evidence that repetitive unrecognized trauma is the cause of the bony changes found in the battered-child syndrome is, in part, derived from the finding that similar roentgenographic findings are present in *paraplegic patients with sensory deficit* and in patients with *congenital indifference to pain;* in both of whom similar pathogenic mechanisms operate. In paraplegic children unappreciated injuries have resulted in radiologic pictures with irregular metaphyseal rarefactions, exaggerated subperiosteal new bone formation, and ultimate healing with residual external cortical thickening comparable to those in the battered-child syndrome. In paraplegic adults, excessive callus may form as a consequence of the lack of immobilization, and the lesion may be erroneously diagnosed as osteogenic sarcoma. In children with congenital indifference (or insensitivity) to pain, identical radiologic manifestations may be found.

To summarize, the radiologic manifestations of trauma are specific, and the metaphyseal lesions in particular occur in no other disease of which we are aware. The findings permit a radiologic diagnosis even when the clinical history seems to refute the possibility of trauma. Under such circumstances, the history must be reviewed, and the child's environment, carefully investigated.

Management

The principal concern of the physician should be to make the correct diagnosis so that he can institute proper therapy and make certain that a similar event will not occur again. He should report possible willful trauma to the police department or any special children's protective service that operates in his community. The report that he makes should be restricted to the objective findings which can be verified and, where possible, should be supported by photographs and roentgenograms. For hospitalized patients, the hospital director and the social service department should be notified. In many states the hospital is also required to report any case of possible unexplained injury to the proper authorities. The physician should acquaint himself with the facilities available in private and public agencies that provide protective services for children. These include children's humane societies, divisions of welfare departments, and societies for the prevention of cruelty to children. These, as well as the police department, maintain a close association with the juvenile court. Any of these agencies may be of assistance in bringing the case before the court which alone has the legal power to sustain a dependency petition for temporary or permanent separation of the child from the parents' custody. In addition to the legal investigation, it is usually helpful to have an evaluation of the psychological and social factors in the case; this should be started while the child is still in the hospital. If necessary, a court order should be obtained so that such investigation may be performed.

In many instances the prompt return of the child to the home is contraindicated because of the threat that additional trauma offers to the child's health and life. Temporary placement with relatives or in a well-supervised foster home is often indicated in order to prevent further tragic injury or death to a child who is returned too soon to the original dangerous environment. All too often, despite the apparent cooperativeness of the parents and their apparent desire to have the child with them, the child returns to his home only to be assaulted again and suffer permanent brain damage or death. Therefore, the bias should be in favor of the child's safety; everything should be done to prevent repeated trauma, and the physician should not be satisfied to return the child to an environment where even a moderate risk of repetition exists.

Summary

The battered-child syndrome, a clinical condition in young children who have received serious physical abuse, is a frequent cause of permanent injury or death. Although the findings are quite variable, the syndrome should be considered in any child exhibiting evidence of possible trauma or neglect (fracture of any bone, subdural hematoma, multiple soft tissue injuries, poor skin hygiene, or malnutrition) or where there is a marked discrepancy between the clinical findings and the historical data as supplied by the parents. In cases where a history of specific injury is not available, or in any child who dies suddenly, roentgenograms of the entire skeleton should still be obtained in order to ascertain the presence of characteristic multiple bony lesions in various stages of healing.

Psychiatric factors are probably of prime importance in the pathogenesis of the disorder, but our knowledge of these factors is limited. Parents who inflict abuse on their children do not necessarily have psychopathic or sociopathic personalities or come from borderline socioeconomic groups, although most published cases have been in these categories. In most cases some defect in character structure is probably present; often parents may be repeating the type of child care practiced on them in their childhood.

Physicians, because of their own feelings and their difficulty in playing a role that they find hard to assume, may have great reluctance in believing that parents were guilty of abuse. They may also find it difficult to initiate proper investigation so as to assure adequate management of the case. Above all, the physician's duty and responsibility to the child requires a full evaluation of the problem and a guarantee that the expected repetition of trauma will not be permitted to occur.

4200 E. 9th Ave., Denver 20 (Dr. Kempe).

References

1. Snedecor, S. T.; Knapp, R. E.; and Wilson, H. B.: Traumatic Ossifying Periostitis of Newborn, *Surg Gynec Obstet* 61:385-387, 1935.

2. Caffey, J.: Multiple Fractures in Long Bones of Infants Suffering from Chronic Subdural Hematoma, *Amer J Roentgenol* 56:163-173 (Aug.) 1946.

3. Snedecor, S. T., and Wilson, H. B.: Some Obstetrical Injuries to Long Bones, *J Bone Joint Surg* 31A:378-384 (April) 1949.

4. Smith, M. J.: Subdural Hematoma with Multiple Fractures, *Amer J Roentgenol* 63:342-344 (March) 1950.

5. Frauenberger, G. S., and Lis, E. F.: Multiple Fractures Associated with Subdural Hematoma in Infancy, *Pediatrics* 6:890-892 (Dec.) 1950.

6. Barmeyer, G. H.; Alderson, L. R.; and Cox, W. B.: Traumatic Periostitis in Young Children, *J Pediat* 38:184-190 (Feb.) 1951.

7. Silverman, F.: Roentgen Manifestations of Unrecognized Skeletal Trauma in Infants, *Amer J Roentgenol* 69:413-426 (March) 1953.

8. Woolley, P. V., Jr., and Evans, W. A., Jr.: Significance of Skeletal Lesions in Infants Resembling Those of Traumatic Origin, *JAMA* 158:539-543 (June) 1955.

9. Bakwin, H.: Multiple Skeletal Lesions in Young Children Due to Trauma, *J Pediat* 49:7-15 (July) 1956.

10. Caffey, J.: Some Traumatic Lesions in Growing Bones Other Than Fractures and Dislocations: Clinical and Radiological Features, *Brit J Radiol* 30:225-238 (May) 1957.

11. Weston, W. J.: Metaphyseal Fractures in Infancy, *J Bone Joint Surg (Brit)* (no. 4) 39B:694-700 (Nov.) 1957.

12. Fisher, S. H.: Skeletal Manifestations of Parent-Induced Trauma in Infants and Children, *Southern Med J* 51:956-960 (Aug.) 1958.

13. Miller, D. S.: Fractures Among Children, *Minnesota Med* 42:1209-1213 (Sept.) 1959; 42:1414-1425 (Oct.) 1959.

14. Silver, H. K., and Kempe, C. H.: Problem of Parental Criminal Neglect and Severe Physical Abuse of Children, *J Dis Child* 95:528, 1959.

15. Altman, D. H., and Smith, R. L.: Unrecognized Trauma in Infants and Children, *J Bone Joint Surg (Amer)* 42A:407-413 (April) 1960.

16. Elmer, E.: Abused Young Children Seen in Hospitals, *Soc Work* (no. 4) 5:98-102 (Oct.) 1960.

17. Gwinn, J. L.; Lewin, K. W.; and Peterson, H. G., Jr.: Roentgenographic Manifestations of Unsuspected Trauma in Infancy, *JAMA* 176:926-929 (June 17) 1961.

18. Boardman, H. E.: Project to Rescue Children from Inflicted Injuries, *Soc Work* (no. 1) 7:43 (Jan.) 1962.

[13]

The Howard Journal Vol 31 No 4. Nov 92
ISSN 0265-5527

The Victim's Charter: A New Deal for Child Victims?

JANE MORGAN* and LUCIA ZEDNER
*Jane Morgan is Lecturer in Law, University of Wales, Aberystwyth
Lucia Zedner is Lecturer in Law, London School of Economics*

Abstract: *Help and support for victims of crime have become key platforms of the government's criminal justice policy in recent years. The* Victim's Charter, *published by the government in 1990, is the first official statement on how victims of crime should be treated and what they are entitled to expect. It addresses, in particular, the three issues which have caused most concern during the last decade: the unsympathetic treatment of victims by the police and courts; obtaining financial compensation; and the need for welfare services such as Victim Support. It may be seen both as the official seal of approval and the culmination of years of endeavour on behalf of victims of crime. In all this discussion there is very little mention of children. The way in which the criminal justice system responds to children and young persons under the age of 17 was the subject of research commissioned by the Home Office and carried out by the authors at the Centre for Criminological Research, University of Oxford. Although a number of innovations have been introduced which relate specifically to child victims, it is argued that much remains to be done to ensure that children receive such help as they may need in the aftermath of crime, and that they are not further victimised by the criminal justice process.*

Since the 1970s there has been an increased interest in victims of crime, both nationally and internationally. This period has seen the emergence both of victim studies and services for victims. The nature and extent of victimisation have received widespread publicity. There has also been a growing recognition that the legal response and intervention by helping professions may make a significant contribution to the overall impact of the crime (Shapland *et al.* 1985). As a result demands have been made for the criminal justice system to become more sensitive to the needs of victims. In 1990 the government itself published the *Victim's Charter* which claimed to be 'A statement of the needs and rights of victims of crime' and set out their 'legitimate rights and expectations' (Home Office 1990). It stated that the police should respond sensitively to victims, keep them informed about the progress of their case and its outcome, and refer them to Victim Support Schemes. Victims should be told about court procedure and provided with adequate facilities in court houses. Information about

---

* Sadly, Jane Morgan died of cancer on 7th July 1992 after a brief illness. The research and the writing of this article was completed earlier this year. She will be sorely missed by her co-author and all who knew her.

the availability of compensation, either via the courts or from the Criminal
Injuries Compensation Board, should be given to victims and they should
have the chance 'of receiving some compensation without being put to
trouble himself or herself'.

In all this, there is very little mention of children. The criminal justice
system has long given special recognition to the vulnerability of juvenile
offenders. However, children who become victims or witnesses to crime
are thrust into an adult system which traditionally does not distinguish
between children and adults. This article describes the policies and
practices which relate to child victims and assesses how far the *Victim's
Charter* is achieving its objectives so far as they are concerned.

The Police and Child Victims: The Specialist Approach to Child Sexual Abuse

At present the only area of national policy which relates specifically to
children is that concerning the investigation of sexual abuse or sexual
assault. The majority of police forces in England and Wales have
specialist officers for investigating these allegations. Historically, this can
be traced back to 1983 when a television programme, which showed a
male detective in the Thames Valley Police interviewing a rape victim in a
particularly unsympathetic manner, brought the plight of victims of
sexual assault to public attention and caused considerable public disquiet.
A Home Office Circular followed which offered advice to Chief Officers on
the handling of investigations of rape and the treatment of victims of
sexual assault (Home Office Circular 25/1983). There was an immediate
commitment on behalf of senior police management to improve
procedures. Many police forces then formed specialist units for the
investigation of allegations of rape. More recently as a result of a series of
highly publicised cases, these policies for adult victims of sexual assault
have been developed and adapted specifically for child victims of sexual
abuse (Home Office Circular 52/1988).

At the same time, the police and social services co-operated in the
development of joint investigation in child sexual abuse cases. One of the
reasons was that such allegations often become known to the police
through other agencies, particularly the social services who have a
statutory responsibility for the welfare of children. Another factor is that
whereas physical abuse can usually be identified by clearly visible
injuries, sexual abuse is rarely identifiable by physical examination alone.
The child's account of what happened is, therefore, crucial to the
establishment of the case (Jones and McQuiston 1988). For this reason,
the child is likely to be interviewed by social workers to establish the facts,
and then again by the police to acquire the necessary evidence. This
duplication of interviewing has caused concern, not least because there is
now considerable evidence of the 'secondary victimisation' which children
are likely to experience as a result. Joint investigation by police and social
workers minimises the number of times a child is interviewed and has
been hailed as an important means of reducing further stress.

295

Such innovations were pioneered in 1986 by the London Borough of Bexleyheath which set up a pilot project involving both the police and the local authority social services department. The training of police officers and social workers together was intended to facilitate the integration of their operational philosophies and to lay the foundations for joint interviewing by the police and social workers. The main priority of the joint management of child sexual abuse cases was agreed to be the welfare of the child victim and other siblings. Criminal justice considerations, such as the arrest and prosecution of the alleged abuser were to be secondary (Metropolitan Police and Bexley Social Services 1987).

Following the implementation of the 'Bexley' project, the joint management and investigation of child sexual abuse cases was endorsed by the government (DHSS and Welsh Office 1988). A national study of child sexual abuse cases shows that joint investigation has now been developed in the majority of forces in England and Wales (Moran-Ellis, Conroy and Fielding 1991).

The establishment of this specialist approach to the investigation of child sexual abuse cases has not been without its problems. These have arisen mainly because of the different operational philosophies of the two agencies concerned (Morgan and Zedner 1992). Although there have been a number of difficulties in implementation, attempts are being made to improve inter-agency procedures both locally and nationally. In principle, the introduction of joint-investigation in cases of child sexual abuse and the philosophy which underlies it is a move in the right direction. In addition there are further indications that the interviewing of sexually abused children will become more 'child centred'. The Criminal Justice Act 1991 contained provisions for the video-taping of an early interview with the child, and a Code of Practice for the conducting of such interviews has been drawn up by the Home Office.[1]

In marked contrast to these detailed policies and procedures to deal with the investigation of child sexual abuse and violence, no guidelines exist as to how the police should respond to children who are victims of other crime.

Our study examines the experiences of over 200 children who were the direct or 'indirect' victims (that is, were present in households where crime occurred or were witnesses to a crime against others) of a wide range of crimes, all of which had been reported to the police. We found that, although most were satisfied with the way in which the police responded initially, in the longer term levels of satisfaction declined markedly. The majority of those who were victims of sexual abuse were pleased with the general police response and all of them were referred by the police to social services for help and support. But the majority of child victims and their families were not kept informed about the progress of their case or its outcome. Significantly, the levels of dissatisfaction at their treatment by the police amongst child victims and their families were markedly higher than those revealed by the 1988 British Crime Survey for adult victims (Mayhew *et al.* 1989). The police referred only a fifth of the direct child victims in the sample – 39 out of 172 – to Victim Support. Only two of the children in the sample were informed of the availability of compensation from the Criminal Injuries Compensation Board (although three others were told about it by friends and four by Victim Support volunteers). None of the children in the sample was told about the possibility that the court might order him or her to be compensated by the offender, although three children, all victims of physical assault, did receive court-ordered compensation, greatly to their surprise (Morgan and Zedner 1992).

Whatever the crime, child victims are particularly vulnerable to secondary victimisation. In recognition of this, those special procedures developed by the police for abuse victims could with advantage be modified for children who are victims of all crime.

The Child Victim/Witness in Court

During the 1980s, the stress which child victims of sexual abuse and violence may suffer when they are required to appear in court received much attention from criminal justice professionals and academics. It was highlighted in the *Report of the Advisory Group on Video Evidence* (the Pigot Report) (Home Office 1989) in 1989 and the Scottish Law Commission (1990) *Report on the Evidence of Children and Other Potentially Vulnerable Witnesses* in 1990. As a result, a number of innovative procedures intended to alleviate the stress caused to child witnesses have been introduced.

During the pre-trial period, the listing of a case can be altered to take account of the needs of the child. In February 1988, the then Minister of State at the Home Office, Mr John Patten, announced that new guidance would be sent to the police and the CPS to ensure 'speedy progress' for child abuse cases: 'the damage done by child abusers to their victims must not be added to by avoidable delay in bringing criminal proceedings' (Home Office news release, 18 February 1988). This injunction was confirmed in a Home Office Circular sent to chief officers of police and the Director of Public Prosecutions issued guidance to the CPS (Home Office Circular 52/1988, 'The investigation of child sexual abuse', (para. 25).

Until 1991, child victims could be required to appear at old-style committal proceedings (under s.6 (i) Magistrates' Courts Act 1980) in a magistrates' court to determine whether there was sufficient evidence to justify committing the accused for trial at the Crown Court. These proceedings were known to be extremely stressful since they were used to test out witnesses to see if they came up to proof. Section 53 of the Criminal Justice Act 1991 provides for certain cases destined for trial at the Crown Court, and which involve children, as either victims or by-stander witnesses, to be taken over by the Crown Court without delay, by-passing committal proceedings. On the day of the court appearance itself, a number of special procedures and facilities intended to alleviate the stress caused to child witnesses have been advocated. It is widely agreed that the child witness should be able to wait well away from the public areas of the court-house and, in particular, that they should not have to be confronted by the defendant. The importance of special waiting provisions cannot be over-estimated: children are often required to attend court for many hours, possibly over a period of days, before being called to give evidence. If a child has spent several hours in a cell-like room or has seen the defendant in the hall, then even the provision of the video-link, discussed below, may come too late to help the child's state of mind.

A number of modified procedures are now in use in some court rooms when children give evidence. These operate at the judge's or magistrates' discretion, subject to objections from the defence. For example, judges and magistrates have the power to exclude the public from the court when a child testifies. The prosecution normally begin by asking for the name and address of the witness. In sensitive cases, such as those involving children, this information may be written down. At Crown Court centres around the country some judges now take off their wigs and robes before a child witness comes into court. Sometimes barristers also remove their wigs and gowns. Seating arrangements may be changed so as to allow counsel to sit next to the child during questioning, to enable the judge to come off the bench, and the child to be removed from the witness box and placed near the jury or alongside the judge. In some cases, a soft-spoken child may be allowed to use a microphone.

The most radical of the reform measures are those that attempt to shield the child victim from direct confrontation with the accused at court: the use of screens to prevent eye contact between witness and defendant or broadcasting the child's live testimony into the court room via closed-circuit television.[2] The first of these techniques to be introduced was the use of screens. These were introduced at the Old Bailey in 1987 and applications for their use subsequently increased dramatically.[3] No statutory authority exists for the use of screens but the judge may rely upon his common law discretion to do what is necessary to ensure that the trial is fair to both prosecution and defence. In *R.* v. *X, Y, and Z* ([1990] 91 Cr. App. 36–43), the Court of Appeal endorsed the use of screens following advice from social workers that some of the children were unlikely to be able to testify if forced to face the defendants in open court. It was held that 'The learned judge has the duty . . . to see that justice is done [which] means . . . he has got to see that the system operates fairly . . . not only to the defendants but also to the prosecution and also to the witness' (*Criminal Law Review* 1990, pp. 515–16). The request for screens may be initiated by the police, parents, or social workers. Although the usefulness of screens has to some extent been overtaken by video technology, they remain a valuable alternative in magistrates' courts where the video link is not in use and for children who do not wish to use the video link even where it is available.

Under the Criminal Justice Act 1988 children under the age of 14 are permitted, with the leave of the court, to give evidence by live television video link in trials involving sexual offences (see, for example, Spencer and Tucker 1987; Spencer 1987). This entails seating the child in a separate room where he or she then testifies in front of a video monitor in answer to questions from counsel in the courtroom, the child's testimony being relayed on a monitor in the courtroom. The *Report of the Advisory Group on Video Evidence* (Home Office 1989) argued strongly that children should not be required to appear in court even if protected by screens or cross-examined by means of the video link:

We recommend that at trials on indictment for violent and sexual offences and offences of cruelty and neglect and at comparable trials in the juvenile courts, video-recorded interviews with children under the age of 14 conducted by police officers, social workers or those whose duties include the investigation of crime or the protection of the welfare of children should be admissible as evidence. Where the offence charged is of a sexual nature this provision should extend to child witnesses under the age of 17. (paras. 2.25 and 2.36)

It recommended that in cases of alleged sexual abuse, violence, or cruelty the court videotape their testimony privately, in advance. The initial interview would be carried out by a trained examiner following a Code of Practice intended to ensure fairness for the accused. Soon after the initial examination, defence counsel would cross-examine the child before the trial-judge out of court. Both interviews should, Pigot recommended, be videoed. At the trial, the tape of the first interview would replace the child's examination-in-chief and the second would replace cross-examination (paras. 2.29 and 2.31).

The Criminal Justice Act 1991 adopted some, but by no means all, of Pigot's recommendations (White 1990; McEwen 1990). Section 54 of the Criminal Justice Act 1991 allowed a video recording of an early investigative interview with a child victim/witness to be played to the jury as the child's evidence-in-chief in cases involving a sexual or violent offence (Birch 1992; Temkin 1990a, 1990b). As mentioned above, a Code of Practice for conducting videoed interviews with child witnesses has been drawn up by the Home Office. Where the tape is admitted, the court will know exactly what the child said when the case first came to light and the child will not have to retell the story from scratch at the trial.

However, the 1991 Criminal Justice Act does not include the Pigot Committee's second main proposal that a pre-recorded examination by counsel in informal surroundings should replace cross-examination in court (Davies 1991). In the Pigot proposals, the defendant would not be present in the room but could communicate with his counsel by audio visual link. The video would then be shown in court without requiring the child to attend. The government considered that such a proposal was in fact likely to increase the number of times a child faced the prospect of cross-examination since it might be necessary to put further questions in court as new evidence arose. If the child had not been required to attend, it could also entail further delays to the court hearing whilst the child was located. In place of Pigot's proposals, therefore, the Act provides that the tape of the initial interview can only be admitted in evidence if the child later attends trial for live cross-examination in the court by video-link. Although the Act, therefore, preserves what is arguably the most harrowing aspect of the trial, it does prohibit an unrepresented defendant in a child abuse case from cross-examining the child victim or by-stander witness in person.

Thus, children are still required to give evidence in person on the day of the trial. It is now widely recognised amongst professionals that appropriate pre-trial preparation of the child witness can make an important difference to their ability to testify, as can the provision of support before and during the trial itself. The provision of a video link on the day of the trial may come too late if a child has spent the period before the case without support. However, in the English and Welsh legal system, there is no single agency with special responsibility to provide support for child witnesses. Neither the *Report of the Advisory Group on Video Evidence* (the Pigot Report) nor the Criminal Justice Act 1991 refers to the preparation of the child witness for giving evidence.

In recent years, attempts have been made by a wide range of individuals and agencies to prepare children for the experience of giving evidence in ways which will not prejudice the rights of the defendant (Spencer and Flin 1990). There are now a number of aids available to prepare a child for appearance in court. A range of materials provide detailed information for children and their parents, and also for professionals providing help and support. For example, the leaflet, *The Child Witness* (Children's Legal Centre 1989) provides information for those dealing with child witnesses, and videos have been produced on court procedures for the training of social workers and health visitors involved in children's cases. Publications such as *Susie and the Wise Hedgehog* (Bray 1989), *Being a Witness* (Children's Legal Centre 1990) and *Going to Court* (West Yorkshire Police 1989; Crown Office and Procurator Fiscal 1989) are directed at child witnesses themselves. But, admirable though these written materials and videos are, they are not adequate in themselves as a means of explaining court procedures to children. It is now recognised that child witnesses need individualised preparation for court. If carried out appropriately this can greatly ease the potential trauma entailed in having to testify (Glaser and Spencer 1990).

Once the child is ready to testify, the question has arisen whether a 'support person' or chaperon should accompany them in court. The only official statement on this is contained in the Crown Court Rules and states that child witnesses under the age of 14 may have a support person with them in the witness room when the video link is in operation (*Crown Court Rules 1982*, Rule 23A para. 10). However, the presence of a support person in court was endorsed, with reservations, by the Court of Appeal in *R*. v. *X*, *Y*, and *Z* ([1990] 91 Cr. App. 42). Lord Lane, the Lord Chief Justice, commended the use of social workers sitting alongside the child witnesses 'to comfort and console them where necessary'. He said 'Plainly, to have anyone sitting alongside a witness is a course of conduct which has to be undertaken with considerable care'. When it took place, the court had to see that nothing improper passed and that no encouragement was given to the child witness to make him or her say something other than the truth (*R*. v. *X*, *Y*, and *Z*). There was no suggestion that the social workers had done anything other than what was proper when they were sitting alongside the witness: indeed the Lord Chancellor, Lord Mackay commended the use of court ushers for this purpose (speaking at a conference on children's evidence in legal proceedings in Cambridge in 1989). But it is clearly preferable for the support person to be someone with whom the child is familiar. However, there is a danger that if a family friend or relative were chosen the person would be ruled inadmissible or inappropriate if he or she were to be called as a witness as well.

The lack of practice directions or agreed guidelines for England and Wales as to what would constitute appropriate preparation of a child for a court appearance is a serious omission. Preparation and support for child witnesses is carried out on an *ad hoc* basis. Although the provision of support both before and during the trial has been advocated, no-one inside or outside the criminal justice system has a clear responsibility to provide information about the court process to child victims and their families; to liaise with others about the child's needs; to assist the child required to give evidence (by arranging an advance visit to the court or by reading the child's statement); to support the child in court, or to explain the court verdict. Support, where offered, is often marred by lack of continuity or by the inexperience of those providing it.

Those systems in operation in Scotland and the United States offer much to commend them. In Scotland the prosecution is responsible for preparation for court. The Scottish Law Commission (1990) *Report on the Evidence of Children and other Potentially Vulnerable Witnesses* acknowledged the value of this and concluded that if children were adequately prepared prior to the trial, the use of new procedures such as video-taped testimony was unlikely to be required in more than a few child witness cases. It stated that 'in the majority of cases – and provided that there has been careful and sympathetic pre-trial preparation of the child – we anticipate that children will be able to give evidence at trial by conventional means . . .' (para. 1.8). It acknowledged that 'a very great deal' is already being done by the Procurator Fiscal in Scotland to prepare child witnesses and recognised that, as a result, 'many children are thought to have been better able to cope with the experience of giving evidence that would otherwise have been the case' (para. 2.10). The US report, *When the Victim is a Child*, also suggested that children who are supported throughout may be effective witnesses at trial even without innovative techniques (Whitcomb *et al.* 1985). The report recognised that giving evidence is not the only cause of anxiety for the child. The period leading up to the trial can also be extremely stressful, while the use of innovative or modified procedures during the court hearing may not help a child who is already upset.

Although in the US many states have adopted laws that permit the use of innovative techniques in court when children testify, in fact the report states: 'Alternatives to traditional in-court testimony have only been used as a last resort. Other reforms aimed at reducing the burden on child victims throughout the investigation and adjudication process, can substantially reduce the need for radical departures from tradition in the courtroom' (Whitcomb 1990). Active Victim-Assistance programmes in America aim to provide support and comfort to child victims throughout the adjudication process. The 'victim assistant' explains the adjudication system, prepares the child witnesses for giving testimony in court, and accompanies them on the day of the trial. Many victim assistance programmes have developed video-tapes, colouring books, dolls'-house

301

size court rooms, and other child-friendly techniques to complement their support efforts.

In Britain there is no tradition of independent representation of a witness in a criminal case. The guardian *ad litem* – an independent representative who advocates the best interests of the child – is available only to children in civil proceedings. In the US, in a small number of states, the role of guardian *ad litem* has been developed to include the role of safeguarding the child's interests in the criminal courts (Whitcomb 1990; Hardin 1986–7). In many ways, the American example offers much that may usefully be adopted in tailoring the British criminal justice system to the special needs of child witnesses.

Compensation for Child Victims

Financial aid in the form of compensation from the criminal courts and from the Criminal Injuries Compensation Board is available for victims of crime. Child victims are no exception (Miers 1990). In 1973, the government introduced compensation orders which might be made by both the Crown and magistrates' courts, involving the payment of a specified amount of money by the offender via the court to the victim. An order might be made in respect of a victim who has suffered personal injury, loss or damage as a result of an offence. The Criminal Justice Act 1982 made it possible to make a compensation order alone and, where given alongside a fine, required that the payment of compensation take priority. Under the Criminal Justice Act 1988 the courts are obliged to give reasons for not ordering compensation to those who are eligible (Miers 1989).

The Criminal Injuries Compensation Board was established in 1964 to administer an *ex gratia* scheme to compensate those who suffered injuries directly attributable to a crime of violence. The scheme was put on a statutory footing by the 1988 Criminal Justice Act (Miers 1989). Compensation in family violence cases became payable for incidents occurring since October 1979. Child victims of violence (whether committed within or outside the family) may be entitled to compensation for their injuries under this scheme, whether or not there has been a prosecution or conviction. This also applies to cases where there is emotional trauma, rather than physical injury as, for example, in cases of sexual assault. Awards of compensation cannot be made for injuries assessed at less than a specified figure (currently £1,000) but substantial sums are awarded for more serious injury. There is a three-year limitation period on making a claim after the incident but this may be waived at the Board's discretion particularly in relation to claims made by or on behalf of child victims (Criminal Injuries Compensation Board (1990) *Twenty-sixth Annual Report*).

In practice, many child victims and their families are not aware of the availability of compensation. Victims depend heavily on the police to inform them about it. Home Office Circular 20/1988 reinforces the advice contained in previous circulars that victims of violent crime should be made aware of the existence of the CICS and of the possibility of compensation from the criminal courts. It stated that 'it remains important that police officers, who in the vast majority of cases are the first to come into contact with victims of violent crime, should bring the scheme to the victim's attention'. In fact, research on adult victims has shown that the police do not routinely inform victims about the availability of compensation either from the offender or the CICB (Shapland *et al.* 1985; Newburn and Merry 1990). These findings were borne out in our study in relation to child victims. Interviews conducted with the police in the course of our research revealed that very few were even aware of the availability of compensation for children. Some mistakenly believed that compensation was not available for sexual abuse within the family, or that the offender had to have been prosecuted successfully before an application could be made. Similarly, there was very little awareness amongst other social and welfare agencies of children's eligibility for compensation under CICS (Morgan and Zedner 1992).

It is not surprising, therefore, that the records of the CICB show that in the past very few claims were made on behalf of child victims. The Board did not collect statistics on the numbers of claims it received relating to children, except within the overall category of 'family violence' and it discontinued collecting data about this category of cases in 1985. The table demonstrates that in the years for which information is available, very few applications on behalf of child victims of family violence were finalised: presumably very few such applications were made.

Year ending 31 March	Cases of family violence finalised	Claims for children finalised
1983	165	5
1984	226	15
1985	239	12

However, during 1989 considerable publicity was given to the fact that child victims were eligible for compensation. Partly as a result of our research, in late 1989 the CICB produced a leaflet about claiming compensation from CICB on behalf of child victims. In part, it was intended to highlight the eligibility of child victims for compensation. As a result the number of claims by, or on behalf of, children increased markedly. The total number of such applications received during the period 1 April 1989 to 31 March 1990 was:

All cases (including those of a non sexual nature)	4,825
All sexual assaults	1,318
Sexual abuse within the family or by a relative	802

The considerable growth in claims made to the CICB on behalf of children is perhaps the most decisive and tangible evidence available of growing recognition of the needs and interests of child victims.

Support for Child Victims

The foremost agency with a duty to protect the welfare of children is, of course, the local authority social services department. This has a statutory responsibility to investigate allegations of child abuse and reports of children considered to be at risk. In addition, social services have a duty to safeguard and promote the welfare of children within their area who are in need, to promote the upbringing of children by their families, and, where necessary, to provide accommodation. The statutory responsibility of this department for child abuse has, to some extent, obscured the need for other agencies to provide services for children who are victims of other crimes. What help there is for such children is provided mainly by the voluntary sector – for example, by helplines and by Victim Support Schemes.

Children who are victims of a wide range of crime come to the attention of Victim Support – the national organisation which exists to give help and advice to victims of crime. Victim Support National Guidelines, issued in 1990, advised local Schemes to accept the referral of children with parental consent if they have experienced volunteers and the back up of professional support. They make an exception, however, of abuse within the family on the grounds that these victims are the statutory responsibility of social services. Over half the 350 Victim Support Schemes receive referrals of children who are the direct victims of crime. All Schemes visit households containing children, such as those where burglaries have taken place. A snapshot survey [carried out by the authors] revealed that in one month (October 1988) 76 of 350 Victim Support Schemes provided support for 367 cases involving 621 children in all. Nearly half of these were domestic burglaries in which children were members of the household. Of the rest, the majority were cases of physical assault against either the child or an adult member of the family (Morgan and Zedner 1992). Victim Support volunteers generally provide support for children in the context of providing support for the family as a whole. In the majority of cases, the volunteers' help was confined to one visit. However, where necessary they provided long-term support, often working alongside other agencies or referring victims to them for specialist help.

Naturally, Victim Support is not able to provide a comprehensive support service for child victims. As we have noted, it is heavily dependent upon the police for referrals; the services which it can offer to child victims and their families are not widely known about by other agencies (Morgan and Zedner 1992).The co-operation of the police is therefore essential. In theory, police officers who deal with victims are well placed to inform them about the availability of this service. Yet our research showed that the majority of police officers were unaware that child victims were eligible for referral to Victim Support. Indeed, by no means all children who come to the attention of the police are referred by them to Victim Support. Where support is offered to child victims and their families volunteers are sometimes prevented from providing an effective service to those children they visit. First of all, they are dependent upon parental co-operation. If this is refused, there is nothing they can do to help the child even if they feel help is needed. Often, particularly where children were indirect victims, parents disputed that their children needed help. In many cases parents do not even consider that their children may be affected. Another factor is that in many cases volunteers have not received enough training about the specific needs of child victims. The primary task of volunteers upon visiting a child victim is to make some estimate of the degree of disturbance suffered by the child and family in order that they may establish the extent of their need for support and assistance. Yet the majority of Victim Support Schemes do not have the required expertise to gauge the psychological impact of crime upon children.

In order to counter these difficulties, Victim Support set up a Demonstration Project in Bedfordshire in 1988 which aimed to raise the profile of the services which Victim Support could offer to child victims; to increase awareness amongst all agencies of child victims and to improve services for them. For example, they provided information about the likely effects of crime on children so that volunteers would be better able to advise parents about the reaction they might expect from their children and how to cope with them. As a result of this project, Victim Support are producing well-defined policy guidelines to determine the nature of the service which volunteers can be expected to offer to child victims and to provide training materials to this end.

Conclusion

It cannot be said that the *Victim's Charter* has ensured a new deal for child victims. The plight of child victims, indeed, their very existence, is only now being fully recognised. While this recognition led to the introduction of a number of innovations during the 1980s, much has still to be done in developing an adequate response to child victims. At present, a child's hope of receiving recognition, compensation or support depends largely on the case being reported to the police. Once it is reported, much rests on the attitudes of the officers involved and their ability to recognise and respond to the child's needs, as well as on more formal police policies regarding investigation.

Access to compensation and support relies heavily on referral by the police or other agencies coming into contact with children. Good systems of communication and co-operation amongst agencies are vital to ensuring that support or, where necessary, specialist help are readily accessible. Much remains to be done to ensure that children receive the help they need in the aftermath of crime and are not further victimised by the criminal justice process. Significant improvements could be made without resort to legislation – and with relatively few financial implications – if there were a better directed use of existing resources. National policy guidelines to all appropriate agencies on the recognition of child victims, their needs and how best to respond to them are urgently needed. Only by such a co-ordinated effort can we ensure that the child victim is no longer the 'forgotten actor' in the criminal justice system.

Notes

[1] See Home Office (1991). This refers to:
  (i) the conducting of the interviews (for example, techniques);
  (ii) the videotaping of the interviews (including what should be available on the monitor to observers of the video-recording and the location of such interviews), and
  (iii) the admonition given to the witness (that is, what the child should be told about telling the truth).

[2] The 1985 US Department of Justice Report *When the Victim is a Child* (Whitcomb 1985), discusses various *ad hoc* techniques to shield child victims from eye contact with defendants, but does not mention the use of screens. In 1988, the Supreme Court struck down an Iowa law permitting the placement of a screen between the defendant and a child testifying about sexual assault (the only state with this provision). The court ruling said that the use of the screen violated the defendant's Sixth Amendment right to confront witnesses. It left open the possibility that use of screens, testimony by closed circuit television, or other methods aimed at minimising trauma to the child victim of sexual abuse might be permitted on a case by case basis where specific witnesses were found to need special protection (*Coy* v. *Iowa* (1988) US Supreme Court).

[3] The principle of screening a witness is much older than this. In *R.* v. *Smellie* ([1919] (xiv) Cr. App. R. 128–130), the Court of Appeal held that if there is a fear that a witness may be intimidated, the witness can give evidence out of sight. Prosecuting Counsel therefore has to establish fear on the part of the witness. Common law requires that the defendant must hear the evidence given.

References

Birch, D. (1992) 'The Criminal Justice Act 1991: children's evidence', *Criminal Law Review*, 262–76.

Bray, M. (1989) *Suzie and the Wise Hedgehog*, London.

Children's Legal Centre (1989) 'The child witness', London: Children's Legal Centre.

Children's Legal Centre (1990) *Being a Witness*, London: Children's Legal Centre.

Crown Court Rules (1982), London: HMSO.

Criminal Injuries Compensation Board (1990) *Twenty-Sixth Annual Report*, Cm. 1365.

Crown Office and Procurator Fiscal (1989) *Going to Court*, Edinburgh: Crown Office.

Davies, G. (1991) 'Children on trial? Psychology, videotechnology and the law', *Howard Journal*, *30*, 177–91.

DHSS and Welsh Office (1988) *Working Together: A Guide to Arrangements for Inter-Agency Co-operation for the Protection of Children from Abuse*, London: HMSO.

Glaser, D. and Spencer, J. R. (1990) 'Sentencing, children's evidence and children's trauma', *Criminal Law Review*, 371–82.

Hardin, M. (1986–7) 'Guardians ad litem for child victims in criminal proceedings', *Journal of Family Law* (University of St Louiseville), *25* (4), 687–728.

Home Office (1989) *Report of the Advisory Group on Video Evidence* (The Pigot Report), London: HMSO.

Home Office (1990) *Victim's Charter: A Statement of the Rights of Victims of Crime*, London: HMSO.

Home Office (1991) 'Video recorded interviews with child witnesses for criminal proceedings' (Draft Code of Practice), London: Home Office.

Jones, D. P. H. and McQuiston, M. (1988) *Interviewing the Sexually Abused Child*, London: Gaskell.

McEwan, J. (1990) 'In the box or on the box: The Pigot Report and child witnesses', *Criminal Law Review*, 813–22.

Mayhew, P., Elliott, D. and Dowds, L. (1989) *The 1988 British Crime Survey* (Home Office Research Study No. 111), London: HMSO.

Metropolitan Police and Bexley Social Services (1987) *Child Sexual Abuse: Joint Investigative Programme: Final Report*, London: HMSO.

Miers, D. (1989) 'The Criminal Justice Act: the compensation provisions', *Criminal Law Review*, 32–42.

Miers, D. (1990) *Compensation for Criminal Injuries*, London: Butterworths.

Moran-Ellis, J., Conroy, S. and Fielding, N. (1991) *Joint Investigation of Child Sexual Abuse: Executive Summary*, Guildford: University of Surrey.

Morgan, J. and Zedner, L. (1992) *Child Victims: Crime, Impact and Criminal Justice*, Oxford: Oxford University Press.

Newburn, T. and Merry, S. (1990) *Keeping in Touch: Police–Victim Communication in Two Areas* (Home Office Research Study No. 102), London: HMSO.

Scottish Law Commission (1990) *Report on the Evidence of Children and Other Potentially Vulnerable Witnesses* (Scottish Law Commission Study No. 125), Edinburgh: Scottish Law Commission.

Shapland, J., Willmore, J. and Duff, P. (1985) *Victims in the Criminal Justice System*, Aldershot: Gower.

Spencer, J. R. (1987) 'Child witnesses and the Criminal Justice Bill', *New Law Journal*, *137* (6330), 1031–3.

Spencer, J. R. and Flin, R. H. (1990) *The Evidence of Children: The Law and the Psychology*, London: Blackstone.

Spencer, J. and Tucker, P. G. (1987) 'The evidence of absent children', *New Law Journal*, 137 (6320), 816–17.

Temkin, J. (1990a) 'Child sexual abuse and criminal justice – 1', *New Law Journal*, *140* (6447) (16 March), 352–5.

Temkin, J. (1990b) 'Child sexual abuse – 2', *New Law Journal*, *140* (6448) (23 March), 410–11.

West Yorkshire Police (1989) *Going to Court*, Leeds: West Yorkshire Police.

Whitcomb, D. (1990) 'When the victim is a child', in: J. R. Spencer *et al.* (Eds.), *Children's Evidence in Legal Proceedings: An International Perspective*, Cambridge: Cambridge University Press.

Whitcomb, D. *et al.* (1985) *When the Victim is a Child*, Washington, DC: US Dept of Justice.

White, R. (1990) 'The Pigot Report', *New Law Journal*, *140* (6445), 300–1.

Date submitted: January 92
Date accepted: May 92

Rape: The All-American Crime

According to estimates by independent criminologists, rape is the most frequently committed violent crime in America today.

I HAVE NEVER BEEN FREE OF THE FEAR OF RAPE. From a very early age I, like most women, have thought of rape as part of my natural environment—something to be feared and prayed against like fire or lightning. I never asked why men raped; I simply thought it one of the many mysteries of human nature.

I was, however, curious enough about the violent side of humanity to read every crime magazine I was able to ferret away from my grandfather. Each issue featured at least one "sex crime," with pictures of a victim, usually in a pearl necklace, and of the ditch or the orchard where her body was found. I was never certain why the victims were always women, nor what the motives of the murderer were, but I did guess that the world was not a safe place for women. I

observed that my grandmother was meticulous about locks, and quick to draw the shades before anyone removed so much as a shoe. I sensed that danger lurked outside.

At the age of eight, my suspicions were confirmed. My grandmother took me to the back of the house where the men wouldn't hear, and told me that strange men wanted to do harm to little girls. I learned not to walk on dark streets, not to talk to strangers, or get into strange cars, to lock doors, and to be modest. She never explained why a man would want to harm a little girl, and I never asked.

If I thought for a while that my grandmother's fears were imaginary, the illusion was brief. That year, on the way home from school, a schoolmate a few years older than I tried to rape me. Later, in an obscure aisle of the local

by Susan Griffin

library (while I was reading *Freddy the Pig*) I turned to discover a man exposing himself. Then, the friendly man around the corner was arrested for child molesting.

My initiation to sexuality was typical. Every woman has similar stories to tell—the first man who attacked her may have been a neighbor, a family friend, an uncle, her doctor, or perhaps her own father. And women who grow up in New York City always have tales about the subway.

But though rape and the fear of rape are a daily part of every woman's consciousness, the subject is so rarely discussed by that unofficial staff of male intellectuals (who write the books which study seemingly every other form of male activity) that one begins to suspect a conspiracy of silence. And indeed, the obscurity of rape in print exists in marked contrast to the frequency of rape in reality, for *forcible rape is the most frequently committed violent crime in America today.* The Federal Bureau of Investigation classes three crimes as violent: murder, aggravated assault and forcible rape. In 1968, 31,060 rapes were *reported.* According to the FBI and independent criminologists, however, to approach accuracy this figure must be multiplied by at least a factor of ten to compensate for the fact that most rapes are not reported; when these compensatory mathematics are used, there are more rapes committed than aggravated assaults and homicides.

When I asked Berkeley, California's Police Inspector in charge of rape investigation if he knew why men rape women, he replied that he had not spoken with "these people and delved into what really makes them tick, because that really isn't my job. . . ." However, when I asked him how a woman might prevent being raped, he was not so reticent. "I wouldn't advise any female to go walking around alone at night . . . and she should lock her car at all times." The Inspector illustrated his warning with a grisly story about a man who lay in wait for women in the back seats of their cars, while they were shopping in a local supermarket. This man eventually murdered one of his rape victims. "Always lock your car," the Inspector repeated, and then added, without a hint of irony, "Of course, you don't have to be paranoid about this type of thing."

THE INSPECTOR WONDERED WHY I WANTED to write about rape. Like most men he did not understand the urgency of the topic, for, after all, men are not raped. But like most women I had spent considerable time speculating on the true nature of the rapist. When I was very young, my image of the "sexual offender" was a nightmarish amalgamation of the bogey man and Captain Hook: he wore a black cape, and he cackled. As I matured, so did my image of the rapist. Born into the psychoanalytic age, I tried to "understand" the rapist. Rape, I came to believe, was only one of many unfortunate evils produced by sexual repression. Reasoning by tautology, I concluded that any man who would rape a woman must be out of his mind.

Yet, though the theory that rapists are insane is a popular one, this belief has no basis in fact. According to Professor Menachem Amir's study of 646 rape cases in Philadelphia, *Patterns in Forcible Rape,* men who rape are not abnormal. Amir writes, "Studies indicate that sex offenders do not constitute a unique or psychopathological type; nor are they as a group invariably more disturbed than the control groups to which they are compared." Alan Taylor, a parole officer who has worked with rapists in the prison facilities at San Luis Obispo, California, stated the question in plainer language, "Those men were the most normal men there. They had a lot of hang-ups, but they were the same hang-ups as men walking out on the street."

Another canon in the apologetics of rape is that, if it were not for learned social controls, all men would rape. Rape is held to be natural behavior, and not to rape must be learned. But in truth rape is not universal to the human species. Moreover, studies of rape in our culture reveal that, far from being impulsive behavior, most rape is planned. Professor Amir's study reveals that in cases of group rape (the "gangbang" of masculine slang) 90 percent of the rapes were planned; in pair rapes, 83 percent of the rapes were planned; and in single rapes, 58 percent were planned. These figures should significantly discredit the image of the rapist as a man who is suddenly overcome by sexual needs society does not allow him to fulfill.

Far from the social control of rape being learned, comparisons with other cultures lead one to suspect that, in our society, it is rape itself that is learned. (The fact that rape is against the law should not be considered proof that rape is not in fact encouraged as part of our culture.)

This culture's concept of rape as an illegal, but still understandable, form of behavior is not a universal one. In her study *Sex and Temperament,* Margaret Mead describes a society that does not share our views. The Arapesh do not ". . . have any conception of the male nature that might make rape understandable to them." Indeed our interpretation of rape is a product of our conception of the nature of male sexuality. A common retort to the question, why don't women rape men, is the myth that men have greater sexual needs, that their sexuality is more urgent than women's. And it is the nature of human beings to want to live up to what is expected of them.

And this same culture which expects aggression from the male expects passivity from the female. Conveniently, the companion myth about the nature of female sexuality is that all women secretly want to be raped. Lurking beneath her modest female exterior is a subconscious desire to be ravished. The following description of a stag movie, written by Brenda Starr in Los Angeles' underground paper, *Everywoman,* typifies this male fantasy. The movie "showed a woman in her underclothes reading on her bed. She is interrupted by a rapist with a knife. He immediately wins her over with his charm and they get busy sucking and fucking." An advertisement in the *Berkeley Barb* reads, "Now as all women know from their daydreams, rape has a lot of advantages. Best of all it's so simple. No preparation necessary, no planning ahead of time, no wondering if you should or shouldn't; just whang! bang!" Thanks to Masters and Johnson even the scientific canon recognizes that for the female, "whang! bang!" can scarcely be described as pleasurable.

Still, the male psyche persists in believing that, protestations and struggles to the contrary, deep inside her mysterious feminine soul, the female victim has wished for her own fate. A young woman who was raped by the husband of a

friend said that days after the incident the man returned to her home, pounded on the door and screamed to her, "Jane, Jane. You loved it. You know you loved it."

The theory that women like being raped extends itself by deduction into the proposition that most or much of rape is provoked by the victim. But this too is only myth. Though provocation, considered a mitigating factor in a court of law, may consist of only "a gesture," according to the Federal Commission on Crimes of Violence, only 4 percent of reported rapes involved any precipitative behavior by the woman.

The notion that rape is enjoyed by the victim is also convenient for the man who, though he would not commit forcible rape, enjoys the idea of its existence, as if rape confirms that enormous sexual potency which he secretly knows to be his own. It is for the pleasure of the armchair rapist that detailed accounts of violent rapes exist in the media. Indeed, many men appear to take sexual pleasure from nearly all forms of violence. Whatever the motivation, male sexuality and violence in our culture seem to be inseparable. James Bond alternately whips out his revolver and his cock, and though there is no known connection between the skills of gun-fighting and love-making, pacifism seems suspiciously effeminate.

In a recent fictional treatment of the Manson case, Frank Conroy writes of his vicarious titillation when describing the murders to his wife:

"Every single person there was killed." She didn't move.

"It sounds like there was torture," I said. As the words left my mouth I knew there was no need to say them to frighten her into believing that she needed me for protection."

The pleasure he feels as his wife's protector is inextricably mixed with pleasure in the violence itself. Conroy writes, "I was excited by the killings, as one is excited by catas-

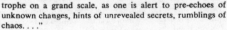

trophe on a grand scale, as one is alert to pre-echoes of unknown changes, hints of unrevealed secrets, rumblings of chaos. . . ."

THE ATTRACTION OF THE MALE IN OUR CULTURE to violence and death is a tradition Manson and his admirers are carrying on with tireless avidity (even presuming Manson's innocence, he dreams of the purification of fire and destruction). It was Malraux in his *Anti-Memoirs* who said that, for the male, facing death was *the* illuminating experience analogous to childbirth for the female. Certainly our culture does glorify war and shroud the agonies of the gun-fighter in veils of mystery.

And in the spectrum of male behavior, rape, the perfect combination of sex and violence, is the penultimate act. Erotic pleasure cannot be separated from culture, and in our culture male eroticism is wedded to power. Not only

should a man be taller and stronger than a female in the perfect love-match, but he must also demonstrate his superior strength in gestures of dominance which are perceived as amorous. Though the law attempts to make a clear division between rape and sexual intercourse, in fact the courts find it difficult to distinguish between a case where the decision to copulate was mutual and one where a man forced himself upon his partner.

The scenario is even further complicated by the expectation that, not only does a woman mean "yes" when she says "no," but that a really decent woman ought to begin by saying "no," and then be led down the primrose path to acquiescence. Ovid, the author of Western Civilization's most celebrated sex-manual, makes this expectation perfectly clear:

. . . and when I beg you to say "yes," say "no." Then let me lie outside your bolted door. . . . So Love grows strong. . . .

That the basic elements of rape are involved in all heterosexual relationships may explain why men often identify with the offender in this crime. But to regard the rapist as the victim, a man driven by his inherent sexual needs to take what will not be given him, reveals a basic ignorance of sexual politics. For in our culture heterosexual love finds an erotic expression through male dominance and female submission. A man who derives pleasure from raping a woman clearly must enjoy force and dominance as much or more than the simple pleasures of the flesh. Coitus cannot be experienced in isolation. The weather, the state of the nation, the level of sugar in the blood—all will affect a man's ability to achieve orgasm. If a man can achieve sexual pleasure after terrorizing and humiliating the object of his passion, and in fact while inflicting pain upon her, one must assume he derives pleasure directly from terrorizing, humiliating and harming a woman. According to Amir's study of forcible rape, on a statistical average the man who has been convicted of rape was found to have a normal sexual personality, tending to be different from the normal, well-adjusted male only in having a greater tendency to express violence and rage.

And if the professional rapist is to be separated from the average dominant heterosexual, it may be mainly a quantitative difference. For the existence of rape as an index to masculinity is not entirely metaphorical. Though this measure of masculinity seems to be more publicly exhibited among "bad boys" or aging bikers who practice sexual initiation through group rape, in fact, "good boys" engage in the same rites to prove their manhood. In Stockton, a small town in California which epitomizes silent-majority America, a bachelor party was given last summer for a young man about to be married. A woman was hired to dance "topless" for the amusement of the guests. At the high point of the evening the bridegroom-to-be dragged the woman into a bedroom. No move was made by any of his companions to stop what was clearly going to be an attempted rape. Far from it. As the woman described, "I tried to keep him away—told him of my Herpes Genitalis, et cetera, but he couldn't face the guys if he didn't screw me." After the bridegroom had finished raping the woman and returned with her to the party, far from chastizing him, his friends heckled the woman and covered her with wine.

It was fortunate for the dancer that the bridegroom's friends did not follow him into the bedroom for, though one might suppose that in group rape, since the victim is outnumbered, less force would be inflicted on her, in fact, Amir's studies indicate, "the most excessive degrees of violence occurred in group rape." Far from discouraging violence, the presence of other men may in fact encourage sadism, and even cause the behavior. In an unpublished study of group rape by Gilbert Geis and Duncan Chappell, the authors refer to a study by W. H. Blanchard which relates, "The leader of the male group . . . apparently precipitated and maintained the activity, despite misgivings, because of a need to fulfill the role that the other two men had assigned to him. 'I was scared when it began to happen,' he says. 'I wanted to leave but I didn't want to say it to the other guys—you know—that I was scared.' "

Thus it becomes clear that not only does our culture teach men the rudiments of rape, but society, or more specifically other men, encourage the practice of it.

II

Every man I meet wants to protect me. Can't figure out what from.

—Mae West

IF A MALE SOCIETY REWARDS AGGRESSIVE, domineering sexual behavior, it contains within itself a sexual schizophrenia. For the masculine man is also expected to prove his mettle as a protector of women. To the naive eye, this dichotomy implies that men fall into one of two categories: those who rape and those who protect. In fact, life does not prove so simple. In a study euphemistically entitled "Sex Aggression by College Men," it was discovered that men who believe in a double standard of morality for men and women, who in fact believe most fervently in the ultimate value of virginity, are more liable to commit "this aggresive variety of sexual exploitation."

(At this point in our narrative it should come as no surprise that Sir Thomas Malory, creator of that classic tale of chivalry, *The Knights of the Round Table*, was himself arrested and found guilty for repeated incidents of rape.)

In the system of chivalry, men protect women against men. This is not unlike the protection relationship which the mafia established with small businesses in the early part of this century. Indeed, chivalry is an age-old protection racket which depends for its existence on rape.

According to the male mythology which defines and perpetuates rape, it is an animal instinct inherent in the male. The story goes that sometime in our pre-historical past, the male, more hirsute and burly than today's counterparts, roamed about an uncivilized landscape until he found a desirable female. (Oddly enough, this female is *not* pictured as more muscular than the modern woman.) Her mate does not bother with courtship. He simply grabs her by the hair and drags her to the closest cave. Presumably, one of the major advantages of modern civilization for the female has been the civilizing of the male. We call it chivalry.

But women do not get chivalry for free. According to the logic of sexual politics, we too have to civilize our behavior. (Enter chastity. Enter virginity. Enter monogamy.) For the female, civilized behavior means chastity before marriage and faithfulness within it. Chivalrous behavior in the male is supposed to protect that chastity from involuntary defilement. The fly in the ointment of this otherwise peaceful system is the fallen woman. She does not behave. And therefore she does not deserve protection. Or, to use another argument, a major tenet of the same value system: what has once been defiled cannot again be violated. One begins to suspect that it is the behavior of the fallen woman, and not that of the male, that civilization aims to control.

The assumption that a woman who does not respect the double standard deserves whatever she gets (or at the very least "asks for it") operates in the courts today. While in

some states a man's previous rape convictions are not considered admissible evidence, the sexual reputation of the
rape victim is considered a crucial element of the facts upon
which the court must decide innocence or guilt.

The court's respect for the double standard manifested
itself particularly clearly in the case of the People v. Jerry
Plotkin. Mr. Plotkin, a 36-year-old jeweler, was tried for
rape last spring in a San Francisco Superior Court. According to the woman who brought the charges, Plotkin, along
with three other men, forced her at gunpoint to enter a car
one night in October 1970. She was taken to Mr. Plotkin's
fashionable apartment where he and the three other men
first raped her and then, in the delicate language of the
S.F. Chronicle, "subjected her to perverted sex acts." She
was, she said, set free in the morning with the warning that
she would be killed if she spoke to anyone about the event.
She did report the incident to the police who then searched
Plotkin's apartment and discovered a long list of names of
women. Her name was on the list and had been crossed out.

In addition to the woman's account of her abduction and
rape, the prosecution submitted four of Plotkin's address
books containing the names of hundreds of women. Plotkin
claimed he did not know all of the women since some of
the names had been given to him by friends and he had not
yet called on them. Several women, however, did testify in
court that Plotkin had, to cite the *Chronicle,* "lured them up
to his apartment under one pretext or another, and forced
his sexual attentions on them."

Plotkin's defense rested on two premises. First, through
his own testimony Plotkin established a reputation for himself as a sexual libertine who frequently picked up girls in
bars and took them to his house where sexual relations
often took place. He was the Playboy. He claimed that
the accusation of rape, therefore, was false—this incident
had simply been one of many casual sexual relationships,
the victim one of many playmates. The second premise of
the defense was that his accuser was also a sexual libertine.
However, the picture created of the young woman (fully

13 years younger than Plotkin) was not akin to the light-hearted, gay-bachelor image projected by the defendant. On the contrary, the day after the defense cross-examined the woman, the *Chronicle* printed a story headlined, "Grueling Day For Rape Case Victim." (A leaflet passed out by women in front of the courtroom was more succinct, "rape was committed by four men in a private apartment in October; on Thursday, it was done by a judge and a lawyer in a public courtroom.")

Through skillful questioning fraught with innuendo, Plotkin's defense attorney James Martin MacInnis portrayed the young woman as a licentious opportunist and unfit mother. MacInnis began by asking the young woman (then employed as a secretary) whether or not it was true that she was "familiar with liquor" and had worked as a "cocktail waitress." The young woman replied (the *Chronicle* wrote "admitted") that she had worked once or twice as a cocktail waitress. The attorney then asked if she had worked as a secretary in the financial district but had "left that employment after it was discovered that you had sexual intercourse on a couch in the office." The woman replied, "That is a lie. I left because I didn't like working in a one-girl office. It was too lonely." Then the defense asked if, while working as an attendant at a health club, "you were accused of having a sexual affair with a man?" Again the woman denied the story, "I was never accused of that."

Plotkin's attorney then sought to establish that his client's accuser was living with a married man. She responded that the man was separated from his wife. Finally he told the court that she had "spent the night" with another man who lived in the same building.

At this point in the testimony the woman asked Plotkin's defense attorney, "Am I on trial? . . . It is embarrassing and personal to admit these things to all these people. . . . I did not commit a crime. I am a human being." The lawyer, true to the chivalry of his class, apologized and immediately resumed questioning her, turning his attention to her children. (She is divorced, and the children at the time of the trial were in a foster home.) "Isn't it true that your two children have a sex game in which one gets on top of another and they—" "That is a lie!" the young woman interrupted him. She ended her testimony by explaining "They are wonderful children. They are not perverted."

The jury, divided in favor of acquittal ten to two, asked the court stenographer to read the woman's testimony back to them. After this reading, the Superior Court acquitted the defendant of both the charges of rape and kidnapping.

ACCORDING TO THE DOUBLE STANDARD a woman who has had sexual intercourse out of wedlock cannot be raped. Rape is not only a crime of aggression against the body; it is a transgression against chastity as defined by men. When a woman is forced into a sexual relationship, she has, according to the male ethos, been violated. But she is also defiled if she does not behave according to the double standard, by maintaining her chastity, or confining her sexual activities to a monogamous relationship.

One should not assume, however, that a woman can avoid the possibility of rape simply by behaving. Though myth would have it that mainly "bad girls" are raped, this theory has no basis in fact. Available statistics would lead one to believe that a safer course is promiscuity. In a study of rape done in the District of Columbia, it was found that 82 percent of the rape victims had a "good reputation." Even the Police Inspector's advice to stay off the streets is rather useless, for almost half of reported rapes occur in the home of the victim and are committed by a man she has never before seen. Like indiscriminate terrorism, rape can happen to any woman, and few women are ever without this knowledge.

But the courts and the police, both dominated by white males, continue to suspect the rape victim, *sui generis*, of provoking or asking for her own assault. According to Amir's study, the police tend to believe that a woman without a good reputation cannot be raped. The rape victim is usually submitted to countless questions about her own sexual mores and behavior by the police investigator. This preoccupation is partially justified by the legal requirements for prosecution in a rape case. The rape victim must have been penetrated, and she must have made it clear to her assailant that she did not want penetration (unless of course she is unconscious). A refusal to accompany a man to some isolated place to allow him to touch her does not in the eyes of the court, constitute rape. She must have said "no" at the crucial genital moment. And the rape victim, to qualify as such, must also have put up a physical struggle—unless she can prove that to do so would have been to endanger her life.

BUT THE ZEALOUS INTEREST the police frequently exhibit in the physical details of a rape case is only partially explained by the requirements of the court. A woman who was raped in Berkeley was asked to tell the story of her rape four different times "right out in the street," while her assailant was escaping. She was then required to submit to a pelvic examination to prove that penetration had taken place. Later, she was taken to the police station where she was asked the same questions again: "Were you forced?" "Did he penetrate?" "Are you sure your life was in danger and you had no other choice?" This woman had been pulled off the street by a man who held a 10-inch knife at her throat and forcibly raped her. She was raped at midnight and was not able to return to her home until five in the morning. Police contacted her twice again in the next week, once by telephone at two in the morning and once at four in the morning. In her words, "The rape was probably the least traumatic incident of the whole evening. If I'm ever raped again, . . . I wouldn't report it to the police because of all the degradation. . . ."

If white women are subjected to unnecessary and often hostile questioning after having been raped, third world women are often not believed at all. According to the white male ethos (which is not only sexist but racist), third world women are defined from birth as "impure." Thus the white male is provided with a pool of women who are fair game for sexual imperialism. Third world women frequently do not report rape and for good reason. When blues singer Billie Holliday was 10 years old, she was taken off to a local house by a neighbor and raped. Her mother brought the police to rescue her, and she was taken to the local police station crying and bleeding:

> When we got there, instead of treating me and Mom like somebody who called the cops for help, they treated me like I'd killed somebody. . . . I guess they had me figured for having enticed this old goat into the whorehouse. . . . All I know for sure is they threw me into a cell . . . a fat white matron . . . saw I was still bleeding, she felt sorry for me and gave me a couple glasses of milk. But nobody else did anything for me except give me filthy looks and snicker to themselves.
>
> After a couple of days in a cell they dragged me into a court. Mr. Dick got sentenced to five years. They sentenced me to a Catholic institution.

Clearly the white man's chivalry is aimed only to protect the chastity of "his" women.

As a final irony, that same system of sexual values from which chivalry is derived has also provided womankind with an unwritten code of behavior, called femininity, which makes a feminine woman the perfect victim of sexual aggression. If being chaste does not ward off the possibility of assault, being feminine certainly increases the chances that it will succeed. To be submissive is to defer to masculine strength; is to lack muscular development or any interest in defending oneself; is to let doors be opened, to have one's arm held when crossing the street. To be feminine is to wear shoes which make it difficult to run; skirts which inhibit one's stride; underclothes which inhibit the circulation. Is it not an intriguing observation that those very clothes which are thought to be flattering to the female and attractive to the male are those which make it impossible for a woman to defend herself against aggression?

Each girl as she grows into womanhood is taught fear. Fear is the form in which the female internalizes both chivalry and the double standard. Since, biologically speaking, women in fact have the same if not greater potential for sexual expression as do men, the woman who is taught that she must behave differently from a man must also learn to distrust her own carnality. She must deny her own feelings and learn not to act from them. She fears herself. This is the essence of passivity, and of course, a woman's passivity is not simply sexual but functions to cripple her from self-expression in every area of her life.

Passivity itself prevents a woman from ever considering her own potential for self-defense and forces her to look to men for protection. The woman is taught fear, but this time fear of the other; and yet her only relief from this fear is to seek out the other. Moreover, the passive woman is taught to regard herself as impotent, unable to act, unable even to perceive, in no way self-sufficient, and, finally, as the object and not the subject of human behavior. It is in this sense that a woman is deprived of the status of a human being. She is not free to be.

III

SINCE IBSEN'S NORA SLAMMED THE DOOR on her patri-archical husband, woman's attempt to be free has been more or less fashionable. In this 19th century portrait of a woman leaving her marriage, Nora tells her husband, "Our home has been nothing but a playroom. I have been your doll-wife just as at home I was papa's doll-child." And, at least on the stage, "The Doll's House" crumbled, leaving audiences with hope for the fate of the modern woman. And today, as in the past, woman-kind has not lacked examples of liberated women to emulate: Emma Goldman, Greta Garbo and Isadora Duncan all denounced marriage and the double standard, and believed their right to freedom included sexual independence; but still their example has not affected the lives of millions of women who continue to marry, divorce and remarry, living out their lives dependent on the status and economic power of men. Patriarchy still holds the average woman prisoner not because she lacks the courage of an Isadora Duncan, but because the material conditions of her life prevent her from being anything but an object.

In the *Elementary Structures of Kinship*, Claude Levi-Strauss gives to marriage this universal description, "It is always a system of exchange that we find at the origin of the rules of marriage." In this system of exchange, a woman is the "most precious possession." Levi-Strauss continues that the custom of including women as booty in the marketplace is still so general that "a whole volume would not be sufficient to enumerate instances of it." Levi-Strauss makes it clear that he does not exclude Western Civilization from his definition of "universal" and cites examples from modern wedding ceremonies. (The marriage ceremony is still one in which the husband and wife become one, and "that one is the husband.")

The legal proscription against rape reflects this possessory view of women. An article in the 1952–53 *Yale Law Journal* describes the legal rationale behind laws against rape: "In our society sexual taboos, often enacted into law, buttress a system of monogamy based upon the law of 'free bargaining' of the potential spouses. Within this process the woman's power to withhold or grant sexual access is an important bargaining weapon." Presumably then, laws against rape are intended to protect the right of a woman, not for physical self-determination, but for physical "bargaining." The article goes on to explain explicitly why the preservation of the bodies of women is important to men:

> *The consent standard in our society does more than protect a significant item of social currency for women; it fosters, and is in turn bolstered by, a masculine pride in the exclusive possession of a sexual object. The consent of a woman to sexual intercourse awards the man a privilege of bodily access, a personal "prize" whose value is enhanced by sole ownership. An additional reason for the man's condemnation of rape may be found in the threat to his status from a decrease in the "value" of his sexual possession which would result from forcible violation.*

The passage concludes by making clear whose interest the law is designed to protect. "The man responds to this undercutting of his status as *possessor* of the girl with hostility toward the rapist; no other restitution device is available. The law of rape provides an orderly outlet for his vengeance." Presumably the female victim in any case will have been sufficiently socialized so as not to consciously feel any strong need for vengeance. If she does feel this need, society does not speak to it.

The laws against rape exist to protect rights of the male

as possessor of the female body, and not the right of the female over her own body. Even without this enlightening passage from the *Yale Law Review,* the laws themselves are clear: In no state can a man be accused of raping his wife. How can any man steal what already belongs to him? It is in the sense of rape as theft of another man's property that Kate Millett writes, "Traditionally rape has been viewed as an offense one male commits against another—a matter of abusing his woman." In raping another man's woman, a man may aggrandize his own manhood and concurrently reduce that of another man. Thus a man's honor is not subject directly to rape, but only indirectly, through "his" woman.

IF THE BASIC SOCIAL UNIT is the family, in which the woman is a possession of her husband, the superstructure of society is a male hierarchy, in which men dominate other men (or patriarchal families dominate other patriarchal families). And it is no small irony that, while the very social fabric of our male-dominated culture denies women equal access to political, economic and legal power, the literature, myth and humor of our culture depicts women not only as the power behind the throne, but the real source of the oppression of men. The religious version of this fairy tale blames Eve for both carnality and eating of the tree of knowledge, at the same time making her gullible to the obvious devices of a serpent. Adam, of course, is merely the trusting victim of love. Certainly this is a biased story. But no more biased than the one television audiences receive today from the latest slick comedians. Through a media which is owned by men, censored by a State dominated by men, all the evils of this social system which make a man's life unpleasant are blamed upon "the wife." The theory is: were it not for the female who waits and plots to "trap" the male into marriage, modern man would be able to achieve Olympian freedom. She is made the scapegoat for a system which is in fact run by men.

Nowhere is this more clear than in the white racist use of the concept of white womanhood. The white male's open rape of black women, coupled with his overweening concern for the chastity and protection of his wife and daughters, represents an extreme of sexist and racist hypocrisy. While on the one hand she was held up as the standard for purity and virtue, on the other the Southern white woman was never asked if she wanted to be on a pedestal, and in fact any deviance from the male-defined standards for white womanhood was treated severely. (It is a powerful commentary on American racism that the historical role of Blacks as slaves, and thus possessions without power, has robbed black women of legal and economic protection through marriage. Thus black women in Southern society and in the ghettoes of the North have long been easy game for white rapists.) The fear that black men would rape white women was, and is, classic paranoia. Quoting from Ann Breen's unpublished study of racism and sexism in the South *"The New South: White Man's Country,"* Frederick Douglass legitimately points out that, had the black man wished to rape white women, he had ample opportunity to do so during the civil war when white women, the

wives, sisters, daughters and mothers of the rebels, were left in the care of Blacks. But yet not a single act of rape was committed during this time. The Ku Klux Klan, who tarred and feathered black men and lynched them in the honor of the purity of white womanhood, also applied tar and feathers to a Southern white woman accused of bigamy, which leads one to suspect that Southern white men were not so much outraged at the violation of the woman as a person, in the few instances where rape was actually committed by black men, but at the violation of his property rights." In the situation where a black man was found to be having sexual relations with a white woman, the white woman could exercise skin-privilege, and claim that she had been raped, in which case the black man was lynched. But if she did not claim rape, she herself was subject to lynching.

In constructing the myth of white womanhood so as to justify the lynching and oppression of black men and women, the white male has created a convenient symbol of his own power which has resulted in black hostility toward the white "bitch," accompanied by an unreasonable fear on the part of many white women of the black rapist. Moreover, it is not surprising that after being told for two centuries that he wants to rape white women, occasionally a black man does actually commit that act. But it is crucial to note that the frequency of this practice is outrageously exaggerated in the white mythos. Ninety percent of reported rape is intra- not inter-racial.

In *Soul on Ice,* Eldridge Cleaver has described the mixing of a rage against white power with the internalized sexism of a black man raping a white woman. "Somehow I arrived at the conclusion that, as a matter of principle, it was of paramount importance for me to have an antagonistic, ruthless attitude toward white women. . . . Rape was an insurrectionary act. It delighted me that I was defying and trampling upon the white man's law, upon his system of values and that I was defiling his women—and this point, I believe, was the most satisfying to me because I was very resentful over the historical fact of how the white man has used the black woman." Thus a black man uses white women to take out his rage against white men. But in fact, whenever a rape of a white woman by a black man does take place, it is again the white man who benefits. First, the act itself terrorizes the white woman and makes her more dependent on the white male for protection. Then, if the woman prosecutes her attacker, the white man is afforded legal opportunity to exercise overt racism. Of course, the knowledge of the rape helps to perpetuate two myths which are beneficial to white male rule—the bestiality of the black man and the desirability of white women. Finally, the white man surely benefits because he himself is not the object of attack—he has been allowed to stay in power.

Indeed, the existence of rape in any form is beneficial to the ruling class of white males. For rape is a kind of terrorism which severely limits the freedom of women and makes women dependent on men. Moreover, in the act of rape, the rage that one man may harbor toward another higher in the male hierarchy can be deflected toward a female scapegoat. For every man there is always someone lower on the social scale on whom he can take out his aggressions. And that is any woman alive.

THIS OPPRESSIVE ATTITUDE TOWARDS women finds its institutionalization in the traditional family. For it is assumed that a man "wears the pants" in his family—he exercises the option of rule whenever he so chooses. Not that he makes all the decisions—clearly women make most of the important day-to-day decisions in a family. But when a conflict of interest arises, it is the man's interest which will prevail. His word, in itself, is more powerful. He lords it over his wife in the same way his boss lords it over him, so that the very process of exercising his power becomes as important an act as obtaining whatever it is his power can get for him. This notion of power is key to the male ego in this culture, for the two acceptable measures of masculinity are a man's power over women and his power over other men. A man may boast to his friends that "I have 20 men working for me." It is also aggrandizement of his ego if he has the financial power to clothe his wife in furs and jewels. And, if a man lacks the wherewithal to acquire such power, he can always express his rage through equally masculine activities—rape and theft. Since male society defines the female as a possession, it is not surprising that the felony most often committed together with rape is theft. As the following classic tale of rape points out, the elements of theft, violence and forced sexual relations merge into an indistinguishable whole.

The woman who told this story was acquainted with the man who tried to rape her. When the man learned that she was going to be staying alone for the weekend, he began early in the day a polite campaign to get her to go out with him. When she continued to refuse his request, his chivalrous mask dropped away:

"I had locked all the doors because I was afraid, and I don't know how he got in; it was probably through the screen door. When I woke up, he was shaking my leg. His eyes were red, and I knew he had been drinking or smoking. I thought I would try to talk my way out of it. He started by saying that he wanted to sleep with me, and then he got angrier and angrier, until he started to say, 'I want pussy,' 'I want pussy.' Then, I got scared and tried to push him away. That's when he started to force himself on me. It was awful. It was the most humiliating, terrible feeling. He was forcing my legs apart and ripping my clothes off. And it was painful. I did fight him—he was slightly drunk and I was able to keep him away. I had taken judo a few years back, but I was afraid to throw a chop for fear that he'd kill me. I could see he was getting more and more violent. I was thinking wildly of some way to get out of this alive, and then I said to him, 'Do you want money. I'll give you money.' We had money but I was also thinking that if I got to the back room I could telephone the police—as if the police would have even helped. It was a stupid thing to think of because obviously he would follow me. And he did. When he saw me pick up the phone, he tried to tie the cord around my neck. I screamed at him that I did have the money in another room, that I was going to call the police because I was scared, but that I would never tell anybody what happened. It would be an absolute secret. He said, okay, and I went to get the money. But when he got it, all of a sudden he got this crazy look in his eye and he said to me, 'Now I'm going to kill you.' Then I

started saying my prayers. I knew there was nothing I could do. He started to hit me—I still wasn't sure if he wanted to rape me at this point—or just to kill me. He was hurting me, but hadn't yet gotten me into a strangle-hold because he was still drunk and off balance. Somehow we pushed into the kitchen where I kept looking at this big knife. But I didn't pick it up. Somehow, no matter how much I hated him at that moment, I still couldn't imagine putting the knife in his flesh, and then I was afraid he would grab it and stick it into me. Then he was hitting me again and somehow we pushed through the back door of the kitchen and onto the porch steps. We fell down the steps and that's when he started to strangle me. He was on top of me. He just went on and on until finally I lost consciousness. I did scream, though my screams sounded like whispers to me. But what happened was that a cab driver happened by and frightened him away. The cab driver revived me—I was out only a minute at the most. And then I ran across the street and I grabbed the woman who was our neighbor and screamed at her, 'Am I alive? Am I still alive?' "

* * *

RAPE IS AN ACT OF AGGRESSION in which the victim is denied her self-determination. It is an act of violence which, if not actually followed by beatings or murder, nevertheless always carries with it the threat of death. And finally, rape is a form of mass terrorism, for the victims of rape are chosen indiscriminately, but the propagandists for male supremacy broadcast that it is women who cause rape by being unchaste or in the wrong place at the wrong time—in essence, by behaving as though they were free.

The threat of rape is used to deny women employment. (In California, the Berkeley Public Library, until pushed by the Federal Employment Practices Commission, refused to hire female shelvers because of perverted men in the stacks.) The fear of rape keeps women off the streets at night. Keeps women at home. Keeps women passive and modest for fear that they be thought provocative.

It is part of human dignity to be able to defend oneself, and women are learning. Some women have learned karate; some to shoot guns. And yet we will not be free until the threat of rape and the atmosphere of violence is ended, and to end that the nature of male behavior must change.

But rape is not an isolated act that can be rooted out from patriarchy without ending patriarchy itself. The same men and power structure who victimize women are engaged in the act of raping Vietnam, raping Black people and the very earth we live upon. Rape is a classic act of domination where, in the words of Kate Millett, "the emotions of hatred, contempt, and the desire to break or violate personality," takes place. This breaking of the personality characterizes modern life itself. No simple reforms can eliminate rape. As the symbolic expression of the white male hierarchy, rape is the quintessential act of our civilization, one which, Valerie Solanis warns, is in danger of "humping itself to death."

Susan Griffin is a feminist and poet. She is currently at work on a trilogy of novellas examining the psychic life of women.

With the rising tide of sexual assaults
women have organized crisis centers to assist the victims

RAPE:
Breaking the Silence

MICHELLE WASSERMAN

The image of the talkative female has inspired many poets and humorists. Ralph Waldo Emerson vowed never to trust three women with a secret unless two were dead. Oscar Wilde concurred: "You can always tell a woman, but you cannot tell her much." Poetic license aside, the so-called talkative sex is often too adept at keeping secrets. Each year in the United States thousands of women and girls are raped, and they are ashamed to discuss their experience, even with their closest relatives and friends.

Because silence among rape victims jeopardizes their physical and emotional well-being, concerned women are organizing to deal with the problem. Rape crisis centers are mushrooming across the country to challenge the myths that perpetuate the silence among rape victims, and to provide a much needed community service.

In its simplest form, a rape crisis center is an emergency telephone line for rape victims who want to find out about legal procedures and health precautions, or who just need to talk. In some cities, small switchboard operations have evolved into networks of para-professional counselors and advocates who provide twenty-four hour confidential service, work in conjunction with local authorities, and educate the community. The Philadelphia group operates from a room in Philadelphia General Hospital. It has a staff of more than fifty volunteers, and its mailing list contains some 300 names. The center in Minneapolis, which is affiliated with a community action project, is equipped with cots and staffed with counselors experienced in leading group therapy sessions.

The first emergency line opened in Washington, D.C., in June, 1972. About ten women, most of them

Michelle Wasserman is a graduate student at the University of Wisconsin and a free lance writer. For background information on this article she visited rape crisis centers around the country and interviewed volunteer and professional counselors. Her travel and research were made possible by a grant from the Fund for Investigative Journalism in Washington, D.C.

rape victims, rented a town house, secured 333-RAPE as their telephone number, and wrote a handbook called How to Start a Rape Crisis Center. They received 200 to 300 calls per month—from rape victims, from local and national media, and from women interested in starting rape crisis centers in their own towns and cities. Before long, the D.C. group became a national clearing house of information and began distributing a monthly newsletter to new rape crisis centers.

The growing interest among women in developing alternative services parallels the rising tide of rape in the past decade. The Federal Bureau of Investigation has estimated that reported rapes increased 146 per cent between 1960 and 1971, and an additional eleven per cent in 1972, when there were 41,890 rapes. Independent criminologists add the important footnote that there are four to ten times as many rapes committed as reported, and that only a small percentage of reported violations end in convictions.

Although the FBI figures do not fully measure the extent of rape today, there is little doubt that the trend is upward. According to the National Commission on the Causes and Prevention of Violence (1969), the rise in rape is part of a general increase in violent behavior in the United States and is largely the result of decaying conditions in urban areas.

But the greater frequency of rape is not the only impetus to the development of crisis centers. Women are realizing that the solutions being offered to the problem are as dehumanizing as the crime itself. They are tired of hearing that the way to prevent rape is to keep their car doors locked and windows shut and never to walk home after dark without a male escort.

I asked a staff worker at the Seattle center if such precautionary measures had any role in an anti-rape program. "Safety precautions are useful but not to the extent that they limit our mobility and prevent us from being free human beings," she replied. A Philadelphia volunteer told me, "Women live according to a rape schedule, whether they realize it or not. Where they live, how they work out their jobs and their transportation, the way they dress at certain times of the day, the way they educate their children, the way they relate to men on the street—everything a woman does conforms to that schedule."

Rape crisis centers are founded on the principle that women cannot and should not be expected to bear the burden of preventing sexual assault—that the root causes of rape are not in a woman's smile or walk, but in a sexist society.

In developing this socio-cultural explanation of rape, women's groups refer to their members' experiences and to one of the few existing studies on the subject. Most studies stress the psychology of rapists. Menachem Amir's *Patterns of Forcible Rape* (University of Chicago Press, 1971), an analysis of 646 rape cases in Philadelphia, is the first major attempt at a socio-cultural approach.

Amir's study indicates that rape occurs in a context of violence rather than passion: "Rape is a deviant act, not because of the sexual act per se, but rather in the mode of the act, which implies aggression, whereby the sexual factor supplies the motive." Avid Hitchcock fans will be surprised to learn that most rapists are not sexually perverted bogey men who hide in bushes and hate their mothers. According to Amir, rapists do not fit into any particular psychopathological category, nor are they more likely than other felons to be psychopathic.

Amir's findings indicate that most rapists are a danger to the community not because they are compulsive sex fiends but because they are violent and aggressive. Their violence is conditioned by cultural norms and the social organization of their environment. Amir discovered that the majority of sexual offenders occupy the lower rungs of the economic and occupational ladder and are between the ages of fifteen and twenty-four. Lower-class males, Amir maintains, learn from their parents and peers that sexual-aggressive conquest is an acceptable substitute for "failures as a man in the economic and social status spheres." Young men glorify exploitative behavior toward women and often participate in group-rapes to demonstrate their "adequacy and maturation." Most rapists, Amir adds, are first-time offenders for sexual crimes, although many have previous records for other offenses.

The reverse side of the myth that rapists are sexual lunatics is the mistaken belief that they are All-American-Boy types in whom the sight of a mini-skirt automatically triggers a physical reaction. Although many offenders fit the description of the All-American-Boy, rape is not typically a spontaneous or impulsive act. Close to seventy-five per cent of the rape cases in Amir's sample were planned. In thirty per cent, the crime occurred between people who lived in the same neighborhood, indicating that the assailant knew the victim or at least had seen her at some time prior to the assault.

Women who staff crisis centers stress Amir's conclusions that rape is a common form of learned behavior. A counselor at the Chicago center told me bluntly, "Rape is the logical consequence of the way men and women are taught to treat each other. Boys learn at an early age that aggression and violence prove virility and masculinity, while girls learn to play hard-to-get." This aggressive-passive role playing perpetuates what a founder of the Philadelphia center calls a "rape society."

Living in a "rape society" and having to conform to a "rape schedule" is a hardship for all women but especially for rape victims. The immediate goal of rape crisis centers is to lessen the burden on the victim by providing her with emergency phone service and constructive counseling.

If a woman calls the crisis line shortly after she has been raped, the counselor's first responsibility is to assess her immediate physical needs. The counselor informs the victim of the nearest hospital or clinic which offers the fastest and best service. Many victims hesitate to go to a hospital because they have heard about the insensitive and often judgmental attitude of many doctors and nurses with respect to rape cases. They are concerned that the hospital will require a report to the police. The counselor instructs the woman on emergency room procedures and tells her of hospitals and clinics that do not insist on police reporting. The counselor also suggests that the victim advise the doctor to perform a test for semen and to make a record of any internal or external injuries, a record that may be helpful in the event she later decides to press charges.

Many victims who call the crisis line are unaware of the availability of the "morning-after" contraceptive pill and may not receive this information at the hospital. Some hospitals provide the pill but neglect to mention its potentially harmful side effects. Upset by the rape, many women forget that they need to take pregnancy and V.D. tests; some do not know that these tests must be administered after a waiting period of several weeks to be accurate indicators. The problems of many victims are often aggravated by hospitals which are remiss in furnishing the proper information, drugs, and tests. At most centers, counselors will offer to accompany the victim to the hospital and to provide transportation.

Another function of a crisis line is to provide information on police procedures. Most crisis centers neither encourage nor discourage women from reporting the incident. The counselor suggests to the victim that reporting may prevent the assailant from committing future offenses. At the same time, the counselor explains that a police interview may call for unnecessary reiteration of a victim's testimony before an audience of unsympathetic detectives. She may be asked embarrassing questions such as, "Did you have an orgasm?" or "How many other times have you had sexual intercourse?" Should a victim decide to report,

21

the volunteer will prepare her for the kinds of questions she will be asked and offer to provide moral support at the police station.

After handling a few emergency calls, counselors find they have no trouble responding to a victim's immediate needs. But the experience of crisis lines is that most calls do not require emergency service. A raped woman does not necessarily respond hysterically. The need to talk often develops slowly, perhaps within several days, but it may be months, or even years after the incident. The questions of victims are not always as clear cut as "Where is the nearest hospital?" or "How do I go about reporting?" A victim will often call a crisis line because she is frightened, depressed, and lonely—and her question, "Can you help me?" has no easy answer.

Many volunteers, even those who have been raped themselves or who have had some professional counseling experience, express concern that they will not be able to handle every crisis. At some centers, training sessions allow beginning counselors to participate in "rap sessions" with victims or role-playing exercises using mock telephone conversations. Other centers bypass the training phase and consult professionals as problems arise. The consensus is that counselors learn best through their experiences with crisis calls and not by way of prescribed rules. As a psychologist who works with the center in Los Angeles told me, "Professional consultation or training sessions can provide a volunteer with only one thing, and that is the confidence that she can indeed be helpful."

In defining the aims of counselors, the key phrases at every center are: show the victim you are concerned, be supportive, be calm and willing to listen, just be there, and be yourself. Volunteers are cautioned to know their limitations and to refer a victim to a professional therapist or agency if that seems necessary.

The experience of crisis centers reveals that a common reaction among rape victims is guilt. I learned from a Minneapolis center volunteer that victims often feel responsible for the incident and ask, "Why did he pick me? What did I do?" They blame themselves for looking attractive or for not putting up a fiercer struggle.

The goal of counselors is to encourage victims to convert feelings of guilt into what a Seattle volunteer calls a "healthy anger." In trying to achieve this goal, rape crisis centers emphasize the strategy of self-help. The self-help approach is supportive, as opposed to directive and authoritarian. Counselors should inform a victim of her options, help her to explore her feelings, and make suggestions. But ultimately, the victim must make her own decisions and initiate her own readjustment.

According to the D.C. handbook, *How to Start a Rape Crisis Center,* self-help "returns to the woman power over her life—something she lost to some extent when she was raped." Also, the nature of crisis counseling dictates that victims be encouraged to make

their own decisions. A New York volunteer told me, "Crisis calls are often a one-shot deal. The victim may or may not call again, and once she gets off the line, no one else can solve her problems."

In several centers, posters hanging near the crisis telephones spell out in colorful bold letters, "EMPATHY NOT SYMPATHY." The Women's Counseling Service in Ann Arbor asserts that empathy—understanding what the victim is feeling—is more helpful than sympathy, a subjective response in which the counselor herself feels as confused or as unhappy as the victim. For example, if a victim appears to feel humiliated or dirty as a result of a rape, a counselor should not respond sympathetically with: "Oh you poor woman. I would also feel humiliated and dirty in your position." A better response is: "It seems that you feel humiliated and dirty. Let's try to understand why you feel this way. Perhaps you shouldn't." Also, a counselor is urged not to use a crisis call as an excuse to propagandize her own views on morality, religion, or even feminism.

Crisis centers have found that the transition from guilt to a healthy anger is often smoother if a victim assumes the responsibility of pressing charges. Volunteers at the Chicago center spend most of their time learning to be para-legal advocates and accompanying the victim through every step of the legal procedure. After the trial, they will encourage the victim to join the group so that she may help others.

The Minneapolis center has found that male counselors often serve as a good foil for a woman's anger. "Talking to a man can also be helpful if a woman has any negative attitude toward men following a rape," one volunteer explained to me. But the consensus at most rape crisis centers is that male counselors will more often than not alienate or intimidate a victim. Volunteers do consider it important to counsel boy friends or husbands who may feel blameworthy or depressed if a woman close to them has been raped. Some men need advice on how to be supportive, rather than authoritarian, overprotective, or reproachful toward the victim.

A raped woman, in addition to feeling guilty, often complains of isolation or loneliness. Many victims are afraid to continue their regular activities and become overly suspicious of strangers. Some centers have organized "rap groups" so that victims can learn that they are not alone in their experiences and responses.

Counselors and advocates realize that many women who call the crisis line have not been raped in the strict legal sense. Many women are raped by their husbands, an act which most states do not recognize as a crime. Also, many callers cannot determine whether or not they have been raped. "We understand that there is such a thing as extra-legal or psychological rape," a Berkeley volunteer told me. "For example, a woman might consent to intercourse because she fears that otherwise the man will never call her again. Later she may feel as if she had been raped, and experience all the feelings of guilt, shame, and loneliness." The policy of the Seattle center is common to centers across the country: "Whether a woman's feelings are real or imaginary, recognizable in court or not, she feels them and we deal with them."

In providing emergency support and empathic counseling, rape crisis centers are seeking to close a gap in community social services. Most centers try to combine their service function with the long range goal of social change.

For example, the New York City Police Department instituted a Rape Investigation and Analysis Unit last January partly because of pressure by the city's anti-rape groups for more sensitive treatment of victims. New York's RIA unit is particularly concerned with boosting arrest rates by encouraging more frequent reporting of offenses. Although rape is probably the most under-reported crime, other violent crimes are also often not reported. Victims of violent crimes may not report because they are afraid of reprisals, or they

doubt that the police can be of any help, or they do not know how to report, or they do not want to take the time. The thirty-three-year-old organizer of the New York RIA unit, Lieutenant Julia Tucker, told me that the level of reportability is lower in rape cases because victims feel ashamed or fear an embarrassing ordeal at the police station. Tucker is trying to correct this situation by offering rape victims the option to speak to a female detective, and by training both male and female detectives in techniques of "crisis intervention."

"It is wrong to measure the effectiveness of the unit only in terms of numbers," Tucker said. "The arrest rate has gone up thirty-eight per cent since we've been in operation, but a more revealing yardstick is the great number of victims who have expressed appreciation and warm feelings toward us." Tucker is pleased that dozens of police departments in the United States and abroad have requested information on how to set up rape units in their cities.

New York's rape crisis center receives referrals for follow-up counseling from the Rape Investigation and Analysis Unit and assists in the collection of data. Other crisis centers are also interested in helping local officials predict the likely behavior of potential rapists. The Seattle group has proposed to the city's police department a "Third Party Reporting System," in which victims who choose not to report might anonymously provide details descriptive of the incident. Such details could be useful in corroborating the testimony of another victim of the same offender who does wish to press charges.

The Chicago center has been successful in keeping a check on pre-trial proceedings. Counselors assist in the preparation of cases by forwarding the information from their own conversations with the victim to state's attorneys. They are also permitted to be present during the victim's interview with the defense attorney.

Rape crisis centers have won positive responses from medical facilities. Hospitals throughout the country are realizing that rape is a public health problem, and that victims require more than a superficial examination for evidence. In Berkeley, for example, a coalition formed after a woman's teenage daughter was raped and was made to wait several hours for treatment. After some negotiation, the local hospital agreed to guarantee private emergency treatment for rape victims by experienced and sensitive personnel, and follow-up care when necessary.

Another function of rape crisis centers is promotion of community understanding and support. Television appearances, speaking engagements, and community meetings provide concerned men with the opportunity to ask questions and offer suggestions. (The majority of rape crisis groups keep their memberships closed to men. Most volunteers feel that exclusiveness enables them to acquire experience in organizing and leadership, skills which men generally have had more opportunities to develop.)

Such participation also gives centers a chance to

CONTACT

Write to the Washington, D.C., group for information on rape crisis centers throughout the country. Copies of *How to Start a Rape Crisis Center* may be obtained for $1.35.

RAPE CRISIS CENTER
P.O. Box 21005
Kalorama Street Station
Washington, D.C. 20009

The address and telephone number of the New York City Rape Investigation and Analysis Unit are:

RIA
New York City Police Department
52 Chambers Street
New York, NY 10007
(212) 577-RAPE

Stop Rape, a manual on self-defense, may be purchased for ninety-five cents from:

WOMEN'S LIBERATION OF MICHIGAN
2230 Witherell
Detroit, MI 48201

23

promote self-defense. According to the volunteers at the D.C. center, self-defense is not a solution to the problem of rape but "only a step in getting control of our lives." They add, "Many rapists could be stopped if women were not socialized to be passive, and discouraged from fighting back."

For those who do not wish to learn judo or karate, crisis centers advocate more basic measures such as biting, pulling hair, blows to the face, and kicks to the knees. A "swift kick to where-it-hurts" is not a foolproof tactic. Men instinctively protect their groin areas, and a kick that misses may throw a woman off balance or incite an assailant to more violent action.

Rape crisis groups agree that acting defensively can help eliminate the need for force. This means looking alert and confident when walking alone, having keys ready before arriving home, using sturdy locks on doors and only last names on mailboxes, and being aware that high heels and large purses limit the ability to run. If there is a suspicious person in an elevator, a woman should not feel silly or paranoid about pushing the emergency button and all the floor buttons. A woman in danger of attack in a residential area should forget conventional etiquette and bang on doors or smash windows if necessary. Women are urged to avoid accepting automobile rides from men, especially at night and if alone.

Weapons such as plastic lemons, aerosol cans, hat pins, lighted cigarettes, stiff hairbrushes, and a container of red pepper may be helpful provided that women realize that such weapons may be used against them. When weapons fail, reasoning with the attacker, relating a sob story, or claiming to have a contagious disease have sometimes proved effective.

Rape crisis centers stress that they are not vendetta groups seeking long sentences, or excessive punishments, such as castration of rapists. A Chicago volunteer assured me that a rigid law-and-order campaign is not useful as a solution because "it doesn't challenge attitudes that cause rape or the system that nourishes it." Aware that prisons are "hell-holes" and that nothing positive is accomplished by convicting an innocent man, anti-rape groups urge a fair trial. But they are concerned that the defendant, not the victim, be placed on trial. Women's groups point out that rape is the only violent crime in which corroborating evidence, such as bruises, cuts, or other signs of active resistance, is usually required for conviction. The requirement is retained despite the advice of many authorities that non-resistance may avert further violence or save a woman's life.

Many rape crisis centers, particularly those in such racially tense cities as Chicago, New York, and Washington, D.C., are prepared to question court proceedings when the conviction of a black man is secured too quickly. At public meetings, the idea that blacks are predisposed to committing sexual crimes especially against white women is exposed for what it is—another link in a long chain of myths. Citing Amir's study and others, rape crisis centers point out that rape is usually not an interracial crime but intra-

racial and intra-community in character. Because rape is a lower-class phenomenon, and because blacks are more likely to be apprehended than whites, black offenders tend to dominate statistical surveys. But black victims are over-represented as well. In only three per cent of the cases studied by Amir was the offender black and the victim white; in four per cent, the offender was white and the victim black.

Even with the success of public gatherings, radio and television panels, and speaking engagements, rape crisis centers have yet to overcome the problem of outreach. Volunteers find it particularly disturbing that only a small percentage of non-white victims call crisis lines. In Washington, D.C., where the majority of raped women are non-white and lower-class, the crisis center has changed the nature of its service. One volunteer told me why. "An emphasis on counseling reflects a white middle-class orientation and will turn off black and lower-class women who regard psychotherapy as an indulgence." The D.C. group now presents itself primarily as an informational and educational center rather than as a counseling service. Other groups feel that the solution to the problem of outreach may be to encourage non-white and lower-class women to develop their own crisis lines.

As I visited crisis centers across the country, I was impressed by the spirit of sisterhood developing among women of all ages and cultural backgrounds around the problem of rape. For example, in many centers, two counselors are on telephone duty simultaneously so that they can discuss difficult calls as they receive them. Periodically center workers get together to talk about the successes they have had or the mistakes they have made as counselors and advocates. There is an atmosphere of satisfaction at crisis centers as women learn how to negotiate with municipal officials, address large groups effectively, or chair a meeting with tact and authority.

Rape center volunteers are as eager to deal with the problems of co-workers as they are to answer a call on the crisis line. One of the founders of the Chicago center told me, "We have to support each other. Many of us were afraid to get involved, afraid that working late hours at the crisis center, having our names published in local newspapers, and appearing on local radio or television would make us more liable to sexual assault. Our families are also concerned about our safety."

Fear is a sensible response to the high frequency of rape. But fear or shame should not muzzle victims. The growth of rape crisis centers may finally break the silence. ☐

Part IV
Remedies and Conclusions

[16]

VICTIMOLOGY: AN INTERNATIONAL JOURNAL
Volume 10, 1985, Numbers 1–4, Pp. 539–559
© 1985 Victimology Inc. *Printed in USA*
0361-5170/85/$1.00 + .10

Victims' Needs and Victim Services: Indications from Research

MIKE MAGUIRE
University of Oxford

The main aim of this paper is to discuss the contribution of recent empirical research from several countries into the "needs" of victims of crime and to draw out the implications of various findings for agencies and organizations that provide services to victims.

The main aim of this paper is to discuss the contribution of recent empirical research from several countries into the "needs" of victims of crime nd to draw out the implications of various findings for agencies or organizations which provide services to victims. However, two reservations must be entered at the start: most of the research described has been concerned with relatively narrow definitions of crime and victims; and the use of the language of needs in relation to victims is problematic and contains certain dangers. It is therefore necessary to preface presentation of the findings with some cautionary remarks, both to put them into context and to acknowledge their limitations.

First, the needs to which reference is made are limited mainly to those experienced by victims of conventional personal and household offenses which have been recorded by the police and which have been committed for the most part by strangers. This excludes important categories of victim which concern many specialist service agencies and politically active groups campaigning for victims' rights: most notably, victims of continuing abuse such as wife–battering, child abuse and racial harrassment.

Secondly, the concept of need can all too easily be associated with paternalistic notions of "magnanimity to the unfortunate." Many victims rightly resent any hint that they should be the object of charity, from the state or elsewhere, and while the satisfaction of need by no means necessarily contains this implication, the use of the term, particularly in countries which rely heavily upon voluntary organizations for victim support, does little to dispel such notions or to advance the case that victims have an *entitlement* to support or assistance. Further, if victims come to be assessed solely in terms of their needs, there is a danger that those who happen to escape serious financial loss, injury or psychological damage (and who thus have no immediately obvious needs in the conventional sense) will simply be ignored. Crime differs from most other producers of need in that it involves a deliberate wrong done by one citizen to another, and it can be argued that victims are entitled to some action to redress that wrong, whatever their personal or material needs.

Finally, there are many doubts in the social policy field about the usefulness of need as an analytic tool for dealing with *any* kind of social problem. Culyer et al. (1972), for example, write that, "The word 'need' ought to be banished from discussion of public policy;" and Armstrong (1983) that, "The idea of 'need' is subjective, transient, fleeting and based on value judgments."

Not only is the term ambiguous, such writers argue, necessitating the construction of confusing taxonomies (such as normative, felt, expressed and comparative needs—Bradshaw, 1972—or objective and conventionally acknowledged needs—Townsend, 1972), but official recognition of need and the standards by which it is judged are highly dependent upon existing welfare ideologies and the constraints within which particular agencies operate (Smith, 1980). Mawby (1983) has been one of the few British writers to recognize the relevance of such policy debates to the victims field, and urges the development of a justice model for services to victims, which goes beyond simply registering and reacting to perceived need on an *ad hoc* basis, towards a rights-based system of entitlements to particular defined standards of agency response.

Nevertheless, despite all the above deficiencies, it has also to be recognized that the term "need" is still familiar currency in policy-making and political circles, and it would be foolish of advocates of victims' rights to ignore its bargaining power. Ultimately, victims are in competition with many other groups which have a claim to attention and resources, and while it is vital to argue their case on the grounds of entitlement, it equally important to present their claim in a more concrete way by making some attempt, however crude, to assess levels of need and to determine what kinds of service are particularly appropriate.

Moreover, it should be remembered that in Britain and several other countries voluntary organizations such as Victim Support Schemes still provide a large proportion of existing services to victims. Such bodies are less concerned with arguments about establishing standards of need or about entitlement to their services, than with discovering where they can be of most practical help with their limited resources. Guidance on questions such as which categories of victim would most benefit from assistance by volunteers, or what proportions require help with problems like repairing damage or claiming compensation, is very valuable to their work, in itself a strong argument for the further development of studies of needs. And finally, there may be food for thought in Brown and Yantzi's (1980) comment that, "the problem of 'needs' with reference to their victimization was neither a novel nor an academic concern for most respondents."

ASSESSING NEED

We are concerned here mainly with attempts to measure the *extent and distribution* of victims' needs. However, it is important first to underline the value of a complementary area of research which also bears upon the kinds of service which might be provided. This is research into the *psychological processes* of reactions to victimization. In particular, clinical understanding of the nature of "post-traumatic stress disorders" and of the stages through which people are likely to pass after suffering serious victimization has developed markedly in recent years, and has contributed to advances in crisis intervention and counselling techniques. Relevant studies are discussed in several papers in Salasin (ed., 1981) and in Smith's (1985) and Weisæth's (1985) papers (see also Bard and Sangrey, 1979; Symonds, 1982; Waller, 1982). The main drawback of such research, however, is that so far it has been based largely on reactions to very serious events, such as the hijacking of aircraft, hostage-taking and rape (indeed, it developed originally from studies of survivors of the holocaust and of brainwashing in prisoner-of-war camps), and it is not clear how generalizable the findings are to victims of less serious crime.

Let us turn now to attempts to measure the extent of victims' needs on a broader basis. Although they overlap considerably in practice, it is possible to identify three distinct approaches which have been used. I shall discuss briefly the relative merits and limitations of each, as well as of the various methods used to collect data, and then move on to summarize the most important and most reliable findings which have emerged.

a) Measurement of 'effects'

The most common approach has been through investigation of the impact of different kinds of crime upon the financial situation, lifestyle, attitudes and mental or emotional stability of samples of victims, from which inferences may be drawn about the kinds of service which are most needed. Despite their methodological limitations (Skogan, 1981; Block and Block, 1984), national crime surveys in several countries (notably the U.S., U.K., Canada and Holland) have produced probably the best available data on levels of financial loss, physical injury and time off work following victimization. They have been, however, much less informative about psychological impact and effects on lifestyle. A limited amount of such information has been gleaned from secondary analysis of their data banks (Blumberg, 1979; Block, 1983; Canadian Federal-Provincial Task Force, 1983; Maxfield, 1984;), but until recently lack of space (and, it has been argued, lack of imagination in their design—Home Office, 1981; Van Dijk and Steinmetz, 1983) has resulted in the inclusion of few relevant or productive questions. While it is likely that such large-scale surveys, by their very nature, have only limited potential in this direction, the 1984 British Crime Survey, in which I was permitted to include a set of questions

about impact on victims and attitudes towards Victim Support
Schemes, provides an example of a welcome trend towards more detailed exploration of particular issues (see also Hough, 1985).

A potentially much more effective instrument for the collection of
accurate impact data is the smaller-scale, more specialized study,
aimed usually at particular groups of victims who are interviewed in
some depth about their experiences. Substantial studies of this kind include Bourque et al. (1978) on burglary and robbery victims, Waller
and Okihiro (1978) and Maguire (1982) on burglary victims, Shapland
et al. (1981 and forthcoming) on victims of serious crimes of violence,
Burgess and Holmstrom (1978) and McIntyre et al (1979) on rape victims, Cunningham (1976) on crimes against elderly victims, Stookey
(1981) on victims of a wide range of personal and household crimes,
and Skogan and Maxfield (1981) on the effects of crime on victims' attitudes and behavior.

A major assumption behind many of these surveys and studies has
been that if one knows the effects of victimization, broad inferences can
be drawn about the needs of those suffering them. Yet while the data
gathered provide a valuable knowledge base, there remains the obvious
difficulty that conclusions about the nature and level of need are likely
to derive substantially from a researcher's (or, subsequently, program
designer's) own perceptions of what various kinds of impact mean for
victims: hence there is a danger of recommending solutions which do
not coincide with victims' subjective understanding of the problems
they face, leading ultimately to the provision of inappropriate kinds of
service.

To take a simple example, a finding that a high percentage of victims suffer unrecovered financial losses could lead to the assumption
of a need for major development of state compensation or insurance
programs. Yet it may also be that many victims experience monetary
loss less as a financial problem than as an integral element of a sense
of having been wronged by the offender. Consequently, deeper, less
tangible needs may be satisfied much better by a small repayment
from the offender than by a larger hand-out by the state (cf. Shapland,
1984). Similarly, findings that a certain percentage of crime victims
are emotionally disturbed by the incident, suffer loss of sleep, or experience fear, do not tell us whether they need simply a sympathetic
ear, sophisticated crisis intervention services, or long-term professional
counselling.

A further difficulty is that impact studies alone do not show
whether particular kinds of need they suggest are largely satisfied by
support or assistance from sources already in existence—for example,
police officers, neighbors, or family members—or whether they remain
unmet and require the intervention of special victim agencies. Thus
while such studies provide useful parameters, they remain only broad
guides to action by service organizations.

b) Self-expressed or 'felt' needs

A second, more direct, approach to the assessment of need has consisted, in essence, of asking victims to identify their own needs. For example, respondents were asked by Brown & Yantzi (1980), Friedman et al (1982) and Stuebing (1984), respectively, "to recall any kind of help they needed that wasn't immediately available," what forms of help or assistance they sought or requested, and whether any of a list of eight crisis needs "had constituted a problem for them personally." In each case, the researchers then went on to ascertain what proportion of these needs had and had not been met by friends, family, the police or other outside agencies.

This approach has the clear policy pay-off of allowing the researcher to come up with a crude estimate of the extent of unmet need which a prospective victim service agency should expect to find among a given population of victims (or, at least, providing a rough idea of the likely "take-up rate" for different kinds of service it may offer). Its main disadvantage is not simply the crudity of the instrument (including in some cases the dubious validity of adding together, as if they were homogeneous, a set of needs as disparate as counselling, repairs and legal assistance, to produce overall percentages of "unmet need") but a much more intractable problem, described succintly by Shapland *et al.* (forthcoming), as follows:

> Expressed needs are to some extent culturally based. They are related to the expectations of victims as to the potential effects of the offence and to their knowledge of what remedies exist.

(N. B. Shapland here uses the term "expressed needs" to refer to what Bradshaw (1972) and other social policy theorists call "felt needs." "Expressed need" is more often used to mean levels of demand measured by calls and requests received by service agencies.)

Her point may be illustrated with another simple example. If certain victims, although deeply upset, have no idea that bodies like victim support schemes exist, they are unlikely to recognize a need for external emotional support: failing to understand that their own bad feelings are a normal reaction to crime, they may be unable to imagine any cure for them beyond, say, suppressing them with tranquilizers. Thus, if a researcher asks questions to the effect: "Do you have any needs which have not been met by the police, friends and family, or other agencies?", negative replies may be received even from victims who (going by past experience) would clearly benefit from support. This problem may be met partly by prompting the respondent with a list of possible needs, although it may then be impossible to distinguish answers reflecting sudden awareness of previously unarticulated needs which are real to the victim, and those reflecting a response along the lines of "that sounds like a good idea."

c) Response to, and demand for, services

The value of a third approach to the assessment of need has tended

544   VICTIMOLOGY: AN INTERNATIONAL JOURNAL

to be underestimated by academics, but, if properly harnessed, the
sources of information it draws upon may ultimately prove to be quite
fruitful. I am referring to attempts to learn from the practical experience of people and organizations actively engaged in the provision of
services to victims. Norquay and Weiler (1981) and Williams (1983)
provide excellent general surveys of a wide range of agencies' experience of, and attitudes towards, victims in Canada and the U.K. These
studies give a useful picture of where victims seek help on their own
initiative and of the kinds of needs they present, but of course do not
tell us anything about those who are reluctant to, or do not know
where to, seek assistance.

A potential source of a fuller picture is assessments by workers or
volunteers who visit victims. For example, Gay et al (1975) analyzed
the report forms on 315 victims completed by volunteers with the Bristol Victim Support Scheme, correlating their assessments of the degree
of emotional disturbance with the social characteristics of the victims—an exercise repeated by several other Schemes since. While
these small studies make no claim to sophistication (the "assessments"
being a quick box-ticking exercise by unbriefed volunteers), it would
not be impossible to set up more rigorous research projects monitoring
careful assessments by experienced helpers.

There is further potential for needs assessment as part of more
general evaluations of existing victim service programs. In the United
States at least, these have been advocated for some time as a vital
component of effective service delivery (Viano, 1978; Salasin, 1981).
Unfortunately, evaluation is complicated by the diversity of criteria by
which success or failure may be judged, and not least by the inevitable
presence of political and ideological considerations: for example, funding for many American programs has been justified substantially on
the hope that they will increase victims' faith in, and cooperation with,
the police and criminal justice system, a factor which may deflect attention away from the real needs of the victim (Elias, 1983; Miers,
1980). Nevertheless, most evaluations reach some conclusions about
the level of need and the appropriateness of the services provided, and
are consequently of interest here.

Chesney and Schneider (1981), evaluating projects in Minnesota,
and Skogan & Wycoff (forthcoming) in Houston, provide examples of
attempts to measure need through an examination of victims' "take-up
rates" of services on offer (what Bradshaw calls "expressed need").
Both studies produce a fairly common finding, that the level of demand
turns out in practice to be lower than initially expected, not only when
the onus is put upon the victim to contact the helping agency, but even
when direct offers of assistance are made to individual victims (as in
outreach programs). Mayhew (1984) uses such evidence as part of an
argument that the incidence of serious consequences of crime for victims may be rather less widespread than conclusions drawn from some
impact research have implied, and that:

> the need among victims for specialized, intensive and largely professional help
> in coping with the aftermath of victimization is in danger of being overstated.

There may well be some truth in these claims, but can the above kind of evidence, from the experiences of victim assistance programs, be used to settle the argument? A major difficulty with this kind of evidence is that the results may be largely a function of the way that the services are presented to the victim. As Mayhew herself concedes, in the Houston project the fact that very few victims responded to offers of assistance from the police may be explained by the use of the telephone, some time after the event, to make the offer: she might have said the same of the Minnesota example, where the outreach element, in which victims were offered crisis intervention services over the telephone, produced few requests for visits. There are early indications from our study of British Victim Support Schemes that victims are much more likely to accept offers of assistance (if only to use the volunteer as a listening ear) if the first approach is made in person, and, even then, only after some time has been spent in establishing a relationship. This phenomenon has been noted in a different guise by Waller (1982), who points out in a footnote that Canadian victim surveys conducted by telephone have tended to uncover less emotional trauma than those using personal interviews. It is another important manifestation of one of the central problems in assessing needs: their identification is highly dependent upon the nature of the relationship between the person seeking to uncover them and the person who possesses them. This theme will be taken up again in the next section.

MAJOR FINDINGS AND THEIR IMPLICATIONS

Despite the many deficiencies of the research so far available, it is possible to make some general statements about victims' needs and to draw out some lessons for service agencies. Owing to lack of space, I shall do no more than mention *medical* needs—which in the U.K. are covered by the National Health Service, but which are very important in the U.S., where it has been found that over one-third of injured victims are not covered by health insurance (Waller, 1982)—and *financial* needs (apart from small emergency funds—see later), which have been widely discussed elsewhere in the context of reparation and compensation. Vital as attention to these needs is, I am here concerned primarily with problems which are more often the concern of victim service agencies, and will discuss only *practical, informational* and *emotional or psychological* needs.

a) Informational needs

Informational needs, although mentioned briefly by many writers and quite often identified as the most common need of all, have until recently received surprisingly little prominence in comparison with others. Those most often identified include advice on crime prevention, insurance and compensation; information about police progress in investigations; and, if an offender has been arrested, information on

whether he is on bail or in custody and the likely dates of court hearings. Moreover, if the victim has to appear as a witness, there is a common desire for a general briefing on court procedures and quite often
a need for specific legal advice.

These kinds of need have emerged, even unprompted, in considerable proportions of cases when victims have been asked to express
their own needs. For example, in Canada, Brown and Yantzi (1980)
found that over 20 per cent of a sample of victims of a wide range of
offenses volunteered a need for information about progress of the case,
compensation or security, the proportion rising to 65 per cent when
prompted responses were included: the majority of such needs remained unmet. Similarly, Stuebing (1984) found 68 per cent of all victims (again after prompting) expressing a desire for information on the
progress of the case and 29 per cent of victims of crimes against the
person needing advice of some kind: 53 per cent and 28 per cent of
these needs, respectively, had not been met. In the U.K., Vennard
(1976) found that over 50 per cent of a sample of victims of assault
whose cases reached court had wanted advice (mainly of a legal nature), but that half of these failed to obtain it, primarily because they
did not know where to go. Again, Maguire (1982) found that one of the
major complaints made by victims about the service received from the
police was that the latter had failed to keep them informed about the
progress of the case, a finding echoed by Shapland (1984) and in some
internal police studies (see Maguire, 1984). And finally, preliminary
analysis of the results of my questions in the 1984 British Crime Survey indicates that more victims of reported offenses express a need for
information on crime prevention or on progress of the case than for any
other kind of service.

Overall, the need for information should, in my view, receive much
more serious attention than it does. Not only may it be important to
the peace of mind and the psychological recovery of the victim, and to
his or her satisfaction with the police or criminal justice agencies
(Maguire 1984), but it is a prerequisite for access to many other kinds
of service. It is clear, for example, that only small proportions of victims have even heard of compensation programs or victim support
schemes (Mayhew, 1984; Ministry of the Solicitor General, 1984) and
that unless information on where to go for particular kinds of assistance is provided by the police or others as a matter of routine, many
who would benefit considerably fail to seek it themselves (Friedman,
1982; Waller, 1982; Stuebing, 1984). There is a strong case, indeed, for
it to be a statutory duty of the police to provide *every* victim with a
card or information sheet about available services, and to officially inform every victim of the outcome of investigations. Both the Canadian
Federal-Provincial Task Force (1983) and the British Home Affairs
Committee (1984) have recently made recommendations of this kind.

b) Practical Needs

The practical needs most often identified include help with clean-

ing up or repairs to damaged property, fitting new locks, replacing stolen documents or credit cards, filling in complex claim forms, transportation (e.g. to and from hospital), child minding, and the provision of
immediate funds. Such needs have been measured several times, with
varying conclusions. For example, while Friedman et al. (1982) found
that they were widespread among victims of burglary, robbery and assault—e.g. with 39 per cent needing to change or repair locks and 27
per cent needing immediate cash loans—Brown and Yantzi (1980)
found much lower levels in a wider range of offenses, even after
prompting (21 and 8 per cent respectively). The 1984 British Crime
Survey, too, will show relatively few victims recalling practical problems and only small proportions of these naming any practical needs
that remained unmet. Some of the variation in findings may be
explained by differences in the types of crime sampled. Research is also
complicated by the facts that family, friends and neighbors often lend
help, and that many victims are fully capable of dealing with practical
problems themselves: in such cases, matters like repairs or compensation claims are less likely to be perceived as a problem or a need. Even
so, most researchers have concluded that, like informational needs, a
considerable proportion of the practical needs identified are not satis-
factorily met. (Friedman puts this figure at around 30 per cent, and
Brown and Yantzi even higher.)

As yet, research on practical needs has produced few firm general
conclusions, but it has at least indicated particular problems which appear to be more commonly experienced by victims of particular types
of crime. For example, it is worth noting from the U.K. Victim Support
Scheme experience that the theft of cash can produce considerable
short-term financial problems for poorer families, particularly at
weekends when there is no access to welfare agencies; and from Shapland (1984) that victims of violent crime are often faced with early expenses in replacing spectacles, clothing, etc. (She also notes that young
self-employed men often suffer financial problems if they have to take
time off work.) Victims of violent crime have also been shown to need
help with transportation if regular visits are required to doctors or hospitals. (20 per cent mentioned such a need to Stuebing and 18 per cent
to Friedman.) Perhaps most striking of all is Stuebing's finding that
44 per cent of victims of crimes against the person needed "someone
to stay with to provide security/protection," of which over one-third
failed to find such shelter.

The major problems in providing practical services are they are
often needed within the first few days after the crime, and that most
victims are either unaware of the availability of help or are reluctant
to ask for it. Hot-line services appear to attract relatively few callers
(Chesney and Schneider, 1981), while even the visits of Victim Support
Scheme volunteers in Great Britain, which generally take place within
two days of the offense, tend to be too late for the most pressing practical problems. (Experiments have been carried out in the U.K. with
groups of offenders on Community Service Orders standing by on call
to undertake repairs under the supervision of a probation officers

linked with Victim Support Schemes, but again the time lag has proved to be a problem.) One apparently successful system for meeting such immediate needs has been that of volunteer service units attached to police stations, such as the Edmonton Victim Services Unit (Canadian Federal Provincial Task Force, 1983), which, provided that police officers attending scenes of crime are properly trained and motivated, allow prompt identification and communication of specific victims' practical needs and quick and efficient service delivery.

c) Emotional Needs

The most difficult area of need to quantify has always been that of emotional or psychological needs. Ideally, measurement has to take account of three dimensions, which can easily become confused: the number of people experiencing emotional reactions or needs of any kind, their severity, and their persistence over time. As will be discussed in the next section, there are few general studies of the persistence of psychological effects and the consequent need for long-term counselling or therapy, a research gap which deserves urgent attention. The other two dimensions have been addressed in several studies, but the results are often confusing, and sometimes contradictory.

As previously mentioned, where emotional problems are concerned, it is particularly unsatisfactory to rely upon victims' self-expressed or felt needs as a measuring tool, owing to the fact that they are often unaware of the possibilities for alleviating stress (counselling, talking about one's feelings, etc). When victims are simply asked to state, unprompted, what needs arose from the offense, the number mentioning a need for emotional support almost invariably emerges as low. For example, Brown and Yantzi found that only ten per cent of their sample volunteered a short term and five per cent a long-term need for "someone to talk to" and Friedman et al. that, even among their sample of more serious crimes, only nine per cent expressed a need for counselling of some kind. However, after prompting, Brown and Yantzi's figure rose to 31 per cent, while Stuebing (1984), who presented interviewees with a list of possible crisis needs, found as many as 47 per cent wanting "someone to talk to after the police had left."

These latter figures are more in line with—though still perhaps lower than—what one might expect from the results of studies attempting to measure the proportion of victims upon whom crime has an emotional impact. Bourque et al. (1978) found that about 80 per cent of a sample of burglary and robbery victims had reacted with nervousness, crying or shaking, and Friedman himself that 75 per cent of burglary, assault and robbery victims had suffered an emotional reaction.

To complicate matters further, in-depth, face-to-face interviews have tended to find a higher incidence of emotional impact than broad survey methods (for example, the latest British Crime Survey finding that "over two-thirds of victimisations were said to have caused no emotional problems"—Mayhew, 1984—creates a very different impression from most of the results quoted above), and the Canadian experience of differing results from telephone and personal interviews (Waller 1982) has been mentioned earlier. Even allowing for differences in the level of seriousness of crimes sampled in the various studies, the range of results is wide. This variation not only illustrates the difficulty of measurement in such a subjective area, but, insofar as it is caused by differences in the research methods used, seems to indicate that victims are reluctant to admit to emotional distress until they have established a rapport with the interviewer. It also suggests the possibility that many victims remain unaware of the link between the offense and present feelings of stress or depression until they begin to discuss the incident. These last two conclusions are supported by the common experience of Victim Support Scheme volunteers in finding early denial of emotional upset later giving way to the expression of deep feelings about the crime.

While the extent of emotional distress can never be measured precisely, there is now sufficient evidence at least to state with confidence (a) that it is by far the most important element to the victim in several particular categories of crime and (b) that quite serious psychological effects, and even (though more arguably) trauma, are experienced by large numbers of victims, even on the most conservative estimates.

Some of the clearest evidence on the first point, apart from the obvious case of sexual offenses (for a good review, see Mazur and Katz, 1979), comes from studies of residential burglary. Ostensibly a property offense, interviews with victims consistently reveal that it regarded much more as a personal offense by those who experience it. For example, in the study by Maguire (1982), 322 victims of burglary were asked what they had found to be the worst aspect of the incident. Over 60 per cent specified "intrusion on privacy" or "emotional upset," while only 28 per cent named "financial loss" or "damage to property," a finding which has been broadly confirmed by other British research since (see Maguire 1984). Friedman et al. (1982), too, whose sample was made up predominantly of burglary victims, concluded that:

> The most common problems (affecting three-quarters of the sample) from which crime victims suffered, were psychological problems including fear, anxiety, nervousness, self-blame, anger, shame, and difficulty sleeping.
> Even when describing practical problems stemming from the crime, three-quarters of the victims described the impact of the crime in psychological terms.

Other crimes in which the component of emotional distress has been found to be particularly prominent include robbery and assault (Lejeune and Alex, 1973; Conklin, 1975; Shapland et al, forthcoming; Stuebing, 1984), while responses to the 1984 British Crime Survey suggest that threatening phone calls and, perhaps surprisingly, vandalism also generate emotional needs in an above average proportion of cases. Finally, Williams (1983) found that the categories of victim most often visiting doctors (for counselling or emotional problems as often as for medical attention) were victims of domestic violence, assault and burglary.

On the second point, it is clear that even if one accepts the most conservative figures on the incidence of severe emotional impact and psychological needs, while they may appear low in percentage terms, the absolute numbers are still high enough to demand serious attention. Thus while "only" 12 per cent of victims in the 1984 British Crime Survey reported that they were "very much" affected by the crime, this grosses up to several hundred thousand people thus affected in Britain each year. With regard to particular crimes where emotional impact is documented in more detail, there is further food for thought. For example, while it is unsurprising that studies of victims of rape, which is a relatively rare event, reveal deep and lasting psychological wounds for very high proportions of victims, there are suggestions that serious trauma may be produced in a broadly similar absolute number of victims of residential burglary. Waller and Okihiro (1978) and Bourque et al. (1978) estimate the proportion of burglary victims suffering "serious trauma" to be around five per cent, from which Waller (1982) calculates that almost 17,000 Canadians and 222,000 Americans annually suffer such trauma as a result of burglary, compared with figures of 23,000 and 800,000 respectively for rape. Similarly, Maguire's (1982) British study indicates that the immediate psychological impact of burglary is "very serious" for about 6 per cent of victims of reported burglary, suggesting that well over 10,000 people are quite badly disturbed by this offense in the U.K. each year.

It has to be admitted that such estimates, like those of Stuebing and Brown and Yantzi, who attempt to calculate the numbers of people in Red Deer City and Kitchener, Ontario in need of services each year, are unavoidably crude and based on many questionable assumptions. Nevertheless, it remains significant that, whatever the definitions of trauma or severe effects employed, most researchers in this field, including myself, have been greatly surprised when interviewing victims at the extent and depth of feelings displayed, even after what appear objectively to be relatively minor crimes. Thus Friedman (1982) writes:

> We were stunned at the general impact of a crime on the victim's psychological state, and at the alterations in daily life which were so often a part of the victimization experience.

Finally, as well as knowledge about the effects of different types of offense, it is important for service agencies (particularly agencies which, like Victim Support Schemes, select those they will visit from large numbers referred by the police) to have some indication of the social characteristics of victims who may be most in need. It has been found with some regularity that women, people living alone, people widowed or divorced, and people from lower socio-economic groups may be more vulnerable to emotional effects than other groups (e.g. Gay et al, 1975; Bourque et al., 1978; Maguire 1982; Stuebing, 1984), with contradictory results where the elderly are concerned. (Here Bourque et al. found no significant difference, and Stuebing even found the elderly to be *less* affected than younger people.) However, such differences have rarely been found to be great and some researchers (e.g. Denton, 1979) have found no significant differences at all. Moreover, it is possible that some categories of victim are readier to admit to emotional effects than others. It therefore seems safest to conclude (Villmow, 1984; Stuebing, 1984; Reeves, 1984) that most service agencies should not give special priority to any one group but should be open to victims of all ages, both sexes and all social classes.

UNSOLVED QUESTIONS

While the kind of evidence discussed above has helped to uncover a huge area of human need which had previously remained virtually unrecognized by governments and social service agencies, it has left many unanswered questions about how best to deal with the problem. Above all, evidence of severe emotional impact, such as crying, trembling or fear, or of emotional needs, such as for "someone to talk to," does not tell us whether, say, sympathy from a neighbor or a policeman would in most cases be sufficient to alleviate the worst effects, or whether there is a need for professional help on a massive scale.

Mayhew (1984) takes the view that the victim movement is in danger of exaggerating the seriousness of what may in most cases be normal short-lived emotional reactions to an unpleasant event, such as occur in response to any other of "life's vicissitudes." She feels, moreover, that unjustified links are too often made between the kinds of impact noted in the studies discussed above and the findings of research concerned with the processes of response to the most serious kinds of victimization (torture, brainwashing, terrorist actions, etc.). For although the kinds of serious emotional distress identified in studies of, say, burglary or assault victims may be superficially similar to the first stages of trauma familiar from the crisis literature (e.g. Symonds 1982; Fields, 1981), there is as yet insufficient evidence to demonstrate that there are frequently long-term reactions of a similar nature. She writes:

> Much of the literature has overemphasized serious types of crime, and these have often been considered alongside a wider range of victimizing events in terms of some current social-psychological orthodoxies—for example crisis theory . . . One effect of this is that the impact of the crime is often presented in emotive terms.

She reminds readers that "crime *in its most typical form* does not usually have serious consequences at least as judged by the more objective indicators of loss or injury," concluding that "routine practical assistance, moral support and reassurance about personal safety" may be sufficient in the vast majority of cases.

In fact, Mayhew's criticisms are aimed primarily at commentators such as Waller (1982), who clearly perceives post-traumatic stress disorders as a fairly common reaction to ordinary crimes such as burglary and sees an important role for trained counsellors and therapists. She is not really in serious disagreement with several of the researchers already mentioned, for they all stress the value of relatively unsophisticated short-term assistance and reassurance, and more than one of these writers note that the level of need for 'counselling' appears to be less than they had first expected. Nevertheless, the question remains open, and it is crucial to the future provision of effective victim services for research to come to clearer conclusions on such issues. Two related gaps are glaringly obvious: the dearth of careful studies of the long-term effects of different types of common crimes, and a similar lack of evidence about what kinds of support are appropriate to and have a measurable effect upon the speed and completeness of victims' recovery from such crimes.

Sparks (1982) rightly comments that "the consequences of these incidents continue, and, for the most part, we have no real idea how long they continue or even exactly what the consequences are." Apart from studies of the very serious case of rape, which suggest severe long-term effects (cf. Burgess and Holmstrom's finding that 26 per cent of victims had not recovered after six years), the only major long-term study so far completed is that by Shapland et al. (forthcoming; see also Shapland, 1981). Here a sample of victims of violent crime were interviewed up to four times over a period of three years. It was found that psychological effects, including depression, anxiety and fear, persisted over long periods for many victims. The sample included victims of rape and sexual assault, a majority of whom, it was concluded, still had "possible emotional needs" two years after the offense, but even among victims of lesser assaults, over 20 per cent were still psychologically affected to some degree after two years. For other types of crime, there are as yet only general indications concerning lasting effects. For example, Maguire's (1982) interviews were carried out on average eight weeks after the offense, when it was found that 65 per cent of burglary victims were still emotionally affected by the incident, although in many cases this amounted simply to vague unease or a tendency to keep thinking about the crime. No firm conclusions could be drawn about how serious a need there might be for services such as counselling at that point, although it does appear significant that when ten of the initial interviewees who had appeared to be worst affected were contacted a year later, all reported continuing feelings of fear, anxiety and distrust of others.

Overall, the consensus of opinion seems to be that most emotional effects wear off within a few weeks or months, victims recovering more or less spontaneously or with normal support from family or friends. This is supported by Brown and Yantzi's finding that a sample interviewed up to a year after the offense presented very few emotional needs, by preliminary results from the 1984 British Crime Survey and by Friedman et al. who estimate the normal duration of the 'crisis period' at about six weeks. Friedman et al. followed up their interviewees after four months and found that most problems which the latter had originally rated as serious were no longer regarded as such at the second interview, even (though to a lesser extent—see later) by victims who had not received much assistance. The implications here are that extra assistance which might be provided by agencies is primarily a means of easing and speeding natural recovery and of making it more complete, and that such assistance need not be of a greatly sophisticated kind (see below). On the other hand, Stuebing (1984), whose interviews spanned periods up to several months after the event, found no significant difference over time in the level of ongoing needs (or, more accurately, ongoing *problems*—the two are confused in his study), such as suspicion and distrust of others (54 per cent) and fear of walking alone or at night (33 per cent). His research provides stronger grounds for regarding agency support as a *prerequisite* for full recovery within a reasonable period, and for help to be pitched at a somewhat higher level than simple short-term assistance.

In conjunction with more comprehensive longer-term studies of the persistence of psychological effects, then, researchers need to develop more sophisticated methods of assessing the *seriousness* of such effects and of determining what levels of support are most appropriate. As Fields (1981) bleakly notes:

> There is no systematic appraisal mechanism through which the consequences of victimization may be assessed . . . We do not know whether there are appropriate services for victims and if there are, what services are appropriate or utilizable by what victims.

And even more fundamental, as Stein (1981) confesses, the considerable literature on crisis intervention has failed to prove that even intervention by trained professionals, let alone by volunteers, actually works where victims are concerned:

> There is precious little hard evidence to support our case for crisis intervention for crime victims. Although crisis intervention has proven its efficacy to the mental health professions, there are no evaluation studies showing the benefits of crisis intervention to crime victims as a particular group in need of its services.

Friedman et al. (1982) is one of the few studies which has attempted to demonstrate that service intervention, even of a fairly unsophisticated kind, has at least *some* effect upon the emotional recovery of victims. It was found that "victims who received all the help they reported needing on the initial interview reported significantly fewer crime-related problems on the follow-up interview than victims who failed to get one or more types of needed assistance" and that "victims who got all the assistance they needed felt more positively about other people than other victims." Unfortunately, the people who failed to obtain help were predominantly from lower socio-economic groups and also reported more serious problems than those who did obtain help, so the samples are not strictly comparable. In our present Oxford study, we are comparing controlled samples of victims visited and not visited by Victim Support Schemes (in terms of anxiety scales and self-reported recovery from the effects of crime) and hope to contribute a little more to this unresearched area. Steinmetz is conducting similar research in Holland. However, much more input is needed from clinically-based evaluative research, to determine what levels of counselling or support are appropriate for what kinds of victim. Haward (1981) is one of the few clinical psychologists in the U.K. to become interested in this area. His work suggests that it is often possible to

predict long-term psychological problems from symptoms displayed
shortly after the offense and from simple personality tests of victims
who experience especially severe immediate reactions, even to offense
like burglary. Guidance of this kind could prove particularly valuable
to volunteers who are at present unable to determine which among
their many clients are at a high risk of long-term problems, and hence
when to recommend referral for professional help.

CONCLUDING REMARKS

The subtitle of this paper refers only to "indications" from research, because, despite a welcome increase in needs-related research
over the past three or four years, it has to be admitted that knowledge
about the nature and extent of victims' needs remains patchy and inconclusive in several important respects. Comparisons between results
are often confusing, owing to major differences in the types of crime
sampled and their levels of seriousness, in the methods used to assess
need, and in the way questions are framed and interviews conducted.
There is often ambiguity and looseness in the use of language, with
writers using terms like "problems" and "needs" interchangeably. Few
researchers have included any measure or indication of the relative
seriousness of different needs (either to the victim, or judged by some
external standard) so a victim on the verge of mental breakdown is
likely to be counted in the same category as a victim who is mildly
shocked. Little is known about the persistence over time of adverse effects from common forms of victimization (burglary, assault, etc). There
are few, if any, reliable evaluations of the effectiveness of different
forms of intervention in alleviating the emotional impact of such
crimes. And, even now, agencies wishing to provide services to victims
could draw very different conclusions from results such as those obtained by Chesney and Schneider (1981) on the one hand, and Stuebing
(1984) on the other, about the basic levels of need for their services and
the likely take-up rates.

Nevertheless, despite all its weaknesses, the kind of empirical research discussed in this paper has already supplied ample ammunition
for the victim movement to support its case for a major reappraisal of
society's response to victimization. It has demonstrated beyond much
doubt that the majority of victims of all kinds of crime experience problems of some kind, however major or minor, and however short-lived
or long-lasting these may be. It has shown that even minor crime can
have a severe emotional impact on victims. It has revealed a widespread need for information, about the progress of police investigations,
about crime prevention and about compensation. It has demonstrated
a need for special service agencies, from which victims of all types of
crime can obtain information, practical help and emotional support. It
has also uncovered an inexcusable phenomenon, not discussed in this
paper, but amply documented elsewhere (e.g. Burgess and Holmstrom,
1978; Chambers and Millar, 1983; Shapland, forthcoming), that of secondary victimization, the creation of extra distress for victims through

insensitive behavior by policemen, court officials or other agents of the criminal justice system. As stressed at the beginning, all these problems can be seen in terms of needs, but it is important to argue for their solution in terms of *rights* or *entitlements* and of a duty upon the state to provide adequate resources to meet them. As Stuebing (1984) correctly argues:

> It is incumbent upon the community to reasonably address these needs and to facilitate recognition by crime victims that their personal troubles are indeed public issues and that victims of crime have a legitimate claim on community resources.

Research has a long way to go before it can provide reliable practical guidance as to the best way to organize victim services: answers to questions about the optimum degree of professionalization and specialization, the most effective means of referral and service delivery, and how best to order priorities among types of offense and categories of victim, largely depend upon more accurate knowledge than presently exists about the effects of crime and the responses which best alleviate these effects. Nevertheless, lessons are already being learned from existing agencies' experience (e.g. Viano, 1978; Reeves, 1984), and I would further pick out two very important general lessons from academic research, both of which, interestingly, emerge less from any particular results than from the very fact that the results overall are variable and confusing!

The first is that there is always a danger of allowing attention to purely practical needs, which are relatively easy to identify, to lead to the neglect of *emotional* needs, which are less obvious and less easy to deal with. (In general, research experience suggests that if you simply ask people what their needs are, they will tell you first always practical and informational problems). The second follows from the fundamental point discussed earlier, that victims' needs are not a fixed, objectively discernible and quantifiable entity: they are in some senses negotiated with the person or agency offering assistance, and the closer that relationship, the more likely they are to emerge. I would therefore assert that one of the necessary prerequisites for a fully effective victim assistance program is the existence of an *outreach* element, whereby victims are individually offered information about the kinds of services available and help in understanding the possible relevance of such services to their own situation. Ideally, as in the British Victim Support Scheme model (Reeves, 1984), volunteers would visit large numbers of victims in their own homes and give each one time and opportunity to define or negotiate their own needs. Where, as will almost always be the case, shortage of resources severely restricts the number of visits that can be made, substitute forms of outreach should be developed, such as telephone calls or letters from the agency, or the routine provision of information sheets and explanations of existing services by the police. Until there is much greater public understanding of the kinds of needs which victims are likely to have, and a climate is created in which it becomes seen as normal rather than exceptional to request services, such outreach elements will remain vital.

556   VICTIMOLOGY: AN INTERNATIONAL JOURNAL

Finally, as stressed at the beginning, this paper has been concerned largely with victims who report conventional types of crime to
the police. It should not be forgotten that many more needs have been
demonstrated at this conference (Lisbon, 1984) in the more 'hidden'
areas of victimization, particularly that which takes place within the
family or between individuals or groups with continuing relationships.
The provision of protection and services for victims of these kinds is
an area which the more conventional and richer agencies should not
leave out entirely from their plans, and not leave them almost entirely,
as at present, to under-funded voluntary groups.

REFERENCES

Armstrong, P.
    1982   "The Myth of Meeting Needs in Adult Education and Community De-
                velopment." Critical Social Policy, Vol. 2, No. 2, p. 29.
Bard, M., and Sangrey, D.
    1979   The Crime Victim's Book. New York: Basic Books.
Block, R. L.
    1983   "Studies of Victimization and Fear of Crime." Washington, D.C.: Depart-
                ment of Justice.
Block, C. B., and Block, R. L.
    1984   "Crime Definition, Crime Measurement and Victim Surveys." Journal of
                Social Issues, 40, 137–160.
Blumberg, M. L.
    1979   "Injury to Victims of Personal Crime: Nature and Extent." In Parsonage,
                W. H., (ed.) Perspectives on Victimology. Beverly Hill: Sage.
Bourque, B. B., Brumback, G. B., Krug, R. E., and Richardson, L. O.
    1978   Crisis Intervention: Investigating the Need for New Applications.
                Washington, D.C.: American Institutes for Research.
Brown, S. D., and Yantzi, M.
    1980   "Needs Assessment for Victims and Witnesses of Crime." Mennonite
                Central Committee, Kitchener, Ontario.
Bradshaw, J.
    1972   "The Concept of Social Need." New Society, 30 March, 1972.
Burgess, A. W., and Holmstrom, L. L.
    1978   The Victim of Rape: Institutional Reactions. New York: Wiley.
Canadian Federal-Provincial Task Force
    1983   Justice for Victims of Crime. Canadian Government Publishing Centre.
Chambers, G., and Millar, A.
    1983   Investigating Sexual Assault. Edinburgh: Scottish Office Social Research
                Study.
Chesney, S., and Scheider, P.
    1981   "Crime Victim Crisis Centers: The Minnesota Experience." In Galaway,
                B., and Hudson, J., Perspectives on Crime Victims. St. Louis: Mosby.
Conklin, J. E.
    1975   The Impact of Crime. New York: Macmillan.
Culyer, A. J., Lavers, R. J., and Williams, A.
    1972   "Health Indicators," in Shonfield, A. and Shaw, S. (eds.), Social Indi-
                cators and Social Policy, London.
Cunningham, C.
    1976   "Pattern, and Effect, of Crime against the Elderly: the Kansas City
                Study." In Goldsmith, J., and Goldsmith, S., (eds.), Crime and the El-
                derly. Lexington, Mass.

Denton, A. R.
   1979   "What They Think/What They Do: A Study of the Perceptions and Serv-
            ice Utilizations of Victims of Violent Crime." Ph.D., thesis, Case Western
            Reserve University (quoted in Villmow, 1984).
Elias, R.
   1983   "The Politics of Evaluating Victim Programs." Paper to Conference on
            Victims of Crime; International Society of Criminology, Vancouver, 1983.
Fields, R.
   1981   "Research on Victims: Problems and Issues." In Salasin, S. E. (ed.),
            Evaluating Victim Services. Beverly Hills: Sage.
Friedman, K., Bischoff, H., Davis, R., and Person, A.
   1982   Victims and Helpers: Reactions to Crime. New York: Victim Services
            Agency.
Gay, M. J., Holtom, C., and Thomas, M. S.
   1975   'Helping the Victims.' International Journal of Offender Therapy and
            Comparative Criminology. 19, 263–9.
Genn, H.
   1982   "Meeting Legal Needs." Centre for Socio-Legal Studies, University of Ox-
            ford.
Haward, L. R. C.
   1981   "Psychological Consequences of being the Victim of a Crime." In Lloyd-
            Bostock, S. (ed.), Law and Psychology. Oxford: SSRC Centre for Socio-
            Legal Studies.
Home Affairs Committee
   1984   Report on Compensation and Support for Victims of Crime. London:
            HMSO.
Home Office
   1981   Public Surveys of Crime: Report of a Workshop held at Sidney Sussex
            College, Cambridge, 6–8 April 1981. Home Office Crime Policy Planning
            Unit.
Hough, M.
   1985   "The Impact of Victimization: Findings from the British Crime Survey,"
            Paper to the Third International Institute on Victimology. Lisbon,
            November, 1984.
Lejeune, R., and Alex, N.
   1973   "On Being Mugged: The Event and its Aftermath." Urban Life and Cul-
            ture, 2: 259–287.
Maguire, M.
   1982   Burlary in a Dwelling: The Offence,the Offender and the Victim. London:
            Heinemann.
Maguire, M.
   1984   "Meeting the Needs of Burglary Victims: Questions for the Police and
            Criminal Justice System." In Clarke, R.V.C. and Hope,T. (eds.) Coping
            with Burglary. Boston: Kluwer-Nijhoff.
Marshall, T. F.
   1984   "Services for Victims of Crime: Research Plans." Home Office, London
            (unpublished).
Mawby, R. I.
   1984   "Victims' Needs, Entitlement and Merit: Towards a justice Model." Paper
            to International Workshop on Victim Rights, Dubrovnik, 1984.
Maxfield, M. G.
   1984   Fear of Crime in England and Wales. London: HMSO.
Mazur, M. A., and Katz, S.
   1979   Understanding the Rape Victim: A Synthesis of Research Findings. New
            York: Wiley.
Mayhew, P.
   1984   "The Effects of Crime: Victims, the Public and Fear." Council of Europe,
            Sixteenth Criminological Research Conference: Research on Victims.
            Strasbourg, Nov. 1984.

McIntyre, J., Myint, T., and Curtis, L. A.
    1979   Victim Response to Sexual Assault: Alternative Outcomes. Washington
               D.C.: Bureau of Social Science Research.
Miers, D. R.
    1980   "Victim Compensation as a Labelling Process." Victimology, Vol. 5, No.
               1, 3–16.
Ministry of the Solicitor-General
    1984   Awareness and Use of Crime Compensation Programs. User Report No.
               2 on the Canadian Victimization Survey. Ottawa: Research and Statis-
               tics Group.
Norquay, G., and Weiler, R.
    1981   Services to Victims and Witnesses of Crime in Canada. Ottawa: Ministry
               of the Solicitor General.
Reeves, H.
    1985   "Victim Support Schemes." Victimology, Vol. 10, No. 1–4.
Salasin, S. E. (ed.)
    1981   Evaluating Victim Services. Beverly Hills: Sage.
Shapland, J. M., Willmore, J., and Duff, P.
    1981   The Victim Complainant in the Criminal Justice System. Oxford: Centre
               for Criminological Research.
Shapland, J. M.
    1984   "The Victim, the Criminal Justice System and Compensation." British
               Journal of Criminology, 24, 131–149.
Shapland, J. M., Willmore, J., and Duff, P.
    Forthcoming Victims in the Criminal Justice System. Farnborough, Hants: Gower.
Skogan, W. S.
    1981   Issues in the Measurement of Victimization. Washington, D.C.: Govern-
               ment Printing Office.
Skogan, W. S., and Maxfield, M. G.
    1981   Coping with Crime. Beverly Hills: Sage.
Skogan, W. S., and Wycoff, M.
    Forthcoming "The Victim Re-Contact Experiment in Houston." Washington, D.C.:
               Police Foundation.
Smith, C. B.
    1985   "Beyond Medical and Police Mandates: Community Responses to Vic-
               tims." Victimology, Vol. 10, No. 1–4.
Smith, G.
    1980   Social Need: Policy, Practice and Research. London.
Sparks, R.
    1982   Research on Victims of Crime: Accomplishments, Issues and New Direc-
               tions. Rockville, Maryland: National Institute of Mental Health.
Stein, J. H.
    1981   "Victim Crisis Intervention: An Evaluation Proposal." In Salasin, S. E.
               (ed.), Evaluating Victim Services. Beverly Hills: Sage.
Stookey, J. A.
    1981   "A Cost Theory of Victim Justice." In Galaway, B., and Hudson, J. (eds.),
               Perspectives on Crime Victims. St. Louis: Mosby.
Stuebing, W. K.
    1984   Victims and Witnesses: Experience, Needs and Community/Criminal
               Justice Response. Working Paper No. 9, Ottawa: Department of Justice.
Symonds, M.
    1982   "Victim Responses to Terror: Understanding and Treatment," in
               Ochberg, F., and Soskis, D. (eds.) Victims 'of Terrorism. Boulder:
               Westview.
Townsend, P.
    1972   "The Needs of the Elderly and the Planning of Hospitals," in Canvin, R.,
               and Pearson, N. (eds.), Needs of the Elderly for Health and Welfare Ser-
               vices. Exeter.

VICTIMS' NEEDS & VICTIM SERVICES   559

Van Dijk, J. J. M., & Steinmetz, C. H. D.
  1983   "Victimization Surveys: Beyond Measuring the Volume of Crime." Vic-
              timology, Vol. 8 No. 1/2 pp. 291–309.
Vennard, J.
  1976   "Justice and Recompense to Victims of Crime." New Society, February
              19th, 1976, 378–380.
Viano, E.
  1978   Victim/Witness Services: A Review of the Model. Washington: U.S. De-
              partment of Justice.
Villmow, B.
  1984   "Criminal and Social Policy with Regard to Victims." Council of Europe,
              Sixteenth Criminological Research Conference: Research on Victims.
              Strasbourg, November, 1984.
Weisaeth, L.
  1985   "Psychiatric Studies in Victimology in Norway: Main Findings and Re-
              cent Developments." Victimology, Vol. 10, No. 1–4.
Waller, I.
  1982   "Crime Victims: Needs Services and Reforms. Orphans of Social Policy."
              Paper at 4th International Symposium on Victimology, Tokyo.
Waller, I., and Okihiro, N.
  1978   Burglary: The Victim and the Public. Toronto: University of Toronto
              Press.
Williams, K.
  1983   Community Resources for Victims of Crime. Research & Planning Unit
              Paper 14. London: Home Office.

About the Author

Mike Maguire is the senior Research Fellow at the Centre for Criminological Research, University of Oxford. He is the author of Burglary in a Dwelling (Heinemann
Educational Books, London, 1982), which is based upon a study including interviews
with over 300 victims of burglary, and of several articles on victims. He has also published work on prisons and parole. He is presently engaged, with the assistance of Claire
Corbett, in an evaluation of Victim Support Schemes in Great Britain, which will be
completed by the end of 1985.

The author's address is: Centre for Criminological Research, University of Oxford,
12 Bevington Road, Oxford OX2 6LH, England.

[17]

JUSTICE FOR VICTIMS

Margery Fry*

A man was blinded as the result of an assault in 1951, and awarded compensation of 11,500 pounds. His two assailants, now out of prison, have been ordered to pay 5 shillings a week each. The victim will need

---

* Miss Fry devoted much of her life to attempts to reform the criminal law and administration and was closely connected with the Howard League of Penal Reform in London. She died in 1957.

192   JOURNAL OF PUBLIC LAW

to live another 442 years to collect the last instalment. A bitter mockery! Have we no better help to offer to the victims of violent crime?

In our modern system of collective responsibility for sickness and injury, we have evolved a machinery for assuring compensation which could well be extended to injuries criminally caused, affording equal benefits to the man who falls from a ladder at work and the man whose enemy pushes the ladder from under him at home.

Modern finance is held together by sharing risks of almost every kind. The private citizen, if he is provident, hedges himself round with insurance on all sides: whether he fears the arrival of twins, or death, or a wet afternoon for the vicarage fete, he seeks the aid of an insurance company. So universal is this practice that burglars have been known to claim that they did no harm to the rightful owners, whose "sparklers" were sure to be well covered.

This principle of clubbing together for mutual protection is venerable in British social life. Early law, with its emphasis on compensation for the victim of crime, could never have worked but for the solidarity which laid upon the offender's relatives (sometimes to the sixth degree of cousinship) the duty of paying up for his misdeeds. It may have been a weakening of the bonds of kinship that led to the formation—as at Exeter and Cambridge in the eleventh century—of guilds whose members were pledged to provide wergild, or blood money, for those who became liable to pay it.

This system of sharing risks by potential offenders (in contrast with our usual method whereby potential victims unite for mutual protection) has a modern counterpart in the compulsory insurance against third party risks for motorists; while the barrow boys of the street markets are said to pay their "obstruction" fines from a common fund maintained for the purpose.

Failing some such supporting group, it is usually futile for courts to award heavy damages for personal injuries; the isolated individual offender can rarely make large amends. What, then, could be done to provide the compensation which the victim ought to receive?

It is old-fashioned now to quote Bentham, but on the tendency of criminal law to pay scant attention to the needs of the victim, he puts it well: "Punishment, which, if it goes beyond the limit of necessity, is a pure evil, has been scattered with a prodigal hand. Satisfaction, which is purely a good, has been dealt out with evident parsimony." He held that "satisfaction" should be drawn from the offender's property, but "if the offender is without property . . . it ought to be furnished out of the public treasury, because it is an object of public good and the security of all is interested in it."

VICTIMS OF CRIMINAL VIOLENCE 193

Is Bentham's proposal useful today? Clearly, so far as offences against property go, any scheme for State insurance would be wrecked by the ease with which it could be defrauded. But crimes of violence against the person are a different matter. Few people would voluntarily wound themselves to obtain a modest compensation, and the risk of successful deception is negligible.

Employers and workmen contribute to cover benefits after industrial accidents, and the logical way of providing for criminally inflicted injuries would be to tax every adult citizen (the dangers of admitting children to benefit are obvious) to cover a risk to which each is exposed.

If the number and nature of crimes of personal violence remained as in 1956, and the victims were compensated, under a funded scheme, on the scale of those who suffer industrial injuries, the cost, after allowing for some savings in respect of National Insurance benefits would be about 150,000 pounds annually. This sum, less than a penny a head a year for the population over fourteen, would not warrant a separate collection, but should be found out of general taxation.

Difficulties would arise, of course, in the case of reported crimes where either no arrest was made or no conviction followed; and a special tribunal would have to be set up to decide upon the existence of an offence in these "cases known to the police."

As with the industrial injuries scheme, there should obviously be no interference with the present jurisdiction of the courts in awarding damages against the aggressor in cases of violent crime, as a supplement to the rather meagre benefits of the scale. But the value of the proposed compensation would not be economic alone. There is a natural sense of outrage on the sufferer's part, which the milder aspect of our modern penal methods only exacerbates. The young hooligan goes to a course of training in Borstal, while the shopkeeper he has "coshed" nurses his grievance with his broken head, gaining perhaps some solatium for a day's work lost giving evidence.

After all, the State which forbids our going armed in self-defence cannot disown all responsibility for its occasional failure to protect. When serious crimes occur in this category the consequences are often terribly tragic. For the family of a murdered man, for the girl whose health has been permanently broken by brutal rape, for the skilled workman who can no longer follow his trade, the simple fact that their hardships had been specially recognized would help to assuage the bitterness of their lot.

In those primitive societies already mentioned the clan of the injured person recognises a duty of ensuring his satisfaction as imperative as that of the aggressor's to help in giving it. The tribe has now broken down and the larger unit of the national inherits both obligations. It is at once the

194   JOURNAL OF PUBLIC LAW

heir of those who claimed due satisfaction for outrage, and of those
united to render it. A slight adjustment in our already wide scheme for
sharing risks would fulfil our double duty.

———————————————

[18]

BRIT. J. CRIMINOL.   Vol. 24   No. 2   APRIL 1984

VICTIMS, THE CRIMINAL JUSTICE SYSTEM AND COMPENSATION

Joanna Shapland (*Oxford*)*

It is only in the last ten years that the role of the victim in the criminal justice system has again risen into prominence. There is now a plethora of research, at least in Britain, considering the victim's experiences, his views and his attitudes. Yet this recent upsurge of interest is in many ways surprising. We have known for some time how vital the victim is to the operation of the criminal justice system. In a simplistic way, one might consider the system, and all the jobs and workings of the professionals within it, as being built upon the actions of two people—the offender and the victim. The numbers and type of cases entering the system, and thereby eventually providing the workload for the courts, prison service and other agencies, appear largely to be determined by the reporting behaviour of victims and witnesses, not action initiated by the police (Clarke and Hough, 1980; Bottomley and Coleman, 1981; Maguire, 1982).

We have, therefore, two contradictory facets of the role of the victim—his practical importance and, in contrast, at least until recently, an ignorance of and an ignoring of his attitudes and experiences by the professionals within the criminal justice system. It is this paradox which is fundamental to our understanding of the victim's attitudes to the system. In this paper I shall discuss the experiences of a sample of victims of violent crime and their attitudes to the criminal justice system and to compensation. I shall consider, first, their experiences with the police and their contribution to the reporting and detection of offences. Secondly, I shall look at their reaction to the courts and to the decisions on conviction and sentencing. The implications of victim experiences, and the possible shape of a more victim-oriented criminal justice system will then be considered. The most common response to the plight of victims appears to be to compensate them—to give them money. However, present methods of compensation have also arisen without much direct reference to victims. Victims' response to compensation will be discussed with regard to their attitudes to the criminal justice system, the effects of the offence on the victim and the availability of compensation.

The study involved 278 adult victims of violent crime from two areas of the Midlands, whose offences had been reported to the police. It was a longitudinal study, involving interviews with the same victims at various stages as they went through the system. Victims were followed for up to

* Research Fellow, Centre for Criminological Research, Oxford University. The research discussed in this article was done in collaboration with Jon Willmore and Peter Duff. It was financed by a grant from the Home Office. A fuller account is being prepared for publication in book form by Heinemann.

JOANNA SHAPLAND

three years and were interviewed between two and four times.[1] In this way it was possible to look at changes in attitudes and to reduce problems of memory loss or overlay due to later events. The sample included male and female victims of physical assaults (causing injuries ranging from bruises, scratches and minor cuts to very serious internal injuries); male and female victims of robberies of the "mugging" type; and female victims of sexual assaults (rapes and indecent assaults). In addition to the interviews with victims, all court appearances of the cases were attended and transcripts made, the police files and any compensation files analysed and police, prosecution, court and compensation agency personnel interviewed.[2] Other recent studies of victims of other types of offence, notably Maguire's (1982) and Howley's (1982) studies of English burglary victims and Kelly's (1982) study of American victims of rape, have found very similar results on some topics, and will also be cited.

The Police: Reporting, Investigation and Detection

In our study of victims of violent crime, victims were found to be vital in the reporting and investigation of cases and also to be essential as providers of evidence for the courts. Between 35 and 41 per cent. of cases (depending on the town concerned) were reported by the victim himself. Another 50 per cent. were reported by other civilians, such as passers-by, neighbours, friends or those in charge of places where the offences happened (for example, licensees or managers of bus stations). This high percentage of the involvement of others is probably due to the violent nature of the offences and the consequent inability of the injured or unconscious victim to report the offence himself. Only three to four per cent. of cases were discovered by the police themselves. Similarly, Maguire (1982) found that the vast majority of burglaries of dwellings were brought to the attention of the police by the victim. The importance of victims to the reporting of crime has been shown in many studies (McCabe and Sutcliffe, 1978; Steer, 1980; Mawby, 1979). The English Royal Commission on Criminal Procedure (1981) has stated: "the overwhelming majority (of offences) . . . is not discovered by the police, but by the public".

Victims are also important in the detection of offenders. Over 60 per cent. of cases in our study were detected as a result of definite information (name or address) supplied by the victim. Another 8 to 13 per cent. were detected as a result of definite information supplied by a witness. Only 14 to 25 per cent. of detections were as a result of police action. Even in Maguire's burglary study, despite the prevalence of cases in which the trail was cold (in 70 per cent. of cases, the victim had been out of the house or asleep in bed for over six hours and had no precise idea of the

---

[1] The first interview occurred as soon as the victim replied to the letter sent about the study. For some victims, whose injuries were serious, this could obviously take some time. The time between offence and first interview ranged from five days to about three months, with the great majority taking place in the first four weeks. Victims were then re-interviewed after the committal to Crown Court, after the outcome of the case and after receiving any compensation (where appropriate).
[2] Further details of the sample and methods may be found in Shapland *et al.* (1981) and Shapland (1982).

VICTIMS, THE CRIMINAL JUSTICE SYSTEM AND COMPENSATION

time at which the burglary had taken place), information given to the police by the victim or a witness was the most important aid to detection of the offender. The usefulness of the victim in this respect does not, of course, deny a role for the police. Without a quick response by the police where victims have themselves apprehended the offender (and over 50 per cent. of cases in our study were reported within five minutes of occurrence), or fast action where a name or address has been supplied, offenders would not be caught. The police may not be the major detection agency in these offences, but they are still responsible for gathering evidence such that the offender, once caught, can be prosecuted.

In our study, a prompt police response was one of the determinants of victim satisfaction at their first contact with the police. But the major factor, as indeed it was throughout the process, was the attitude of the police officers and the concern they expressed, rather than what they actually did with the case—a concern with process rather than with outcome. The great majority of victims (over 75 per cent.) were satisfied or very satisfied with the police at their first contact. What impressed them was the manner of the police ("she was marvellous, she listened to everything") and whether they appeared to take the case seriously. The few victims who had a negative reaction gave comments such as: "I was crying but no sympathy—just pen and paper—just as if it were happening every day to them—just one of a crowd, but you think you're the only one" (indecent assault victim).

Similarly, burglary victims are concerned that the police should listen carefully, and perform the almost ritualistic fingerprint dusting and questioning that would indicate to them that the police are taking the case seriously (Maguire, 1982; Howley, 1982). Howley has pointed to the discrepancy between police and victim attitudes. Police officers thought that it was important to appear "professional" and "efficient"; whereas victims were, above all else, looking to the police for support, reassurance and personal contact. Three-quarters of Howley's victims expressed satisfaction with police action, but caring and supportive attitudes were the main subject for victim praise. Apparently uncaring or casual attitudes were the most frequent source of criticism. The concern, again, was with process rather than outcome.

Very similar results were found in a study of a very different offence—rape—from a very different criminal justice system—the United States. Kelly (1982) found that her rape victims rated the police highly (76 per cent. were satisfied with patrol officers and 80 per cent. with detectives), but were disturbed about insensitive questioning and any tendency on the part of the police to regard the victim not as a person, but as evidence. It is, therefore, the attitude of the police during initial contacts that determines victim satisfaction.

This concern with attitude and with treatment continues during the police investigation of the offence. By the middle of the investigation in our study, however, the initial high levels of victim satisfaction with the police were starting to decline. This was due largely to lack of information,

JOANNA SHAPLAND

for which the police were blamed. By the end of police and court processes, there was a significant decline in ratings of satisfaction with the police handling of the case[3] and also a decline in attribution of positive qualities to the police generally (so that the police were rated on five-point adjectival scales as being significantly less efficient, less over-worked, more offensive, less fair, less bureaucratic, more crooked and less helpful). There were even 14 per cent. of victims who would not report a similar offence to the police in future.[4] This lower level of satisfaction persisted over the two or three years after the offence, as did victims' memories of their experiences. The major reason for dissatisfaction was lack of information, and a consequent feeling that the police did not care:

> "They should have let me know. I haven't been kept informed at all."
> "Up to the bloke's arrest I was very satisfied—they were pretty good—then they didn't tell me anything. So I suppose you'd have to put unsatisfied."
> "I'm very annoyed—a two-minute phone call would do to tell us when the case is on. If they want help they should look after the people who do help them."

The need for information was present throughout the process. Victims wanted to know whether the offender was caught, what the charges were, whether he was in custody or on bail (a matter where, interestingly, the facts were less frightening than fear of the unknown), when the court appearances would be, whether the victim would have to give evidence, whether the offender was convicted and what the sentence was. The most important of these was, however, the outcome, whether it be conviction and sentence or just that the offender had not been caught, the police had no further leads and were filing the case. Eighty-eight per cent. of victims felt that they should have received some notification of the result of the case, and most of these put the responsibility on the police.

Again, a need for information occurs for victims of other offences. Maguire's (1982) burglary victims complained that, after the first few days, they had heard nothing further about the case. Only 24 per cent. had received any notification of police progress. Those who praised the police usually did so in terms of the "trouble they took" over the case. Howley's (1982) victims also criticised police who did not report developments. For Kelly's (1982) rape cases, victims' assessments of how they were treated by both police and prosecutors were more favourable if they were provided with information, consulted and included in their case. Indeed, the most important prediction of satisfaction with prosecutors was

[3] On a five-point scale from very satisfied to very dissatisfied, there were significant decreases in satisfaction from first contact with the police to the first interview (Town 1: $p<0.001$); from first interview to after committal of the case to the Crown Court, where relevant (Town 2: $p<0.05$); and from the time of the first interview to after the outcome of the case (Town 1 and Town 2: $p<0.001$). There was then no difference between ratings after the outcome of the case and after the completion of compensation processes, where applicable, six months to two years later. All tests were t-tests for paired data.
[4] A study in the Dutch Antilles (Spickenheuer, 1982) has also suggested that prior victimisation reduces willingness to report, if previous police action was regarded as unsatisfactory. Major reasons for dissatisfaction were the little trouble taken by the police and lack of information.

VICTIMS, THE CRIMINAL JUSTICE SYSTEM AND COMPENSATION

not the verdict, but victims' assessment of how they were treated. The rule was: the more the contact, the greater the satisfaction.

The Outcome and Court Processes

At the outcome stage, again, it appeared that process was more important than the actual result of the case. Perhaps surprisingly, in our study, as in Maguire's, victims were often quite happy if the police did not catch the offenders, provided that they felt that the police had been interested and had kept them informed. They wanted, however, to be told the outcome clearly and fully—to know that enquiries were no longer continuing.

Victims were, again, not particularly punitive either in the sentence that they would wish their offender to get or in their reactions to the sentence that those offenders who were convicted finally received. Their suggested sentences seemed to be very much within those of current English sentencing practice. They did, however, feel that compensation for the offender should have played a much larger part than in fact it did (only 20 per cent. of victims whose offenders were sentenced received compensation orders and many of these were for small amounts). These reactions on sentencing are not just confined to the victims of violent crime, as in our study. The recent British Crime Survey (Hough and Mayhew, 1983) has also suggested that: "victims' recommendations are broadly in line with present practice", and that compensation is important. Over 10 per cent. of victims of all crimes favoured compensation as the major disposal for their offender. It may be argued that the equivalence between victim views and current sentencing practice is not an argument for any particular level of sentencing, but a reflection of knowledge gained through media reporting. However, it can be said that, first, the idea of the "hanging, drawing and quartering" victim is a myth and, secondly, the idea of court-based compensation is received favourably (given that compensation as a sole sentence has only just been introduced by the Criminal Justice Act 1982).

In the court process itself, when victims did attend court to give evidence (or managed to find out when the court appearances were and attended out of interest), it tended to be the peripherals of the court system that caused problems: the lack of facilities, cramped surroundings, sitting next to the defendant with consequent feelings of intimidation, lack of notice at the Crown Court, inadequate recompense for their costs and, above all, lack of information and knowledge of when the appearance was and what they would have to do. The actual experience in the witness-box, contrary to previous analysis, did not cause great distress to the majority of victims. The apparent lack of interest of the prosecutor (who tends not even to meet witnesses or victims beforehand) was more seriously regarded:

> "I was nervous, frightened because I hadn't been to a trial before. They didn't try to help me in any way—the prosecution solicitor should have

135

JOANNA SHAPLAND

explained to me what was going to happen—it would have been easier. I
didn't even know there was a solicitor until it started."

Kelly (1982) describes almost identical feelings in her American rape
victims. Victims were bothered by a lack of information—about their legal
status and about court procedures. They were frightened by subpoenas
and by grand juries. They felt excluded from their cases. They were
particularly annoyed at lack of consultation over plea-bargaining or re-
scheduling of court appearances. It was felt that the judicial system had
little regard for the victims' well-being.

A Victim-Oriented Criminal Justice System

So, there is the paradox. The criminal justice system depends heavily
upon victims for the reporting and detection of offences and for the
provision of evidence in court. Yet, it does not appear to value the victim.
The concern with attitudes, information and consultation shown by
victims in our study and in others is an expression of the need to be
valued, to be wanted and to be considered as an important participant.
The system is not geared to the perspective of the victim. There appears
to be a mismatch between the victim's expectations of the system and the
system's assumptions about victim needs. The police, for example, have
become, in Howley's (1982) words: "preoccupied with technical efficiency,
whereas victims look to police for support and reassurance". Prosecutors
and court staff are concerned with processing the ever-growing numbers
of defendants through the system in the fastest and most economical way.

It does not seem that the system ignores the victim because he is
perceived as a threat. Indeed, the victims in our study were not expressing
a desire to take over the criminal justice system. They did not want
decision-making power—they were happy that the decisions to charge, to
prosecute and to sentence, should be left with those who are taking them
today. Eighteen per cent. of victims did, however, express some interest
in the possibility of using a mediation dispute regulation procedure (see
Chinkin and Griffiths, 1980). There were some areas where victims wished
for consultation before decisions were taken—on whether charges should
be pressed or dropped at court and on whether information about victims
should be given to the press. But the major requirements were for
information and for help—not as charity but in exchange for the very
considerable time and effort the victims themselves put in at a time when
they were injured or shocked.

The changes in the criminal justice system necessary to approximate
more closely to the present expectations of victims are not major or
structural ones. They are primarily attitudinal. The victim's problems in
participating in the criminal justice system may be seen to stem from his
lack of status, or even accepted role within that system. If the victim is a
non-person in the eyes of the professional participants, at least as far as
the day-to-day functioning of the system is concerned, then he will not be
informed or consulted as a matter of course. Even if those participants

VICTIMS, THE CRIMINAL JUSTICE SYSTEM AND COMPENSATION

accept the desirability of retaining his goodwill (because of his possible evidential usefulness), any information flow will tend to be one-way. The victim will be told what is deemed necessary or helpful to tell him. It is only if the victim is seen as being an important partner in the criminal justice system that the flow of information will become automatically two-way and consultation will occur. For example, the victim might have the right to know the outcome of the case and be able to determine how this information is presented to him.

However, changes to approximate more closely to present victim expectations would involve teaching the professional participants in the criminal justice system that the victim is to be treated courteously, kept informed and consulted about all the stages of the process. They involve treating the victim as a more equal partner. That, however, would imply a greater emphasis on the role of the victim and, potentially, less emphasis on the role of the offender and that of the legal profession. This might include a shift in working practices of the professional participants that might initially appear to involve more work, more difficulty and more effort but, paradoxically, may result in easier detection, a higher standard of prosecution evidence and fewer cases thrown out at court.

Attitudes are, however, not absolute. They depend upon expectations and upon knowledge of the system. So, if the system changes, so will the attitudes and expectations of victims. At the moment, the similarity of victim attitudes over offences and in different systems is extraordinary. It tends to suggest similar roles for victims and a similar perception of victims in different countries and in different systems. If, however, we change our criminal justice system, if, say, we adopt the more victim-oriented system suggested by the findings of these studies, we may merely produce a system more rounded in its concerns but no less adversarial than at present. Or we may, in so doing, alter victims' attitudes and expectations so that, by a gradual process, a different model emerges, one perhaps closer to a mediated consensus model of dispute regulation. Such a development would produce a very different form of criminal justice system, which would have implications both for the offender and for the professional representatives involved.

Victim Assistance—Society's View of Victims

We have seen that the victim's dealings with the police and courts are characterised by his status as a non-person. Strangely, the area of victim assistance and compensation seems very similar. The major projects aimed at fulfilling victims' needs have been set up without regard to, or even investigation into, victims' expressed needs. We now have a plethora of schemes to give aid and assistance to victims, and this area is one of the fastest growing fields of voluntary effort. In Great Britain, there is state compensation to victims of violent crime (the Criminal Injuries Compensation Board—CICB); compensation from offenders as part of the sentence of the court (compensation orders) or, in a few new schemes, as part of pre-trial diversion; Victim Support Schemes to provide emotional and

JOANNA SHAPLAND

practical assistance, starting immediately after the offence; and other groups offering practical, emotional and financial help to victims of particular offences (Rape Crisis Centres, battered wives' refuges, etc.). In the United States, there are also victim/witness assistance projects to provide advice and help at court (National District Attorneys Association, 1977).

The reasons given when setting up these schemes vary. Some are apparently victim-centred. State compensation, for example, has been justified on many grounds. One is the humanitarian and social welfare idea that the state should compensate those who suffer hardship occasioned by criminal violence.[5] Others have suggested that the Government or even society is responsible for its failure in preventing the crime against the victim and so has some moral obligation to reimburse him (Burns, 1980). The notions of equitable justice and of reciprocity in social relationships have also been raised. These are based on the premise that the victim has suffered through no fault of his own. A sense of injustice or even of "outrage" may then arise in the population which can only be satisfied by compensation of the victim (Thorvaldson and Krasnick, 1980). The reason finally adduced in the setting up of the CICB seems to combine elements of the first and third: compensation should show "social solidarity or the desire to express public sympathy for the victims of crime" (Home Office, 1978).

Other reasons for setting up state compensation schemes have not been so seemingly victim-centred. American schemes have been advocated to improve the satisfaction and promote future co-operation of the victim with the criminal justice system. Alternatively, Miers (1983) has argued that most schemes are essentially "political"—they play on the desire of the public to compensate victims but merely state the desirability of so doing rather than setting up effective means to produce compensation. They "make a public statement about crime and the values which are embodied in criminal justice and welfare programmes".

Whatever the justification cited for a particular scheme, the parameters of schemes are similar. Although all state compensation schemes stress the need to consider and compensate the particular harm suffered by the individual applicant (and so the applicant is asked to provide full details of his expenses, losses and suffering), the decision-making process is one-way. The scheme decides who is eligible and what expenses may be claimed in each case, according to the guidelines used to set it up.[6] There may be no consideration of what harm victims do suffer, or whether the compensation scheme is meeting any need expressed by victims. State compensation is given from state to victim, according to rules devised by the state.

[5] Considerable discussion of these issues may be found in Miers, 1978; Burns, 1980; Thorvaldson and Krasnick, 1980; Harland, 1978.
[6] The applicant, as in the case of the CICB, may of course appeal if he feels that the guidelines have not been followed.

VICTIMS, THE CRIMINAL JUSTICE SYSTEM AND COMPENSATION

This ignoring of the expressed needs of victims is strange. For all except the "political" purposes of compensation, reference to victims would seem to be necessary. If we never look at the reactions of victims, how can we discover whether suffering is alleviated, expenses or losses recompensed, moral status restored, or co-operation with the criminal justice system increased? Even if we have only a "political" purpose (and this is predicated on one or other of the alternative purposes being supported by that society), we may find that public statements about the worth of victims, which are later shown to be hollow, may rebound on any who set up such ineffective schemes.

On what basis are schemes for victim aid and assistance set up, if not according to the expressed needs of victims? They seem to reflect the views of society as to the nature of victims and the needs they are considered to have. If we consider state compensation again as an example, this contains the idea that compensation should be awarded only to "innocent victims". In England and Wales, for example, the Report of the Working Party which set up the CICB (Home Office, 1961) stated that any scheme should be "based mainly on considerations of sympathy for the innocent victim". Two assumptions have flowed from this. The first is that there are undeserving victims which the state has no "moral" obligation to compensate (for example, if the crime "arises directly from undesirable activities of the victim"). The second is that there will be fraudulent claims: the scheme "should provide as many safeguards as possible against fraudulent or exaggerated claims". Both of these have been amplified by the fact that state compensation is public money, which has to be accounted for. The results have been the inclusion in the CICB scheme of descriptions of various categories of undeserving victims (who are to be denied compensation or given only a partial award) and the feeling amongst those administering the CICB that everything the claimant says is to be checked. As the administrative officers said in the course of the present study, "All information given on the application form is checked". From considering the files, there seemed to be almost a presumption in some cases that applicants would tend to or try to exaggerate. Considerable correspondence could take place over small sums.

Another prevalent view is that assistance is given on the basis of sympathy, to give help, aid, even charity to victims. The voluntary sector may be encouraged to play a large part (for example, the victim support scheme movement), on the basis that victims, like the poor, deserve charity. Such aid may, however, tend to be concentrated on those seen to be the most obviously deserving and innocent. The most obvious example of this is the concentration, at least in rhetoric, on the elderly, especially old ladies who are the victims of robbery.

Even compensation from the offender, which, in Britain, takes the form of compensation orders from the courts, has been set up to provide an alternative to civil legal procedures for victims, so that they may obtain financial assistance more quickly, more easily, and at less potential cost. As a result an apparent tension between the supposedly civil nature of the

JOANNA SHAPLAND

award and its place in a penal sanction has been perceived by legal commentators and by prosecutors and justices' clerks (Shapland, 1982).

In other jurisdictions, the benefits to the criminal justice system in terms of the victim's greater co-operation have been stressed. Unfortunately, both the present study and that of Doerner and Lab (1980) in the United States have failed to find any spin-off benefit of compensation on attitudes to the criminal justice system. The award of compensation affects attitudes to the compensating authority itself (the state scheme or, in the case of compensation from the offender in Britain, the courts) but not attitudes to other parts such as the police.

The prevailing view in terms of society's attitudes to victims and victim assistance appears to be that it is the deserving, innocent victim who should be compensated or helped and that that help should be given as a form of charity. It is the schemes themselves which will decide who fits this stereotype. Assistance, being charity, is not a right and should not be questioned by the recipient.

The Effects of the Offence on the Victim

Before moving on to look at victims' views of society's provision for their needs, one must, first, consider the effects of crime on the victim. These effects are not confined to the immediate consequences of the offence—physical injury, shock, loss of property, time off work or financial losses. They can intrude into most of the areas of the victim's life, producing a change in his relationships with members of his family, neighbours, friends or work colleagues. There are also the costs involved in being a victim in the criminal justice system, though these are rarely acknowledged in any form of assistance offered to victims. Some are direct costs—the time, transport fares and potential loss of earnings involved in helping the police to investigate and prosecute the offence. Others are more long-term and more indirect. They include the stress and worry over the weeks, months or, in a few cases, years the case may take to finish. During this time the victim may be called upon to help the police and may constantly be on the alert to be a witness at court.

Crimes of violence appear to produce substantial immediate effects on their victims. Only nine per cent. of victims in our study had been entirely free of effects from the offence itself by the time of the first interview. Some obviously required medical attention, almost all expressed some wish for emotional support and reassurance. The role of friends and relations was significant here, but some victims were isolated or the offence was such that they found it difficult to talk to those they knew well (for example, in some sexual assault cases). In initial contacts with the police, which took place at this time, the manner of the police was found to be very important. Victims wished the police to be considerate and give the impression that they were taking the offence (and the victim) seriously.

VICTIMS, THE CRIMINAL JUSTICE SYSTEM AND COMPENSATION

Figure 1: *Effects suffered by victims at different times since the offence.*

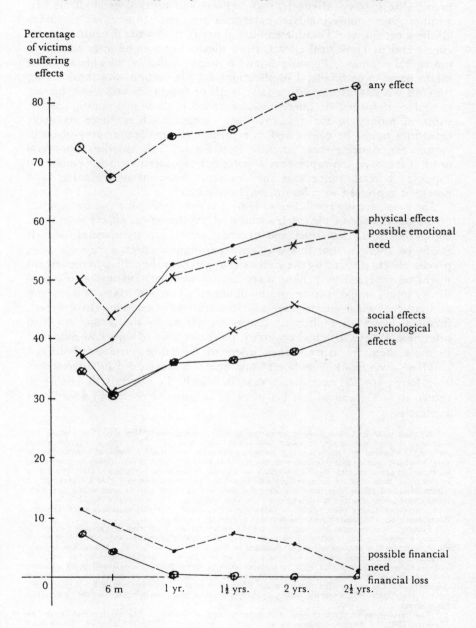

JOANNA SHAPLAND

Figure 1 shows the percentages of victims suffering various effects at different times.[7] The effects have been divided into the broad categories of financial loss, physical effects, social effects and psychological effects.[8] In addition, three more inclusive categories are used. "Any effect" includes all these categories. "Possible emotional need" represents the sum of social effects and psychological effects, since these appear to be inter-related in individual victims. "Possible financial need" includes all effects which might have some financial implications for the victims. So, those losing time off work, those requiring false teeth or spectacles and those having to replace damaged clothing would be added to those mentioning specific sums of money in the financial loss category. These three inclusive categories might be considered to represent the maximum proportion of victims experiencing some potential need for aid. The "possible emotional need" category then represents a potential expressed wish for emotional support or reassurance and the "possible financial need" category a potential expressed wish for financial assistance.

The most striking result from Figure 1 is the persistence and consistency of the prevalence of physical, social and psychological effects over time, compared to the low level and decrease over time of financial loss.[9] It might be thought that this was an experimenter effect, except that the precise effects suffered by the victims changed over time. Pain in movement might be replaced by aching scars in cold weather. Disruption of social life by injury might turn to an unwillingness to go out. Many of the social and psychological effects were also confirmed by relatives. In contrast, financial losses were often no longer important by the second or third interview. Where they had occurred, most victims had somehow managed to meet them by using money intended for other purposes (holidays, children, even food) or by borrowing. Some, however, did suffer considerable hardship (for example, a case in which the victim was unable to return to work, and so lost his income, because he could not afford new spectacles).

[7] At each interview, victims were asked the open-ended question: "Has this offence made any difference to your way of life, to whom you see or where you go?" They were then prompted to include the effects of injuries (where applicable) and changes to their life at home, at work and in the neighbourhood, but no specific effects were suggested at any time, nor was the victim prompted about his replies at previous interviews. It is possible to calculate the interviews relevant to each time period in two ways, both of which produce very similar results. The one shown in Figure 1 represents the effects described at the next interview after the time shown (since victims were asked to tell the interviewers about any effects suffered since the last interview). The alternative would be to count only interviews taking place within a particular time period, but this produces more apparent fluctuation due to the lower number of interviews involved in each period.

[8] Financial loss includes any statement by the victim which mentioned any specific amount of money, whether for loss of earnings, damaged or stolen property or medical expenses. These would all come under the heading of special damages in any compensation award. Physical effects cover both temporary physical suffering such as headaches or pain while performing everyday activities; and permanent disfigurements such as scars or missing teeth. Social effects could occur at home (holidays disrupted, family concern, etc.), at work (victim changes job, perceives that he is treated differently, etc.) or concern the victim's social life (victim does not go out alone, will not go to pubs, etc.). Psychological effects include worry, anxiety, depression and their symptoms in the victim or in his relatives.

[9] The persistence of effects is echoed in other studies of victims of different types of crime (see Maguire, 1982, for English burglary victims; Brown and Yantzi, 1980, for Canadian victims of all types of crime).

VICTIMS, THE CRIMINAL JUSTICE SYSTEM AND COMPENSATION

There were, of course, differences between the effects suffered by victims of physical assaults, sexual assaults and robberies. Physical assault victims suffered less effects overall, yet the percentages were still over 60 per cent. at the outcome of the cases or even two years afterwards. Throughout all four interviews with victims, physical assault victims were more likely to suffer physical effects. Sexual assault victims were more prone to psychological effects than were physical assault or robbery victims.

Effects, Needs and Perceived Needs

The effects described above are victims' perceptions of the effects of the offence and the criminal justice system—whether the victims felt an effect was important enough to mention it to the interviewers. They are not measures of the severity (perceived or actual) of those effects. Nor are they measures of need. Suffering an effect does not necessarily imply the existence of a need for any particular kind of support. Indeed, it is impossible to measure "actual" need. In our study and in others, it is found that those victims who suffer the worst perceived effects are not necessarily those who would fit the stereotype of the most affected victim. In addition, expressed needs are to some extent culturally based. They are related to the expectations of victims as to the potential effects of the offence and to their knowledge of what remedies exist. If victims do not know that victim support or assistance schemes exist, or that compensation may be available from the courts or from the state, then they may only be able to formulate a diffuse wish for emotional support or for compensation.

But this is not to suggest that effects or expressed needs are unimportant. The effects which victims said they had suffered were sufficiently immediate for the victims to have presented them as significant to the researchers. They were not prompted about any particular kind of effect. Some of these effects were alleviated by informal support by family and friends. Others were stated as unfulfilled needs. One might consider the effects that victims said they had suffered as drawing the outer boundaries of expressed need for the present system. If the system changes, the expectations and, thus, the effects and expressed needs will also change. Some effects will be coped with informally. Others form the unfulfilled needs of those particular victims and may be the basis on which they judge how responsive a system is to them.

Victims' Views of Society's Response

We have already stated that victims' views on victim assistance will be determined, to some extent, by the present response of society—their knowledge and expectations of those forms of assistance that are available. Victims' views may, therefore, change as different schemes are set up, or as publicity about schemes becomes more widespread. Rather than discussing victim reactions to particular details of schemes, it may be more useful to consider whether victims agree with the societal view postulated above, and whether there are any expressed needs which are not catered for in any way at present.

143

JOANNA SHAPLAND

These views need to be seen against the background of two factors. The first is that the victims of violence in the present study tended not to be suffering from financial loss at the time at which they received compensation (see Figure 1). Financial need, where present, was concentrated in the first few weeks or months after the offence. It is extremely unlikely that any system of state compensation or compensation from offenders can meet this need (certainly the time scale of both the CICB and court compensation orders preclude this). Compensation is thus judged against a background of mental, not financial, suffering.

The second factor, and one of the most striking findings of the present study, is that over half the victims did not know of any means to obtain compensation, although between 57 and 64 per cent. would have wished it. The views of those who experienced one or other of the sources of compensation are, therefore, the views of that minority who did find out and so were able to apply. There was no evidence that any more of this minority were eligible for compensation than those who did not know about the possibilities. The almost accidental selection of those to be compensated by the CICB, in particular, is contrary to all the purposes that have been put forward to justify state compensation to victims. This ignorance of practical possibilities for compensation was not because victims did not want compensation—57 per cent. definitely wanted compensation and another seven per cent. were undecided. Knowledge about compensation was, however, the most important determinant of whether victims applied for compensation.

The views of those who did apply for or receive compensation showed a common pattern, whatever the source of the money. If the money was regarded as compensation (and Social Security benefits did not fall into this category) then it was not the actual receipt of the money that was important, but the judgment which that award represented about the suffering and position of the victim. The only purely financial aspect seen to be important was special damages, particularly expenses actually incurred by the victim (as opposed to lost wages). This is perhaps not surprising, given the low extent and persistence of expressed financial need.

How, then, did victims view state compensation and compensation by offenders? They regarded compensation not as mainly a matter of money or of financial assistance (charitable or otherwise), but rather as making a statement about the offence, the victim and the position that the criminal justice system was prepared to give to the victim. Even the element of payment in proportion to suffering and loss was subordinated to this symbolic function. This was most obvious in victims' enthusiasm for compensation from offenders as part of the sentence of the court. It also appeared in victims' comments on the operation of the CICB, particularly in their support for the idea of state compensation as a right for all eligible victims.

To victims in the present study, therefore, compensation was seen not according to the societal view as charity doled out to innocent, deserving

VICTIMS, THE CRIMINAL JUSTICE SYSTEM AND COMPENSATION

victims, but according to the very much older view of compensation as restitution—as the giving back or recompensing to the victim what he has lost, not only materially but symbolically and in terms of suffering. Compensation awards, either from the state or from the offender, were perceived as society's judgment on them as victims. This has two implications for compensation. First, compensation should be based primarily on the offender with the state as back-up. Victims saw compensation orders as part of the sentence, not as primarily a civil measure. They did not expect "full" compensation from impoverished offenders. They did, however, expect the courts to make such orders a priority in sentencing. Victims who received compensation orders were significantly more satisfied with the courts than those whose offenders received a different sentence. This desire for recognition by the courts is very similar to victims' reactions to the rest of the criminal justice system.

Secondly, the tariff for compensation might follow not the present civil scale but a rather differently-weighted criminal scale. Such a criminal scale would pay more regard to mental effects—the social and psychological effects of Figure 1. It would also be based on a concept of "seriousness" of the offence from the point of view of the victim—not that of the individual victim in a particular case, but what victims might be expected to suffer as a result of that type of offence.

It may be useful to go into more detail about this concept, as it is still unfamiliar to us to think of criminal matters from the point of view of the (average) victim. It would involve different elements and weightings of the contributing factors from those derived from the point of view of the offender (or of "society"). It might, therefore, involve consideration of the perception of the victim, "I might have died", rather than that involved in a consideration of the offender's culpability, "he might have considered that I would nearly die", or that of civil proceedings, "I did nearly die".

The seriousness of a crime includes consideration not only of its consequences to the victim but also the symbolic gravity of the offence and the fact that the victim has suffered from a crime (rather than an accident). The victim might be said to have been brought unwillingly into contact ("stained") with crime. The symbolic gravity of a crime might include several elements; for example, whether it puts the victim at risk of personal physical harm or merely touches his possessions or, perhaps, whether the offence was intentional. Intentional violence may be considered more hurtful and, therefore, harmful by its recipient than negligent or accidental violence. A scale of seriousness of offences from the point of view of the victim may thus bear a considerable resemblance in its constituent elements to scales of seriousness from the point of view of the offender or of society—hardly surprising, given the cultural continuity. However, the combination and weighting of those elements will be different.

Let us consider an award of compensation under this new criminal tariff as opposed to the civil tariffs now operating. Some parts of the award will be similar. There will still be a division into expenses paid out (special

JOANNA SHAPLAND

damages) and the more general symbolic sum. But, under the criminal tariff, expenses incurred during participation in the criminal justice system would obviously be included. In the civil scale, the general sum ("pain and suffering") is mainly based on the consequences of the offence—the injuries suffered. There is, however, no particular reason why the actual sums paid under the civil tariff should have the values they do at present. The criminal tariff would include the elements of consequences (with a greater weighting for mental effects), symbolic gravity and criminal nature of the offence, but these would probably not be additive, at least in a simple fashion, since they tend to be interrelated. It would not be necessary that the total award should be greater than the present civil award.

Let us take two examples. One would be an offence of high symbolic gravity but low consequences (for example, a knife blow which was deflected and merely scratched the skin). Here, the general part of the award would be higher under the criminal tariff than the civil, since the symbolic gravity would be high. The other example is potentially much more difficult. It is the opposite case, where the symbolic gravity is low but the consequences high (the eggshell or thin-skull case, in which a slight blow or push with no deliberate intention causes serious injury). If the total amount of money available under the criminal scale were to be the same as that available under the civil, then the victim would receive much less under the criminal scale. If we wish compensation to operate as a welfare system (perhaps because we do not have a full welfare system for those disabled as a result of accidents or, indeed, any other cause), then this will be seen as a major stumbling-block to the use of a criminal scale. If, however, compensation is to be a statement about the victims of crime, then it might be argued that such social welfare considerations are irrelevant—we cannot attempt to mitigate any general lack of welfare provision by giving it only to victims under a rubric of compensation.

This need for recognition and for symbolic status in compensation does not preclude the parallel wishes of victims for emotional support and help. The two seem incompatible only in organisational systems, not in the recipient. Many victims did receive all the support they needed informally from friends, relatives and workmates. Only five per cent. of victims did not refer to the involvement of other individuals at some stage. However, victims also expressed a desire for greater help and support both from the police and from a specialised victim-support agency. Slightly more than a third of victims said that they would have liked help from a victim-support scheme during their own case (such schemes were available to a minority of victims in the study). This help would cover practical and informational matters as well as emotional support.

A Victim-Centred System for Compensation and Victim Assistance

A system constructed according to the experiences and wishes of the sample of victims in the present study would have four parts. The first would be provision for immediate and emergency payment of expenses

146

VICTIMS, THE CRIMINAL JUSTICE SYSTEM AND COMPENSATION

incurred and wages lost. It would also include payments for damaged clothing, spectacles and teeth and the cost of travel to hospitals, doctors, etc. It would be an emergency service, and so would be widely publicised. Many victims would not use it, being able to cope with such items themselves. It should, however, cover the expenses of those who have no such reserves. The requirement for immediacy has two implications. First, it will not be possible to conduct exhaustive investigations into whether the offence is a crime of violence or into all the financial resources of the victim. Secondly, the process of application should be simple and speedy. This implies a locally-based distribution agency.

The second part would be a system for practical, informational and emotional support for victims. It would assist victims to claim emergency payments and compensation and would publicise services. It would also refer victims to more specialised agencies (such as psychiatric services, housing services, refuges, etc.). It would, with the agencies involved in the criminal justice system, attempt to co-ordinate services for victims, so that the agencies, not the victims, would have to iron out inconsistencies and incompatibilities. It would make as much use as possible of past victims in this, to ensure that the process of assistance remains victim-centred.

The third part of the system would be an increased use of compensation orders by the courts, amounting almost to a presumption that compensation would be considered in every case. The information required to assess the value of such orders should be routinely gathered during the investigation of the case by the police or prosecution (possibly using a system similar to that introduced in Scotland). If the court wishes to gather more evidence, or there is a query about the effects cited, then the victim might be called to give evidence. Victims should always be notified of the making of such an order (in the context of informing them of the outcome of the case). They should then receive regular reports on the progress of payment of the order and on any enforcement action taken by the court. Failure to pay compensation should be treated at least as seriously as failure to pay fines. Throughout, the victim should be treated with care and consideration by those employed in the criminal justice system.

The fourth stage of the process would act as a back-up (admittedly a very substantial one) to the third. This would involve a body such as the CICB, set up on a statutory basis to provide compensation as a right to those deemed to be eligible. The scheme should be widely publicised. For both the third and fourth parts of the system, awards might not necessarily be based on damages awarded in the civil courts, but would be according to the criminal scale discussed above.

Implications of Victims' Views

In victims' interactions with the criminal justice system, it was the attitude of the personnel of that system to the victim that was the chief determinant of victim satisfaction. In general, the system appeared to regard the victim as a non-person and so failed to accord him sufficient respect and concern.

JOANNA SHAPLAND

In the field of compensation and victim assistance, the problem is subtly different, though the faults, as perceived by victims, are similar. It is not that the victim has not been thought of, or aid not attempted. It is that those attempts appear to have a different basis to that wanted by victims. The victim does not wish to be in the position of accepting gratefully what financial assistance he may be offered by the courts or the state. He expects, not only to receive redress and recompense for the crime committed against him, but, moreover, to be considered as an important part of the criminal justice system. The desires of victims are the same in both spheres; the changes necessary to society's views of the victim are rather different.

To approach a victim-centred system, society's view of the victim would need to move from the black-and-white, deterministic picture of the deserving, innocent victim to a more realistic appreciation of what affects victims and who they are. Those who suffer most may be not the stereotypical elderly victim but those who are assaulted at work and feel unable to continue at that job, or those who are self-employed and lose not only their own but their family's livelihood. The situational and life-style factors associated with victimisation, such as going out to pubs and clubs in the evening (see for example, van Dijk and Steinmetz, 1982), would need to be appreciated not as provocation by the victim "causing" the offence, but as the reality of crime.

Allied with this change in the societal view of the victim would be a change in perceptions of compensation and of victim assistance. These would embody neither solely a rights-based approach nor solely a welfare approach. Rather, they would be based on respect for the victim, leading both to rightful recompense and to practical, informational and emotional help. These would be set within a criminal justice system, with the focus on compensation from offenders rather than state compensation. Interaction between victim and system during investigation, prosecution and the provision of assistance would be a two-way process on a basis of more equal partnership.

REFERENCES

BOTTOMLEY, A. K. and COLEMAN, C. (1981). *Understanding Crime Rates*. London: Gower.

BROWN, S. D. and YANTZI, M. (1980). *Needs assessment for victims and witnesses of crime*. Report prepared for the Mennonite Central Committee and Ministry of Correctional Services, Province of Ontario, Canada.

BURNS, P. (1980). *Criminal Injuries Compensation*. Canada: Butterworths.

CHINKIN, C. and GRIFFITHS, R. (1980). "Resolving conflict by mediation". *New Law Journal*, January 3, 6–8.

CLARKE, R. V. G. and HOUGH, J. M. (1980). *The Effectiveness of Policing*. London: Gower.

DOERNER, W. G. and LAB, S. P. (1980). "The impact of crime compensation upon victim attitudes toward the criminal justice system". *Victimology*, 61–7.

VICTIMS, THE CRIMINAL JUSTICE SYSTEM AND COMPENSATION

HARLAND, A. T. (1978). "Compensating the victims of crime". *Criminal Law Bulletin*, 203–24.

HOME OFFICE (1961). *Compensation for Victims of Crimes of Violence*. London: H.M.S.O. Cmnd. 1406.

HOME OFFICE and SCOTTISH HOME and HEALTH DEPARTMENT (1978). *Review of the Criminal Injuries Compensation Scheme: Report of an Interdepartmental Working Party*. London: H.M.S.O.

HOUGH, M. and MAYHEW, P. (1983). *The British Crime Survey*. Home Office Research Study No. 76. London: H.M.S.O.

HOWLEY, J. (1982). Victim-police interaction and its effects on public attitudes to the police. M.Sc. thesis, Cranfield Institute of Technology.

KELLY, D. (1982). "Victims' reactions to the criminal justice response", paper delivered at Law and Society Association meeting, June 6th, 1982, Toronto, Canada.

McCABE, S. and SUTCLIFFE, F. (1978). *Defining Crime*. Oxford: Basil Blackwell.

MAGUIRE, M. (1982). *Burglary in a Dwelling: the Offence, the Offender and the Victim*. London: Heinemann.

MAWBY, R. (1979). *Policing the City*. Saxon House.

MIERS, D. (1978). *Responses to Victimization*. Abingdon: Professional Books.

MIERS, D. (1983). "Compensation and conceptions of victims of crime." *Victimology*, **8,** 204–212.

NATIONAL DISTRICT ATTORNEYS ASSOCIATION (1977). *Commission on Victim Witness Assistance*. Final evaluation report.

ROYAL COMMISSION ON CRIMINAL PROCEDURE (1981). *Report*. London: H.M.S.O.

SHAPLAND, J., WILLMORE, J. and DUFF, P. (1981). *The Victim in the Criminal Justice System*. Final report to the Home Office.

SHAPLAND, J. (1982). *Compensation to Victims of Violent Crime*. Final report to the Home Office.

SPICKENHEUER, J. L. P. (1982). *Bevolking en criminalitet op de Nederlandse Antillen*. W.O.D.C. no. 34, Ministerie van Justitie, Nederland.

STEER, D. (1980). *Uncovering Crime: the Police Role*. Royal Commission on Criminal Procedure, Research Study no. 7. London: H.M.S.O.

THORVALDSON, S. A. and KRASNICK, M. R. (1980). "On recovering compensation funds from offenders". *Victimology*, **5,** 18–29.

VAN DIJK, J. J. M. and STEINMETZ, C. H. D. (1982). *Beyond Measuring the Volume of Crime*. Ministry of Justice, The Hague, Netherlands, no. LIII.

[19]

VICTIMOLOGY: AN INTERNATIONAL JOURNAL
Volume 4, 1979. Number 2. Pp. 198-213

Some Recent Theoretical Developments in Victimology

EZZAT A. FATTAH

Simon Fraser University, Burnaby, British Columbia

During the past 10 years the study of victims of crime which, in the fifties and early sixties was in an embryonic stage, has strongly affirmed its presence as one of the most promising branches of criminology. While still facing attacks and criticisms similar to those directed at criminology several decades ago, victimology is slowly coming of age in academic and professional circles and is gradually achieving worldwide recognition as an integral part of criminology. This paper analyzes the current status of victimology and some recent trends and developments in theoretical and applied victimology.

During the past 10 years the study of victims of crime which, in the fifties and early sixties was in an embryonic stage, has strongly affirmed its presence as one of the most promising branches of criminology.

While still facing attacks and criticisms similar to those directed at criminology several decades ago, victimology is slowly coming of age in academic and professional circles and is gradually achieving worldwide recognition as an integral part of criminology, as shown by:

1. A rapidly growing body of literature on victims of crime and victimization.
2. A series of international symposia on victimology of which the first two, organized by Professors Drapkin and Schaefer respectively, were held successively in Jerusalem (September 1973) and Boston (September 1976). The third, organized by Professor Schneider, was held in Muenster, West Germany in September 1979.
3. An international institute on victimology organized by Professor Emilio Viano held in Bellagio, Italy in July 1975.
4. An international journal devoted entirely to victimology founded and edited by Professor Viano and published in Washington, DC by Visage Press.

This paper analyzes the current status of victimology and some recent trends and developments in theoretical and applied victimology.

Victimology has recently undergone a metamorphosis from a "victimology of the act" to a "victimology of action." In its infancy victimology was essentially the victimology of specific crimes: victimology of violent crimes, i.e., homicide: victimology of sexual offences, i.e., rape; victimology of property crimes, i.e., burglary and fraud.

Current victimology is concerned with affirmative action for the victims of crime. The theoretical advances in victimology resulting from

RECENT THEORETICAL DEVELOPMENTS   199

efforts of pioneer victimologists have recently been overshadowed by major developments in the applied field intended to alleviate the plight of the victim, to provide the latter with the services, aid and assistance s/he needs and help him/her overcome the injurious effects of victimization. Several factors have contributed to the current trend:

1. An unmistakable swing to the right in public opinion and among personnel of the criminal justice system, not only in the United States and Canada, but in many other countries. The rightist position on crime and justice issues has always voiced strong criticism of the tendency toward milder penalties and claimed the welfare and rights of their victims (Miller, 1973). It insists society's first and foremost responsibility in the area of criminal justice is to the victim of crime and demands more attention and concern be given to the victim. One of the positive consequences of the recent shift to the right has been to sensitize criminal justice professionals and the general public to the plight of the victim and to focus the public's interest on the sufferings of those criminally victimized. One can observe this trend in recent titles such as, Pity the Criminal Less, More His Innocent Victim (Feeney, 1973) or Victims of Crime or Victims of Justice, a program sponsored by the Criminal Justice Section of the American Bar Association (1977).

2. The mounting influence of feminist movements. In their crusade against male chauvinism, supremacy and domination, women's liberation movements have adopted the cause of rape victims and battered wives. This has resulted in many studies on rape and conjugal violence against female spouses, and in several publications about rape from a feminist perspective. Women's movements have also been influential in setting up family-crisis centers and rape-relief centers in many countries.

3. A general decline of basic, fundamental research on criminology and a growing popularity of applied research in criminal justice. The rising popularity of applied research can be traced to many factors, not the least of which is the availability of money for this type of research in the United States from the Law Enforcement Assistance Administration and other organizations.

FROM STATIC CRIMINOLOGY TO DYNAMIC VICTIMOLOGY

The beginnings of victimology were basically etiological. Even a cursory reading of the early writings in victimology tend to support this view. The first systematic study of the victims of crime is Von Hentig's book, The Criminal and His Victim, published in 1948 by Yale University Press. The part dealing with the victim, Part IV of the book, contains one chapter entitled "The Contribution of the Victim to the Genesis of the Crime." Von Hentig's aim was to provide a dual frame for the study of crime as a substitute for, or at least as an alternative to, the traditional, unidimensional approach focused on the offender. Until that time, criminological explanations of criminal behavior centered on the sociocultural characteristics, the biological abnormalities and the psychological peculiarities of the offender. Most theories, whether attempting to define causation or association, offered only static explanations.

The traits approach completely ignored or deliberately minimized the importance of situational factors in actualizing or triggering criminal behavior. The study of the victim, his characteristics, his relationships and interactions with the victimizer, his role and his contribution to the genesis of the crime seemed to offer great promise for transforming etiological criminology from the static, one-sided study of the qualities and attributes of the offender into a dynamic, situational approach that views criminal behavior as the outcome of dynamic processes of interaction.

> Since criminal behavior is dynamic, it can only be explained through a dynamic approach, where the delinquent, the act and the victim are inseparable elements of a total situation which conditions the dialectic of the antisocial conduct. (Fattah, 1976)

Traditional, conventional explanations of criminal behavior not only failed to explain why certain individuals with certain characteristics commit crimes while others having the same characteristics do not, but they never offered an explanation of why that particular person committed the crime at a particular moment, in a specific situation, against a specific victim. Victimology seemed to offer the possibility of integrating predisposing factors with triggering or actualizing factors, individual variables with situational variables. Through victimology it appeared possible to develop a dynamic model encompassing the perpetrator's motives and the sufferer's attitude, the criminal's initiative and the victim's response, one party's action and the other party's reaction. This, however, remains largely an unfulfilled promise.

THE CONCEPT OF VICTIM-PRECIPITATION

Attempts to shed light on the victim's actual role in initiating, inducing, provoking, triggering or facilitating the crime and attempts to develop an explanatory model of crime incorporating the attitude and behavior of both the offender and the victim have suffered a setback as a result of severe criticism of the concept of victim-precipitation. The concept is being attacked in several quarters on various grounds. Among the critics are some feminists who are genuinely concerned about the high acquittal rate in rape cases and the humiliation and mistreatment of many rape victims at the hands of the criminal justice system. Surprisingly, most of the criticism is leveled not at the concept of victim-precipitation itself but at the way it has been operationalized, not at the notion that victims of crime may in certain cases initiate or trigger their own victimization but at how precipitation has been defined. Female students of rape were particularly incensed by Amir's (1967) imprecise definition of victim-precipitation in his study of rape in Philadelphia. Clark and Lewis' (1977) position is typical of Amir's critics. In their book, Rape: The Price of Coercive Sexuality, published in 1977, they write

> Amir's unquestioning acceptance of the male perspective is not unique; it is a widespread feature of male-dominated society. But when this general bias is carried

RECENT THEORETICAL DEVELOPMENTS

into the social sciences, it becomes an academic endorsement of the rapist's point of view, and an excuse for blaming rape upon its victims.

Unfortunately, some of the critics extended their attacks on victim-precipitation to the whole discipline of victimology accusing it of being "the art of blaming the victim" and of attempting to disculpate the offender and to inculpate the victim (Clark and Lewis, 1977). The following quotations from the previously mentioned book by Clark and Lewis are examples of the criticism campaign mounted against the young discipline of victimology:

> In the social sciences, victim blaming is becoming an increasingly popular rationalization for criminal and deviant behavior . . . over the past few years, victim blaming has become institutionalized within the academic world under the guise of victimology.

> The male researcher finds his escape in victimology. He seeks the problem's cause in the behavior of its victim, and goes on to persuade himself and the public at large that by changing that behavior, the problem can be controlled. In this way, the study of victimology becomes the art of victim blaming.

With the continuing criticism of victim-precipitation it is becoming increasingly clear that at least part of the critique is prompted by a failure to grasp the subtle distinction between the behaviouristic concept of victim-precipitation as used in etiological studies of crime for explanatory purposes and the legalistic concept of victim provocation used in criminal courts for the sake of determining the criminal responsibility of the accused, for settling the issue of guilt and for choosing the optimal penal sanction. The frequent use in victimological writings of words borrowed from legal terminology such as "guilt," "culpability," "responsibility," "blame," etc. has only contributed to the confusion. And titles such as Nicht der Mörder, der Ermordete ist Schuldig (Franz Werfel, 1920), The Murdered One, Too, Is Guilty (Lydia Sicher, 1936) and Is the Victim Guilty? (Fattah, 1971) have provided extra fuel for attackers.

Despite the growing criticism of victim-precipitation, there is little doubt that the concept, as originally conceived by Marvin Wolfgang in his study of criminal homicide in Philadelphia (1958), is basically a sound one. In Levine's words (1978), the concept met the need for a straightforward definition of the essential nature of the offender-victim interaction via the parties' overt and objectively ascertainable behavior during its course. In particular, in those cases where criminal victimization is the outcome of a long or brief interaction between the doer and the sufferer, it is practically impossible to understand the offender's motives and to explain his behavior unless the interpersonal dynamics of both protagonists are examined and all situational variables are analyzed. This analytical process ineluctably includes the study of the victim's attitude and behavior side by side with the offender's perceptions and definition of the situation. In contrast with the static concepts of victim vulnerability or victim proneness, victim-precipitation is a dynamic concept which allows a better understanding not only of why the crime was perpetrated but also why it occurred in this particular context against this specific victim. That the concept has been defined too broadly or operationalized too loosely in one or several studies is no reason to dismiss it altogether or to challenge its validity and its potential utility, when correctly applied, to the explanation of the dynamics of criminal behavior. For instance, one can hardly take issue with Wolfgang's classic formulation of victim-precipitation according to which:

> The term victim-precipitated is applied to those criminal homicides in which the victim is a direct, positive precipitator in the crime. The role of the victim is characterized by his having been the first in the homicide drama to use physical force directed against his subsequent slayer. The victim-precipitated cases are those in which the victim was the first to show and use a deadly weapon, to strike a blow in an altercation—in short, the first to commence the interplay of resort to physical violence.

The cases cited by Wolfgang to illustrate victim-precipitated homicide leave no doubt as to the soundness of the concept.

In his study of forcible rape, Amir (1967, 1971) used a broader and less precise definition. Clark and Lewis (1977) claim that Amir "confuses victim's behavior with the offender's interpretation of that behavior." They blame him for never reaching the logical conclusion ". . . that it is the offender's mistaken interpretation which precipitates rape."

Though Amir's methodology and working definition of victim-precipitation are in many ways deficient, Clark and Lewis' critique fails to recognize the importance of the participants' subjective definitions of the situation in which they are involved, to the explanation of their actions and responses. The offender's perception of the victim's attitude and his/her subjective interpretation of the victim's behavior are important clues to the understanding of his/her personality, motives and crime although from a legal point of view they may not constitute sufficient grounds for reducing the charges against him/her or for mitigating the punishment. Criminal courts and compensation boards have to decide whether the offender was right or wrong in his/her perception, whether his/her interpretation and definition of the situation were correct or incorrect, whether s/he was justified in inferring what s/he inferred and in acting the way he did. All these are important elements for the determination of guilt and for the compensation decision. Behavioral scientists, on the other hand, are interested in explanation not justification, in understanding the behavior not rationalizing it, in etiology not in guilt or innocence, in the interpersonal dynamics that led to the crime not in legal excuses and extenuating circumstances. Defense lawyers may, in their attempts to get the charges reduced or to obtain lenient treatment for their clients, blame and assign a culpable role to the victim. But it would be farfetched to interpret the behavioral explanations of causative forces as attributions of fault or imputations of guilt. The challenge to the behavioral scientist lies in discerning actual perceptions and sincere interpretations from ex post facto rationalizations.

The use of explanatory concepts such as victim-precipitated, victim-facilitated, victim-initiated, victim-induced and victim-invited criminality to describe the victim's role in the causative process should in no way be interpreted as an attempt on the part of the social scientist to blame the victim or to hold him responsible for the crime.

Referring to the victim's negligence or carelessness and pointing out the victim's reckless, heedless or imprudent behavior are the victimologist's way of emphasizing the importance of situational variables and of stressing the close link between certain crimes and environmental opportunities. Similarly, when, for instance, in a case of a wife who killed her husband, reference is made to the woman's perpetual maltreatment at the hand's of her spouse, this is not to be construed as a deliberate effort to blame the victim and to disculpate the killer. It is an attempt to explain the motives for the killing and to analyze the chain of events that finally led to the commission of the crime.

Victimologists' assertions that certain victim attitudes or behaviors may favor, encourage, facilitate or trigger the perpetration of certain crimes reflect a genuine desire to draw attention to the conflict that sometimes exists between the protective function of the law and the unwillingness of some victims to be protected. This conflict is evident in the case of laws on statutory rape which prohibit among other things consensual heterosexual intercourse between teenagers under the age of consent. It is also present in the case of laws prohibiting the sale of liquor or pornographic material to juveniles or forbidding them access to specific places such as racetracks or gambling casinos. By pointing to the victim's failure to protect himself/herself or his/her property, victimologists are trying to demonstrate how reluctant some victims are to use devices designed for their protection. It is not paradoxical that car drivers must be compelled to use seat belts by legislation and threat of criminal sanctions?

FROM VICTIM-OFFENDER RELATIONSHIPS TO VICTIM/OFFENDER ATTITUDES

Victimology previously focused on characteristics of victims of specific crimes, causal role of the victim and patterns of victim-offender relationships. However, with the exception of cases where the victim is a direct precipitator in the crime, learning a primary or secondary relationship exists between the victim and the offender usually does not help in explaining the motivation or activities of the two parties. Modern victimology has extended the interpersonal perspective from a typology of relationships to the reciprocal attitudes of the victim and offender and to their perceptions of one another.

This has been one of the most important theoretical developments in victimology in recent years. Not only did it open a new horizon in the study of victim-offender interactions but it opened a new avenue for the understanding of the dynamics of criminal behavior. Furthermore, research in this area will have important practical applications in the field of prevention, criminal rehabilitation and victim education and treatment.

The Offender's Attitude to the Victim

Several criminologists (Sutherland, 1937; Redl and Weinman, 1951; Cressey, 1953; Cressey, 1953; Sykes and Matza, 1957) have discussed the offender's attitude to the victim and drawn attention to the role offenders' perceptions of actual and potential victims play in the rationalization and selection processes. Recently, those perceptions and the extent they are influenced by the culture have been highlighted in the evergrowing literature on rape. Victimological studies of other categories of victims also indicate that by stigmatizing certain individuals or groups, society legitimizes their victimization and designates them culturally appropriate targets for criminal attacks.

The Desensitization Process

Crimes such as homicide, assault, rape, robbery or fraud, usually involve physical or material harm to the victim. Many involve infliction of pain and suffering on a fellow human being. Not all criminals are insensitive or devoid of feelings of pity and empathy. To avoid the moral tension, the feelings of guilt and remorse associated with and resulting from the crime, they desensitize themselves against the plight and sufferings of the victim. The desensitization process also serves to counteract the force of internalized social sanctions, to overcome the moral inhibitions and to appease the delinquent's conscience. The legitimization of the act, the denial and reification of the victim and the devaluation of the sufferer are mechanisms in the desensitization process (Fattah, 1976).

While criminologists and victimologists were advancing the theoretical paradigm of the use of the victim as an agent of self-legitimization. several similar psychological studies were undertaken. Social psychological studies support the deindividuation and derogation models of desinhibition. They showed when the victim is not seen as an individual a state of deindividuation may result which will lower inner restraints. They also showed victim derogation and victim denigration lead to reduced feelings of responsibility and a lessened post-aggression dissonance.

> If the subjects can attribute to the victim characteristics that deserve to be punished, then the harm can be seen as appropriate and just. (Lerner, 1974).

It is less dissonant with self-concept for people to believe that they have hurt a bad person than a good one, so in order to minimize the dissonance attendant to the perpetration of harm, they tend to perceive their victims as possessing negative traits. Thus, derogation of one's victim may be an attempt to justify one's behavior toward the person (Cialdini et al, 1976; Bersheid and Walster, 1969).

Social psychologists' explanations of the derogation/denigration process are mostly inspired by Lerner's (1974) "just world hypothesis" and revolve around people's need to believe in a just world. However, the process seems to be an indication of the delinquent's attempt to desensitize himself, to justify his harmful behavior and to rationalize his injurious actions. This is confirmed by studies conducted by Cialdini et al (1976) who found evidence the mediator of the victim derogation phenomenon in the Lerner situation is not a tendency to believe in a just world but a tendency to justify one's complicity in the harm doing.

The analysis of the desensitization process will shed light on the forces which transform a socialized. seemingly normal individual into an uninhibited, ruthless aggressor capable of committing acts of extreme cruelty and savagery and a person who is at odds with his own system of moral values, without empathy or compassion for the victim and without guilt or remorse. Furthermore, enhancing the delinquent's awareness of the victim and sensitizing him/her to the victim's sufferings may develop into an effective technique of criminal rehabilitation.

Offenders' Stereotypes of Probable Victims

Although there are few studies in this area, they indicate that delinquents stereotypic definitions and consensually validated images of victims exist. Hermann and Julia Schwendinger (1967) observed a tacit agreement among delinquents that the victim was a worthless human being. Their data reinforced the assumption that delinquents tacitly hold a common attitude toward the victim.

Sutherland (1937) provided a good description of the stereotype that con men have of their probable victims: "suckers who are gloating over their prospective gain . . . with larceny in their souls . . . and with little sympathy for those they are hoping to beat."

Many students of rape insist that rapists have a devalued image of the female. They see her as a sexual object, as a piece of property that has to consent, submit and suffer. Male drivers also seem to have stereotypes of female hitchhikers. They see them as desiring, consenting, willing or at least taking a chance of being raped. This greatly influences their interactions with female hitchhikers to whom they give a ride and distorts their conception of what has happened. In their minds there was no crime—it was not rape, it was available sex.

Cross-cultural studies can be extremely valuable in examining and comparing delinquents' stereotypes of victims and understanding how cultural interpretations of victims' behavior contribute to the selection of the target, the motivation and rationalization of the act.

Offenders' Perceptions of Deserving Victims

Victimological studies show delinquents make subtle distinctions between appropriate and inappropriate targets for victimization and draw a sharp line between those who can be victimized and those who cannot (Sutherland, 1937; Thrasher, 1947; Sykes and Matza, 1957; Dynes and Quarantelli, 1970). Two categories of victims are particularly vulnerable to criminal victimization: the culpable victim and the culturally legitimate victim.

The Culpable Victim

Ex post facto attribution of guilt and responsibility to the victim is not a new phenomenon. For ages, phrases such as "he has himself to blame," or "he had it coming to him" or "he asked for it," used to indicate the victim shared part of the responsibility for what happened to him/her. Victimology, however, drew attention to the mental process of rationalization in which "blaming the victim" is used as a technique of neutralization. This process differs from ex post facto justifications because it precedes rather than succeeds the commission of the crime and enables the delinquent to neutralize his/her inhibitions, to silence his/her conscience and to avoid post-delictum feelings of guilt, shame or remorse.

The anteriority of the victim's guilt rids the potential delinquent almost completely of guilt. It makes it possible for him/her to legitimize the act, to redefine it as retaliatory justice, to deny responsibility and to blame the victim. Blaming the victim, even in the cases where the victim is completely innocent, is not a process of intentional distortion. In many cases, the criminal is convinced of the victim's guilt. This is true in many cases of passionate crimes, as it is in the crimes of paranoiacs. The passionate crime is characterized by a justiciary attitude on the part of the offender, an attitude which is one of the conscious and justifying motivations of the crime. In crimes motivated by revenge and many political crimes the injurious act is seen and perpetrated as an act of justice and a rightful form of retaliation.

The technique of blaming the victim is also evident in the crime of genocide, where the extermination of a minority is viewed as desirable, useful, necessary and justified. Preceding the acts of genocide, the minority is blamed for many types of social and economic ills. In this way compassion for the group is eliminated and its annihilation appears a just and legitimate end (Fattah, 1976).

Blaming the victim is by no means limited to violent offences or offences against the person. In tax evasion the act is seen as a rightful reprisal against a government that imposes high taxes. Treason can be legitimized as a retalitory act against an unjust, autocratic and oppressive regime.

The Culturally Legitimate Victim

The concept of the culturally legitimate victim was first used by Weiss and Borges in 1973 to describe victims of rape. They pointed out that socialization and especially sex-role learning exploit males and females and produce victims and offenders. A male-dominated society, with most positions of power and influence occupied by men, tends to establish and perpetuate the woman as a legitimate object for victimization.

> Social processes prepare the woman for her role as a potential victim and provide the procedures to make her a socially approved or legitimate victim for rape (Weiss and Borges, 1973)

In primitive societies, adolescent gangs and political extremist groups, acts of violence against the members of the out-group are tolerated and sometimes encouraged while violence against members of the in-group is condemned. The normative system in those societies or groups designates members of the out-group as legitimate and appropriate targets for violent and physical aggression. A national survey of attitudes toward violence in the United States found that "excluding people from groups to which one feels related can serve as a rationalization justifying violence toward them," or make violence inflicted on such people more easily acceptable (Blumenthal et al, 1972; Conklin, 1975).

The use of the strap in schools for misconduct, the use of violence to discipline or control the behavior of inmates in penal institutions and the flogging of offenders guilty of certain crimes are seen as legitimate forms of violence and those on whom such punishments are inflicted are seen as appropriate, deserving targets.

In most jurisdictions, forcible sexual intercourse with one's wife is not considered a criminal offence and does not qualify as rape. If a wife is raped by her husband she is a culturally legitimate victim. The concept extends to many other forms of violence within the family. Children are considered legitimate targets for the use of physical force in the process of training and control and husband-wife violence has been regarded as legitimate by the police and the courts.

Straus (1975) points to the doctrine of spousal immunity which exists in many jurisdictions in the United States and prevents a wife from suing her husband for assault and battery. Quite often police do not make arrests in such cases. The training manual of the International Association of Chiefs of Police (1965) recommends that no arrests be made in such cases. Straus feels that police share the implicit legitimacy of spousal violence provided resulting injuries or destruction are within limits. Furthermore, most state victim compensation schemes exclude from eligibility for compensation cases of violance between husband and wife.

In many countries, the unfaithful wife exemplifies the culturally legitimate victim. In those countries the husband who kills his wife is exempted of any punishment or treated with extreme leniency.

Proximity and Distance, Closeness and Remoteness

To commit certain crimes the offender must decrease the physical proximity and increase the affective distance to the victim. The commission of a harmful act against a remote, intangible and impersonal victim evokes less moral resistance and requires less psychological courage than an attack directed against a close, perceptible and tangible target.

In his laboratory experiments, Milgram (1974) examined the effect of the closeness of the victim on the subjects administering the electrical shocks. Milgram hypothesized correctly that by bringing the victim closer to the subject, by rendering the victim more salient to the subject and thus enhancing the subject's awareness of the victim's suffering and distress, the subject's performance will be regulated to some degree and his obedience to the experimenter will decrease. The experiments revealed that obedience to the experimenter reduced as the victim was rendered more immediate to the subject: 35 percent of the subjects defied the experimenter in the remote condition, 37.5 percent in voice-feedback, 60 percent in proximity and 70 percent in touch-proximity.

Milgram notes in the remote situation the victim's suffering possesses an abstract, remote quality for the subject. The subject is aware in a conceptual sense that his/her actions cause pain to another person. The remote condition allows the subject to put the victim out of his/her mind. When the victim is close it is more difficult to exclude him/her from thought. In the proximity conditions the subject may sense that s/he has become more salient in the victim's field of awareness and consequently becomes more self-conscious, embarrassed and inhibited when punishing the victim (Milgram, 1974).

Sympathetic concern for the victim and heightened awareness of the victim's suffering are inhibiting forces. Unfortunately, most of the time they are not sufficient to prevent the crime from being committed.

The Victim's Attitude Toward the Offender

Research concerning cases where there was some personal interaction or face-to-face dealings between the offender and victim is in its infancy. It has been observed that in some cases of kidnapping, hostage-taking and hijacking, particularly when it lasted days and weeks, the victim reacts with a positive rather than a negative emotional response to the victimizer and such an initial response may develop into a deep emotional attachment or a strong affective bond.

Some researchers believe such affective ties result from the state of dependency that develops between the hostage and keeper, and the kidnapped and captors. Others explain it by using the Freudian concept of the "identification with the aggressor," while others point to the strong feeling of gratitude a survivor feels toward his/her captor because the captor spared his/her life.

> Most experiences, particularly those of a prolonged character, reliably suggest the development of an empathy between the terrorist and the hostage victim. It is suggested by some that, in prolonged cases, a state of dependency develops between the hostage and his keeper, to the extent even of giving rise to serious ethical and identity problems on the part of the victim. (Cooper, 1976).

The Stockholm Syndrome

The Stockholm Syndrome is the dramatic and unexpected realignment of affections, to the positive bond between hostage and captor and to the feelings of distrust or hostility on the part of the victim toward authorities (Ochberg, 1977).

The term was coined after a Swedish incident in 1973. Following a bank hold up in Stockholm, two robbers held bank employees hostage in the bank's vault from August 23 to August 28. It was reported that an affective tie developed between one of the female hostages and one of the offenders. Following their release, the victims asked that mercy be shown toward the offenders. Although the Stockholm syndrome does not always occur, it does not seem to be too infrequent. Similar affections have been described in various kidnappings and seiges.

Ochberg (1977) says positive bonds do not form immediately, but are usually established by the third day. He pinpoints four factors which promote the Stockholm Syndrome: intensity of the experience, duration, dependence of the hostage on the captor for survival and distance of the hostage psychologically from authority.

The Hijackee Syndrome

The Hijackee Syndrome is a similar phenomenon and it is the experience of passengers on a hijacked plane, train or bus who emerge from the experience with warm praise for the hijackers instead of reacting to their victimization with rage, anger and outrage. Dr. Hubbard, author of a book on the skyjacker, said in an interview with Time Magazine (October 1976) that hijackers cash in on widespread hostility to authority. Once the air passenger believes he will not be killed, he can view his captor as a dashing desperado lashing out against the establishment. Hubbard adds that sometimes victims also see the hijacking as a free ticket to adventure and personal publicity. Moreover, because the hijacker does not use all the force available to him, the passengers are grateful.

A similar opinion was expressed by psycholinguist Murray Miron who noted that a hijacker builds admiration through sheer menace.

"Someone who holds your life in his hands rewards you every time he doesn't kill you. Even so little a reward as permitting the passengers to light up a cigarette or go to the bathroom acts as a subtle link to the captor."

Psychiatrist Lawrence Freedman explains that the coalescing of the aggressors and hostages into a united group deploring the intransigence of outside authorities who refuse to meet the hijackers' demands is a manifestation of what Freudians call "identification with the aggressor" referring to childrens' identification with a punitive parent-figure and their incorporation of his aggressive qualities.

Such an explanation, however, as Ochberg (1977) points out ignores the fact that the hijackers' victims do not necessarily incorporate the terrorists' violence. Ochberg leans more towards the gratitude hypothesis:

> It seems rather that hostages successfully deny the danger engineered by the terrorists. Having separated this from awareness, they are overwhelmingly grateful to the terrorist for giving them life. They focus on the captor's kindnesses, and not his acts of brutality. Intellectual appreciation of the terrorists' cause may be related to this irrational affection, but the relationship is not complete. That is, one can love a captor and not his cause, and vice-versa. (Ochberg, 1977).

FROM THE FUNCTIONAL RESPONSIBILITY OF THE VICTIM TO THE SOCIAL RESPONSIBILITY TO THE VICTIM

In 1968 Stephen Schafer, one of the pioneers in victimology, published a monograph for which he intentionally chose the reverse title of Von Hentig's book written twenty years earlier. In his book, The Victim and his Criminal: A Study in Functional Responsibility, Schafer discusses what he calls "The functional responsibility of the victim," the responsibility of the victim for his own victimization and his duty to do everything possible to prevent it. Though Schafer's treatment of the concept is condensed into two pages the following quotation explains what he meant by the victim's functional responsibility,

> Also, it is far from true that all crimes 'happen' to be committed; often the victim's negligence, precipitative action, or provocation contributes to the genesis or performance of a crime. The norm-delineated functional role of the victim is to do nothing to provoke others from attempting to injure his ability to play his role. At the same time, it expects him actively to prevent such attempts. This is the victim's functional responsibility.

Schafer's book contains a plea for revival of the victim's importance, recognition and respect for the victim and his/her injury and an adequate system of compensation and restitution to the victim.

In the current climate surrounding the criminal justice system and the punitive mood of the general public, Schafer's ideas about the functional responsibility of the victim would be regarded as heretic. But his request for adequate compensation and restitution to the victim has been heeded by most Western societies.

Questions asked at the 1977 annual meeting of the American Bar Association Section of Criminal Justice illustrate the growing awareness of the plight and needs of the victim. In his introduction B. James George, Jr. asked, "Are the victims of crime also the victims of the criminal justice system itself? Does the system give the victim any rights . . . while it religiously keeps watch to preserve the rights of the defendant? Should victims of crime be eligible to receive compensation from the state, restitution from the offender—or civil damages from third parties?"

The same questions were asked two years earlier at the International Study Institute on Victimology in Bellagio, Italy. The section dealing with "The victim and the justice system" made several recommendations considered a charter of victims' rights. The group affirmed the victim's right to compensation and restitution and stressed the victim's need to be treated fairly and humanely by the criminal justice system and society.

EFFECTS OF VICTIM CHARACTERISTICS
ON CRIMINAL JUSTICE DECISIONS

Until a few years ago little research had been done concerning whether the victim of a crime has an impact on the outcome of the criminal justice process in handling his/her case. Consistent with the general concern about the victim in the last five years, there has been growing interest in the role of the victim in the criminal justice process and this has generated a number of empirical studies.

Studies demonstrate observers are likely to be influenced in their assessment of responsibility and guilt and in their choice of the appropriate punishment for the aggressor by the characteristics of the victims. There was also a dearth of empirical research based on actual cases to demonstrate the extent victim characteristics and behavior influence criminal justice decisions.

The victim can influence the criminal justice process through the decision whether or not to report the incident. This initial decision is important because in most cases the mobilization of the criminal justice apparatus is usually contingent upon the victim's complaint.

Support for this assertion comes from studies of police activities in some American cities which showed the majority of police work is initiated by citizens and a small percentage is initiated by the police themselves (Black, 1970). Once the victim has reported the incident to the police, subsequent decisions at different stages in the process are influenced by the victim's characteristics and behavior. Studies show the police decision to proceed; the prosecutor's decision to file a charge or to dismiss the case, once an arrest was made; the prosecutor's selection of charge; and the final outcome of the case are influenced by the victim. They also show the wishes and desires of the victim are usually considered and complied with by police and prosecutor except in serious offences where the victim is unwilling to formally proceed with the charges.

Provocation by the victim in some jurisdictions constitutes a legal excuse while in others it is an extenuating circumstance. In cases when the behavior of the victim does not qualify as provocation in the legal sense, such behavior may result in a reduction of the charges, a more lenient sentence or a verdict of non-guilty. Wolfgang (1958) found that in Philadelphia,

A significantly smaller proportion of offenders in victim-precipitated homicide (62 percent) than in non-victim precipitated homicide (82 percent) were found guilty.

RECENT THEORETICAL DEVELOPMENTS   211

The victim can also influence decisions of the criminal justice system in two other ways: a) the way s/he is perceived by the actors within the system: the police, the prosecutor, the courts; b) the way s/he behaves as a witness. Studies of victim's impact on criminal justice decisions identify those characteristics likely to have a significant influence on the criminal justice process. Two sets of characteristics were examined that were linked to the final outcome of a case:

1. Personal characteristics of the victim. These include socio-demographic characteristics, such as race, sex, age, occupation, social class, status and respectability. They also include personality characteristics, such as emotional disturbance; physical characteristics, such as attractiveness; offence-related characteristics, such as victim-offender relationship; severity of injury and loss.
2. Behavioral characteristics of the victim. A distinction is usually made between the behavior of the victim prior to and during the commission of the offence, such as prior criminal history, addiction problems, sexual conduct, as well as victim's participation in, or precipitation of, the offence; and the behavior of the victim as a complainant and as witness throughout the pre-trial and trial phases.

FROM OFFENDER-CENTERED PREVENTION TO VICTIM-BASED PREVENTION

Crime prevention, whether through punishment or rehabilitation, is offender-centered. Through its special preventive effects punishment is supposed to deter the punished offender from repeating his/her offence or from committing other offences. Through its general preventive effects, punishment is supposed to dissuade others from following the criminal's example. Rehabilitation is aimed at preventing recidivism by bringing about positive changes in the offender.

Current skepticism regarding the effectiveness of punishment and rehabilitation as preventive tools has re-emphasized the need for new crime prevention techniques. Modern strategies of crime prevention stress the link between crime and opportunities and advocate hardening criminal targets as the most effective way of preventing crime.

In contrast with traditional prevention, the modern approach emphasizes temptation/opportunity situations created by potential victims and aims at reducing the opportunity factor through measures taken by potential victims or police.

REFERENCES

American Bar Association/Section of Criminal Justice
    1977   "Victims of Crime or Victims of Justice?" Proceedings of the Annual Meeting in August 1977. Washington, DC: American Bar Association.
Amir, M.
    1967   "Victim Precipitated Forcible Rape." Journal of Criminal Law, Criminology and Police Science 4:493.
    1971   Patterns of Forcible Rape. Chicago: University of Chicago Press.

212   VICTIMOLOGY: AN INTERNATIONAL JOURNAL

Bersheid, E. and E. Walster
    1969   Interpersonal Attraction. Reading, MA: Addison-Wesley.
Black, D. J.
    1970   "Production of Crime Rates." American Sociological Review 35:733–748.
Blumenthal, M. et al.
    1972   Justifying Violence: Attitudes of American Men. University of Michigan.
Cialdini, R. B. et al.
    1976   "Victim Derogation in the Lerner Paradigm. Just World or Just Justifica-
                tion?" Journal of Personality and Social Psychology 6:719–724.
Clark, L. and D. Lewis
    1977   Rape: The Price of Coercive Sexuality. Toronto: Womens Press.
Conklin, J.
    1975   The Impact of Crime. New York: MacMillan.
Cooper, H. H. A.
    1976   "The Terrorist and the Victim." Victimology 2:229–239.
Cressey, D. R.
    1953   Other People's Money. New York: Free Press of Glencoe.
Dynes, R. and E. L. Quarantelli
    1974   "Organizations as Victims in Mass Civil Disturbances." in Drapkin and
                Viano (eds.), Victimology. Lexington, MA: Lexington Books.
Fattah, E. A.
    1971   Is the Victim Guilty? Montreal: University of Montreal Press.
    1976   "The Use of the Victim as an Agent of Self Legitimization: Toward a Dy-
                namic Explanation of Criminal Behavior." Victimology 1:29–53.
Feeney, D. G.
    1973   "Pity the Criminal Less, More His Innocent Victim." Canadian Society of
                Forensic Science Journal 1.
International Association of Chiefs of Police
    1965   Training Manual
Lerner, M. J.
    1974   "Social Psychology of Justice and Interpersonal Attraction." in Hutton (ed.),
                Foundations of Interpersonal Attraction. New York: Academic Press.
Milgram, S.
    1974   Obedience to Authority. New York: Harper and Row.
Miller, W.
    1973   "Ideology and Criminal Justice Policy: Some Current Issues." Journal of
                Criminal Law and Criminology 2:141–154.
Ochberg, R.
    1977   "The Victim of Terrorism-Psychiatric Considerations." Paper presented at
                an international seminar in Evian, France.
Redl, F. and D. Weinman
    1951   Children Who Hate. New York: Free Press.
Schwendinger, H. and J. Schwendinger
    1967   "Delinquent Stereotypes of Probable Victims." in M. W. Klein (ed.), Juve-
                nile Gangs in Context. New York: Prentice Hall.
Sicher, L.
    1936   "The Murdered One, Too, Is Guilty." International Journal of Individual
                Psychology 4.
Straus, M. A.
    1976   "Sexual Inequality, Cultural Norms and Wife-Beating." Victimology
                1:54–70.
Sutherland, E.
    1937   The Professional Thief. Chicago: University of Chicago Press.
Sykes, G. and D. Matza
    1957   "Techniques of Neutralization: A Theory of Delinquency." American Socio-
                logical Review 22:664–670.
Thrasher, F. M.
    1947   The Gang. Chicago: University of Chicago Press.
Weiss, K. and S. Borges
    1973   "Victomology and Rape: The Case of the Legitimate Victim." Issues in
                Criminology 8:71–115.

RECENT THEORETICAL DEVELOPMENTS   213

Werfel, F.
     1920   Nicht der Morfer, der Ermordete ist Schuldig. Munich: Kurt Wolff Verlag.
Wolfgang, M. E.
     1958   Patterns in Criminal Homicide. Philadelphia: University of Pennsylvania
                 Press.

About the Author

   Ezzat A. Fattah is a professor at the School of Criminology, Simon Fraser University
in Canada. An internationally known victimologist, he is the author of several articles and
books in the field.

   For reprints of the article contact the author at the Department of Criminology, Simon
Fraser University, Burnaby B.C., Canada V5A 1S6.

Name Index